# PRAISE FOR *PLAYING WHILE WHITE*

"Leonard's voice and mind lend both gravity and dexterity to the modern sporting landscape, applying academic insight to this most secular world."
                                                    **—BOMANI JONES**, ESPN

"Systemic racism is often explored within the contexts of many of our institutions: government, education, criminal justice. *Playing While White* thoughtfully engages in a discourse around the privilege that whiteness affords, highlighting the ways that white athletes and whiteness are profiled as innocent, desirable, smart, and exceptional. This is in sharp juxtaposition to the way that Black bodies continue to be policed and profiled, demonized and denigrated both on and off the field. This poses the following query: do Black lives matter in the world of sports? Leonard's brilliant and thorough analysis of the institutionalized racism that is perpetrated in sports is one that we must all delve deeper into, and grapple with, as a society."

**—MICHAEL ERIC DYSON**, AUTHOR OF *TEARS WE CANNOT STOP: A SERMON TO WHITE AMERICA*

"Leonard is one of our most brutally honest truth tellers. He uses sports as a lens to understand how sports can both challenge and perpetuate institutionalized racism. This is a book for the conscious sports fan and people unafraid to discuss these issues with candor and clarity. I can't recommend it enough."

**—DAVE ZIRIN**, SPORTS EDITOR, *THE NATION*

"Leonard's in-depth investigation at how whiteness operates in sports (and, in turn, our society at large) is smart, cutting, nuanced, and, above all, important. It is a necessary work for this time."

—JESSICA LUTHER, AUTHOR OF *UNSPORTSMANLIKE CONDUCT: COLLEGE FOOTBALL AND THE POLITICS OF RAPE*

"Few have talked about race and sports with the passion and critical acuity of David J. Leonard. With *Playing While White*, he takes the road less paved and turns his attention to Whiteness, exploding the myths of privilege and entitlement that we are all too willing to assign to Black athletes."

—MARK ANTHONY NEAL, AUTHOR OF *LOOKING FOR LEROY: ILLEGIBLE BLACK MASCULINITIES*

"Issues of white privilege, and broader considerations of 'whiteness' as social construction, are critical to contemporary US social and political discourse. In *Playing While White*, Leonard expertly explicates the extent to which sports play an important role in constructing and privileging white identity politics in American society."

—JOSHUA I. NEWMAN, AUTHOR OF *EMBODYING DIXIE: STUDIES IN THE BODY PEDAGOGICS OF SOUTHERN WHITENESS*

"Examines the effects of the dominant racial ideology on American sports and highlights the ways that whiteness is privileged above other racial identities. *Playing While White* will appeal to sports fans interested in ways to explain the racial disparities in American sports."

—LORI LATRICE MARTIN, AUTHOR OF *BIG BOX SCHOOLS: RACE, EDUCATION, AND THE DANGER OF THE WAL-MARTIZATION OF PUBLIC SCHOOLS IN AMERICA*

# PLAYING WHILE WHITE

## PRIVILEGE AND POWER
## ON AND OFF THE FIELD

*David J. Leonard*

UNIVERSITY OF WASHINGTON PRESS

*Seattle and London*

University of Washington Press
www.washington.edu/uwpress

LIBRARY OF CONGRESS CATALOGING-IN-PUBLICATION DATA
Names: Leonard, David J., author.
Title: Playing while White : privilege and power on and off the field /
    Dr. David J. Leonard.
Description: Seattle : University Washington Press, 2017. | Includes bibliographical
    references and index.
Identifiers: LCCN 2016050498| ISBN 9780295741871 (hardcover : alk. paper) |
    ISBN 9780295741888 (pbk. : alk. paper)
Subjects: LCSH: Racism in sports—United States. | Sports—Social aspects—
    United States. | Whites—Race identity—United States.
Classification: LCC GV706.32 L46 2017 | DDC 306.4/83—dc23
LC record available at https://lccn.loc.gov/2016050498

**TO DR. HARRY EDWARDS**
You saw something in me, long before
I knew I could play on this level.
Thank you for planting a seed, for teaching
the world that sport is more than a game.


**TO DR. CEDRIC ROBINSON**
You nurtured my intellectual curiosity and reminded me
that my work is important. You told me that I matter.
I hope this work, and everything I do, makes you proud.

# CONTENTS

# ACKNOWLEDGMENTS

Intellectual work is a process, a difficult and challenging process. This book is the end result of hours of labor—reading, thinking, and writing. This is never a solo exercise. Knowledge production is a team game. I am grateful that I have so many teammates who lifted me up, who pushed my thought process, who encouraged me, and who otherwise supported me during this journey. I am everything because of this unconditional love.

I am thankful to those on whose shoulders I stand intellectually. I am grateful to the many scholars and thinkers, intellectuals and activists, who continue to shape my thinking on sports, American culture, race, and racism. To those who have given me a platform, edited my work, and supported me—Jamilah Lemieux, Darnell L. More, Jeff Chang, Bob Wing, Cynthia Fuchs, Jamilah King, Kevin Merida, Raina Kelley, Dave Zirin, Mark Anthony Neal, Jenée Desmond-Harris, Tamura Lomax, Vincent Thomas, Robert Reese, Alexander Leichenger, Douglas Hartman, Jabari Asim, Monica Casper, Michael Tillery, and Bomani Jones—as well as to those who have encouraged, taught, and pushed me: thank you.

I am honored to have an amazing intellectual community that nourishes my own analysis and in whose presence in my life is priceless. Thank you MAN, Deborah, Cole, Rich, LG, Stephanie, Nitasha, Vernadette, Theresa, Safiya, Camille, Sanford, Aureliano, Jeffrey, Leigh, Kiese, Kimberly, Simone, Deborah, Rebecca, Imani, Koritha, Julius, Heidi, Ayana, Danielle, Jeffrey, MLH, JP, Kishonna, Julius, Simone, Treva, Regina, T2, Danielle, Lori, Paula, Alondra, Mary, Carmen, Gaye, Sarah, and Robin.

Ebony: Thank you for being that friend, the person who encourages me. You have my back and always stand in my corner. Your messages always give me the boost I need to keep pushing.

Stacey: Although we were separated by thousands of miles, multiple time zones, and our busy schedules, I could not have finished this book without you. As you finished your own brilliant book, I was continuously inspired and reminded of our collective mission. I am blessed to be your academic Boo.

Jenny: I have known you almost my entire life, and I am a better teacher, scholar, partner, parent, activist, and person because of you. You teach me about life, about sports, and everything in between.

Thank you, Jorge Moraga, for your editorial assistance with this project. Not only did your interventions make the book that much stronger, but also your words of encouragement sustained me on so many levels. You are the future of sports studies, and for that I am grateful.

Thanks to Pat, Sue, Ana Maria, and Cerissa. Thanks to Dean DeWald and CAS for the necessary support to bring this book to life.

Thanks to everyone at the University of Washington Press. Thanks to Niccole Coggins, Charles Wheeler, Margaret Sullivan, Rachael Levay, and everyone who may have touched this book for your polishing efforts. And HUGE thanks to Larin McLaughlin; you are my editor for life. Thank you for your support, editorial genius, and friendship. Each is priceless, as are you.

Mom and Dad, thanks for encouraging a love of sports, a love of critical thinking, and a passion for justice.

Amanda and Ollie: You make me smile, you give me hope, and you always help me keep my eye on the ball.

Much love and respect to Rea and Sammy for their patience, support, and the endless days of shenanigans.

And to Anna, thank you for always believing in me. Whether listening to my analysis, pushing my thinking, or simply helping me get through a day, everything I do is a testament to your friendship, partnership, and love.

# PLAYING WHILE WHITE

# INTRODUCTION

O VER the past several years, I have found myself moving back and forth between writing on sports and #BlackLivesMatter. In a given week, I would write on Johnny Manziel and Ferguson, Missouri; on Trayvon Martin and white collegiate athletes; on Mike Brown and NASCAR. While these topics may seem disconnected, the centrality of race, of the production and consumption of blackness and whiteness, of criminalization and the racial formation of innocence in each space reveal the connective tissue of their themes, subjects, and issues.

The same sorts of racial logics and stereotypes that produce national mourning for mass shootings in suburbs, that contribute to a culture of racialized fear resulting in countless dead black bodies at the hands of police, operate in a sports world that routinely redeems, forgives, and humanizes white athletes, all while criminalizing and policing black athletes. The same sorts of logic that turned Trayvon Martin's hoodie into a criminal uniform and mandated a dress code in the NBA[1] contribute to a sporting arena that celebrates the individuality and colorful personality of trash-talking, pants-sagging, style-producing white athletes. Never mind Bill Belichick's hoodie or corporate profits from the popularity of these sartorial choices. Race and racism are central to sporting culture, just as they are central to discussions of the criminal justice system, policing, and the American political landscape.

What binds these discussions together is not simply intellectual or discursive; it is not purely ideological or a matter of shared themes, but exists in my biography, in my personal stories, and in my social location. To look at sports, and to look at the ways that society makes #WhiteLivesMatter on and off the field at the expense of people of color, is to look in the mirror. As I stare into my white face, I am forced to interrogate my own whiteness (and masculinity and heterosexuality). I see my own privilege, and reflect on the ways I have been profiled as innocent, smart, hardworking, having the potential to change, scrappy, and tough on the playing fields, in school, in the streets, and at the workplace. I cannot help but think about the numerous examples where I have gotten a pass, been forgiven, been "normalized," and been visible (except when being invisible meant getting a pass).

Throughout my life, I have not just made mistakes: I've broken the law, acted like a "thug" and a "punk," and engaged in irresponsible and contemptible behavior. This took place in the streets, in school, and on the athletic field, where I would routinely cross the line, talking trash, and playing dirty with little regard for the consequences. Had I not been a middle-class white kid, these actions surely would have led to a technical foul, my ejection, or other forms of punishment. As a high school athlete, I was celebrated for my willingness to get into fights on the field and court; I brought toughness and passion to the game. I protected others; I led and inspired others. If I made a mistake, I grew from it, taught others, and became better. When I talked trash and played with a "chip on my shoulder," it was recast as something worthy of celebration. I was a good kid; I was a kid who was #PlayingWhileWhite.

My "indiscretions" and "misdeeds" came without consequences. I was neither punished nor defined by these unseemly behaviors; when I skipped part of baseball practice to get alcohol for a party to be held at my house I was punished with a few extra laps. When I started a fight during a handshake, I was not even questioned. When I talked trash instead of shaking hands after a game, I dealt with no repercussions. When I encouraged a beanball war, I was sternly spoken to even as many saw me as the victim. The stories are endless, and they are not limited to my sporting identities.

Neither my whiteness nor my community was put on trial, and I was most certainly not condemned to death. Instead, my indiscretions and behaviors on and off the field were recast as teachable moments in which I would be given the opportunity to learn and grow. They were considered to be part of my maturation, and were celebrated as necessary and productive mistakes. These are the privileges of being perceived as an innocent, an angel—of being white and middle-class. I was profiled over and over again, and I cashed in on that profile. This is my story and the story of so many other white athletes; all of us playing sports that are both defined by whiteness and shaped by assumptions about whiteness.

❖　❖　❖

In 2013, America fell in love with yet another white male athlete. With Tim Tebow out of the NFL (we would have to wait another three years for the spectacle of his baseball career), Lance Armstrong having betrayed America's trust, no marquee white basketball or boxing star, and a sporting world dominated by the likes of LeBron James, Tiger Woods, Serena Williams, and Robert Griffin III, white America put its future in the hands of the newest great white hope: Texas A&M's Johnny Manziel. Embracing his "swagger" and "personality," his "grit," "passion," and "never quit attitude," white America was captivated by Manziel, who became known as "Johnny Football." Even those who criticized and condemned his destructive behavior did so from a place of disappointment—that is, they expected him to be a good kid, play by the rules, and make good decisions, rather than act like *other* athletes. Gregg Doyel encapsulated Johnny Football nation, when he wrote in "Still a Johnny Football Fan; Not Crazy About Johnny Manziel, the Person." "The swooning will continue for Johnny Football, because he remains one of the most charismatic players I've ever seen. . . . There's a reason Manziel rocketed into full-fledged stardom midway through his freshman season at Texas A&M, before he was allowed to speak to the media, before he took to Twitter to reveal himself in pictures and tweets. He was a star because we loved the way he played, and I'm determined to hang onto that love no matter how unlikeable he has become off the field."

Doyel was correct. The world would continue to watch every move made by Johnny Manziel for two more years, irrespective of bad play, bad behavior, or his ultimate fall from the pinnacle of white adoration. Such swooning was driven by nostalgia for the "good old days" and by the pleasure garnered from the prospect of the newest white quarterback. While reflecting the desire to see Manziel through narratives of white exceptionalism ("he's different") and white bootstrapism (never mind his wealth and class privilege), Manziel Mania was driven by the desire to protect him from the supposedly unfair criticism, expectations, and pressure that rendered him a victim.

Manziel stepped into a cultural moment of panic, anxiety, and loss. Despite the long tradition of white quarterbacks, aided and abetted by stacking, stereotypes, and positional discrimination, Manziel was imagined as both an outsider and a "new sort of quarterback" who was challenging the perceived dominance of the black quarterback. Evidenced by the visibility of the San Francisco 49ers' Colin Kaepernick, the Carolina Panthers' Cam Newton, and the Seattle Seahawks' Russell Wilson (and the past successes of Donovan McNabb, Randall Cunningham, and Warren Moon), the white community was seen as losing their hold on the quarterback position. Johnny Football, like Tebow, had the potential to reverse this course, providing hope to those imagining loss. Never mind that in 2013, the quarterback position remained overwhelmingly white; Manziel offered the discursive pleasure of making the quarterback great again, of making football great again, and of "making America great again."

The cultural power of the quarterback—as the field general, leader, and brains of the team—is wrapped up in hegemonic definitions of white masculinity.[2] The position is often defined by signifiers of white athleticism, including leadership, intelligence, and hard work. Daniel Buffington summarizes the research as follows: "White male athletes are often presented as being harder workers (Murrell and Curtis 1994; Wonsek 1992), superior leaders (Jackson 1989), more team oriented (Davis and Harris 1998), and more mentally astute (Hoose 1989; D. Z. Jackson 1989) than their Black counterparts."[3] The value placed upon the quarterback on and off the field reflects these racial tropes. The power afforded Johnny Manziel, Aaron Rodgers, Peyton Manning, Tom Brady, or others, points to the entrenched nature of these ideas, and the cultural power of the white quarterback.[4]

Race has everything to do with Johnny Manziel's movement through the sporting world—just as it has everything to do with Tim Tebow (the former NFL quarterback), Ryan Braun (the once-suspended MLB player), Marshall Henderson (the often-suspended yet celebrated college former basketball player), Andrew Luck, Josh Hamilton, Kevin Love, Oscar Pistorius, NASCAR, Hope Solo, Ryan Lochte, and Michael Phelps. Race helps us to understand how Colin Kaepernick and countless black athletes are demonized and threatened for bringing their disrespectful politics into sports at the same time that countless white athletes and coaches are empowered to support Donald Trump with few questions about respect, the values of his campaign, or the message they sent in their support. Whiteness is privilege on and off the field. Whiteness matters.

❖   ❖   ❖

*Playing While White: Privilege and Power on and off the Field* explores how and why whiteness matters within contemporary sports and what that tells us about race and racism in the twenty-first century. It documents how #PlayingWhileWhite means being seen as a leader, being celebrated as an intelligent athlete, and being praised for embodying the positive values found in our sporting landscapes; it means that "mistakes" beget redemption, celebration, and endless possibility; it means being seen as unselfish, as lacking ego, and as a role model. #PlayingWhileWhite means exoneration and innocence; it means epitomizing a culture of individuality, freedom, and choices. For the black athlete, trash-talking and other indiscretions off the field result in narratives about "thugs" who don't respect the game, widespread debates about role models, values, morality, and punishment. The same behaviors in white athletes generate stories about passionate players who simply need to mature. When black players yell at teammates, they are seen as selfish hip-hop ballers; for white players, this behavior is a sign of a desire to win and a commitment to leadership.

Black athletes, from Jack Johnson to Muhammad Ali, from Allen Iverson to Richard Sherman, from Dez Bryant to Odell Beckham Jr., from Serena Williams to the latest brash, trash-talking athlete of color, are routinely ridiculed, demonized, and even criminalized for their behavior. The same cannot be said of white athletes, from Larry Bird and John Stockton to Michael Phelps and Johnny Manziel. In fact, #TrashTalkingWhileWhite is at times used as evidence of a calm demeanor, a passion for the game, a level of fearlessness, competitiveness, and swagger. #PlayingWhileWhite is the ability to talk trash and receive accolades as a wordsmith for the very practice that for black athletes results in vilification.

*Playing While White* thus explores the power and privileges that result from whiteness. The wages of whiteness can be seen in the narratives and tropes of intelligence, leadership, redemption, and individuality. As evidenced by the careers of Manziel and Tebow, the second chances afforded to Ryan Braun, Josh Hamilton, and Hope Solo, the redemption of Michael Phelps and Ben Roethlisberger, the protection of NASCAR and coach Joe Paterno, and the celebration of violence and hooliganism in hockey and soccer, not to mention countless more examples, #PlayingWhileWhite remains an entrenched privilege within contemporary sports. White privilege has no salary cap and cannot be put on the waiver wire.

This book takes up several key themes that are central to understanding the racial dynamics of multiple sports and athletes: (1) White nostalgia—contemporary sports often waxes nostalgic for the moment when sports were more about the game and less about the money, when athletes were role models, and when passion, hard work, and determination were central to sporting cultures.[5] (2) Part of the power of white nostalgia rests with a celebration of (and belief in) the brains-over-brawn trope. The value and desirability of white athletes is believed to stem from their intelligence, as opposed to their athleticism. Reflective of a larger history of white supremacy, sporting discourses have long celebrated white athletes for their cerebral approach to the game. Although indicative of the persistence of "old racism," the celebration of white athletes as "heady" or "intellectual" ballplayers without a specific racial marking embodies the nature of new racism. The celebration of intelligence (as opposed to black athleticism) demonstrates the persistence of racial schemas within a "post-racial" sporting context. (3) Seen as lacking the physical gifts of their teammates and opponents, white athletes are celebrated for their work ethic. While they are doubted and discouraged for their lack of pure athleticism, the media and public discourse find power in a narrative steeped in bootstrapism, hard work, and determination. In keeping with the hegemony of neoliberalism, meritocracy, and the larger celebration of individual accomplishment, the narrative of hardworking white athletes has resonance outside the playing fields. White sporting masculinities based on intelligence, hard work, and the determination to pull oneself up by one's own sneaker laces are seen as both unique and desirable on and off the field. (4) Public sporting discourse not only celebrates white intelligence as unique and exceptional, but also praises the character that white athletes bring into contemporary sporting cultures. In a sporting world in which black athletes routinely face criticism about their attitude, style of play, or lack of love for the game, white athletes are celebrated as different, as conveyers of fresh values who can redeem sports, save it, and make it great again.

From media commentary to the games themselves, from online chatter to the larger discursive positioning of sports celebrities and events, *Playing While White* focuses on the ways that sports culture narrates a sports world defined by exceptional whiteness, victimized whiteness, transgressive whiteness, marginal whiteness, and redemptive whiteness.

The first three chapters of the book focus on the narratives, tropes, indexes, and stereotypes associated with white athletes. Whether imagining white athletes as leaders, scrappy, intelligent, competitive, passionate, underdogs, perseverant, or determined, sports becomes a staging ground for the creation, production, articulation, and dissemination of the signifiers of whiteness. The image and meaning of whiteness, grounded in a system of white privilege and antiblackness (white supremacy), operate not only on the field and in America's sporting arenas, but also in every American cultural, economic, political, or lived space.

Chapters 4 through 6 focus on the ways in which whiteness is imagined as antithetical to criminality. The profiling of white bodies—athletes or otherwise—as inherently innocent not only over-determines narratives surrounding white indiscretion and law-breaking but also allows for the entry of white athletes into the narrative pathways of redemption and forgiveness that are not accessible to black athletes.

Chapter 7 looks at the ways that sports sell sex and the ways that race and gender operate within sports media narratives. Highlighting the privileges of #PlayingWhileWhiteAndMale, this chapter also focuses on the disparate experiences of black and white women athletes.

Chapter 8 offers a different approach. Whereas every other chapter looks at multiple sports anchored by a particular narrative and profile of whiteness, this chapter focuses specifically on NASCAR. Bringing together many of the themes central to #PlayingWhileWhite, the chapter traces how NASCAR embodies the power and privileges of whiteness within sporting culture.

The final two chapters examine whiteness as playing the right way and whiteness as victimhood. While analyzing specific narratives saturating sporting discourses and the ways in which white athletes are profiled, these chapters emphasize how the celebration of specific inscriptions and profiles of athletic whiteness, and the nostalgia for a previous (segregated) generation of sports work dialectically. To imagine white athletes as playing the right way or as victims is to give voice and credence to the index of white athletes as smart and scrappy.

In each chapter, I focus on the ways that sports humanize whites, a privilege invaluable inside and outside the arena. From the profiles and characteristics available to white athletes to the innocence and redemption afforded to white athletes, from the endless sports and opportunities to the celebration and sympathy afforded white athletes, sports make clear that white athletes matter, and that the successes and contributions of white athletes matter the most. This isn't just a story about sports or the sports media; it's a story about the very fabric of the United States.

As such, this book looks at the ideological power, the financial capital, the material benefits, and the cultural appeal of white athletic bodies. It examines the lessons taught and the cultural power in a myriad of athletes and sports. Whether manifested in Johnny Football and Danica Patrick, Tim Tebow and Oscar Pistorius, NASCAR and collegiate lacrosse,[6] Ben Rothlisberger and Roger Clemens, on the soccer pitch or the hockey rink, with Joe Paterno, Kevin Love, Marshall Henderson, Maria Sharapova, Tom Brady, Rob Gronkowski, Michael Phelps, Ryan Lochte, or numerous other examples, *Playing While White* documents how it is the power and resonance of whiteness that anchor the pedagogies of sport, more than the game or athletic success, and more than the talent, the jump shot, the rocket arm, or the sweet swing.

Looking across a spectrum of sports, this book thus examines the many ways that white athletes and white sporting cultures are celebrated, sold, and made visible because of power and privilege; ultimately it's bigger than the game, it's about the love, power, and the desirability of whiteness. It's about ideological appeal, financial need, and narrative fulfillment made available through white athletic bodies within the sporting landscapes of the twenty-first century. It is about the production and pedagogies of whiteness, processes that shape the playing field, the schoolyard, the criminal justice system, the economic sphere, and the political landscape.

### PLAYING WHILE WHITE: PRIVILEGE AND POWER IN SPORTING ARENAS

Ruth Frankenberg defines whiteness as a "location of structural advantage" and a "standpoint, a location from which to see selves, others and national and global orders."[7] In her estimation, "whiteness is a site of elaboration or a range of cultural practices and identities, often unmarked and unnamed or named as natural or 'normative' rather than specifically racial."[8] While others emphasize the intimate relationship between whiteness, power, and the production of a racialized Other, Frankenberg focuses on how whiteness is defined by privilege and the unnoticed structural advantages. Similarly, bell hooks explores the constructions and production of whiteness, noting that American discourse defines whiteness as "synonymous with goodness." Collectively, she notes, we have been "socialized to believe the fantasy that whiteness represents goodness and all that is benign and non-threatening."[9] George Lipsitz further notes that "whiteness never works in isolation; it functions as part of a broader dynamic grid created through intersections of race, class, gender and sexuality."[10]

Although academic discourses have recently sought to render whiteness as a visible racial category of significance, given "the wages of whiteness" and the "possessive investment in whiteness," its meaning and existence tend to remain overlooked as "if it is the natural, inevitable, ordinary way of being."[11] Dominant discourses and representations render whiteness as "a privileged place of racial normativity."[12] Joe Feagin and Hernan Vera further note that "one difficulty in studying the white self is that until recently, it was an invisible and non-regarded category, even difficult to name and not perceived as a distinctive racial identity. Even today, most white Americans either do not think about whiteness at all or else think of it as a positive or neutral category."[13]

While ultimately seeking to decenter and demystify whiteness, *Playing While White* focuses on whiteness as part of a larger discussion of antiblack racism and the structures of power. In examining privilege, race, masculinity, commodification, gender, and countless other issues, *Playing While White* examines the ways that racial profiling shapes the narrative, identities, and experiences of athletes, leading to separate and unequal experiences. It uses sports, and the profiling of white athletes, to spotlight antiblack racism within and beyond the sporting arena.

Reflecting on the ways that whiteness becomes desirable, normalized, different, victimized, minoritized, under attack, and the embodiment of goodness, *Playing While White* argues that ultimately the power of white athletes reflects the investment in whiteness, one that accounts for risks and payout, and the physical, material, political, and economic value of white athletic bodies.

It works to analyze, and expose "the everyday, invisible and subtle, cultural and social practices, ideas, and codes that discursively secure the power and privilege of white people, but that strategically remains unmarked, unnamed, and unmapped in comparison to society."[14] As noted by Richard Dyer[15] and Henry Giroux,[16] examining whiteness (within the sporting arenas and beyond) seeks "to make whiteness strange."[17] According to Dyer, "as long as race is something only applied to non-white peoples, as long as white people are not racially seen and named, they/we function as a human norm. Other people are raced, we are just people."[18] Still, unmarked whiteness anchors sporting cultures, naturalizing whiteness as a source of physical dominance, creativity, and sexual prowess.

Interrogating the narrative, textual, and contextual renderings of whiteness within sporting cultures makes "whiteness [become] unfrozen . . . as ensembles of local phenomena complexly embedded in socio-economic, socio-cultural and psychic interrelations. Whiteness emerges as a process, not a 'thing,' as plural rather than singular in nature."[19] Focusing on the structures of antiblack racism and the privileges of #PlayingWhileWhite as well as the lived, felt, and enduring realities of racism, this book examines the ways that race matters on (and off) the field.

The white athletes and sporting practices discussed within this book personify the normalization of whiteness on two levels that one might assume exist in contradiction. From Johnny Manziel to Hope Solo, from Josh Hamilton to Marshall Henderson, from collegiate athletes to Tom Brady, they are imagined as good kids who may make mistakes, but in no way are seen as representative of their community, even though the deployed narratives and available tropes are reflective of "the pedagogical lessons of whiteness."[20] These sporting examples teach us not only "how white people are represented, how we represent ourselves—images of white people or the cultural construction of white people,"[21] but how whiteness is lived, unpoliced, and free. White athletes are defined by the ubiquity and invisibility of this whiteness.

Yet, the presence of white bodies on and off the court and their place in the sportscape[22] reflect the hegemony of a sporting world that remains "black" and "white." "Blacks remain 'raced,' primarily as athletes, and whites prevail 'unmarked as racial subjects' in the role of spectators, the media and administrators."[23]

Whiteness is not limited to the sidelines, press boxes, and bleachers but is present on the field and within the narrative offering of sports. In order to understand the popularity and importance of white athletes, white teams, and white sports, it is important to understand the historical context of production. The new golden age of the white athlete reflects a multi-decade search for the "great white hope" to usher in the end of "the golden age of black athletics."[24] The spectacle, celebration, and hyper-visibility of the white superstar and the white peripheral athlete reflect the ideological and media search for the "great white athlete."[25]

The whiteness that white athletes, teams, and sports bring to the table is important, irrespective of its purported invisibility. The benefits and privileges are lived and grounded in material reality. The ability to transcend the regimes of surveillance that police hip-hop's "ballers of the new school"[26] allows white athletes to cash in on the privileges or "wages of whiteness," a Whiteness 2.0 without the markers of racial otherness. This demonstrates the utility of whiteness inside and outside of the arena.

The production of whiteness in white athletes is significant because of the broader racial landscape defined by claims of post-raciality and persistent inequality.[27] Kimberle Williams Crenshaw notes that dominant racial discourses, from popular culture to news media, consistently teach "that the absence of certain attributes accounts for the continued subordination of blacks."[28] New racism is evident, imbued, and perpetuated in the sporting landscape. Narratives of success, and those who pathologize failure with arguments about culture, individual choice, and values, are a fixture of new racism and the sporting landscapes. "The importance of race and the enduring fact of racism are relegated to the dustbin of history at a time in American life when the discourses of race and the spectacle of racial representation saturate the dominant media and public life," writes Henry Giroux. "The politics of the color line and representations of race have become far more subtle and complicated than they were in the Jim Crow era."[29] Cultural differences mark and rationalize the existence of inequality. As Amy Elizabeth Ansell notes, contemporary racial discourse "utilizes themes related to culture and nation as a replacement for the now discredited biological referents of the old racism."[30] The (idealized) white athlete does important work in the production of these racial discourses.

The white athletes that anchor this work are able to reap the benefits of whiteness because of both old and new racism, and because of the "racial scripts"[31] that imagine success and failure in culturally and racially deterministic ways. Encounters and experiences within the arena of sports, the criminal justice system, and the American media are overdetermined by the power of whiteness. The prospects of being seen as innocent, intelligent, smart, scrappy, heady, a team player, passionate, and a free spirit has material, ideological, and psychic value; the prospects of being celebrated, redeemed, commodified, and humanized are all reflective of the power of whiteness and embedded in America's racial DNA.

❖ ❖ ❖

Contemporary sports, given its market and media saturation, its integrated nature, its premium on masculinity, and the societal investment in athletic practices, lays an important foundation for the contemporary white imagination.[32] The fantasies and meanings of whiteness, blackness, and colorblindness emanate from playfields and sporting arenas, from talk radio, the Internet, and the televisual representations of ESPN.

Amid post-racial fantasies,[33] sporting cultures exist as an important site in the trafficking of racial ideas, narratives, and ideologies. Alongside the claims of colorblindness are the daily utterances of whiteness and racial otherness; the cashed-in wages and denied funds resulting from persistent racism are visible both on and off the field. "Sports is thus every bit a part of our trans/national landscape, a place inhabited by heroes and villains," write Michael Giardina and Michele Donnelly. "It is an open book of storylines, bold and beautiful, a history of the present told through box scores and movie scripts, [and] SportCenter highlight reels."[34] These sport pedagogies are central to the lessons of race and nation, class and gender, sexuality, and the dominant frames that guide public discourse. These stories, in different forms, emanate from a place of longing and loss, adoration and fantasy, heroization, and the celebration of whiteness.

Despite the visibility of blackness within American sporting cultures and the diversity of a globalized sporting life, whiteness is central to the commodification and consumptions of athletes and the sports they play. Whiteness and its relationship to antiblack racism are the oxygen and foundation for sporting cultures. Whiteness is central to understanding sporting narratives and the deployed frames used to process narratives involving crime, drugs, sexuality, opportunity, and other transgressions.

*Playing While White* works to document the ways in which sports render whiteness as "benign and non-threatening"; it looks at the ways in which whiteness is imagined, deployed, and consumed within sporting cultures, reflecting on power and privilege as well as costs and consequences. It reflects upon the invisibility of whiteness and the ways that sports teach what it means to be white in contemporary society.

This book accepts the task of analyzing, deconstructing, and contextualizing contemporary white athletes and the privileges they enjoy on and off the field. It looks at a culture of empowerment and empathy, a culture of redemption and excuses, and the ways that white athletes are emblematic of the power of whiteness. Given the importance of sport within contemporary culture and its existence as "one of the few places in American society where there is a consistent racial discourse,"[35] it is crucial that we offer critical, in the moment scholarship that reflects on the "wages of whiteness" on and off the sporting field. Given the unrelenting evidence that #AllLivesDoNot Matter, it has become a crucial time to reflect upon these pedagogical moments, because each one tells us something about sporting cultures in the twenty-first century and the continued power and privilege of whiteness. Guided by themes of innocence, intelligence, redemption, law and order, culture, leadership, criminality, and accountability, this book works to show what's bigger than the playing field, and most certainly bigger than a game.

*Playing While White* enters into societal discussions visible in our newspapers and on our websites, in our homes and work places, through a critical examination of several recent developments, spectacles, and changes, seeking to answer a fundamental question: what do these events and corresponding reactions/discourse reveal about race, class, gender, culture, and the American sports arena?

❖   ❖   ❖

The orientation of this book builds on W. E. B. DuBois and David Roediger's idea of "the wages of whiteness." Roediger,[36] who builds on DuBois's discussion of whiteness in *Black Reconstruction*[37] argues that in exchange for "whiteness" and the privileges granted from admission into this exclusive club, working-class whites pushed aside their class-consciousness and alliances with workers of color. Ruling elites bought compliance and silence from white workers through the appeal and privileges of whiteness. Sports continue to do this work.

*Playing While White* reflects on the ways that sports, through the validation of white athletes and white sporting cultures, through its demonization and policing of athletes of color, and through its advancement of a white hegemony, resembles a bank ATM machine where the wages of whiteness are withdrawn and deposited each and every day.[38] Borrowing from Kyle Kusz,[39] who documents the crisis and the revolt of the white athlete in post-1980s America, *Playing While White* argues that the anxiety resulting from the integration of American sports, the growing visibility of black athletes in a globalized corporate and new-media-driven sports culture, and even the election of Barack Obama have prompted further payouts that appease and satisfy the appetites of white fans.

Amid this heightened insecurity, ESPN and fans, sporting leagues and commentators alike, have placed their bets on the cultural, physical, ideological, and economic appeal of white sporting masculinity. Whiteness within sports is both a wage coveted by athletes, fans, and corporate powers and a calculated wager that works to provide security and preserve power in a moment of perceived instability. Herein lies the core argument of *Playing While White*.

This text also takes this discussion into the twenty-first century by recasting the wages of whiteness within discourses of racial profiling. Whereas discourses around profiling focus on the ways that antiblack racism contributes to differential treatment from the police—such as stop-and-frisk—this book works to show that within a society anchored by white supremacy, both people of color AND whites are profiled on and beyond the playing field. While people of color, whether driving, walking, or flying, face the burdens of profiling that result in surveillance, policing, and the presumption of guilt, whites cash in on the power of whiteness when profiled as innocent, law-abiding, intelligent, or moral. While black athletes live under a cloud of suspicion, stereotype, and demonization, white athletes play without burden, without skepticism, and without dehumanizing stereotypes. White athletes are individuals, innocent and desirable, celebrated and sought after, praiseworthy and contradictory. They are human and celebrated as such. *Playing While White* highlights the ways that contemporary sports embody these pedagogical lessons, providing power and privilege to white athletes and fans alike. Playing, performing, and competing while white have numerous benefits and privileges, all of which tell us about the power of whiteness on and off the field.

# CHAPTER 1

# THE SCRAPPY WHITE LEADER

*For him, there is no "I" in team.*
*A true leader.*
*A paragon of virtue.*
*A role model on and off the field.*
*A floor general.*
*Disciplined.*

THESE are just some of the clichés routinely directed at American athletes and coaches alike, at least those who are white and male. It is telling that the same descriptors associated with leadership, inside and outside of sports, mirror the tropes, stereotypes, and hegemonic profiles traditionally reserved for white males. White men are leaders, captains of industry, and role models; they have the requisite talents and temperament to inspire others to fulfill their greatness.

Compare these descriptors to criticisms commonly directed at black and brown athletes, such as Kobe Bryant, Allen Iverson, Dez Bryant, Terrell Owens, Odell Beckham Jr., Richard Sherman, Cam Newton, Russell Westbrook, Colin Kaepernick, and Yasiel Puig. What binds their experiences together within the larger issue of demonization is the trope of selfishness. Each has been demonized for being a bad teammate, for putting self in front of the team, and for otherwise caring more about personal success than winning. This is the exact opposite of the narrative afforded to numerous white athletes such as Johnny Manziel, Brett Favre, Larry Bird, John Stockton, Tom Brady, Tim Tebow, Ben Roethlisberger, Kevin Love, Aaron Rodgers, and Bryce Harper.

As a member of the Cleveland Cavs and Miami Heat, LeBron James was routinely vilified for putting himself in front of the team through his free agency moves, while Kevin Love was celebrated for teaming up with LeBron James in Cleveland. As with white coaches, from Vince Lombardi to Phil Jackson, white athletes benefit from entrenched ideas that whiteness is unselfishness, determination, scrappiness, intelligence, and a desire to win: that is the recipe for leadership.

Within white supremacist discourses, definitions of leadership center around whiteness and maleness. Dominant white racial frames imagine blackness as "emotional," "lazy," "selfish," and "violent," and therefore unfit to lead. Similarly, Asianness is typically profiled as "timid," "weak," and "feminine," all of which prove ineffective in a leader, whether quarterback, coach, CEO, or president. As noted by Edward Said in *Orientalism*: "There are Westerners, and there are Orientals. The former dominate; the latter must be dominated, which usually means having their land occupied, their internal affairs rigidly controlled, their blood and treasure put at the disposal of one or another Western power."[1] This sort of racist logic extends to black bodies, which are imagined as undisciplined and therefore incapable of governing and leading.

This chapter takes up the question of leadership and the tropes surrounding team, teammates, ego, and unselfishness. While focusing readers' attention on the celebratory narratives surrounding Tim Tebow, Johnny Manziel, and other white "leaders," it looks at the ways that "field generals" and captains, those who purportedly make their teammates better, are defined through whiteness. Such designations reflect not only the ways that whiteness maps onto the aesthetic, moral, and attitudinal dimensions of leadership, but also how tropes of scrappiness, morality, hard work, and selflessness operate within discourses of leadership.

The profiling of leaders as white males is not limited to white male bodies as evident in the honorary designation of Michael Jordan, Tim Duncan, Derek Jeter, Russell Wilson, and Stephen Curry as selfless team leaders. Not coincidentally, each also appears on the Mount Rushmore of post-racial or post-black athletes. Having transcended the scripts reserved for black athletic bodies, these five stars have been read through the tropes of white leadership, reaffirming the hegemony of #WhiteLeaderMan. Their exceptionality is coded in their apolitical demeanor, their quiet disposition, their color, stature, and other markers that put them outside of the definitions of hegemonic blackness. As exceptions, as celebrated black athlete leaders, they also become evidence of post-raciality, denying the profound ways that racial profiling constrains leadership narratives and the job position. Antiblack racism creates a world where being white means being perceived as without ego, unselfish, interested in putting the team first; and as being a leader with the requisite values to guide a team to athletic success and to provide a role model to teammates.

## THE FIELD GENERAL:
## (WHITE) QUARTERBACKS AS LEADERS

With the exception of the coach,[2] no other sports figure is celebrated as the quintessential leader like the football quarterback. Described as the field general, the coach on the field, a born leader, and the team's brain, the quarterback is imagined as the ultimate leader on and off the field. "The professional quarterback is unquestionably the most important, dominating position in all of sports. He not only handles the ball on almost every offensive down, he also represents the team," writes Alan Webber in the *Washington Post*. "He's the face of the franchise, the persona of the team, the focus of the coverage, the gem of endorsements. When the team wins, he's the hero (and usually the MVP). When it loses, he's the goat (and the one whose failure gets scrutinized, sometimes publicly by his own teammates)."[3] While such laudatory praise reflects the responsibilities of the quarterback—calling plays, communicating with the coach, calling audibles—and the visibility of the quarterback, which results in increased media attention and celebrity, the longstanding whiteness of the quarterback is central to the discourse around leadership.

The narrative surrounding quarterbacks as natural born leaders reflects the entrenched whiteness associated with position. "This pattern of racial inequality has been referred to as the 'mediocrity is a white luxury' phenomenon," writes Merrill Melnick.[4] "Also of interest to sport researchers is the apparent racial segregation by playing position in some team sports (the 'stacking' phenomenon)."[5] Given the history of positional segregation, and the playground-to-quarterback pipeline,[6] the dialectics between whiteness, quarterback, and leadership is not surprising. According to Daniel Buffington, "In American football, Black athletes tend to be overrepresented in peripheral positions such as wide receiver and defensive back, whereas White athletes tend to be overrepresented in central positions such as quarterback and center."[7] *Whiteness* and *quarterback* are such entangled concepts that it is almost impossible to imagine either without the other.[8] According to Andrew Billings: "The quarterback position remained the most frequently stereotyped position in sports. Often, sports teams had predominantly Black players but usually had a White quarterback directing the offense, fulfilling the two most common stereotypes of ethnicity in sports: (a) the perceived superiority of White athletes in measures of intelligence and work ethic (Birrell 1989; McCarthy and R. L. Jones 1997); and (b) the presumed athleticism ('born athletes') on the part of Black athletes (D. Z. Jackson 1989; Staples and T. Jones, 1985; Whannel 1992)."[9]

Because the quarterback is associated with leadership, and because white masculinity is mapped onto leadership bodies, it is no wonder that white football players are pushed into the field general position. In recent years, the linkages between whiteness, quarterback, and leadership were on full display with Peyton Manning.

As a member of football's first family, Peyton Manning's leadership skill is widely revered. His near obsession with the game, his propensity to study film, and his purported commitment in practice are cited as evidence of his leadership skills. According to the discourse, his success is about more than statistics and wins but the determination and confidence that he shows each and every day. According to Gary Burnison:

> Survey[s] shows that at any leadership level, like President, CEO, or sports figure—the great leaders rise above and represent the team more than themselves. Leaders demonstrate that they are in charge and in control. And part of being in charge is their belief they will overcome the odds and win—and they do. Much of this is driven by their aura of confidence, a presence that permeates the culture. This is apparent in Peyton Manning's deep belief that he and his team will make it. He carries that through in his off the field demeanor. Anyone can just look into his eyes and see the deep confidence of an unshakable winner. . . . He has the intangibles that make a leader great.[10]

Similarly, fellow leadership expert Alan Webber celebrates Tom Brady's leadership qualities, which are more valuable than his laser accuracy or his feel for the game: "Achievements aren't what make Tom Brady who he is. That's not what has taken him from good to great, either as a quarterback or as a leader. What marks him a role model for leadership is his approach to the game: personal humility and professional will."[11] As if to further make clear the racial subtext in both the celebration of Brady and the qualities associated with leadership, Webber praises Brady for his discipline, preparation, selfless drive, and his focus on making his teammates and team and, implicitly, America itself, better: "His imprint is on his team, not his ego. He's never satisfied with his own performance. He knows that he can do better, should do better, has to do better. He also knows that he has to lead by example. . . . It's this kind of selfless drive coupled with professional will that not only makes Brady better, and makes the team better, but also sends a message to the younger players."[12]

Confident, yet humble; knowledgeable yet willing to learn; successful yet never content: these are the qualities celebrated in Manning,[13] Brady,[14] Drew Brees,[15] Andrew Luck,[16] Aaron Rodgers,[17] and countless other (white) quarterbacks.

With rare exception—such as the Seahawks' Russell Wilson[18]—the white quarterback is both the benchmark and example of the types of leadership necessary in today's sports culture. No wonder black quarterbacks—Colin Kaepernick, Cam Newton, Robert Griffin III, Michael Vick, and Donovan McNabb—have been widely criticized for their lack of leadership, lack of toughness, and inability to elevate the games of others.[19] In a recent ESPN ranking, Jameis Winston's position as the seventeenth-best quarterback in the league was justified with this assault on his leadership skills:

> "Winston's buffoonery just didn't show up," an offensive coordinator said. "They found a way to play very, very tough on offense and they found a way to hand the ball off a lot, which took tons off him. What they did down there was one of the best-kept secrets going, and it saved the kid. I thought they rallied around him and I was happy for him. He talks out of his ass, and I was just never sure if there was a real guy in there and whether he could really, truly bring people together and lead them. They helped him, and he did it.[20]

The racial scripts are clear not only in the criticism of his intangibles and lack of leadership, but in the praise for his coaches. Still, denial that race matters is widespread within modern sports culture.

While holding onto narratives of colorblindness, the discourse makes clear that leadership definitions are not about race or gender. Instead, it imagines true leadership as resulting from work ethic and passion for the game. To work hard and love the game comes through respecting the sport. Such respect and the passion for the game (scrappiness) is why some guys leave it all on the field, offering gutsy performance. This is what leadership looks like.

It is also about winning. Winners are leaders; leaders are winners. If you win, you are more likely to be seen as a leader. At least that is the narrative of the dominant discourse. Yet, this isn't always the case, as evidenced by the demonization of Cam Newton and Colin Kaepernick as selfish, of Ohio State's Cardale Jones as lacking the requisite mind-set to lead a team. Yet Tim Tebow,[21] who won very seldom after college, and Johnny Manziel, who didn't win titles at any level, have been positioned as pure leaders, inspiring their teammates to maximize their talents.

Writing about Tim Tebow, who is routinely described as a winner, a leader, and as someone players would follow into a "fox hole," Donald Wood sees Tebow's leadership as bigger than calling plays or leading the team to wins: "While most people think of QBs as the on-field leaders that show up every Sunday, it's the actions that those players take behind the scenes that have their teammates trusting and respecting them. . . . The NFL should have their crack team of overpaid employees analyze what makes Tebow such a good leader and build a model to help other quarterbacks that don't know how to lead a team some idea on how it's done. Maybe Tebow should teach a class. Leadership 101."[22]

Praised for his soft-spoken, lead-by-example approach, his "mental toughness,"[23] and his commitment to winning, for several years Tim Tebow was the poster child for sports leadership. His successes, his on-the-field struggles, and his approach to retirement are all pointed as evidence of his leadership. "Possibly because Tebow grasps something about leadership that [other coaches] have yet to learn: It's not about domination but about persuasion. Someone who tries to force others to do his bidding isn't a leader; he's a warlord. Leadership only works when other people find you credible and grant you their cooperation," writes Sally Jenkins in the *Washington Post*. "So what exactly is that mysterious quality called leadership? It's not exactly charisma; it doesn't hurt that Tebow gleams like a superhero, but the worst despots are charismatic too. It's not exactly talent, either. According to experts, one reason we struggle to define it is because we look at it from the wrong side up."[24] Tebow's integrity, confidence, decision-making, clarity, and consistency are what make him a good leader. His religious faith was consistently cited as evidence of his leadership skills. In a society purportedly without a moral fabric, especially on America's sporting fields, Tebow was seen to bring a level of stability to his team. He was seen as the perfect leader, because he brought discipline, morality, and an ethos that turned his (black) teammates into more productive ballers and citizens. According to Steve Tobak, a CBS Money commentator, Tebow's leadership qualities highlight the importance of faith and family:

Have faith. There's absolutely no doubt that Tebow's religious faith drives his faith in himself. And that, in turn, drives his teammate's faith in him, which seems to inspire the entire team to perform at a ridiculously high level and win against all odds. . . . Inspiration is inspiring. Faith is self-fulfilling. . . . Culture is key. Growing up with a strong family unit, sense of community, and system of ethics and beliefs—as Tebow did—is really important in leadership. I think people with a strong cultural background are more effective at creating a strong corporate culture. They also tend to make building team spirit a priority.[25]

Noting how players "respond to him" and how he inspires players to exceed their potential, former Pennsylvania governor Ed Rendell identified Tebow's greatness as about more than stats: "One intangible the so-called experts often overlook is one I think makes for truly great quarterbacks—leadership. Tebow might not be the best passer in the NFL, or anywhere close to it, but his leadership can produce victories. He did it for Denver, but never got the chance for the Jets."[26]

Tebow's ineptitude on the field, from his inability to move an offense, his extremely low completion percentage, and even his struggles on the baseball field all became evidence of his leadership qualities. Because he made his teammates better and won despite his failures, he was a good leader. In spite of his inability to throw touchdowns or secure first downs, he was able to lead his team to victories. Therefore he must be a great leader. His failures became part of the leadership narrative. It requires toughness to continue to battle in the face of endless incomplete passes (or strike outs) and media scrutiny. His ability to move forward spoke to his leadership abilities; the fortitude required to compete and guide a team toward victories even as pundits questioned one's talents reflected his leadership skills. This sort of logic anchored the discourse surrounding Tebow, embodying the ways that his profile as white quarterback, as Christian field general, propelled the mythology of Tebow as winner and leader. So did the narrative of Tebow being unathletic. To compensate for these inadequacies, he played with an edge, he was scrappy, and he worked hard, all of which not only enhanced his play but also served as a model for his teammates. While necessary because of his purported deficiencies, because he was just an "average Joe," his discipline, his scrappy never-die attitude made him into a top leader.

## SCRAPPY, HARDWORKING EVERYMAN:
### LEADING BY EXAMPLE

As conceptions of whiteness and leadership entwine, the definitions of what makes a good leader, what inspires teammates to reach their own greatness, all work through hegemonic definitions of whiteness. To be a white athlete is to be a leader; to be a white athlete is to be a scrappy and gritty player, whose motor never stops, whose "drive never relents," and whose determination is unmatched. These qualities are consistently noted.

In its list of the ten scrappiest players in baseball, the *Bleacher Report* inadvertently highlights the aesthetics (and racial subtexts) of scrappiness. In every context, scrappiness translates to hits and outs (or catches/tackles in the NFL; basket/rebounds in the NBA) and leadership: "Whether it's diving for out of reach grounders, running hard to first every time they make contact, or fearlessly tracking down flies headed straight toward the fence, these players make the most out of their time on the field. Although grinders usually go somewhat unnoticed not being as flashy and naturally talented as some of their teammates, these guys will always have a place in my heart."[27]

Baseball has long monopolized the scrappy discourse, because of its place as a national pastime within American folklore as emblematic of the nation's democratic exceptionalism.[28] In recent years, reflecting the dialectics between it and militarism, because of the staging of a particular vision of masculinity, and because of its popularity, football has emerged as the principal site for the production of narratives of scrappiness and leadership.

Seen as "too small, too slow,"[29] Wes Welker had relatively successful college and NFL careers. Defying expectations, Welker used these doubts, rooted in stereotypes about whites, to fuel his pursuit of ambition. His success was attributed to his work ethic,[30] his intelligence,[31] his scrappiness,[32] and his dedication.[33] According to Jeff Howe, "It would, however, be a mistake to think Welker's success . . . derives solely from the practice field. Yet, that's where his work begins. Welker has been counted out so many times that he doesn't understand the purpose of downshifting gears. The next second he lets up would be the first."[34] Similarly, Monique Walker makes clear that despite being an elite athlete and a Pro-Bowl player, Wes Welker was an everyman. "There are Wes Welkers everywhere. He is the scrappy receiver on the high school football team. Or he is the smallish player with bursts of quickness hidden among his college teammates."[35] As he could relate to others, he was a leader, who inspired not only his teammates but also boys throughout the nation who were able to see themselves on the field because of people like Welker.

Likewise, for Christopher L. Gasper, who describes Welker as a real-life Rudy, as "5-foot-nothing, and a hundred-and-nothing pounds" and as someone stifled by his "diminutive stature," he was a superstar, an MVP. His contributions on and off the field were just as important: "The humble, hard-working wide receiver with the Oklahoma twang and incomparable game has stepped up and filled a leadership void, risked life and limb to keep the chains moving."[36]

What is striking with this narrative is how Welker's scrappiness and intelligence are seen as exceptional, as necessary compensation for his diminutive size and his deficient athleticism. More importantly, the narrative defines these qualities in relationship to his skills as a "leader." He inspires his teammates and others inside and outside the league to dedicate themselves to their craft, to maximize effort, and to otherwise elevate their game. Through his action, he is motivating players to be professional, to be disciplined, and to focus on becoming the best NFL players and men possible. "It's been for the better, as his teammates at each level have raised their games to follow his lead, and his counterparts in the NFL have compared Welker's passion at practice to some of the best players in the league at nearly every position."[37]

As an undrafted free agent, Welker reportedly had to work for everything; these experiences and his approach to the game have made him into an important leader. That because of his size and (supposed lack of) athleticism, that because he was never handed anything, and that because he was often underestimated, he had become a tremendous leader. Through his words and actions he was a powerful role model to his teammates. According to Isaiah Burse "It's funny how he was an undrafted free agent, too, and he became so successful. Just seeing him is kind of like a dream. For me, it's like I know I can do it. If he can do it—not taking away from his ability or anything—but I know if he can do it, I can do it. I want to learn everything from him so I can be successful, as well, in the future."[38]

The story of Welker is not unique (it is a similar story afforded to Tim Tebow and Johnny Manziel), nor is it limited to football; we see this kind of narrative emerge about David Eckstein (baseball), Matthew Dellavedova (basketball), Dustin Pedroia (baseball), Nik Stauskas (basketball), Aaron Craft (basketball), and many more. "David Eckstein is more than a 'scrappy' little player," Bill Shaikin notes, in his commentary, that there must be "an unwritten rule that every story about David Eckstein must describe him with that adjective."[39]

Matthew Dellavedova, the Cavaliers point guard, found himself in several skirmishes during the 2015 and 2016 NBA playoffs, resulting in debates about whether he was a dirty player or simply scrappy and hardworking. According to Charles Barkley, "He doesn't have the talent of some of the others, so he has to be a pest."[40] To stay in the league, to get onto the court, he needed to be scrappy, and to have a "motor" unlike his peers. Like his scrappy peers, his contribution is one of leadership, inspiring his teammates to sacrifice their bodies, to hustle, and do the "little things."

And then there is Aaron Craft, a former star point guard from Ohio State University, and who, according to sport media blogger Matt Yoder, was never seen as a true athlete. "Nobody ever talks about Craft's natural talent or athletic ability— the consensus is he only gets by on pure scrappiness and fundamentals and being a 'lunch pail guy' as if anyone actually still carries those around these days."[41]

Celebrated for his "grit"[42] for his "all-around scrappy-do" approach to the game,[43] "hustle and intensity,"[44] as "a scrappy and heady senior,"[45] and as "scrappy and gutty and feisty,"[46] Aaron Craft embodied the hegemonic media scripts governing white players, as well as the connections made between being "scrappy" and being a leader. Bill Raftery once "described Craft as having 'a toughness in that jersey that belies the angelic countenance.'"[47] Over and over again, we see the imposition of whiteness and the signifiers branching from the broader tree in the narratives surrounding white athletes.

The *Boston Globe* once portrayed the Boston Red Sox's Dustin Pedroia as "the national pastime's epitome of pluck, a trash-talking scrapper who outplayed expectations at every level, from T-ball to the bigs, grinding his way to stardom."[48] According to his college coach, "Dustin always had a chip on his shoulder, like a fighter going into the ring who is trying to prove he belongs. He was special from day one. I wish every coach had a chance to coach a Pedroia."[49] His grit, work ethic, and determination have made him a great player. He was a self-made man. At least that was the media narrative circulated over and over and again.

Noting the power in the myth, Tommy Craggs highlights how the commodification of Pedroia, especially in the post-steroid era, is wrapped into his position as the scrappy white leader:

> Pedroia's story has lined up neatly with a story baseball desperately wants to tell about itself, here at the dawn of what we're now all solemnly calling the Post-Steroid Era. Two years into Pedroia's career, in fact, it has already been smoothed into myth: the tiny Everyman who, by dint of sheer effort and uncommon grit, without the benefit of size or Norbolethone, manages to pull himself through the early chapters of an Alger novel and become

a superstar. The little infielder who could. A grinder. Plucky. Scrappy—always scrappy.[50]

In his article, "On Pedroia, Gonzalez and Perceptions," Peter Abraham further argues that irrespective of facts Dustin Pedroia is routinely reduced to the "scrappy" player:

> Pedroia is scruffy, he says funny things to the media and he looks like he really cares. Therefore we all assume he's clutch and plays hard and really cares. That he is shorter than most players leads us to believe he's a great overachiever. Terry Francona used to say all the time that Pedroia "wills" himself to be great. Pedroia is not an overachiever. He played college baseball for a major program (Arizona State) and was a second-round draft pick. He has ridiculously quick hands, tremendous hand-eye coordination and he's strong. He doesn't will himself to do anything any more than any other player can. It's an insult to his ability to suggest he's an overachiever. Pedroia is an excellent player because he has excellent skills and works hard to make them better, not because he's Scrappy McScraperson.[51]

Just as the term *leadership* is a dog whistle signaling whiteness, so is the use of the term *scrappy*. It is reserved for white players, and seeks to define their success through tropes of hard work, determination, guts, and perseverance. As with narratives of intelligence, the scrappy frame emerges from the racial script that presents black players as physically advantaged and athletically privileged, thus forcing white players to compensate for their deficiencies with scrappiness.

According to a blogger at *Deadspin*, "as we all know by now, 'scrappy' is a meaningless, arbitrary, clichéd adjective that sportswriters use to describe baseball players they like. Often, these players are small, white, terrible at baseball, David Eckstein, or all four of the above."[52] Similarly, Matt Yoder offers a powerful list of descriptors reserved for white athletes:

> These crutches and code words are common in the sports world, where a player's race all too often decides what kind of player he or she will be. It's not exclusive to American sports either. You're never going to hear Pro Bowl DE Cameron Jordan complimented with having a high motor, but that's seemingly the only phrase that is allowed to describe J. J. Watt. Another good example came

in the Wild Card Playoffs on the weekend when Mike Mayock called Chiefs QB Alex Smith "sneaky athletic" even though he had over 1,000 rushing yards at Utah and had one of the most notable TD runs by a QB in playoff history. He's not 'sneaky athletic' at all. He's just athletic. . . . Here's the top White Guy Code Words to look out for so that you can avoid using them only for white athletes and be more progressive in your sports fandom. Case in point, I think all of these have been used to describe Dustin Pedroia.

1. Scrappy
2. High motor
3. Gamer
4. Sneaky athletic
5. Gritty
6. Winner
7. High IQ
8. Good fundamentals
9. Plays the game the right way
10. Lunch pail guy
11. Heady and/or cerebral
12. Deceptive speed
13. Gym rat
14. Intangibles
15. Gets the most out of his abilities
16. Has a lot of heart
17. Grinder
18. Out-hustles
19. Someone you'd love your daughter to date
20. David Eckstein
21. Wes Welker type
22. Coach's son
23. Faster than he appears [53]

Commenting on the ways that national media describes Danny Woodhead as "scrappy," despite the fact that many of his peers are of the same stature, and play with the same level of fearlessness and ferocity, Tommy Craggs points to the ways that whiteness over determines the narrative. "Woodhead is a 'small,' super-fast running back in a league with no great shortage of them. The difference is that little Danny is blessed with sufficient amounts of Vitamin D to get called scrappy over and over in the national media." [54]

#PlayingWhileWhite means being labeled as scrappy and determined; it means being celebrated for intangibles that translate into white athletic success on-the-field and in the locker room as inspiring leaders.

In 2014, *New Yorker* columnist Jonathan Chait penned "What White People Don't See When They Watch Basketball." Focusing on media coverage of University of Michigan basketball, Chait notes how #PlayingWhile White means being seen as tough, smart, gritty, and scrappy:

> A couple of years ago, the basketball team I root for, the University of Michigan, had a player named Zack Novak. Everybody loved his story. He was slow and pudgy coming out of high school, recruited by nobody, and offered a spot at Michigan. Turned out he could play, at least some. He was only six foot three, but he played power forward, compensating for his lack of size and skill with unrelenting effort. . . . If you watch college sports, you know the kind of player I'm talking about. Right: a white guy. . . . Watching him hang in there on the low block against opponents five or six inches taller every game was a constant miracle. He was a gritty, hustling, tough, smart overachiever.

Chait connects Novak's career to that of Nik Stauskas, who despite having a flashy game, being a collegiate superstar, often talking trash, and playing the game with swagger, was another Novak. His grit, toughness, work ethic, and intelligence were often noted.

Chait also juxtaposes the Stauskas/Novak story with that of Jordan Morgan, another Michigan player, who in Chait's eyes embodies the basketball "rags-to-riches" story:

> The thing is, there is a player on the team this year who's almost exactly like Zack Novak. His name is Jordan Morgan. In high school, he was pudgy, slow, and small. No major conference programs except Michigan offered him a scholarship. But he physically transformed himself and has become, like Novak, an amazing overachiever. As a six-foot-seven center, he's almost as undersize for his position as Novak is. He won't shoot unless he's within a couple feet of the basket, and often not even then, because opposing players can often swat away his shot attempts. Instead he spends most of every offensive possession throwing his body around the court, setting screen after screen to open up shots for

his teammates. He uses leverage, smarts, and unrelenting effort to gain every inch of advantage fighting against opposing centers. Morgan is a fifth-year senior who already graduated with a degree in engineering, and is studying for a master's degree in manufacturing engineering. But the announcers don't talk about this stuff even one-tenth as often as they did Novak. And when they do, they don't use terms like "gritty," "unselfish," "scrappy," and "smart." My explanation is that it is because . . . he's black.

Unfortunately, like so much of this part of the discourse, Chait reduces these stereotypes and media representations to individual prejudice and implicit bias rather the structures of antiblack racism. He too recycles narratives of white victimhood (although his inclusion of Morgan pushes the conversation in important ways), revealing how the privileges of whiteness operate in these moments. #PlayingWhileWhite means cashing in on the privileges while becoming a victim at the same time.

The likes of Tebow, Pedroia, Stauskas, Welker, and countless brethren all cash in on these scripts: they are leaders because they are gritty and work hard; they are good locker room guys; role models; leaders; glue guys; guys who can fit in; and sources of inspiration. Yet, they are also imagined as victims, which for Chait and others becomes part of why they are successful: to challenge those stereotypes and profiles, as well as the doubters and haters, each competes in a way that makes them invaluable.

Victimized by stereotypes that "white men can't jump," that they are slow and physically weak, this part of this narrative recasts white athletes as having a distinct experience from their black counterparts. Seen as scrappy/gritty/motor/determined stereotypes, white athletes, thus, are burdened with unfair expectations and prejudices, which of course constrains opportunities and how coaches, teammates, opponents, and fans see them. The discourse of white victimhood erases the ways that these racial logics and scripts not only shape the experiences of African American athletes but also exist as an anchor of white supremacy.

To look at the tropes of scrappiness requires examining discourses and practices that see black athletes as "lazy," "entitled," and lacking the requisite skills to be a leader. The #PlayingWhileScrappy (being a white athlete) frame just as the hegemony of the #PlayingDespiteLazy frame (being a black athlete) is one based in antiblack racism.

The racial importance of the scrappy trope, and its links to the ways we imagine leadership, victimhood, and athlete of year's past through whiteness, can be powerfully seen in the infamous career of Johnny Manziel.

Notwithstanding his propensity to talk trash,[55] his endless rap sheet, which includes multiple arrests, a sense of entitlement on steroids,[56] demotions resulting from lying to his coach, betrayal, and so much more, Manziel's career was one in which he was continuously held up as an example of an all-American kid fighting to lead his team toward victory.

## JOHNNY FOOTBALL: A REAL LEADER

Irrespective of the trash-talking,[57] the off-the-field difficulties,[58] the limited résumé (only two years of college football), the fact that his entourage once included Drake and LeBron James, and other distractions, the rise of Johnny Manziel was all about his supposed role as team leader. Skip Bayless once described him as a "rare specimen" who has the potential to "lead" a team to the promised land. He was a "proven leader" and a "winner."

His whiteness has everything to do with this fanfare and his being seen as a leader;[59] while Manziel has come and gone, the narrative and the type of coverage he experienced provide a window into the value and meaning of contemporary sporting whiteness. Whether celebrated as a crusader, a throwback, a passionate and determined young man, or as someone who, despite size and whiteness, is dominating the quarterback position, Manziel embodies the pedagogies of sporting whiteness. He is the embodiment of the power and privileges resulting from #PlayingWhileWhite. Even in those moments of disappointment, the media's narrative focused on his unfulfilled potential as a leader to not only his teammates but to countless (white) kids who looked up to the "improbable" superstar.

The celebration of Manziel was as much the wages of white "swagger" as anything else. Bucky Brooks made this clear:

> The term "swagger" is overused in sports today, but Manziel's game is dipped in confidence and self-belief. He seemingly walks on the field with a boulder-sized chip on his shoulder, yet his teammates respond to his bodacious leadership style. Watching the Aggies rally back from an enormous deficit, I witnessed Manziel's teammates feed off his energy and enthusiasm.[60]

The narrative of "Johnny Football" as quintessential leader reached new heights following the 2013 Chick-fil-A Bowl game where Texas A&M came back from a larger deficit.[61] Down by several touchdowns, Manziel was seen screaming at his teammates on the sidelines only before *he* led them to a monumental win.

In wake of their victory, his "pep talk," his encouraging words, his passionate plea to his teammates (as opposed to a tirade or public belittlement of his teammates) was cited as reason for their comeback and evidence of his leadership qualities. Never mind the failures to lead the team in the first half; never mind the improvements shown by the defense in the second half of the game; never mind his team's superiority to a Duke team that played over its head for thirty minutes—it was all about Johnny Manziel.

His legend—fueled by the mythology surrounding his career, his profile as a scrappy leader, and his reported toughness = his whiteness— was fully visible. In "Statement Game: How Johnny Manziel Silenced His Critics with Last Night's Performance," Trevor LaFauci noted:

> It was his actions on the sideline that gave us a different look at Manziel. Throughout A&M's comeback there was one constant: Manziel firing up his teammates. He pulled aside star receiver Mike Evans in the first-half after Evans got his second unsportsmanlike penalty to talk to him. He huddled with his offense on the bench and got them riled up. He raised his arms to the crowd to pump them up.

Similarly, a report in *Sports Illustrated* framed Manziel as a team-first guy who cared about his team's success and ultimately doing whatever it took to win.

> Johnny Manziel marched back and forth on the sideline during the first quarter of Texas A&M's game against Duke in the Chick-fil-A Bowl. Moments after the Blue Devils had prevented the normally prolific Aggies from reaching the end zone for a third straight series, a fiery Manziel got in the face of several teammates as A&M stared at a 14–3 hole early in the contest. . . . Manziel wasn't pointing fingers. Instead, the electric quarterback, playing perhaps his last game in a Texas A&M uniform, was demanding accountability.[62]

While comparing Johnny Manziel to Allen Iverson, minus the tattoos, cornrows, and skin color ("he comes from a much more privileged background"), Tony Lee celebrated their similar leadership styles and abilities. Identifying his "heart," his "stature," and his determination as why he has the necessary leadership skills, Lee concluded:

Manziel showed he had the intangibles—being a leader on the field and deftly handling interviews—to succeed in the NFL. Manziel was the team's emotional and spiritual leader during the game. He implored his defense to "take it from them. . . . And after the game, Manziel was Tom Brady-like in his interviews. He's grown, as can be seen in the post-game interview where he says all the right things about loving his coach and teammates.[63]

His intelligence, heart, and "intangibles" are what make him a great leader. He yells because he is passionate; he screams because he has to bring that energy since presumably he lacks the "physical talents" to lead and succeed. #PlayingWhileWhite.

Herein lies a core element of the racialized celebration of Johnny Manziel and the privileges baked into whiteness: #PlayingWhileWhite means constantly being imagined as an inspirational leader. Manziel, like many white quarterbacks before him, embodies hegemonic notions of white masculinity and its association with leadership. He has the requisite skills to inspire and galvanize his teammates—his whiteness is central to that ascribed role.

Whereas Manziel is celebrated for leading, for encouraging his teammates to reach their potential, for "rallying the troops,"[64] for being "the team's emotional and spiritual leader,"[65] for helping his team as they "feed off his energy and enthusiasm,"[66] black athletes often face questions about their motives and effectiveness as leaders. Black athletes are routinely demonized as combative, selfish, and as "cancers" to their teams.[67] For example, in the aftermath of the Dallas Cowboys' wide receiver Dez Bryant getting in the face of quarterback Tony Romo and tight end Jason Witten, Bryant was vilified in the media. He was described as "selfish,"[68] as having "flipped out,"[69] and as "lacking class and maturity."[70]

Jason Whitlock used the sideline confrontation as a moment to not only criticize Bryant but to recycle a culture of poverty narrative that demonized single-parent black homes. Whitlock lamented "Dez Bryant's inability to control his emotions," which, to him, is "a family dysfunction issue." While acknowledging the effects of the war on drugs, divestment from public schools, and mass incarceration, Whitlock continued his focus on the "dysfunctional" (black) families:

> Dez Bryant is swirling in a cultural tsunami every bit as destructive and powerful as climate change.
>
> Its victims are primarily black and brown, but Hurricane Illegitimacy is a not black or brown problem. It's an American

problem that is denied and exacerbated on the left and mischar-
acterized and exploited on the right.

Like climate change, Hurricane Illegitimacy is powered by
man-made factors:

1. A lack of proper restraints on welfare entitlement
   programs for single mothers and fathers. . . .
5. Our collective lack of courage and resolve to combat
   popular-culture forces that celebrate, normalize and profit
   from baby-mama and criminal culture.

Because of this melting-pot-country's history, we've been condi-
tioned to identify the race of a person misbehaving and examine
the racial implications. We would be far better served looking at
the family history.[71]

It is not uncommon for black athletes, particularly those who are demonstra-
tive, animated, and passionate, to be called out as selfish, mean, destructive,
crazy, difficult, and otherwise not good teammates. For example, throughout
his NBA career, Kobe Bryant was denounced as selfish, as a distraction, as
a bad teammate, and as someone who didn't make his teammates better.[72]
From his shot selection to his salary, he was demonized as someone who
didn't put the team first. During the 2012–13 season, Kobe Bryant called out
Dwight Howard for his lackadaisical play:

We don't have time for [Howard's shoulder] to heal. We need
some urgency. . . . [Howard] has never been in a position where
someone is driving him as hard as I am, as hard as this organization is. It's win a championship or everything is a complete failure.
That's just how [the Lakers] do it. And that's foreign to him.[73]

Few praised Bryant's comments. Instead, many in the media denounced
him for "throwing Dwight under the bus" and not supporting him. This was
nothing new for Bryant, who has never been identified as a good leader.
His yelling at teammates was rarely seen as encouragement or support but
rather as anger and ego. "The root cause of the Lakers' dysfunction has been
consistent for 15 years. It is Kobe Bryant's ego . . . Kobe emasculates his big
men," noted Jason Whitlock.[74] Similarly, in 2002, ESPN's Mike Greenberg
wrote, "Everything Kobe says and does these days gives the impression he is
playing for himself. That's not the way to win a title. This isn't about what is
best for Kobe; it's about what is best for the Lakers and the league. And what
is best for both of them right now is for Kobe to go away." Such critiques are

rooted in a broader discourse that sees blackness as a dysfunctional cultural movement that encourages misogyny, materialism, selfishness, and contempt for the accepted, civilized, and established (white) values of both the sports world and society as a whole. Even when athletes like Johnny Football or Tim Tebow embody the athletic styles or the imagined cultural disposition associated within blackness, they get a pass.

Johnny Manziel rarely faced accusations of selfishness. Despite berating teammates and taunting opponents as a college athlete, spending more time in Vegas than at the Browns' facility while a professional, or, reportedly not being able to "put down the weed," the rap on Johnny was almost never that he was a selfish pariah or a toxic influence. His love for his teammates and his leadership abilities were rarely questioned. Instead, his yelling was reconstituted into evidence of his passion for winning and his yearning to elevate the game of his brothers; his Twitter confrontations became seen as proof of his willingness to defend his teammates; his off-the-field difficulties were reimagined as reminders of his ability to deal with the pressure and still succeed; his troubles were used to humanize him and reflect on his future maturation. #PlayingWhileWhite.

## MANZIEL AS FREEDOM FIGHTER

The power of whiteness has been a defining element in Manziel's career, and the power of white privilege was fully visible in the aftermath of a 2013 investigation of Manziel for allegedly signing autographs illegally. Noted as evidence of the NCAA's hypocrisy, as part of the sham of amateurism, as proof that student athletes were indeed indentured servants,[75] as reason why the NCAA should start paying student athletes,[76] the narrative positioned Manziel as changing the landscape of college sports.[77] He was leading to change, battling the injustices within collegiate sports. He was a "trailblazer."[78] For media and fans alike, the prospect of his being suspended for allegedly receiving payment for autographs was outrageous. It was evidence of the hypocrisy of the NCAA.

Noting the many ways the NCAA and countless others profit from "Johnny Football," Dan Wetzel wrote, "Forget outrage. Forget arguing that a guy such as Manziel should be able to profit off his own likeness (which he should). Forget mocking the light penalty—does he get a timeout in the corner, too? Forget even again debunking the ridiculous notion of 'amateurism' that college sports exploits."[79] While acknowledging Terrelle Pryor before him, "Manziel's greatest act as a college football player is exposing this absurdity in all its glory."[80] Of course, the situation involving Pryor, who was suspended for selling memorabilia, did not elicit widespread calls for reform, or sympathetic media reports; the criminalization of Dez Bryant or Reggie Bush, both of whom were punished under the NCAA's draconian rules, did not lead to celebratory narratives that positioned them as good in the face of the pernicious NCAA.

Amid the many reports, questions, and uncertainties was an emergent narrative of Manziel as "game-changer," as someone who would rightly battle the injustices of the NCAA. With "Manziel Case Was Tipping Point," Jen Engel recast the one-time football player by day, partier by night as a collegiate freedom fighter. His defiance, his refusal to play by the NCAA rules, and his "show me the money" approach to autographs were all seen as part of a plan to bring down the NCAA. Manziel was a game-changer, a transformative hero within a larger history of struggle. "Once upon a time in this country, there were ugly, racist, tyrannical rules dictating where a black person could sit on a bus. There were all kinds of these laws, actually, created and defended by the racists who benefited from them," notes Engel. American racism ended because an "everyday woman named Rosa Parks, who had grown tired of being tired" said no. She "was merely the tipping point for many Americans long since tired of these immoral laws." Manziel was also tired, albeit of the NCAA making money off his labor, name, and signature. Consequently, Engel finds that Manziel, too, will lead us to the promised land of reform.[81]

The Parks reference demonstrated a lack of substantive understanding of Rosa Parks's activism,[82] the larger history of the black freedom struggle, the level of terror experienced by African Americans inside and outside the movement,[83] the persistence of racism, or those activists fighting collegiate athletic injustice. It reflects the power of colorblind racism—claims that racism no longer represents an obstacle, seemingly ignoring the persistence of racism as evidence by discriminatory subprime loans, stop-and-frisk, mass incarceration, racial profiling, job discrimination, police shootings, the rise of Donald Trump, and anti-immigrant scapegoating.[84] It also embodies the power of whiteness.

Manziel is no Rosa Parks. Rosa Parks trained, sacrificed, and participated in the Civil Rights movement. In fact, he's no James Reeb, Michael Schwerner, Viola Liuzzo, Andrew Goodman, Anne Braden, or Bob Zellner either. All were active participants in the black freedom struggle, sacrificing tremendously.[85] Their participation, as whites, elicited national attention and sympathy, a strategy employed by the movement as part of an effort to elicit support by highlighting white pain.[86] While Engel and others tried to make such an argument—that Manziel, because of his popularity and status, would elicit outrage toward the NCAA—the failure to account for race and class demonstrates a major shortcoming. Worse yet, the individuals listed above participated in a movement alongside countless others who sacrificed greatly for the cause. Manziel was a movement for and about himself. A movement is not "Johnny Football," his friends, and his permanent marker.

Rather than join a movement, partner with a group like National College Players Association, #AllPlayersUnited, or voice his support for unionization or Ed O'Bannon's lawsuit against the NCAA's use of student athlete likenesses within video games,[87] Manziel followed in the footsteps of his capitalist forefathers: he got paid. And he barely got punished for the reported rule violation.

And for that, according to Engel, he is Rosa Parks. He is a tipping point. She writes, "On a much less historically significant scale, so it is with Johnny Football—and no, this is not intended in any way to compare the vast evil of Jim Crow to an incompetent NCAA investigation, or to slings from TV commentators."[88] While Engel had previously chastised then Ohio State quarterback Terrelle Pryor for rules violations, Manziel's refusal to abide by NCAA rules was evidence of his sacrifice, his courageous stance, and his willingness to lead college athletics toward a new chapter.

Dave Zirin brilliantly challenged the Johnny Civil Rights leader narrative. By erasing his privilege, the comparison is myopic in that Manziel, not yet "an accidental activist," is no Rosa Parks, who for many was "the mother of the movement":

> By comparing the two, Engel does more than trivialize the bravery of Parks. She traffics in a myth about who Parks was and why she chose to fight the indignities of the Jim Crow South. In Engel's telling—and this is the kindest possible interpretation—Manziel, like Parks, is the unconscious activist thrust by circumstance into firing the first shots at an unjust system. [89]

Zirin and others[90] made the many problems of the comparison clear. However, as easy as it is to dismiss Engel, her reclamation of Johnny Football and her denial of the racial implications here ("This has absolutely zero to do with race. What I believe to be true is, after years of watching black kids, white kids, and mostly poor kids of all colors villainized for accepting a free sandwich or plane fare to go home and attend a funeral or, God forbid, wanting a cut of the billions of dollars they make for people not doing much in the way of heavy lifting, this was America's tipping point.") was commonplace.

Contrary to mainstream perceptions, race has everything to do with Johnny Manziel; surely, his whiteness matters. It mattered when Engel recast this moment as "a tipping point"; it mattered when commentators used this moment to spotlight the hypocrisy of the NCAA; it mattered that "he's just twenty" and "he's behaving like other college students" were common defenses of his daily transgressions. His whiteness and hetero-masculinity mattered when Deion Sanders blamed Manziel's struggles on his girlfriend.[91] It mattered as he was celebrated as the greatest quarter-back since Johnny Unitas, despite the fact that in 2012 he lagged statistically behind Oregon's Marcus Mariota (who wasn't even invited to New York for the Heisman festivities). It matters with the excuse-making, the multiple chances, the media focus on his every move, and the widespread concern that he succeed in spite of his trials and tribulations.

Manziel's whiteness matters whether looking at his popularity, the celebration of his "fiery personality,"[92] the dim spotlight on his "issues," and the celebration of his ability to change collegiate sports or even the quarterback position. "Somehow, America loves Johnny Football. We love him so much that we're now ready to overthrow the NCAA and the stupid rulebook that might deny us the privilege of watching Manziel attempt to duplicate his improbable freshman season. We love this rich, pampered, Justin Bieber-wannabe so much that we're now apparently ready to deal with the fraudu-lence of amateurism," writes Jason Whitlock.[93]

While Whitlock sees this in abstract terms, it should be clear how racism operates here: the desire to see Manziel as the ultimate victim is rooted in a history in which the abuse or the exploitation of white bodies, particularly elite males, elicits mainstream media coverage that registers different lev-els of empathy, outrage, and action. Manziel embodies the historic project of imagining whiteness as under siege, as threatened, and as victimized. Central to this history is the "sense of victimization, outrage, resentment, and resurgent—if misplaced—pride of White racial projects."[94] According to Jason Silverstein, the "racial empathy gap" manifests itself within a myriad of spaces, which would presumably include a sports culture where white athletes and those of color elicit very different emotions: "The racial empathy gap helps explain disparities in everything from pain management to the criminal justice system. But the problem isn't just that people disre-gard the pain of black people. It's somehow even worse. The problem is that the pain isn't even felt."[95] The racial empathy gap is real in sports.

It's not a coincidence that black athletes such as Reggie Bush, Ter-relle Pryor, Spencer Haywood, who challenged the NBA's rule forbidding high school players from going straight to the league,[96] Curt Flood, whose sacrifices and protests resulted in free agency within Major League Baseball,[97] and more recently, Ed O'Bannon,[98] have been demonized as ungrateful, greedy, selfish, and criminal, while Manziel has been reimagined as a victim of the horrible NCAA. He's a hero, whereas Pryor is selfish; Manziel is an agent of change, while Bush is self-interested. This is no coincidence, but part and parcel with the logic and rules of American racism.

The ability to see Manziel, the son of a wealthy Texas family, as a victim of the NCAA, is a not-so-subtle reminder of how racism operates within contemporary America. Because of his whiteness, the dominant narrative sees Manziel as a victim of exploitation. Black athletes are illegible in this context.[99] This isn't simply about empathy, but the ways in which America's race-colored glasses over determine who is seen as innocent, as victim, and as righteous leader standing on principles irrespective of the consequences.

With black athletes, the emphasis is always on how they have been compensated with an education, with the opportunity to attend a college or university.[100] The subtext here is that without a scholarship and without athletics, they would not be on campus— that is, they are not deserving of a college education, the chance to attend a university, or societal respect and visibility without sports.[101] As such, irrespective of the millions generated through blood, sweat, and tears, primarily African American football and basketball players should be content since without the NCAA they would be "stuck in the ghettos." Such racist assumptions seem to rationalize the systemic exploitation of college athletes and the celebration of Johnny Manziel as deserving of compensation.

This sort of racist logic mirrors that of major league baseball, and, for that matter, that of transnational capitalism. A Colorado baseball scout seemed to justify the exploitation of Latin American baseball players—the horrible work conditions and the abysmal signing bonuses—by highlighting the "opportunity" otherwise unavailable, saying: "These guys, if they don't play in the big leagues they're going to end up selling mangoes in the street for the equivalent of a quarter."[102] The ability to see the exploitation of Johnny Manziel and not that of his African American peers reflects this worldview. Whereas he doesn't need the NCAA or football in order to attend college and be successful, black athletes are presumed to attend America's universities only because of football and basketball. Whereas Johnny should be paid, black athletes should be grateful.

Irrespective of successes on or off the field, irrespective of hard work and dedication, irrespective of bloated coaches' salaries, billion-dollar TV deals, free advertisement, and a collegiate athletics programs paid for by football and basketball teams, the Terrell Pryors, Nigel Hayeses, and Reggie Bushes of the world need to just shut up and be grateful because without the NCAA, they would be "selling mangoes."[103] They are paid with opportunity; Manziel already had opportunity (and a Benz), so the NCAA better dig into those corporate-lined pockets.

Manziel was also imagined as a victim of racial stereotypes and prejudice. He's a leader of the "silent majority." *He's* the victim of racism. Manziel was a victim because he didn't act "white," because he had "ghetto tendencies"[104] and because he "played like a black quarterback."[105] Such narratives not only further white victimhood but work through a myriad of racist stereotypes. According to Clay Travis, "Johnny Manziel plays like a 'black' quarterback. Deep down, a great deal of the animosity Manziel has provoked has come for this reason, because lots of white people don't like the way Manziel carries himself both on and off the field." Travis hammered home Manziel's place as a victim, as someone held to unfair standards and judged because of his whiteness, because of his class status:

> Manziel has become our own national Rorschach test. Is he an entitled brat who is playing the game in a classless manner, or is he an irreverent rebel whose brilliance owes much to his individuality? Your answer probably tells us a ton about you. . . . Because people of all races, rightfully, believe that rich white kids don't have to always play by the same rules as the rest of us. Those who focus on this element of Johnny Football believe that he received favorable treatment from the NCAA because he's rich and white. They point to other athletes, typically black and poor, who have been treated less fairly than Manziel. They believe that if Manziel was black, America would have a different opinion of him than they do now. This story isn't so much about Manziel as it is a worldview rooted in race and class—the idea that even in 21st century America, some of us still aren't treated equally. That resentment is down deep in your core beliefs. Even as you watch him play, a part of you thinks that this is yet another moment when the world treats someone else more fairly than it does you and yours.

One of the five groups he sees as unfairly judging and discriminating against Manziel is made up of those whites, who "hate Johnny Manziel because he's not playing like you believe a 'white' athlete should play." He identifies this victimization as follows:

Many of these people are older and white, but all ages are represented. They believe there's a proper way for a white quarterback
to conduct himself and that Johnny's flouting all those rules. It's
interesting that Manziel represents a new racial dynamic in our
country. Ask him who he patterns his game after, and he name
drops Vince Young and Mike Vick. He hangs with Drake in his
free time. Johnny's a rich white kid who identifies with black culture as much or more than he does with white culture.[106]

Describing Manziel as "the most scrutinized athlete in college sports history,"
Travis spotlights (and embodies) the excuse making, the sense of victimization, and the signifiers associated with whiteness and new racism.[107]

    This helps us understand the differential responses to Manziel and Bush,
Pryor, Hayes, and Dez Bryant. The failure to account for race, to look at
double standards, to compare the punishments and vitriol experienced
by Manziel, to those directed at Reggie Bush, Terrelle Pryor, and Dez Bryant reflects a yearning to see college sports through a binary of student
athletes versus the NCAA. Recognizing the inequities not only undermines
this narrative but the broader adherence to a post-racial sports world.
Manziel's experiences not only illustrate the hypocrisy and exploitation that
is collegiate sports, but the ways that sports and countless other institutions
work to the benefit of whites in America. Allen Barra, in "Johnny Manziel,
Trailblazer: The NCAA Is a Total Joke, Again," reflects on the racial double
standards evidence with Manziel:

> Let's not choose to exonerate Manziel. He is an astonishingly
> spoiled and self-absorbed young man who knowingly put his
> school's football program and his own teammates in jeopardy
> by his actions. And unlike Reggie Bush, he doesn't even have the
> excuse that his family needed the money. That, though, isn't really
> the issue. The issue is that Johnny Manziel has revealed the first
> genuine crack in the NCAA's armor.[108]

The fact that Bush, Pryor, and countless other examples didn't result in
making a "crack in the NCAA armor" says it all. It is no wonder that in a few
short months, the NCAA had sealed that crack, thus preserving a system
of exploitation and abuse disproportionately endured by young black men.
    #PlayingWhileWhite is the ability to fight the system and receive praise
for waging a battle bigger than self. It is also the ability to never have to
fight because you are rightly compensated. Whereas NCAA basketball and

football players, disproportionately African American, are exploited with little outrage from the public,[109] whereas black student athletes are punished for selling autographs, memorabilia, or simply getting a few hundred dollars, athletes from Olympics sports, disproportionately white, can cash in on their athletic talents.[110] Just as white athletes, from lacrosse to swimming, from wrestling to soccer, have greater access to high school teams and resources that form the pipeline to college scholarships,[111] which are paid for by football and basketball revenues, these same athletes are able to receive cash bonuses during the Olympics without threatening their collegiate eligibility.[112]

While #PlayingWhileWhite is about narrative and rhetorical celebration, it is also about material conditions, opportunities and the privileges that come with being white. To swim or wrestle, to receive money for winning a gold medal and not a national championship in football, are tied up in the structures of antiblackness, whiteness, and white supremacy.

## CONCLUSION

In a column about Colin Kaepernick's questionable future as a quarterback, David Whitley remarked that he didn't look like a leader because of his tattoos. Citing Michael Vick and Terrelle Pryor as other examples of those who don't look like quarterbacks (but not Big Ben and Alex Smith, both of whom have tattoos), Whitley argued that to be a leader meant to follow in the footsteps of other quarterbacks who were leaders, to be "clean-cut," and white. "Neither exactly fit the CEO image, unless your CEO has done a stretch in Leavenworth or has gotten Ohio State on probation over free tattoos." In other words, because all three have tattoos and because those who have tattoos look like criminals, they lack the skills necessary to lead. The "NFL quarterback is the ultimate position of influence and responsibility. He is the CEO of a high-profile organization, and you don't want your CEO to look like he just got paroled."[113]

The criminalization of black athletic bodies through discourses of tattoos is nothing new. A 1997 article from the Associated Press similarly imagined tattoos as markers of criminality and dysfunctionality: "Tattoos always have been popular among inmates, sailors, bikers and gang members. Now they're showing up in increasing numbers in the NBA." In 2009, Kyle McNary identified tattoos as why the "NBA [was] almost unwatchable." Describing those with ink as people who "lack self-esteem" and as individuals saddled by "poor decision-making skills," McNary imagined the proliferation of tattoos as an epidemic destroying the league.[114] At the core of these debates was leadership. Those who have tattoos are imagined as selfish, as driven by ego, as without control, as influenced by hip-hop culture, and as criminal. These are not the qualities seen as essential for leadership.

From the first sentences of his column— "San Francisco's Colin Kaepernick is going to be a big-time NFL quarterback. That must make the guys in San Quentin happy"—to its constant description of people with tattoos as looking as though they are on parole, Whitley sees a tattooed body as a criminal body, incapable of leadership. Questioning Colin Kaepernick's leadership skills, which are seen as essential for quarterback position, creates a binary between the "criminal body" and the leadership body, between the black and white bodies inside and outside of America's sporting arenas.

Embodying a level of nostalgia for Johnny U, and even John Elway, fears about the lost power of white masculinity play through this piece. As the quarterback is seen as the key to success—the leader most essential to a team's greatness—anxiety emanates from the lost cultural power imagined to accompany the declining significance of the white quarterback. Reflective of a broader discourse, the criminalization of the tattooed body not only signifies and represents a signifier of antiblack racism, commonplace within sporting cultures,[115] but the ways that the stereotypes regarding black athletes are used to deny their leadership qualities. Contemporary sports culture consistently represents black male athletes as "overly physical, out of control, prone to violence, driven by instinct, and hypersexual." These characteristics, along with the tattoos themselves, are markers of being "unruly and disrespectful," "inherently dangerous," and "in need of civilizing."[116] Those with undesirable bodies and culture are not leaders themselves, but are in need of leaders who can discipline, control, and, if necessary, facilitate the removal of the tattoos.

From Tom Brady to Peyton Manning, from Tim Tebow to Johnny Manziel, from Vince Lombardi to Joe Paterno, from Coach K to Bill Belichick, from Steve Nash to Dustin Pedroia, white athletes and sporting figures are imagined as leaders. Positioned as sources of inspiration, as individuals who have the requisite discipline and values, who have overcome doubts, physical limitations, and stereotypes to not only pull themselves up by their bootstraps—or shoe strings—but to lead others who are incapable of succeeding on their own.

This narrative contributes to a sporting landscape that not only produces a disproportionate number of white quarterbacks, point guards, managers and coaches, general managers, athletic directors, and others in leadership positions, but also shapes media and public discourse, resulting in praise for white athletes in ways rarely experienced by their black, Latino, or Asian counterparts.

The impact of this sort of racial profiling, of the hegemony of racial scripts that see white masculinity as an essential ingredient to leadership, extends beyond the sporting landscapes. From the political arena to the workplace, from the military to America's restaurants, from education to presidential campaigns the dominance of the trope that sees white (men) as natural born leaders perpetuates inequality while normalizing it not as the result of bias and institutional racism but as racial difference. #PlayingWhileWhite is to be seen as scrappy, as feisty, as team oriented, as a leader not because of race and racism but because of performance. Without them, every team would be lost. There is a whole lot of power and prestige in whiteness.

# CHAPTER 2

# HE GOT BRAINS

*Whiteness and Intelligence on and off the Court*

O N the eve of the 2011 NBA lockout, Bill Simmons, then with ESPN, took to the airwaves to lament the intelligence of NBA players:

> What are [Kevin] Garnett's credentials, exactly? During one of the single biggest meetings (last week, on Tuesday), Hunter had Kobe Bryant, Paul Pierce and Garnett (combined years spent in college: three) negotiate directly with Stern in some sort of misguided "Look how resolved we are, you're not gonna intimidate us!" ploy that backfired so badly that one of their teams' owners was summoned into the meeting specifically to calm his player down and undo some of the damage.[1]

Beyond trotting out the "angry black man" trope, which is widely deployed by the NBA punditry when describing protests and resistance from its players, and blaming the players for the lockout, Simmons's evidence of incompetence hinges on the amount of formal college education of Pierce, Bryant, and Garnett. People were losing their jobs, and fans losing their NBA season because of the stupidity of uneducated (black) players.

In "Behind the Pipes: Into the Arms of the NHL," while explaining why he started going to hockey games, Simmons not only cites the lockout, but the decision-making of NBA players: "I don't trust the players' side to make the right choices, because they are saddled with limited intellectual capital."[2]

The racial paternalism in both articles is striking as are his efforts to resuscitate Hernstein and Murray's *Bell Curve* and its conclusions about race and intelligence.[3] Given this history, and the continued demonization of black athletes,[4] we are left with an argument that the NBA faced a lockout because those who possess the requisite intelligence and the proper fitness have failed to control their inferior players who are too stupid, too undisciplined, and too clueless to understand the business and the economics of the league, not to mention the politics and media issues surrounding it.

Playing on longstanding tropes of black intelligence and discipline deficiencies,[5] Simmons's criticisms of the players cannot be understood outside of a larger history where the IQ of African Americans has been questioned, rationalizing discrimination, segregation, and inequity. Joe Feagin, citing research from the National Opinion Research Center, which points to the connections between racial stereotypes about welfare, work ethic, and intelligence, highlights the ways that intelligence is seen on racial terms. "A majority of whites still stereotype black people as violence-prone, inclined to live on welfare, and disinclined to hard work, and a substantial majority still stereotype black Americans as unintelligent."[6]

As evident in Simmons's words and other examples noted in this chapter, these same ideas govern the world of sports. Abby L. Ferber argues that the "Success in the field of athletics also does nothing to undermine the historical propensity to reduce black men to their bodies. Sporting success fulfills white supremacist fantasies; it furthers the profiling of blackness as savage, physical, and as distinct from whiteness."[7] According to Jay Coakley, the successes and athletic prowess of white athletes is attributed to "fortitude, intelligence, moral character, strategic preparation, coachability, and good organization."[8]

Delia Douglas, in her discussion of the Williams sisters, highlights how binaries, and the trope of the good and bad black body, have been central to a white supremacist project: "Historically, white supremacist logic has long relied on the 'the use of a dichotomous code that creates a chain of correspondences both between the physical and the cultural, and between the intellectual and cognitive characteristic' (Hall 1997, 290). In this context, blacks were understood as more body than mind."[9] Mercurio and Filak further highlight the connective tissue between racial formation, sporting institutions, and white supremacist ideologies: "Stereotypes based on race have been present in sports for decades. In the case of making clear demarcations between how whites and blacks play the game."[10]

Alongside the historic practice of imagining black athletic success as evidence of physical rather than mental prowess, through body not brain, the framing of white athletes as hardworking, intelligent, and driven by a moral center furthers racial division. The dialectics between race and intelligence anchor the sporting world. Mercurio and Filak conclude that, "the stereotype most often attached to race is one of talent versus intelligence. Writers, coaches, and social critics have openly or subversively stated that Black athletes rely on athletic abilities whereas White athletes rely on intelligence."[11] White supremacist ideologies impact media discourse and the opportunities afforded to athletes. "In the sport of football, this leads to the perception that Black athletes are not equipped to play the 'smart' positions."[12] Similar circumstances play out in basketball and baseball as well as within school and job opportunities. Race, the racist assumptions about intelligence embedded in racial markers, shapes the play field in every aspect of life, illustrating the fallacy that is meritocracy.

The racial discourses surrounding intelligence are as American as apple pie, and they are baked into its very crust. Michael Eric Dyson describes such rhetoric as central to the history of American white supremacy: "Skepticism about black intelligence and suspicion about black humanity have gone hand in hand throughout the history of this country in feeding the perception that black people don't quite measure up."[13] Writing about black male athletes and processes of representation, Ben Carrington invokes Frantz Fanon, who links the incompatibility of blackness and intelligence within the white imagination. Carrington notes Fanon's exploration of the ways in which blackness was conceptualized and envisioned through white supremacy:

> When Fanon gives his white patients a word association test, it is significant to note how often his respondents mention either sports, or prominent black athletes of the period. Fanon informs us that the word, "Negro brought forth biology, penis, strong, athletic, potent, boxer, Joe Louis, Jesse Owens, Senegalese troops, savage, animal, devil, sin." For Fanon, the black male was the repository of white fears, fantasies and desires, and of all of these constructions, there was one figure above all others that held a central place within the colonial imaginary: "There is one expression that through time has become singularly eroticized: the black athlete."[14]

The illegibility[15] of the intelligent black athlete is not only evident in the demonization of black athletes, and the ridicule directed at athletes like Odell Beckham, Jr., Colin Kaepernick, Adam Jones Jr., Cam Newton, Carmelo Anthony, Shaquille O'Neal, Terrell Owens, Chad Johnson, and Charles Barkley, but in the ubiquitous celebration of the intelligent white athlete.

The examples are countless; there seems to be an unending stream of media narratives that celebrate and attribute intelligence, IQ, or their brains as reasons for success.[16] While not limited to the football field, the smart and intellectual (white) athlete often becomes a trope reserved for the (white) quarterback. Among others, Ryan Fitzpatrick, Peyton Manning, Tim Tebow, Johnny Manziel, Andrew Luck, and Tom Brady have all been celebrated as intelligent.

This chapter, thus, takes up the question of intelligence and racial coding within America's sporting landscapes. The hold of these scripts, stereotypes, and profiles embodies the centrality of racial definitions of intelligence to white supremacy. To be white is to be driven by mind, intelligence, intellect, thoughtfulness, and the brain; to be black is to be driven by physicality, emotion, rawness, and the body.[17] By looking beyond narratives of IQ, intelligence, and #PlayingWhileSmart, this chapter also reflects on the ways racism shapes discourses around style/creativity on the playing field. In other words, whereas white athletes are imagined as successful because of their mind, intellect, and knowledge, black athletes are seen as cashing in on their creativity, spontaneity, and style, which is imagined as both a binary with intelligence and a source of compensation for deficiencies in this regard. These racial scripts shape conversations about athletic success, and broader perceptions of intelligence, education, job preparedness, and the American Dream.

While focusing on Tim Tebow, Andrew Luck, and Peyton Manning, this chapter also takes up the question of how and when athletes of color become "intelligent" within sporting landscapes. Myron Rolle (football) and Shane Battier (basketball) have each been celebrated as smart ballers, as aberrations of sorts, and as racial exceptions. Just as white athletes buttress white supremacy, the celebration and visibility of these intelligent and exceptional black athletes represents an important race denial card. Still, their intelligence and bodies are defined through whiteness, further demonstrating the entrenched connections between intelligence and race, on and off the field.

#PlayingWhileWhite means being inscribed as successful not just because of athletic ability and hard work, but as holding the requisite intelligence to excel in and dominate the physically demanding world of sports.

## ALL-SMARTY TEAM

Type in "smartest" and "athletes" on Google, and countless lists will appear that celebrate sporting MENSAS. The *Sporting News* named the twenty smartest athletes, and provided player biographies that included SAT scores, languages spoken, alma maters, and "nerdiest thing ever done."[18] Of the twenty, the vast majority were baseball players (seven) or quarterbacks (four); equally apparent from the list was that intelligence is the purview of white males, with no women on the list and only four athletes of color. Sam Acho, Grant Hill, Shane Battier, and Myron Rolle were all included, despite the fact that all but Acho were either retired or near retirement at the time of publication.

The *Bleacher Report* offered a more extensive list with its "35 Smartest Athletes of All Time."[19] It described its intervention as one working to counter stereotypes, to shine a spotlight on the sophistication and intelligence of America's sports stars. "Athletes are typically stereotyped as 'meatheads.' While the media loves to report on the countless academic violations from student athletes, there are still tons of very bright athletes in professional sports." Yet, it, like so many of the lists, reinforces hegemonic fictions regarding intelligence, athletes, and race. At one level, it nostalgically locates the intelligent athlete as a "relic," no longer visible within today's sports world. The inclusion of Bill Bradley (basketball), Ken Dryden (hockey), Bryon White (football), Alan Page (football), Jeremy Kramer (football), Jim Bouton (baseball), Dick Kazmier (football), and Bill Walton (basketball) locates intelligence as part of a bygone era. Reflecting the power of sporting nostalgia, the discourse around intelligence becomes an opportunity to celebrate and reconfigure the past as one of purity and beauty. As discussed previously, race codifies discourses of intelligence. The era of white players was the era of smart players; the time of white dominance was one of cerebral athletes who brought fundamentals and a textbook understanding onto the court, producing a better product.

The focus on a previous generation's athletes reflects how the criteria for intelligence rest with post-athletic-career accomplishments, partly because intelligence is seen as something that can be identified on a résumé. The narrative conflation of intelligence and professional accomplishment, especially if one had an Ivy League education, invariably privileges white males, reinforcing longstanding stereotypes about race and intelligence.

The descriptions found within these lists also reinforce the binaries between athleticism and intelligence. For athletes, their on-the-field successes are the result of athletic talent (and hard work), yet their off-the-field accomplishments embody their intelligence. There is little, if any, room for discussion of athletic intelligence or the athletic benefits of thinking processes and deductive reasoning on the playing field and court. Intelligence is a currency that is useful within the classroom, the courtroom, business enterprises, and even the operating room.

Rhetorically and narratively, it is interesting to examine the purported evidence of intelligence. What emerges are very distinct racial narratives where white athletes are presented as intelligent because they went to exceptional schools, had amazing GPAs, and have gone on to accomplish things in industries and institutions that require brilliance and book knowledge.

> CHRIS NOWINSKI: The Harvard-educated former WWE star has made huge strides in the battle against concussions and head injuries in the NFL. Nowinski, who studied Sociology while in school, has become the face of the fight against concussions in contact sports, and routinely reaches out to athletes to secure their brains to be studied after their deaths.
> RYAN FITZPATRICK: The Harvard-educated QB had a big year this season in Buffalo, and looks like he'll head into next season as the starter. Fitzpatrick, who scored a 1580/1600 on his SAT, majored in Economics while in school.
> CRAIG BRESLOW: The Oakland Athletics pitcher was recently named the smartest athlete in all sports by *Sporting News*. The Yale-educated Breslow got a 1420 on his SAT's, and a 34 on his MCAT's (the average score is a 28), and was accepted into NYU's Medical School. Breslow graduated with a 3.5 GPA with a degree in Molecular Biophysics and Biochemistry. [20]

Conversely, the black athletes included receive less robust narratives that define their intelligence less by their intellectual prowess, knowledge, or communication abilities and more by their accomplishments and interests.

> Dhani Jones has made a bigger name for himself off the field than on it . . . . Dhani's travels and television exploits have gained him a following amongst nerds. Jones is one of the most well read athletes in the league, and one of the best-traveled.
> JAMAL MASHBURN: While Mashburn may not be the most eloquent NBA commentator, he is a very successful businessman. After making over $75 million throughout his career, Mashburn has parlayed his NBA success into success in the restaurant world. He's the owner of 34 Outback Steakhouses, 37 Papa John's, and also an owner of franchises of Dunkin' Donuts and car dealerships in Kentucky.
> GRANT HILL: The seven-time NBA All-Star first starred at Duke, where he majored in History. Hill is an avid reader and collector of art. [21]

Hill, Mashburn, and Jones are described as smart because they like to read, collect art, and travel, and because of their financial success. They are smart for athletes; they are different from their peers and therefore worthy of celebration. Compare this to Fitzpatrick, Breslow, and Nowinski whose intelligence is quantified through conventional metrics and other narrative dimensions. They are cosmopolitan, civilized, intellectual, and well-rounded. They could be successful in any industry, in any space.

These lists and so much of the discourse surrounding intelligence use conventional markers of intelligence, such as SAT scores, GPA, and college attendance. This is especially the case with several white athletes, whose academic biography is presented as evidence of their brilliance. Given the widespread evidence about the cultural and racial biases of SAT testing,[22] and the racial and class histories of the Ivy Leagues,[23] the embrace of these metrics of intelligence not surprisingly privileges white athletes.

## HE GOT BRAINS

White athletes are often celebrated as role models, as leaders, and as hard workers because of their intelligence.[24] They model how to play the right way: they see the court; they are able to out-smart their opponents and elevate the play of their teammates. They understand a "good shot," how to run a "route properly," and the fundamentals of the game. Intelligence produces results. The use of their intellects is essential because of the purported lack of athleticism and physical prowess of white athletes. In other words, white athletes compensate for their deficiencies—lack of speed, strength, and athleticism—with cunning, smarts, and athletic intelligence. They are playing chess while others are running sprints. The efforts to compensate for athletic limitations also propel white athletes to "work hard," to put time in at the gym to develop into world-class athletes. To recognize shortcomings and commit to improving is further evidence of intelligence.

As with other industries, where a white sounding name is the ultimate résumé booster,[25] whiteness is a source of privilege throughout sports culture because of assumptions about intelligence. According to Casey Gane-McCalla: "Black athletes are usually given credit for their 'natural athleticism,' while whites are credited for their 'hard work,' 'discipline,' and 'knowledge of the game'; as if Black athletes are naturally given the gift of great athleticism, and white people become great athletes through hard work, discipline and intelligence."[26]

Often framed in opposition to Magic Johnson, Larry Bird, the "Hick from French Lick" was routinely celebrated as a heady and smart basketball player. "Larry Bird was the individual microcosm of everything good about both basketball and sport itself. He possessed the full range of requisite skills; an unsurpassed work ethic; a simple, direct value system; a thorough understanding of team dynamics," wrote Bob Ryan. "What separates the Truly Irreplaceable from even the Superstars is a quality that takes intelligence and instinct and savoir faire and ties them into some unspoken empathy with the fans."[27]

Similarly, after Steve Nash joined the Lakers, then coach Mike Brown celebrated his arrival by focusing on his basketball IQ, intelligence, and leadership abilities: "With his intelligence, he's a guy that can fit in well." Dismissing him as defensive liability because of his lack of speed, Brown argued, "He'll know where his help is built into or where his help is coming from and as long as he keeps funneling the ball to his help and he works hard, which he'll do, he'll be fine. He's extremely intelligent. I don't foresee any problems with Steve on that end of the floor."[28]

More recently Matthew Dellavedova has picked up the mantle of the tough, smart, feisty white basketball player. Described as an "unlikely star," Dellavedova emerged as a force on the Cleveland Cavaliers because of his competitiveness, fearlessness, aggressive play, and intelligence. "The six-foot, four-inch Dellavedova says he can dunk, but athleticism has never been his thing. He made his mark in what has become his NBA specialty: scrappiness," wrote Jared Zwerling during the 2015 playoffs. According to one Western Conference scout, "He plays every minute like it's his last. He's gritty and rugged, and he's very intelligent. . . . There's nothing exceptional about his game, but he plays with high energy and makes open shots. That's what most coaches want from their role players."[29]

This is not simply about the descriptors given by play-by-play announcers or adjectives used within media stories. Even as racial stereotypes saturate media narratives, profiling white athletes as smart, cerebral, and intellectual, these same biases impact opportunities and jobs. This is about who gets drafted; it is about positional segregation; it is about longevity; who is seen as a good practice player, and who might be a successful coach or general manager. To be a white athlete comes with numerous benefits beyond the field as well.

At Deadspin.com, Fischer-Baum, Gordon, and Haisley examined the 2014 scouting reports from CBS, ESPN, and NFL.com, indexing the types of adjectives used to describe black and white players. Its findings mirror the literature in that white football prospects are frequently celebrated for their IQ:

Intelligent: 2.48 per 10,000 words for white players;
    0.67 per 10,000 words for black players
Intelligence: 3.51 per 10,000 words for white players;
    1.16 per 10,000 words for black players
Smart: 6.13 per 10,000 words for white players;
    2.32 per 10,000 words for black players
IQ: 1.13 per 10,000 words for white players;
    0.36 per 10,000 words for black players
Thinking: 0.15 per 10,000 words for white players;
    0.04 per 10,000 words for black players[30]

The reporters found that black and white football prospects were divided into two separate categories, making it clear that race shapes who is seen as intelligent and who is seen as athletic and creative. Their conclusions mirror years of literature. Whereas black football players are seen as athletic, naturally gifted, creative, innovative, extemporaneous, improvisational, and physically superior, white athletes are celebrated for their intelligence, ability to follow rules, traditional work ethics, and team orientation.[31] These racial scripts—black athleticism and white intelligence—work in concert with one another.

The purported lack of athleticism forces white reliance on IQ, intelligence, and other intangibles. It leads to smarter approaches to the game. Todd Boyd, in *Am I Black Enough for You*, identifies a dialectical relationship between race and the narratives surrounding players and style of play:

> Textbook basketball is akin to classical music, wherein performance is centered on the replication of a supposedly superior style. Musical sophistication is determined by one's proximity to the original; deviations are considered errors. This privileging of the original seems to permeate much of Western culture. Mastery of the form is achieved through one's ability to replicate at the highest level. With this in mind, those who operate in the tradition of textbook basketball can be clearly linked to the recurrent Western ethos of replication.
>
> Playground basketball, on [the] other hand, is much like jazz in the sense mastery of form depends upon one's ability to improvise, to create on the spot, to engage in full-court transition games that foreground style. The celebration of style through improvisation, consistent with much of African American culture, has a great impact on the selling of the NBA to the American public.[32]

Whereas whiteness represents the prescribed, traditional, coach-driven "textbook or formal" style, black style exists in the creative, undisciplined, free-flowing, and reactive sports performance.

Although specific to basketball, Boyd's discussion is evident in media discourses surrounding the pocket passer versus the running quarterback,[33] and the "scrambling quarterback"[34] being more athletic[35] compared to the dropback quarterback, who relies on his knowledge of the defense. It can also be seen in the histories of positional segregation that has led whites to dominate those positions associated with intelligence in football (the quarterback, the center, the middle linebacker), basketball (point guard), and baseball (catcher, pitcher, and shortstop).

Racially defined styles of play, notions of intelligence, mental toughness, and mental agility shape these discussions. #PlayingWhileBlack is seen as reacting, utilizing one's God given talents and physically dominating, while #PlayingWhileWhite requires intelligence, guile, determination, and a focus on out-smarting one's opponent. The dominance of this ideology inside and outside the sporting landscape speaks to why whites dominate the smartest players lists. It is no wonder that whites continue to dominate those "thinking positions"[36] most notably the position of quarterback.

## THE GREAT WHITE QUARTERBACK

As noted in chapter 1, while baseball is frequently invoked as "America's pastime," football is America's conscience, ethos, and ideology all wrapped up into one violent spectacle. Embodying everything that is America—violence; masculinity; hyper-capitalism; sexism; consumerism; American exceptionalism; racial hierarchy—on steroids, football is a window into the nation's history and soul. As such, the place of the quarterback—as leader; as general; as the literal and metaphoric head of the team—and the persistent racial segregation of this position[37] elucidates the centrality of race and racism not only on the gridiron but in America at large. To examine the quarterback and the "possessive investment"[38] in his whiteness is to peel back the curtain on American racial ideology. It is no wonder that many in the history of American sporting discourses have sought to protect the position, to preserve its whiteness. While discrimination from the coach and other decision makers preserves a "racial cartel"[39] on the field, the ubiquitous naming of leadership and intelligence as core requisites, along-side the profiling of these characteristics as both essential to whiteness and antithetical to blackness, has perpetuated a football culture in which white and quarterback are virtually synonymous.

The eternal search for "the great white hope"[40] is not limited to boxing as NFL teams and their media partners have long needed a white quarterback. "White men were/are insecure in their manhood and prefer to rig the games of life to ensure their success and maintain their status as the supposed 'Alpha Male,'" writes Desi Cortez. "I'd contend that wet dream evaporated eons ago, starting with Jack Johnson, Jesse Owens and Joe Louis from the early 20th century on most people knew White men were crafting their own success by excluding Blacks and other people of color from participating in mainstream society—but given the advancements made in equality of opportunity the Great White Man myth has been exposed, end of fairytale."[41]

The search or preservation of white-only positions is not simply about restricting access and denying opportunity but defining the position in a way in which only whites need apply. The focus on intelligence, in a society that denies intelligence to people of color, virtually guarantees the continued dominance of whites as quarterbacks, coaches, and general managers. The profiling of white quarterbacks as dominating because of their brains can be seen within the narratives surrounding today's (white) quarterbacks.

For example, Andrew Luck embodies the ways that the media describes white quarterbacks as intelligent on and off the field. His play calling, his QBR (Total Quarterback Rating), and the purported infrequency of interceptions are all signs that "he has brains." In "A Dichotomy of Brains and Brawn," Rick Reilly chronicles Luck's emergence as one of the league's superstars because of his intelligence.[42]

Yet, Luck is not simply a smart quarterback; he is smart. He went to Stanford, he had a 3.48 GPA, and he majored in Environmental Engineering. He uses words like "vociferous," "cognizant," and "implemented." For Reilly, Luck is unique because while his IQ is off the charts, he's also tough: "That's the baffling thing about this son of two law school graduates. Luck's the oddest combination of lobes and lats. He's both brains and brawn. He doesn't just crack the safe, he then picks it up and carries it out of the bank."[43]

Careful not to emasculate Luck with narrative about a "Stanford nerd" and his Roget's vocabulary, Reilly and others are quick to highlight his toughness and physical prowess alongside his intellectual strengths. He is not the weak white athlete who must use cunning and IQ to overcome physical ineptitude, but instead the perfect blend of brains and brawn.

Similarly, Aaron Rodgers has been anointed as the next great quarterback because of his work ethic, his intelligence, and his understanding of the game. In "Rodgers Preparing to Assume Control," Lori Nickel celebrates the future Hall of Famer as someone who has worked to become successful and has capitalized on his own intelligence:

But what Rodgers says isn't as important as what he has done. Rodgers had near perfect attendance in all of three off-season voluntary workout sessions and quarterback school lessons. He's improved his nutritional habits and disciplined himself in the weight room. He's handled a delicate situation as a former No. 1 draft pick and Favre's successor with intelligence and maturity. He's memorized coach Mike McCarthy's playbook and worked his way around the locker room bonding with players.[44]

Compared to Rodgers, Tom Brady, and Andrew Luck, Peyton Manning is a card-carrying MENSA genius: He is Albert Einstein in cleats. In "Hard Work Behind Manning's Genius; 'Pretty Driven,'" Mike Klis celebrates his intelligence like no other:

> Manning has long been considered the NFL's smartest quarterback. His cerebral reputation was primarily incited through his demonstrative commands at the line of scrimmage—well away from the secretive huddle and in front of God, a fan-filled stadium and television audience. What his many observers may not realize, though, is Manning's mind is not a gift so much as it has been developed. Genius was less a birthright than the product of mental exercise. . . . Manning's mind is not wired in a way where he suddenly gets the urge to draw equations on the chalkboard, like Matt Damon's character in *Good Will Hunting*. Nor is Manning like Russell Crowe's character in *A Beautiful Mind*.[45]

Celebrating "his brains,"[46] as "someone who can see things faster,"[47] as one of the NFL's "smartest QBs,"[48] as the "smartest man in the NFL,"[49] as "the smartest player I've ever been around,"[50] and as a genius on and off the field,[51] the Manning origin story is one that focuses on his intellect. His brilliance is evident in his play calling, his "Wonderlic score,"[52] his propensity to study film, and his "Omaha" audibles.

While seeming to discount Manning's athleticism, the simplicity of the Colts offense,[53] the defensive prowess of the Broncos, the privileges of growing up in the Manning household (access to trainers and coaches; knowledge garnered from growing up around football), and any number of other factors, explanations about his career generally circle back to his intelligence. His success was the result of the combination of his intelligence and discipline and the athletic talents of his wide receivers. Challenging this binary, Michael Smith, in "Students of the Game Foes Are Often Left Smarting," sees the success of Brady and Manning as not simply the result of their own intellects, but also proof of the intellectual prowess of their receivers and coaches:

> Start with the film-buff quarterbacks, the Colts' Peyton Manning and the Patriots' Tom Brady. "Smart" is a word often associated with both of them. They know the assignments of every member of their offense, and do all that they can to learn everything about the other teams' defense. Not much surprises them. Trick questions don't fool them. Manning and Brady's respective go-to receivers, Marvin Harrison and Troy Brown, are precise route runners who know how to read coverages and get open. And you'll find several sharp guys along both offensive lines.[54]

For Smith, intelligence is something every player brings to the table. Such a profile is not unique even though intelligence is more legible in certain positions and bodies, which are disproportionately white.

Whether looking at the quarterback, the middle linebacker, the football center, basketball point guard, or the pitcher or catcher, as well as those narratives surrounding white coaches, it is clear that the intelligence narrative is, for the most part, reserved for whites. Yet, there is also a place for those exceptions who not only reify America's racial logic but the hegemony of colorblindness.

## IMMIGRANT NARRATIVES AND
## THE INTELLIGENCE EXCEPTION

Although #PlayingWhileWhite often means being seen as an athlete who uses mind as much as body, as being successful because of intelligence, intellect, and the rapidly firing synapses that allow one to see the game at a different level—something that happens rarely for athletes of color—the intelligence narrative is afforded to some exceptions. The "he got brains" narrative is not for white athletes only. In fact, deployments of narratives of exceptionalism work to disarm the obvious racial tropes and discourses operating through discussions of intelligence. Colorblind racism requires exceptions that work to prove that race doesn't matter. To believe in a post-racism meritocracy requires a belief that it is one's work ethic, set of values, culture, and intelligence[55] rather than privilege or discrimination that determine outcomes.

As noted by Ferber, "the good guy space reinforces colorblind racism. By embracing the successful good guys, Whites can tell themselves they are not racist, and they can blame African Americans for their own failures."[56] This is not simply about success stories that substantiate claims about the fulfillment of the American Dream within a post-racial moment. These exceptional stories bubble to the surface because their elements—whether in the form of narratives of hard work, intelligence, or morality—authenticate narratives that blame and pathologize those living in poverty inside ghettos, suffering an American nightmare. Writing about Michelle Alexander's *The New Jim Crow*, Bill Quigley highlights the importance of racial exceptions within discourses of colorblindness:

> During Jim Crow, individual black success was a threat to the prevailing system of control. Today, the opposite is true. The current caste system depends, in no small part, on black exceptionalism. Mass incarceration is predicated on the notion that an extraordinary number of African Americans (but not all) have freely chosen a life of crime and thus belong behind bars. A belief that all blacks belong in jail would be incompatible with the social consensus that we have moved "beyond race" and that race is no longer relevant. So we as a "colorblind" society need to have some black people doing well, ones we like. We therefore embrace certain types of black people — those who make whites comfortable and don't challenge the status quo. Their success actually helps to rationalize the treatment of the rest.[57]

Sports do important work here. The popularity of Michael Jordan and Stephen Curry purportedly proves that race doesn't matter. The success of Tony Dungy and Doc Rivers supposedly demonstrates that black coaches have opportunities within today's sportscapes.[58] The ascendance of Cam Newton and Russell Wilson becomes part of the story that purportedly proves that positional segregation is no longer in practice. The commercial successes of Kobe Bryant, LeBron James, Stephen Curry, Odell Beckham, Kevin Durant, Cam Newton, Russell Wilson, and Richard Sherman speak to a shifting racial landscape. The athletic opportunities, successes, and commercial opportunities available to Serena and Venus Williams,[59] Simone Biles, Simone Manuel, Gabby Douglas, and Tiger Woods[60] highlight racial progress, not only proving a colorblind present, but the existence of post-racial meritocracy: those who work hard, who play the game the right way, and who have the requisite cultural values will succeed and be compensated. Those who fall short, make bad choices, and lack the requisite skills are left behind.

The power of exceptions—as evidence of post-raciality and proof that inequality is the result of choices and cultural differences—anchors discussions of intelligence within the sports world.[61] There are many examples (Freddy Adu, Tim Duncan, Luol Deng, Christian Okoye, Hines Ward, Jeremy Lin, the Ogwumike sisters, Emeka Okafor, Yao Ming, Tony Parker) of athletes of color who are celebrated for their intelligence, their work ethic, and their values.[62]

Not coincidentally, many who become the exceptions, who are cited as "intelligent athletes," who embody the brainiac baller, who are noted as proof that anyone can make it, who are praised as model athlete minorities are the sons and daughters of immigrants or immigrants of color themselves. They are imagined as distinct and different, as exceptions not simply because they grew up in a different environment, as part of a "different" culture, but because these experiences and differences produce unique tools, values, approaches, and levels of intelligence.[63]

In a story that has long been denied to African American athletes, with its emphasis on single mothers, poverty, absentee fathers, and cultures of poverty, the efforts to link the athletic success of immigrant athletes of color and white athletes to family values, intelligence, work ethic, toughness, determination, and other values ultimately normalizes racial inequality while maintaining a stance that race doesn't matter. In explaining success through individual choice and culture, the immigrant and white athlete narrative reinforce an ideology of bootstrapism, meritocracy, and cultural explanations of success.

In this context, I want to conclude this chapter by focusing on Myron Rolle and Shane Battier, each of whom, in different ways, spotlights the importance of the exceptional narrative. The discourse surrounding each of these players exemplifies the hegemony of whiteness as intelligence (and intelligence as whiteness), the entrenched stereotypes about unintelligent African American athletes, the dialectics between athleticism (or lack thereof), intelligence, and success, and dominant narratives about colorblindness.

Myron Rolle embodies the exceptional immigrant athlete discourse.[64] Portrayed as an immigrant, a student that happened to play football, and as someone unlike his peers, Rolle's story reveals these entrenched stereotypes. Instead of emphasizing the true uniqueness of his life story, and his skill, the media discourse consistently uses his narrative to legitimize the stereotypes of other black athletes.

As a Rhodes Scholar who played Division I football, he is rare. Of the 20,000 men who have played in the NFL, only two others have been Rhodes

Scholars. And they were of a previous generation. Yet Myron Rolle became a point of juxtaposition for other (African American) athletes that simultaneously normalized the stereotypes of the stupid and educationally disinterested black athlete and the smarty-pants white athlete.

A profile in the *New York Times* noted that he was only one of two football players who had taken chemistry and biochemistry in fourteen years, and the other was a walk-on. Celebrated for his "intellect" and "his mind" a feature in *SB Nation* furthers a story of exceptionalism, much of which is centered on his intelligence and education. According to Aaron Gordon:

> When Rolle was 3 years old, he moved with his parents and four
> brothers from the Bahamas to Galloway Township, N.J. His father
> worked for Citibank and Myron grew up in a solidly middle-class
> home in a family devoted to achievement, education and love. As
> a promising student and athlete, Rolle accepted a scholarship to
> attend The Hun School of Princeton, a prestigious preparatory
> school, where he stood out on several levels.[65]

Whereas others choose their college based on promises from coaches or other "frivolities," he picked a school that would prepare him to fulfill his lifetime dream of becoming a neurosurgeon.

Being different also made things difficult for Rolle, who found it hard to fit in with his teammates whose IQs and interest in school clearly did not match his:

> During workouts the next summer for the Seminole football
> team, Rolle didn't fit in. Many of his teammates came from dif-
> ficult backgrounds, where their families had to choose between
> buying food and keeping the lights on. . . . Looking back, Rolle
> realizes he had no idea how to conduct himself around them,
> tucking his shirt, wearing glasses and using, as he puts it, "proper
> speech." His teammates didn't see a football player, they saw a
> nerd, a square.[66]

While highlighting the costs and consequences of being seen as different, spotlighting the ways that NFL teams read Myron Rolle as "too smart" to be a great football player, Justice B. Hill, with "Former FSU Star Myron Rolle Paid Cost for Being Different," reinforces a narrative that limits intelligence to white athletes and those who are not seen as "black:"

Rolle shows what can happen to someone who is "different" than he's expected to be. . . . He placed his books ahead of his football aspirations.

While he wanted a look at the NFL, Rolle longed to be a neurosurgeon.

But that's not what we expect from a football player, particularly a Black football player.

Chiseled body?

Yes.

Fearlessness?

Yes.

Nerdish?

No!

A muscular, fearless Black man finds obstacles in his path when "bookish" and "nerdy" are attached to his résumé. But his résumé doesn't include a stop in the NFL, a league where he fit in as well as he did with a certain group of folk who favor Black men who are crass and unschooled, folk who see "proper English" and education as unbecoming of a brother.[67]

The bifurcation of *athletic/intelligent, black/white,* and *tough/bookish* is central to the Rolle narrative. As he is both athletic and intelligent, tough and bookish, he is an exception; he embodies those qualities and characteristics that are seen as distinct in white athletes and in black athletes. What makes him unique is that he embodies both.

While the "he got brains" narrative is often reserved for the transnational, immigrant, and white athlete, those African American athletes (Grant Hill, Shane Battier; Robert Smith, Jonathan Martin) who are imagined as different, as unusual because of their class status, where they grew up, their family structure, and their skin color, are also celebrated for their brains. Whether being mixed-race or attending an Ivy League, the discourse of difference preserves the whiteness and colorblindness of the gifted sporting discourse. Attending Duke or having a white parent reinforces the idea that proximity to whiteness is in essence proximity to intelligence and to cultures that value smarts. Growing up in a culture and community of thinkers and learners carries over onto the court, propelling those who may lack the skills or athletic talent or physical prowess into the upper echelons of sports success.

A *New York Times* profile of Shane Battier embodies the ways that intelligence functions within the binary that positions "run-of-the mill" African American players in opposition to those exceptions:

In basketball there is only so much you can plan, however, especially at a street-ball moment like this. As it happened, Houston's Rafer Alston was among the most legendary street-ball players of all time—known as Skip 2 My Lou, a nickname he received after a single spectacular move at Rucker Park, in Harlem. "Shane wouldn't last in street ball because in street ball no one wants to see" his game, Alston told me earlier. "You better give us something to ooh and ahh about. No one cares about someone who took a charge."

The Rockets' offense had broken down, and there was no usual place for Alston, still back near the half-court line, to go with the ball. The Lakers' defense had also broken down; no player was where he was meant to be. The only person exactly where he should have been—wide open, standing at the most efficient spot on the floor from which to shoot—was Shane Battier. When Daryl Morey spoke of basketball intelligence, a phrase slipped out: "the I.Q. of where to be." Fitting in on a basketball court, in the way Battier fits in, requires the I.Q. of where to be. Bang: Alston hit Battier with a long pass. Bang: Battier shot the 3, guiltlessly. Nothing but net.[68]

Whereas Alston, a "street baller," excels because of his creativity, swagger, attitude, and athleticism, Battier brings IQ, intelligence, and smarts, allowing him and the team to excel.

From Battier to Luck, from Brady to the immigrant narrative, sports does ample ideological work, teaching us all about race and its realness with respect to intelligence.

### CONCLUSION

In 1994, Richard Hernstein and Charles Murray published what would become the "New Republican" bible:[69] *The Bell Curve: Intelligence and Class Structure in American Life*, a "book that gave standardized tests—and the racist ideas underpinning them—a new lease on life."[70] As noted by Stephen Jay Gould, *The Bell Curve* reflected the widely held belief that "social inequalities" were the "dictates of biology."[71]

Five years later, Jon Entine published *Taboo: Why Black Athletes Dominate Sports and Why We're Afraid to Talk About It*, a book that built upon the "intellectual and scientific" tradition of attributing black athletic success to genetics and psychological differences based on race. It too saw sports and its racial demographics as "dictates of biology."[72] Or for the likes of Harry Edwards another book based on the racist ideas of biological determinism. According to Edwards:

> The idea of race-linked, biogenetic-based excellence is a palpable myth. You can no more tell who is going to be a great athlete by racial heritage than you can tell who is going to be a great pianist by the space between their thumb and pinkie. . . . Entine's book carries implications of a lack of competitiveness and discipline as far as African-Americans are concerned. And to that extent, it reinforces myths about African-Americans being more instinctual, animalistic, and less inclined toward intellectual and moral development. . . . Jon Entine's book gives us the opportunity to reflect upon the fact that these highly virulent, racist notions– backed up by pseudo-scientific nonsense from the 18th and 19th centuries–are still out there, and from time to time, find fertile ground in which to grow and sprout. . . . For the same reason that you see very few black airline pilots. It's not that we can't fly the planes. It's that socio-cultural circumstances and opportunities limit our prospects.[73]

For Entine and his brethren, circumstances or socially-produced opportunities were secondary to inherent biological differences. If racial difference explains sports success or the types of athletic endeavors undertaken, then surely such differences have resulted in other sorts of social arrangements.

Hernstein and Murray (along with Entine) were merely giving voice to a longstanding tenet of white supremacy: white intellectual superiority and black intelligence deficiency. "The races vary intellectually and morally, just as they do physically," noted Madison Grant.[74] He further remarked, "It has taken us fifty years to learn that speaking English, wearing good clothes, and going to school and church does not transform a negro into a white man". [75] Not only concluding that race was real, that race was biology, and that "biology was destiny,"[76] such thinking normalized and naturalized difference and inequality. The necessity of segregation, and the resulting inequality was encoded in biology and measured in IQ tests. According to Ibram Kendi, for eugenicists, social Darwinists, and other racialist scientists, "Standardized tests became the newest 'objective' method of proving Black intellectual inferiority and justifying discrimination."[77]

The popularity of *The Bell Curve* and *Taboo* reflects the centrality of the racial mind/body discourse within white supremacy and its relationship to sporting cultures. The ubiquity of this language, these tropes, and commonplace narratives that profile white athletes as smart and black athletes as "natural athletes" is merely an extension of the history.[78] It reflects the encoding of these ideologies within America's racial DNA all while doing the work that instills these ideas from one generation to the next.

Whether embracing cultural or biological arguments, white supremacist ideologies focus on racial difference, on the profiles that operate within the broader racial hierarchy, to explain why whites dominate the quarterback position and the coaching ranks, compared to the wide receiver position or basketball, where African Americans have excelled in recent years. According to this narrative, the racial sporting landscape isn't evidence of racism, historic or otherwise, but instead a product of different skills and talents encoded in racial DNA and cultural baggage.

Just as race operates outside the arena, the hegemony of narratives, descriptors, tropes, and rhetorics locating intelligence and brainpower as reasons for white athletic success, as opposed to physicality, athleticism, and body type for black athletes, normalizes and rationalizes inequality in sports and beyond. Racial profiling and the efforts to create an IQ hierarchy within sports contribute to a racial logic that divides athletes and communities.

# CHAPTER 3

# TALKING TRASH (WHILE WHITE)

*A Betrayal of Tradition or a Sign of Competitive Leadership?*

When I retire, I'll get Ricky Hatton to wash my clothes and cut my lawn and buckle my shoes. Ricky Hatton ain't nothing but a fat man. I'm going to punch him in his beer belly. He ain't good enough to be my sparring partner. —FLOYD MAYWEATHER JR.

I'm just looking around to see who's gonna finish second.
—LARRY BIRD, ON HIS CHANCES OF WINNING
THE 1986 THREE-POINT SHOOTING CONTEST

I'm not worried about the Sacramento Queens. Write it down. Take a picture. —SHAQUILLE O'NEAL

They can't stop a nosebleed, twenty-fifth in the league, and we the ones that get disrespected. —BART SCOTT

I can't really hear what Jeremy [Roenick] says, because I've got my two Stanley Cup rings plugging my ears. —PATRICK ROY

Tell your girlfriend to stop cheering for me. Or tell your wife and kids to stop cheering for me. —KEYSHAWN JOHNSON

I'll call the President. President, we need the National Guard! We
need as many men as you can spare! Because we are killing the
Patriots! So call the dogs off! Send the National Guard, please!

—SHANNON SHARPE, DURING A ONE-SIDED
VICTORY AGAINST NEW ENGLAND

After the fight I'm gonna build myself a pretty home and use him as a
bearskin rug. Liston even smells like a bear. I'm gonna give him to the
local zoo after I whoop him. —MUHAMMAD ALI, 1964

Your . . . wife tastes like Honey Nut Cheerios.

—KEVIN GARNETT TO CARMELO ANTHONY

TALKING trash is central to sports; reflecting the competitiveness of
sports, the ways that sports imagines masculinity, and the violence of
sports, the practice of verbally assaulting one's opponent is nothing
new. The above epigraphs illustrate how trash-talking transcends generation, sport, and race. It takes place on and off the field; players, coaches,
general managers, and owners do it.

The existence of the sports media requires players to talk trash. Yet, that
isn't the lesson gleamed from the sports media, which continuously reduces
trash-talking to the immorality and dysfunction of today's athletes. Linked
to blackness and the hip-hop generation, presented as evidence of unsportsmanlike conduct that betrays tradition and honor of year's past, and as a
source of decay in the values of sports and its utility as a source of role models,
trash-talking is imagined as a pollutant that is destroying the sports fabric.
That is, unless the required white body, the right mouth, the right sport,
and the right context is in place for the one talking. For example, during
the 2016 Olympics, white athletes, from Michael Phelps to Lilly King, were
given a pass for wagging their fingers and talking trash toward their opponents. Their winning without the requisite humility was positioned apart
from trash-talking, refashioned as equal parts nationalism and joy. Within
the context of the Olympics the same cannot be said for either the men's
basketball team or America's sprinters who were expected to be quiet and

humble so as to not embarrass the nation. The right and beauty of talking trash are clearly not afforded to every athlete equally.

In many ways, trash-talking is as American as apple pie. It can be found in sports and popular culture, in academia and politics, and within our own folklore. What is more emblematic of talking trash, of taunting and puffing one's chest with brazen bravado, than the trope of American exceptionalism? Telling the world "We are the greatest," that we are not only exceptional but a shining city on the hill, is the ultimate trash talk. It is so grandiose and arrogant that it puts Ali to shame.

Despite its resonance throughout society, the idea of trash talk remains wedded to modern sports culture. More specifically, trash-talking is imagined as a new sporting phenomenon that has materialized with integration and the increased influence of hip-hop. This chapter, thus, takes up the racial discourse surrounding trash-talking. It examines the ways that the presumed links between verbal jousting and blackness shapes its place within modern sports. The entanglement of talking trash and blackness produces a discourse that sees rhetorical banter through a lens of pathology and criminality; that is, when it comes from a black voice and body, trash-talking is threatening and dangerous. For white athletes, talking trash is almost illegible. Yet when seen as part of the game, it represents something different: a sign of passion, competitiveness, and evidence of the beauty of sports.

The whole adage says that, "One person's trash is another man's treasure" is apt here because within the sporting landscape one person's trash-talking is trash, corruptive, corrosive, and undesirable, but another's is a treasure that is worthy of celebration. As part of the larger theme of #PlayingWhile-White, and the dialectics that exist between privilege and antiblack racism, this chapter focuses on the many different ways that trash-talking is seen/normalized/rendered invisible within the white body.

Focusing specifically on the example of Johnny Manziel, especially in comparison to the experiences of Richard Sherman, it argues that not only do white athletes get away with talking smack they are celebrated for their verbosity; unlike their black counterparts, they are protected from the regimes of regulation and demonization, and are allowed to play with the pleasure and agency to talk, move, and engage in the psychological warfare of sports.

## THE CULTURE WARS OF TRASH-TALKING

At one level, trash-talking is seen as part and parcel of male sports—it is a "manly art." The acceptance of trash talk in hockey, NASCAR, baseball, and boxing, through both celebration and erasure as evidence of normalization, highlights the dialectics between constructions of (white) masculinity and the practice of talking trash in sports. It is no wonder that Nigel Collins sees the history of trash talk in boxing as distinct from sports in general, writing, "But boxers are not just athletes and they don't play. They are fighters, and that changes everything."[1] Similarly, in *Manly Art*, Elliott J. Gorn highlights how sports journalists throughout history have celebrated the trash-talking abilities of John L. Sullivan for his "creative swearing, his clever epithets for opponents and prodigious boasts about himself."[2] While reflecting the specific history of trash-talking within boxing, reflective of the cultural acceptance of violence and brash individuality within the ring, the racial specificity is worth thinking about here. Jack Johnson,[3] Muhammad Ali, and Floyd Mayweather, among others, were (and are still to this day) routinely chastised for their rhetorical blows inside and outside the ring. Larry Atkins, with "In This Corner, The Man Who Invented Trash-Talking," makes clear his disdain for Ali the trash-talker and its long-term impact on sports culture:

> While I admire and respect Ali's tremendous boxing skills and the fact that he spoke his mind and stood for his convictions by sacrificing the prime of his career when he shunned the Vietnam draft on religious grounds, I couldn't stand his trash-talking, self-promotion, showmanship, arrogance and disrespect for his opponents. While he floated like a butterfly and stung like a bee, his words also stung many. Ali set the stage for everything that many people today don't like about modern-day athletes—dancing in the end zone, taunting fans and opponents, etc. He wrote poetry that predicted in which round he would beat his opponent. Ali referred to himself as "The Greatest," and for years he compared Joe Frazier to an ugly, stupid gorilla and called him an "Uncle Tom." He reportedly mocked Joe Louis for losing his money and for being inarticulate.[4]

Similar discourses govern a myriad of sports,[5] whereupon there is a right way to engage in competitive banter that inspires fans' interest and spawns competition all while being respectful to opponent and tradition.

At another level, the complex relationship between sports and trash-talking evident in efforts to see good trash-talking as an art form, as about a psychological edge. As opposed to unsportsmanlike and ego-driven trash talk of today's athletes, the talk of a different generation was part of the game. Celebrated as part of the masculine spirit of athletics, the individual competition, the art of trash-talking is often located at the annals of history.

As one examines the various online lists of the "greatest trash-talkers," the nostalgia becomes clear. Athletes of a previous generation (who played before integration and into the 1970s and 1980s) are much more common to be found in this context than with other lists, which seemingly privilege the here and now. Likewise the trash-talking of this previous generation is often depicted as "kinder" and "gentler," governed by rules that didn't allow for personal attacks, the "N-word" and efforts to humiliate your opponent.[6] For example, Tyler Leli notes, in offering a preface to his list of trash-talkers, which is dominated by already-retired athletes, "There is no doubting that the move away from allowing players to be as reckless towards their opponents has happened because of a precious few incidents that stained the images of leagues like the NBA, NFL, NHL and MLB, but there are certainly people who still long for the golden ages of trash talk."[7] Similarly, Richard Lapchick argues, "Those who are older know that trash-talking has been part of basketball and football for a long time." Yet, over time "the language has changed, and the form is different."[8] Citing "disrespectful language" and "trash-talking," Julie Pfitzinger describes a troubling sports world, that has spilled over from the professional ranks into recreational leagues where fun and learning lessons is supposed to be primary.[9] According to Frank White, a game official:

> In our adult society, there is a real lack of civility, and it's spilling over to the young people. The tone of games has changed, in subtle ways, to the point where things have become more aggressive and there is more verbal bullying among players. This is not your father's sports world—it's a F**king new era.[10]

These shifts, evident in the ubiquity of trash-talking and taunting, reflect the intrusion of hip-hop,[11] with its emphasis on bravado and battles, the commercialization of sports,[12] and a lack of civility within modern sports.[13] According to Jason Silverman:

> Trash talk, the practice of boasting and insulting one's foes on court or afield, may be one of our culture's most beloved, and most reviled, phenomena. Commercials from athletic companies such as Nike often glorify trash-talking, suggesting that bad manners are essential to good basketball. But critics see in trash talk the decline of sportsmanship and consider it yet another sign of society's general loss of civility.[14]

Others see this change as a consequence of modern sports media and social media, which has contributed to an erosion of societal mores while breaking down the boundaries between the athletes and the outside world. Nigel Collins waxes nostalgic, boasting of the good old days while putting contemporaries to shame for their infantile and sophomoric attempts at talking trash. For him, trash-talking in boxing isn't what it once was:

> The growth of trash talk has been greatly enhanced by television, the Internet, and social media. Television allowed millions of people to see and hear boxers in ways fans never had before, and if one of them said something noteworthy, the word spread quicker than ever. The Internet ratcheted up the intensity, and social media gave everybody, including the fighters, unlimited access to new modes of expressing themselves. Whether that's been a good thing is a matter of personal taste.[15]

As with so much of sporting culture wars, hip-hop and blackness is often identified as the problem, the source of erosion and corruption. "If you listen to today's music, specifically hip-hop and rap, there's a clear message there about not respecting authority," notes Ed Tapscott, a former college basketball coach and NBA executive. "It preaches a kind of rugged individualism, not in a cowboy kind of way, but in a verbal confrontation kind of way. The music world has attached itself in many ways to sports and a lot of young athletes react to that music."[16]

For some the culture of trash-talking reflects modern sports, which creates entitled and spoiled athletes.[17] According to Dr. Steven Ortiz:

> Spoiled-athlete syndrome begins early in sports socialization. From the time they could be picked out of a lineup because of their exceptional athletic ability, they've been pampered and catered to by coaches, classmates, teammates, family members and partners. As they get older, this becomes a pattern. Because they're spoiled, they feel they aren't accountable for their behaviors off the field. They're so used to people looking the other way.[18]

For others, the danger of trash-talking is the impact of bad role models,[19] lack of sportsmanship,[20] the focus on winning,[21] the declining values of sports,[22] trash-talking as a gateway to crime off the court,[23] and an overall sports culture that is mired in crime and dysfunction.

What is striking with the discourse is how much of it conflates trash-talking and taunting during game action with criminal misconduct.[24] As with the media discourse surrounding Tiger Woods, which linked his infidelity to the crimes of several different athletes arrested for everything from drugs to violent crime, the media framing offers little room between yelling "you can't guard me," and drugs, dogfighting, or murder. "Once upon a time, after all, the public—and coaches and team owners too—expected athletes to stand for certain ideals of civility, self-mastery, respectability, and fair play that provided an example for all citizens," write Anderson and Reinharz in "Bring Back Sportsmanship." "In place of the sportsman, the gladiator has appeared, substituting naked aggression for the sportsman's fidelity to rules, restraint, and civility."[25]

Writing about the NBA's "crackdown on trash-talking and taunting" in 1994, which was fueled by the cozy relationship between sports and hip-hop culture, evidenced by the ascendance of Allen Iverson, the Fab 5, UNLV, and "U"—University of Miami[26]—the *Seattle Times* lamented Gary Payton's mouth, calling on him to emulate his more "humble" and quiet peers. "Bad-mouthing opponents is the mother's milk of fights and brawls. It sets a terrible example for kids who idolize their NBA heroes."[27] Responding to this editorial, one reader similarly lamented trash talk as a threat to kids and society as a whole:

> Uncivilized, disrespectful behavior has too often been acted out before a screaming enthusiastic crowd that influences juvenile minds. They see this as a method of getting attention—and getting some recognition they could not get any other way.
>
> There are too many pro-sport stars who behave as human beings who can serve as role models to our young. This is just one element in the puzzle contributing to wayward behavior and criminal acts and violent crimes. The earlier a young boy or girl can realize that it is not acceptable to act like an animal the greater opportunity you have of having them conduct themselves in a civilized manner with their families, friends and neighbors.
>
> Trash is trash is trash—and those who both act this out and admire it should be made to feel terribly uncomfortable.

This would become even more draconian in 2004 following the Palace Brawl, which furthered a narrative of both nostalgia and outrage at the criminal costs and consequences of the influence of urban (black) youth culture and hip-hop.[28]

Focusing on the centrality of antiblack racism within America's culture wars, as evidenced by the protection of whiteness, the demonization of black bodies, and the rendering of blackness as problem alongside the signifiers of whiteness as benign and desirable, Stuart Hall, who notes that "blackness is never innocent or pure,"[29] argued that the constructions of blackness as criminal, as threatening, guided politics in the 1980s:

> [T]he themes of crime and social delinquency, articulated
> through the discourses of popular morality, touch the direct expe-
> rience, the anxieties and uncertainties of ordinary people. This
> has led to a dovetailing of the "cry for discipline" from below into
> the call for an enforced restoration of social order and authority
> "from above." This articulation for the bridge, between the real
> material sources of popular discontent, and their representation,
> through specific ideological forces and campaigns, as the general
> need for a "disciplined society." It has as its principal effect, the
> awakening of popular support for a restoration of order through
> imposition: the basis of a populist "law-and-order" campaign.
> This in turn, has given a wide legitimacy to the title of balance
> within the operations of the state toward the "coercive" pole,
> whilst preserving its popular legitimacy.[30]

Likewise, Herman Gray argues the emergence of a post-Nixon conservative movement successfully reduced "blackness as a marker of internal threats to social stability, cultural morality, and economic prosperity."[31] This is nothing new; it is central to the project of white supremacy, "which has been premised on the inherent inferiority of blacks and the equally fallacious assumption of the superiority of whites by whites," writes Kimberlé Williams Crenshaw. "Within traditional white supremacist paradigms, blacks were imagined to be lascivious, emotional, and childlike, while whites were regarded as industrious, pious, rational, and mature."[32] The panics surrounding blackness, its scapegoating, and the efforts to source problems to the black community not only replicate longstanding cultural projects that locate broader social and cultural problems through black bodies in general, and hip-hop specifically,[33] but also simultaneously exonerate whiteness and America as a whole.

The rising influence of black popular culture, the visibility of black celebrity, and the election of Barack Obama heightened these stakes through the early part of the twenty-first century. The regulation and outrage regarding trash-talking, particularly from black athletes, and the normalization and acceptance of competitive banter from white athletes are reflective of the broader issues and the centrality of antiblack racism. To be sure, #PlayingWhileWhite protects white athletes from these culture wars, racial panics, and the cultural anxieties that emanate from the ideologies of white supremacy. It protects white athletes from debates and surveillance surrounding trash-talking. Antiblack racism and resulting culture wars and panics empower whites to express themselves, use trash-talking for a competitive edge, and otherwise get verbal.

There is little evidence that trash-talking is new, is dramatically different now, or is a product of today's me-first generation, hip-hop swagger. Yes, hip-hop, with its emphasis on lyrical battles, braggadocio, and banter, influences contemporary trash talk. The influence of hip-hop on sports trash talk is evident in the importance of the dozens and the competitive nature of the cypher within rap, graffiti, and break dancing cultures. Yet, chatter on-the-field as a widespread practice is not new, preceding hip-hop. According to Chuck Smith, a former NFL defensive lineman, "People have been talking trash for decades. It's about creating a competitive advantage because the myth in the NFL is that everybody is mentally strong. That really isn't accurate."[34] Similarly, Taylor Buckley rebuffs the historic revisionists, noting the importance of trash-talking through the history of sports and in competition in general:

> Some say trash talk needs silencing. They act like it's new and bad. Wrong. It's tradition, part of history just getting a keener edge. Experts have traced its origins variously to Larry Bird, Muhammad Ali and even to Babe "I'll-smack-this-one-roughly-to-Salt-Lake-City" Ruth. But actually trash talk dates to the Battle of Trenton, when George "I-can-toss-a-silver-dollar-to-the-moon" Washington rattled that unsuspecting Hessian general from his Christmas Eve stupor, stared him in the eye and said tauntingly: "Your mother wears combat boots!" (A phrase which nowadays is usually enunciated in its shortened form: "Yo mama!"). Trash talk is part of the underpinnings of all competition.[35]

Still, leagues and media alike continue to see trash-talking as a symptom of the perniciousness of hip-hop, a culture destroying the moral, economic, and cultural fabric of sports. These racial panics elicit both the formal regulation[36] and media shaming, highlighting the stakes within these purported debates about sportsmanship and the art of talking trash.

While nothing new, the politics of racial nostalgia[37] and the racialization and criminalization of trash-talking result in different levels of policing.[38] Indeed, basketball and football have been sites of ample discussion and the ultimate establishment of rules prohibiting trash-talking, taunting, and excessive celebration. The visibility of black bodies and the presumed influence of black culture contribute to the culture wars that prompt discipline and punishment surrounding touchdown dances and smack talk.[39]

Outside the most intense sports sites, media discourse rarely addresses trash talk in hockey, golf, NASCAR, swimming, or even baseball. While the experts on smack talk, and those creating lists for the Mount Rushmore of trash talk include baseball and hockey, alongside of tennis, swimming, and other "refined" and "civilized sports," the public and mainstream media as a whole rarely see trash talk within these sports cultures.

Similarly, athletes such as Larry Bird and John Stockton, notorious for their own verbal battles, are rarely seen as problems in this regard. They embody sportsmanship and correct values. Lamenting the retirement of Wayne Gretzky and Larry Bird, the *Telegram & Gazette* not only bemoaned the declining civility and values of sports, evident by trash-talking, but marked those fleeting values in the play of Larry Bird:

> Unfortunately, such gracious—dare we say gentlemanly? — behavior in pro sports is rare. The norm? Trash talk, cheap shots, breast-beating and mocking victory dances around fallen opponents—not to mention even more deplorable behavior off the court and field by these well-remunerated role models. It is a sad commentary that such refreshing qualities as modesty, sportsmanship and candor have become so rare in the pro ranks that, when glimpsed in a Larry Bird or Wayne Gretzky, they are occasions for joy.[40]

Like John Stockton, Tom Brady, Michael Phelps, Rob Gronkowski, and Andrew Luck, the constructed image of Bird belies the historic memory of his competitors, which was that Bird talked trash, took cheap shots, and otherwise did whatever necessary to win. The image represents the embodiment and the power in #PlayingWhileWhite: the white athlete is always seen as a moral, capable role model.

Embodying the illegibility of taunting and such banter within those sports and from those bodies of whiteness, discussions focus on blackness. This not only shapes the location (which sports, when), but the manner in which trash-talking is discussed and the types of anxieties projected. Media discourses rarely discuss trash-talking as part of the game, nor as a talent and skill set that requires intelligence and wit. Even those who explicitly or implicitly link trash-talking to black culture rarely provide historic or cultural analysis. No mention of the cultural practices of signifying, or the dozens; no discussion of oral traditions or cultures of resistance. Rather, it is constructed as evidence of mean-spiritedness, declining values, criminal influences, and a lack of respect for game and opponent.

Mainstream discourse and media representation of trash-talking consistently associate it with blackness, simultaneously dehistoricizing and decontextualizing this placement. Naturalizing and pathologizing its locality, the discourse sees trash-talking as a symptom, and evidence that blackness is essentially disruptive, uncontrollable, and a source of "cultural degeneracy." The realities of racism are not simply felt by those black athletes who experience media scorn or who deal with fines and suspension, but by white athletes, who have the power to talk trash, a right codified by a system of racism. Take Rob Gronkowski or Tom Brady, who can dance, taunt opponents, and talk trash. Rather than a sign of disrespect, it becomes an indicator of their passion. Neither is alone. This unearned advantage provides white athletes with the ability to use this psychological tool. White athletes are able to utilize mental tricks alongside their athleticism without the same level of scrutiny and media backlash.

Consequently, white athletes are able to convert the art of trash-talking into a commodity, as a source of revenue and praise, even as their black peers face a different set of rules. In an effort to highlight these racial double standards, especially in a moment defined by claims of post-raciality and colorblindness, the rest of the chapter is dedicated to Johnny Manziel and Marshall Henderson, both of who have cashed in on the illegibility of white trash-talking. Whereas Richard Sherman faced a different set of rules, Johnny Talker and Marshall Heckler #PlayWhileWhite, allowing for a whole lot of chatter with little noise from a media that is quick to tell Sherman, Beckham, Russell Westbrook, Yasil Puig, Serena Williams, and even Ali to "shut up and play."

### JOHNNY TALKER

Johnny Manziel, the once famed college football player turned mediocre NFL star turned professional bust and TMZ star, has always liked to talk trash. From his making money gestures to the endless banter on the field, from his Twitter beefs to his public conflicts, his career has been defined by his propensity to rhetorically challenge his opponents, opposing teams, fans, and the media. During his freshman year, he was known to take to Twitter to wreak havoc on his critics. In one instance, he fired back at a fan who dared to question his talents with a picture of his Heisman Trophy. In another tweet, he celebrated his team's Bowl victory, challenging those who noted the absence of a championship victory.

While his responses were more than appropriate, the level of celebration from a media that is quick to chastise athletes for responding to fans, for engaging media critically, and for otherwise putting their own voice out there is striking. "Johnny Manziel sending a tweet about championships mattering a day after video and pictures of him enjoying his life lit Twitter afire leaves him open for criticism, as a titleless player in a ring-mad society" wrote Andy Hutchins.[41] "But Johnny Football sees and reacts to criticism on Twitter like he does pressure on the field. When you make fun of Johnny Manziel, you are making fun of someone who will give it right back—then crow about his Twitter following. You can't win. Just enjoy it." The often-deployed narratives about humility, respect, and keeping quiet rarely applied to Manziel, who, in fact, was celebrated for his brash and fearless attitude on and off the field. Just as scrappiness and hard work were innate to white athletes, indicative of leadership qualities, Manziel's trash talk became evidence of his passion and leadership abilities. His whiteness contributed to an alternative reading of his words and his trash-talking swagger.

This should be of little surprise given that the cultural intrusion of blackness—those cultural practices associated with black bodies—is consistently imagined as corruptive and destructive. Writing about the demonization of the black underclass, Robin D. G. Kelley discusses "the cultural and ideological warfare that continues to rage over black people and the 'inner city' as social problems."[42] Highlighting the importance of situating contemporary antiblack racism within America's post–civil rights culture wars, Kelley writes:

> The culture wars continue to rage each day in the streets of urban America, in the realm of public policy, in the union halls, and at the workplace. . . . The "ghetto" continues to be viewed as the Achilles heel in American society, the repository of bad values and economic failure, or the source of a vibrant culture of resistance. Depending on who is doing the talking/writing ghetto residents are either a morally bankrupt underclass or a church-going, determined working class living in fear of young riffraff. Whatever the narrative and whoever the source, these cultural and ideological constructions of ghetto life have irrevocably shaped public policy, scholarship, and social movements.[43]

George Lipsitz similarly describes America's racialized culture wars in the following way: "Ignorant of even the recent history of the possessive investment in whiteness . . . Americans produce largely cultural explanations for structural problems." The erasure of these structural changes codified in racism and the cultural narratives leads to the demonization of communities all "while hiding the privileges of whiteness by attributing them to family values, fatherhood, and foresight—rather than favoritism."[44]

Within these racial culture wars, #PlayingWhileWhite means excessive celebration, talking trash, bravado, and taunting[45] in absence of those governing narratives of moral, cultural, and racial panic.[46]

And Johnny Football cashed in on the absence of either surveillance or public shaming when it comes to trash-talking. Manziel has the requisite class and racial standing to engage in practices that have long been lamented as "what's wrong with youth culture, or today's athletes," and thus is celebrated for his passion and love of the game exhibited by his propensity to taunt and trash-talk.

The celebratory tone of Manziel's trash-talking was on full display after his initial game of his sophomore season. Following a tumultuous off-season and a suspension during the game's first half, Manziel entered the game against Rice, taking little time to send a message. After scrambling for a first down, he made "an apparent trash-talking autograph gesture to a Rice defender,"[47] which resulted in a personal foul. Add to this, he was seen throughout the game taunting Rice with both his money-counting gesture and his trash talk. While this was met with some criticism, his "swagger" was met with celebration and adoration. Described as having "having fun," as "entertaining,"[48] or engaged in "playful chatter,"[49] as responding to the "mind games"[50] and trash-talking, Manziel's on-the-field behavior was either dismissed or celebrated as part of his unflappable disposition. Clay Travis responded to his first game with celebration with the requisite praise and celebration: "God bless you, Johnny. Thanks for being back."[51] Chris Greenberg noted that, while some had hoped for "a chastened and subdued Johnny Manziel," they got instead the return of Johnny Football.[52] Graham Watson offered the common reframe that painted Manziel as merely responding to the unfair criticism and scrutiny directed at him:

> Manziel could have left it alone, turned a deaf ear, instead he
> yelled back and made a motion like he was autographing some-
> thing. After he threw his first touchdown pass, he rubbed his fin-
> gers together like he was handling money. Several emailers have
> said the money signal has been something Manziel has used since

last season, but given his recent run-in with the NCAA, which interviewed him on suspicions of taking money for autographs, he should have thought better about using the motion fresh off suspension.[53]

At worst, he was dismissed as "childish," but such narratives were couched in celebratory tones that saw Manziel as simply a passionate kid whose emotions had gotten away from him for a brief minute. And his potential to grow-up and reign in this passion was almost a given. The media, his coaches, and others just needed to give him time.

Bucky Brooks, with "Don't Throw Johnny Manziel Out with the Trash Talk," offered a powerful reclamation of Manziel not as a selfish, brash, and arrogant player but as someone just having fun, someone blessed with a "gladiator mentality" fueled by competitiveness and greatness: "I believe his swagger and intensity are strong points of his game, and a major reason why the college football world fell in love with him a season ago."[54]

While getting a pass, especially in comparison to black athletes—from Jack Johnson to Muhammad Ali, from Allen Iverson to Richard Sherman, from Dez Bryant to Odell Beckham, from Serena Williams to the latest brash trash-talking athlete of color—what is telling with Manziel is how trash-talking is used as evidence of his calm demeanor, his passion for the game, his fearlessness, his swagger, and his competitive nature, and not the outcome of his incivility, racial makeup, and/or criminality. No mention of his selfishness or his impulsive disposition, even after being cut from the Browns, getting suspended from the league, or his countless encounters with law enforcement. #PlayingWhileWhite means the ability to talk trash and receive accolades for the very practice that has always resulted in the vilification of black athletes.

## A WORDSMITH WITH A PASSION FOR THE GAME: BEING MARSHALL HENDERSON

Described as a colorful personality, an entertaining gunner, enigmatic, passionate, crazy, flamboyant, eccentric, and full of swagger, Marshall Henderson, a shooting guard from Ole Miss in 2011–13, was loved by many. More than his game, his talent, or success, it was his "antics" that propelled both the love and attention. Whereas his black peers are routinely criticized for disrespecting the game, exhibiting poor sportsmanship, talking trash, and serving as poor role models, Henderson is a breath of fresh air, a wordsmith, who brings energy and passion to the game.[55] The power and privileges of #PlayingWhileWhite are immense with Henderson.[56] His rap sheet (which is discussed in chapter 5), his ability to move from school to school in absence of the labeling and scrutiny experienced by his black peers who are seen as mercenaries disinterested in school, and his behavior[57] and performance on-the-court all illustrate his privileges in operation. For example, although he averaged fifteen shots a game and shot less than 40 percent from the field, media narratives consistently depicted him as a scorer and an offensive talent. Sure, he was the fourteenth leading scorer in Division I during the 2012–13 season, but he also had the lowest shooting percentage of any player in the top forty. Echoing the media narrative of him as a scoring machine, Henderson would spend ample time on the court telling the world of his greatness.

Given the sordid history of integration at Ole Miss, the "ghosts of Mississippi,"[58] and the historic mistreatment directed at African American students at this "rebel campus," it is not surprising that Marshall Henderson elicited praise. Henderson's boastful, trash-talking approach was recast as odd or different, but nevertheless exciting and nonthreatening. Frank Schwab described his behavior during the 2013 season as follows:

> On one play in the second half, Henderson was leaning left to go back down to the defensive end, then shifted right to reach out and save a ball going out of bounds. He grabbed it and immediately nailed a 3-pointer over Florida's Casey Prather, who was closing hard. Then college basketball's most outrageous player enjoyed the moment, to say the least.
>
> He did the "3 goggles." Then he did the landshark, with his thumb to his forehead with his hand as a shark fin. Then when he came back after a timeout was called, he did Florida's traditional Gator chomp back down court to taunt the fans. Later the ABC cameras found a kid who was imitating the landshark. Yes, many probably think America's youth imitating Henderson is the sign the apocalypse is near.
>
> No, Henderson doesn't care if anyone was bothered by his antics. He was the one popping his jersey at the end, after Kenny Boynton's 3-pointer for the Gators rimmed out and the Rebels were SEC champions. Henderson is having fun with his villain persona.[59]

He was imagined as a good kid, who is entertaining on the court, and like other (white) college students, off the court. According to Tom Ley:

That floppy-haired kid who goofily poses for pictures while wearing three-goggles is somehow the same maniac in the GIF at the top of the page. That's what makes Henderson so intriguing. His on-court behavior clearly comes from some deep, dark *Helter Skelter*ish part of the soul, but off the court he's a perfectly sane, self-aware young man who does not at all seem like a human acid flashback.[60]

Matt Rybaltowski likewise celebrated Henderson for his individuality and willingness to express himself freely: "In an age of political correctness and the contrived sound bite, Marshall Henderson is an anomaly, a free-spirit college basketball hasn't seen since Jason Williams brought his killer crossover to Gainesville in the late 1990s. Dating back even further, it's not a stretch to consider Henderson a Bill Walton in a shooter's body."[61] Talking smack, taunting, trash-talking, getting in trouble, and not listening to authority figures such as his coach are recast as signs of individuality and free-spirited nature.[62]

While embodying the power of whiteness, as Teflon, as protection, Henderson's ability to engage in (mis)behavior with impunity is also about basketball and his whiteness. His appeal—like Johnny Manziel's, like the flashy basketball styles of Jason "White Chocolate" Williams, Grayson "the Professor" Boucher, and "Pistol" Pete Maravich—is rooted in his perceived mastery over the style and athletic skills long associated, albeit critically, with black athletes. Speaking about the popularity and aesthetic choices of Justin Timberlake, Imani Perry told Marc Lamont Hill during a Huffington Post Live segment that within the American imagination "there is a sonic preference for blackness, but there is a visual preference for whiteness."[63] Similarly, within the white sporting imagination there is an athletic preference for blackness, but there is a visual preference for whiteness. Marshall is exhibit A.

When Henderson taunted fans, talked trash, or simulated smoking weed after draining a three, he was praised for the "joy" and "passion" he played with each and every night. When Henderson threw ice into the stands of his school's student section following a bad call, his actions resulted in few consequences;[64] apparently, for a twenty-four-hour sports media that searches for and creates stories, the event was not even newsworthy. Instead, the narrative consistently depicted Henderson as fearless, determined, and passionate. By failing to acknowledge that every athlete is not entitled to taunt Florida or Auburn fans, throw ice into the student section, shoot with reckless abandonment, yell at his coach, punch another player, and get arrested on multiple occasions, media discourses turned his privilege into an unremarkable right.

Few athletes are celebrated for giving the finger to tournament fans and talking trash because they are entertaining, different, and "good for the game."[65] And then there is Marshall Henderson. Matthew Sturgeon, in "College Basketball Is More Fun with Ole Miss Sharpshooter Marshall Henderson," deployed the "fun" and free-spirited narrative with little irony:

> Why would anyone like this guy? And how in the world is he good for the game of college basketball?
>
> I'll tell you why; he's *different*. Henderson is tough, fearless, and doesn't fit the mold of how college athletes are supposed to act. He rubs people the wrong way and greatly angers the opposition. And while it may seem like his attitude is "me me me," that couldn't be further from the truth. The guy plays with incredible passion, and his love for winning and the game of basketball itself was very apparent after that NCAA Tournament loss last March. . . . If he was such a problem or "thug" he'd no longer be on the Ole Miss team. . . . If he was that big of a distraction, or a cancer to the team, he wouldn't last.[66]

Whereas black ballers are continuously criticized for selfishness—"there is no 'I' in *team*"—and demonized for putting ego in front of team by trash-talking, Henderson's aspiration to "get his money," and his propensity to taunt fans, was imagined as a sign of his being free spirited. Over and over again, he was celebrated for saying what was on his mind, even if his mind seems to begin and end with himself.

It is a striking moment of hypocrisy where not only did Henderson get a pass for his trash-talking, self-promotion, and his shot selection, because he is imagined as exceptional. In an age of media scrutiny, where (black) athletes are routinely criticized for deviating from the prescribed scripts, the celebration of Henderson from the same media that makes millions from telling today's (black) student athlete to shut up and play, is the embodiment of antiblack racism.

In 2012, Cardale Jones, a student athlete at Ohio State University, had the audacity to tweet: "Why should we have to go to class if we came here to play *football*, we ain't come to play *school*, classes are *pointless*." He was pilloried, critiqued, and cited as evidence of what's wrong with today's student athlete. He was suspended for one game for his 140-character protest. There were no headlines about his refreshing challenge to political correctness and no celebratory articles about his free spirit or about the passion Jones shows for his sport. When Nigel Hayes, a student athlete at the University of Wisconsin, held a sign describing himself as a "broke college student" in protest against the exploitation of collegiate athletes,[67] he faced widespread condemnation. Few celebrated or praised his message; even less described him as carefree or passionate about these issues.

For Henderson not speaking out on social issues or fighting for a cause bigger than himself meant that he was not threatening. So was his whiteness. He was consistently praised for his individuality and for his refusal to accommodate societal demands that he "shut up and play." The consummate trash-talker, he, of course, shared in his own celebration, noting, "That's just who I am, on and off the court, I like to wear my hat, my hoodie, and some shades." Yet, as Charles Modriano, a blogger and sports activist, noted in an interview with me, his ability to be himself, to express his own individuality is the essence of white privilege. "Young African-American men have no such luxury—on or off the court. At worst, wearing a hoodie can help get you killed like Trayvon Martin, and on just an average New York City day, it will get you 'stopped and frisked.'" His bravado, his performative masculinity, one that allows for the devaluing and disrespecting opponents, and his propensity to taunt fans and fellow players, are not only accepted but recast as refreshing and colorful. He is a good kid and therefore any behavior, even though those routinely described as that of thugs, is given a pass. The good kid pass is wrapped up in his whiteness. He is the anti-Richard Sherman, which is true, but within media discourse the evidence provided is not Sherman's Stanford education, his work in the community, or his greatness on the field, but rather that one is seen as a colorful kid and the other a thug[68] representative of today's (black) athlete gone wild.

### AMERICA'S WORST NIGHTMARE:
### YOUNG, BLACK, AND TALKING TRASH

In the final seconds of the 2014 NFC title game, Richard Sherman dropped back into coverage where he ultimately tipped a pass away from the San Francisco 49ers' Michael Crabtree, who was just inches from a game winning touchdown. Resulting in an interception, Sherman's efforts secured a victory and a trip to the Super Bowl. Immediately after the game, Sherman told Erin Andrews:

"Well, I'm the best corner in the game!"

Andrews: "O.K. then."

Sherman: "When you try me with a sorry receiver like Crabtree, that's the result you're going to get! Don't you ever talk about me!"

Andrews: "Who was talking about you?"

Sherman: "Crabtree! Don't you open your mouth about the best! Or I'm going to shut it for you real quick!

The interview heard around the world set off Twitter and the rest of the Internet. Called a "thug"[69] and countless other racist epithets, Sherman was chastised for his brash and cocky trash-talking. Calling his act "classless," John Devine noted, "Trash-talking isn't an art. It's garbage. Nothing good comes out of it."[70] Identifying Sherman as yet another NFL player of questionable character, Devine saw Sherman as antithetical to "sportsmanship."

We harped on Terrell Owens and Chad Johnson for years for their antics on the sidelines. We saw Ray Lewis do it for years. Why is this different? I think Sherman said it best himself earlier last week when he uttered, "If we were allowed to do what we do on the football field in public, we'd probably all be in jail."

No, crucifying an individual on national television doesn't warrant a jail sentence.

But it crossed the line.

You can't shoot off your mouth in high school or college football without serious ramifications. No taunting and no trash-talking. It's called sportsmanship.

Michael Cohen concurred, lamenting Sherman as "immature," "unprofessional" and "someone unable to control his emotions." Describing his postgame remarks as a "tirade," he further noted:

He is a brash, bold trash-talker on the football field. But for all his glory, he still has a lot to learn about sportsmanship. . . . Sherman's actions *were* classless and, what's worse, violated one of the few basic norms that exist in sports, namely to treat your opponents with a modicum of respect. . . . At a time when middle and high schools are rolling out anti-bullying programs, trash-talking should not be given the "boys just being boys treatment." On the football field, talking trash is, for better or worse, part of the game. We're inured to its public displays. Off the field, it is the language of bullies—a tool that the strong use to terrorize the weak and the vulnerable. It's hardly an ethos for young people to embrace. [71]

Commissioner Roger Goodell, who did not offer similar statements about Riley Cooper[72] and Richie Incognito,[73] both of whom used the N-word yet were afforded redemption, criticized Sherman for his post-game comments: "It's an emotional game, and you see a young man who comes off the field and he's pumped up, and there's so much excitement in the stadium, but no, I'm not cheering for that. . . . He took away a little bit from the team."[74] Terrence Moore felt similarly, arguing, "Sherman's persona is dangerous, along with the shallow-thinking folks who support him and his ever-flapping tongue."[75] Ignoring countless studies to the contrary[76] Moore used the moment to offer a sociological explanation for the rightful outrage:

> Consider, too, that a large percentage of black youngsters raised by single women are latchkey kids, which means they come home to an empty dwelling to fend for themselves over long stretches of time. So many of those youngsters get their idea of how to survive and prosper from older folks in the neighborhood. Either that, or they look toward the most visible people they see on television. Actors, rappers, athletes. Which is why Barkley was a role model back then to millions, and which is why he remains one today—whether he likes it or not. The same is true of Sherman. And on that score, he was a loser on Sunday. So Sherman deserved what he got in the aftermath.[77]

Beyond becoming yet another sports commentator who not only waxes sociological when discussing black athletes (but not white athletes), and recycling the Moynihan Report, which in 1965 identified single-family homes as the source of poverty within the black community, Moore parrots the broader discourse that seemingly identifies the duty of (certain) athletes to become role models, embracing the responsibility to teach youth desirable values and behavior. More often than not, these expectations and the shaming that comes with failure to be a role model is directed at black athletes.

Such arguments are rarely extended to the likes of Henderson, Gronk, Brady, Bird, or Manziel. Their trash-talking, celebratory dances, taunts, tweets, and gestures simulating their getting paid don't elicit outrage or theorizing about what they are doing to the kids. #PlayingWithWhiteness means not having to be accountable or analyzed; Manziel is just Johnny "Football"; Marshall is just being Marshall; and for Bird, Gronk, or Brady, trash-talking is a sign of their competitive edge. For them, to be #Brash-WhileWhite is to display confidence, to play with an edge, and spirit, which means everything is all right. This is clearly very different from the reactions resulting from Cam Newton dabbing, Odell Beckham dancing, or Richard Sherman telling the world about his greatness.

William C. Rhoden explains the reaction to Sherman as reflective of an American ethos that loves and hates brashness, confidence, and cocky dispositions: "We love to hate trash-talkers because that sort of attitude goes against the grain of an invented and false American modesty. At the end of the day, we are as narcissistic a culture as they come, which is why—at the end of the day—we grudgingly admire people like Sherman."[78]

Yet, what's clear in looking at Manziel versus Sherman, or Tom Brady, who in the wake of Deflategate was celebrated for his ability to talk trash, is that white America is deeply uncomfortable with African American trash-talkers; the sight and sound of black emotion, whether anger or joy, whether frustration or passion, elicits ample reaction, dissection, and commentary. Bravado and confidence, like rage, is unacceptable in association with blackness. Whiteness plus brashness is not only acceptable but also desired and celebrated. Arturo Garcia offered a brief summary of the racially based differential responses:

> All too often, when white players engage in trash talk, it's coded as Being A Competitor, or Being Fearless. The legend of Peyton Manning, for instance, wasn't derailed in 2003 when he went on live television and ripped "idiot kicker" and then-Indianapolis teammate Mike Vanderjagt during the Pro-Bowl. . . .
>
> It's not like Manning is the only one getting a pass: New England's Tom Brady yells at his teammates in public and NFL—excuse me, National Football League—pundits trip over each other to tell you he's "showing his passion for the game." Sherman actually pointed out on Fox Sports that, contrary to his squeaky-clean rep, Brady is an inveterate trash-talker in his own right; he just does it when the television cameras aren't looking. Yet no one is appalled or distressed by this revelation.
>
> Meanwhile, Dallas' Dez Bryant argues with his quarterback, and a network analyst tells him to "grow up." White quarterbacks wear baseball caps backwards and it's an everyday thing; San

Francisco's Colin Kaepernick does it, and a Buffalo newspaper's
NFL beat writer complains that he's being unprofessional. Richie
Incognito reportedly uses racist slurs in the course of bullying
Miami teammate Jonathan Martin, and it's "locker room culture";
Martin leaves the squad and he's "soft."[79]

As was apparent from the media responses, the erasure of the specifics of
what happened on the field, the larger history of trash talk, and the "signifying going on" all contributed to criticism and racial panics directed at
Sherman.

Many of the media and Twitter pundits reasserted "common sense"
understandings of black athletes, reiterating the narrative of Sherman as
an immature, selfish, and petulant child who represents what is wrong
with modern professional sports culture. Reflecting the longstanding
project of constructing black athletes as "bad boys," which, in the end,
"works to reinforce efforts to tame their 'out of control' nature,"[80] Sherman
was yet another problem. Whether depicting his rhetoric as indicative of
a lack of sportsmanship and a win-at-all-costs mentality; by representing Sherman as a bully, as scary, or as selfish; or through focusing on his
trash-talking, extravagance, bravado, and material flash, the demonization
of Sherman illustrates how his body (and his body of work) functions as a
contested site of the social significance of black athletes in the twenty-first
century.

The post-game criticisms were not simply about Sherman, but, rather,
they evoke the contested history of black athletes and their place in white-
run sporting industries geared at largely white consumers. As noted by
Imani Perry, in *Prophets of the Hood*, popular culture (including sports)
exists not only as a site for the construction and dissemination of ideas
about blackness, but also as a space where "the isolation of black bodies as
the culprits for widespread multiracial social ills" becomes commonplace.[81]
Even those examples where Johnny Manziel has been subjected to criticism
for his behavior, especially after the twentieth "indiscretion," the scope and
depth of such commentary is nowhere comparable to that which has been
directed at Sherman, Serena Williams,[82] or Dez Bryant.[83]

In other words, whereas, Johnny Football, Marshall Henderson, Tom
Brady,[84] and Aaron Rodgers[85] may be critiqued for their antics or exuber-
ance, the passions exhibited by black athletes are rarely seen as positive or as
evidence of their humanity. Instead they signify weakness, selfishness, and
an inability to control emotions. While Brady and Rodgers have earned the
right to tease their opponents, the same is not the case for too many black

ballers. Instead, #TalkingTrashWhileBlack is seen as yet another intrusion of hip-hop, its pathologies, dysfunctions, and disparate values. It is a threat to sportsmanship, team, and honor in competition: to Western civilization itself.

The differential responses are not just telling us about sporting cultures but the ways that privilege and power operate within a larger landscape. The reason Richard Sherman (or Cam Newton and Odell Beckham) elicits panic and outrage reflects the danger seen in black bodies that lack "discipline," "that are not under control." It reflects the same sort of ideologies that normalize school suspension rates, foster racial profiling, and otherwise sustain systemic inequality.[86]

Whereas, at worst, Henderson and Manziel are criticized for poor judgment as individuals, Sherman becomes a moment where hegemonic tropes about blackness, hip-hop, and black masculinity become circulated. He's representative (and his post-game passion is imagined as indicative of some pathology and some problematic values); at worst Manziel, Henderson, and others are exceptions (their behavior is also cast as exceptions to who they really are). More likely, they are celebrated as yet another reminder of the playfulness, innocence, and beauty of sports.

TALKING TRASH OR HONORING THE DEFEATED?
TO BAN OR NOT TO BAN, THAT IS A WHITE QUESTION

In 2014, reports emerged that NFL would consider instituting a penalty for use of the N-word on the playing field.[87] Like the regulation, policing, and double standards that follow trash-talking, the discourse surrounding the N-word is both ironic and based on racial contradictions and hypocrisies. This is from a league that has maintained an active defense of the R**skins[88] as a legitimate and honorific name for one of its more popular franchises and the one from the nation's capital. This from a league, and its media partners, that celebrates (white) players that talk junk as evidence of their competitiveness and passion for the game. At worst, each word highlights the entrenched racism of sports culture, and society at large, and a refusal to confront white power.

One word is read as a racial slur, and only a racial slur, and must not be uttered even as the structures of violence, degradation, and inequality remain entrenched in society; this same word is worthy of banning not just because of its symbolism and its connection to a history of antiblack violence but because it is uttered in the context of demeaning and disrespecting trash talk. The other word, despite linguistic, historic, and psychological evidence[89] is framed as anything but a racial slur that can be used in marketing, media coverage, and fan cheers. Trash talk is thus at the core of the differential responses. Black athletes, who are imagined as the source of the "N-word," must be controlled through public shaming and punishment. But the example in which the league and its teams are taunting an entire community with racism and with celebration of state violence is tradition.

Additionally, the N-word is taken to be a reference to the bad old days of racism, best forgotten; a reminder of the unresolved history of slavery and the social death that rendered blacks as property to be exchanged and exploited. As part of the NFL's effort to sell itself as a post-racial promised land, the debate over the N-word functions inside a narrative that simultaneously sees the (white) NFL as a source of power and racial liberation as opposed to its (black) players, who, with trash talk, use of the N-word, and thug conduct are obstacles to racial progress.

The R-word, on the other hand, is preserved as a tradition and ideal with claims to a so-called time after race. Our "raceless" present is more a trademark, a valuable piece of property from which Dan Snyder, the league, media conglomerates, and countless others make obscene profits from distortion and dehumanization.

And it is hard not to see in this pattern that some kinds of racism matter; some types of utterances, rhetorical violence, and trash talk elicit discomfort and unease; some can be seen and described, and demand public action, while others remain invisible, unspeakable, and unmoving.

After a season that began with Riley Cooper white player, drunk at a concert, calling a security guard the N-word because he felt slighted (see chapter 6 for further discussion), and ended with a damning report on the culture of the Miami Dolphins' locker room—in which use of the same word figured prominently in the bullying of Jonathan Martin—it is perhaps understandable that the NFL wanted to police this "incivility," if not outright hate. Yet, the regulation of certain bodies, slurs, and trash-talking is more about who is seen as a threat to civility and order rather than objective marker of these threats.

The NFL's refusal to deal with violence, to abandon the R-word, to address the absence of diversity within the league office and within front offices, or address institutionalized racism in its many forms, yet police the N-word or "excessive" celebrations says a lot about its mission and racial politics. The focus on trash talk and player-uttered slurs obfuscates the antiblack and anti-Native racism all while obscuring the powers and privileges of whiteness inside and outside of the NFL. This is ultimately about regulating (black) players—their utterances, their agency, and their bodies. Just as the

Palace Brawl was used to rationalize and justify the NBA Dress Code, the elimination of straight-from-high-school players, and countless other initiatives that disciplined and punished the NBA's primarily black players,[90] Goodell and the league seemingly used Riley Cooper, Richie Incognito and the growing debate around the N-word to increase its power. Being a #CommissionerWhileWhite (is there any other way to be commissioner?) is about repackaging hegemony, and the consolidation of power as benevolence, kindness, and social good.

This was all about respect, decency, and discipline, as defined by Roger Goodell and his corporate partners. This was all about control; it was about power, the politics of respectability, discipline, and punishment, about selling corporate multiculturalism, and regulating the voices and bodies of its primarily black players. This is why the focus has been on black players, on discipline, on the lack of respect that these trash-talking, endzone dancing, and taunting that "today's players" show for the game, each other, and social norms.

Even critics of the R-word like Peter King[91] praised the proposal to penalize the use of the N-word. An editorial in *Indian Country Today* celebrated the move, yet demanded that these protections be extended to other marginalized and disparaged communities. "Eliminating racism and the use of racist language from the NFL is a worthy and long overdue goal, but it cannot be confined to just one race," writes John F. Banzhaf III: "The use of the word 'n*ggers' is reprehensible, especially in this day and age, but so are the use of words like 'ch*nks,' 'w*tbacks,' 'r*gheads,' and 'r*dskins.'"[92]

That the NFL refuses to #DropTheName and actively attempts to rid the league of the N-word (as well as endzone dances, helmet removal, not standing for the national anthem, and trash talk) with more vigor than it has shown with head trauma, reflects a shared logic. The Washington DC team mascot purportedly exemplifies honor whereas using the N-word, kneeling for the anthem, and talking trash with banter or dances conveys dishonor and disrespect. Together, both serve as cases of how the white saviors have the power and potential to discipline and redeem "savaged" Others under the guise of twenty-first century multicultural sporting culture.

Some critics see these contradictions as self-serving, even callous cynical hypocrisy.[93] While acknowledging these patterns, it is important to think about the shared history and the centrality of white power through it all. And the proposed rule change and the defense of the Washington DC franchise must be read as efforts to protect white power while maintaining control over discourse and keeping the voices and bodies of people of color in their prescribed places. Despite appearance to the contrary, both the refusal to

#DropTheName and the push to #DropTheSlur simultaneously reflect the NFL's rejection of challenges to racism. Each seeks to preserve white power and profitability; each privileges white desire ahead of anything else. Each points to a desire to protect white supremacy and an impotent multiculturalism. Each speaks to the desirability of whiteness. The commodification and celebration of white trash-talking whether on playing fields or society as a whole, elucidates the value afforded to white bodies, as the index of civilization and marker of goodness.

To be sure, the discomfort with trash talk, combatting the N-word, and not changing the Washington DC football team name, and thus maintaining Native American branded monikers, is all about being a #FanWhileWhite, #OwningWhileWhite, and profits.

The preservation of one slur and the efforts to punish the use of another slur is also about money; the regulation of trash-talking in one space and the acceptance of the dehumanization of an entire community in another demonstrates the power of #OwningWhileWhite. Clearly Dan Snyder and the NFL generate billions of dollars through the commodification of anti-Indian racism. It would be a mistake to see the proposed rule as anything but a shrill capitalist move that seeks to profit off a crafted image of the league. It would be a mistake to ignore the importance of selling respectable, disciplined, and desirable NFL players.

Surely fearful about potential lawsuits regarding hostile work environments, the NFL is also using this moment to position itself as a leader in the fight against racism. As with the NBA, with its dress codes, regulation of trash-talking, and efforts to produce more disciplined and likable black players who will be judged by the content of their character and the quality of their play rather than the color of their skin. For some, the NFL efforts to regulate all forms of trash talk are about challenging societal stereotypes. Jason Whitlock sees the potential ban as "progress":

> Stipulating and enforcing a policy that NFL players, particularly black NFL players, refrain from using the N-word on the playing field isn't complicated, racist, hypocritical or an abuse of power.
>
> It's progress. No different from the NBA stipulating and enforcing a policy that required its players to dress like young professionals when sidelined and attending games. When initially floated and subsequently enacted, the shortsighted and simple-minded crowd pilloried commissioner David Stern's dress code as bigoted and out of touch with modern hip-hop America.[94]

Ultimately, the NFL is branding itself as a force of multiculturalist good and progress in sports. This is why Bird, Brady, Henderson, and Manziel can talk trash without concern; this is why NASCAR and hockey are able to taunt without much outrage. Clearly, accounting for the "ontological problem" of blackness[95] is not a burden that white athletes live with. Evidently, challenging racial stereotypes is not a part of #PlayingWhileWhite.

Sports culture is one where Richard Sherman's trash-talking prompts outrage and endless commentary on what his use of the English language says about today's athletes, today's youth, and the deleterious impact of hip-hop on society. Similarly Cam and Odell dancing, Joey or Yasiel flipping bats or otherwise playing baseball the "wrong way," and even Colin Kaepernick's kneeling elicits criticism that focuses on how they disrespect their opponents, fans, and society as a whole.

On the other hand, for Tom Brady, Johnny Manziel, Larry Bird, Marshall Henderson, and other white ballers, trash-talking communicates feistiness, competitiveness, passion for the game, and efforts to use any tool in the name of victory. As discussed in chapters 1 and 2, trash-talking is filtered through a narrative of white athletic intelligence and leadership, resulting in different conclusions for black and white athletes.

As we will see in the next chapter, race and racism shape discourses around crime just as they do our understanding of leadership, intelligence, athleticism, or morality, as shown by who can trash talk with impunity. Not only does the widespread practice of viewing white athletes through a prism of innocence and black athletes as criminals lead to different treatment and media narratives but it determines which athletes need to be controlled and disciplined and which ones can operate freely or even find redemption after minor missteps. In the end, #PlayingWhileWhite means having the ability to engage in behavior—whether talking trash, naming your team a racial slur, or violating the law—that more often than not is neither remarkable nor worthy of punishment.

CHAPTER 4

# WHITE THUGS?

*Crime and the Culture of Innocence*

ROM a history of slavery and lynching, through the persistent realities of racial profiling, mass incarceration, and daily instances of violence, the connection between dehumanization and criminalization
has been central to white supremacy.[1] Evident in virtually every American
space, "young + black + male is equated with reasonable suspicion, justifying arrest, interrogation, search, and detention of thousands of African
Americans every year."[2]

Sports reveal these entrenched realities; it also exists as a vehicle that perpetuates a world where black and brown bodies are hyper-criminalized. This
chapter takes up the question of crime and sports, demonstrating how race,
gender, and class not only shape the responding discourses and the differential levels of accountability but also influence ensuing spectacle and panics that follows sporting crimes and misdemeanors. It looks at how criminal
activity and misdeeds so often define black athletes, even though athletes in
general commit fewer crimes proportionally to their place in the population.[3]

Given America's racial history and entrenched ideologies that connect
race and crime, it is no wonder that an arrest or accusation against a black
athlete results not only in a recounting of past indiscretions on and off the
field but also an effort to contextualize through listing similar and dissimilar
incidents. For example, in the aftermath of the 2003 arrest of Kobe Bryant on charges of rape,[4] several media outlets connected his arrest to an
epidemic of NBA players arrested for DUI or drugs as opposed to linking
to larger discourses surrounding sexual violence, or masculinity inside and
outside of sports. We can also see this in the efforts to connect Ray Rice to
Adrian Peterson where their arrests for domestic violence and child abuse
led to discussions about athletes and crime as opposed to those focused on

issues of male violence. This sort of epidemic narrative infrequently happens with white athletes, where incidents are often framed in isolation of broader issues of white athlete crime, crime in the white community, or even crime in sports.

Rather than looking at the widely known cases involving superstar athletes, and those accused (and sometimes convicted) of the most serious crimes, I want to focus on the efforts to excuse and minimize everyday lawbreaking. Before that discussion, I think it is important to briefly talk about race and crime, the ways that crime and race operate within sports media discourses, and also the complexity and messiness within these discussions.

Race matters when discussing media coverage of more serious crimes within sports culture. There are countless examples that speak to the public fascination with black athletes and crime: O. J. Simpson,[5] Kobe Bryant,[6] Aaron Hernandez,[7] Mike Tyson,[8] Jameis Winston,[9] Adrian Peterson,[10] Michael Vick,[11] and Ray Lewis.[12] The literature highlights the ways that race has shaped media discourses and public consumption of arrests and trials, and notes how the criminalization of blackness anchored and shaped a myriad of cases.

Much of the popular discourse surrounding these cases reproduced, both directly and indirectly, hegemonic ideas about race and crime, furthering narratives about "thugs," the pathologies of "inner-city culture," "super predators," and the dangers of unchecked black masculinity. This can be seen in the narratives, the levels of coverage, and the larger implications that develop in the aftermath of these cases. For example, so often media coverage about crime and sports focuses on football and basketball players, ignoring athletes in other sports like baseball and hockey, all while erasing larger sociological data on crime among males of a similar age.

What is difficult here is that any conversation about whether race shapes the media narratives and public reaction becomes a discussion about guilt or innocence. We saw this with several high-profile cases, from O. J. Simpson to Mike Tyson, from Kobe Bryant to Aaron Hernandez. For example, to reflect on the racial scripts and narratives directed at Aaron Hernandez[13] is not about exonerating him or getting into his guilt or innocence. To spotlight the way race operates offers a window into the logics of American racism. To reflect on racial double standards between the media discourses surrounding Hernandez compared to Oscar Pistorius[14] need not turn into a conversation about whether "the race card" is being used to excuse the crimes committed by the former New England football star. This is not about deflection or distraction. It is about reflecting on the very different narratives that formed about two athletes convicted of murder. Hernandez was often portrayed as inherently evil, as a "gangsta" and a "thug," and as a ticking time bomb. He had manipulated his employers and his fans into believing he was a good guy when in reality he was a coldblooded killer.

On the other hand, Pistorius has been portrayed as a sympathetic figure, and has been humanized through an extensive focus on his unfortunate turn from heroic Olympian to killer. In fact, some sought to explain the shooting as an outgrowth of white fear in crime-plagued South Africa.[15] For Pistorius, killing his girlfriend, Reeva Steenkamp, marks just one chapter in his life;[16] for Hernandez, the killing of Odin Lloyd offers a window into his core character, serving as a representative chapter in his life. Noting these distinct differences, and their significance given the larger history of race in America, does not represent a commentary on their specific legal cases.

Efforts to compare US women's soccer captain Hope Solo to Adrian Peterson or Ray Rice followed a similar pattern. That is, discussions about how race shape these media discourses—for Peterson, reports about his "whupping" his child; for Ray Rice, in the aftermath of the release of a video showing him brutally hitting his then-fiancée, Janay Palmer; for Solo, in the aftermath of her arrest for domestic violence—often devolve into accusations against those who cite double standards or note how race operates as trying to let Peterson or Rice off the hook. Those who argued that corporal punishment is not unique to black communities[17] or that domestic violence cuts across racial, gender, and class lines as part of the criticisms about the coverage afforded to Peterson and Rice were often met with the accusation that these are just excuses.

Likewise, to reflect on race, to elucidate the many differences between the abovementioned cases and that of Hope Solo or MMA's War Machine should not become merely an effort to excuse or downplay the seriousness of domestic violence or the specific details in each case.

To talk about antiblack racism with respect to the media coverage of Jameis Winston or Kobe Bryant is not an invitation to treat either as victims, perpetuate myths about false accusations, or otherwise use the impact of racism to undermine accusations of sexual violence. To be clear, "the odds that you will be falsely accused of rape are basically the same as the odds that you or someone in your family will be hit by lightning. Your odds of being falsely accused of rape are about the same as your odds of being attacked by a shark."[18] We must talk about these facts, about rape culture,[19] while also underscoring the historic and contemporary racism within and beyond the criminal justice system.

Moreover, to say that race matters is not to say that other factors, from the popularity of sports to the intersections of race, class, sexuality, and gender, don't influence discourse as well.[20] In other words, it can be possible to talk about how the media's coverage of Hope Solo's arrest for domestic violence often became an opportunity to humanize her, to present her as "flawed" but redeemable, as a victim of a "checkered past," all while providing an explanatory narrative about why she may have done terrible things.[21] She was able to cash in on her whiteness and its privileges even as sexism shaped both media and public consumption of her arrest. In other words, we must talk about racism and sexism. The media narrative that followed Solo's arrest provides a chance to highlight institutional sexism and the ubiquitous efforts to make comparisons between men and women as a practice of exoneration and denial. Jennifer Doyle makes this clear in her essay, "Sexism, Hope Solo and 'the Domestic Violence Case No One is Talking About'":

> For the media pundit, all of these cases are all the same. This is, in fact, how sexist and racist ideologies work—the media discourse will move towards a "there are two sides to the story" structure. Given that there is *no way* to produce a story of Janay Palmer as the aggressor from the image of her knocked unconscious, we must find some other woman—a woman who is violent just like men are violent.[22]

We can see similar developments within discourses concerned with sexual violence. As one examines media and public discourses surrounding Kobe Bryant, Mike Tyson, and Jameis Winston, especially in comparison with those involving Yale's Jack Montague,[23] who was expelled following accusations of sexual violence, members of the Duke lacrosse team accused and ultimately exonerated of sexual violence,[24] Ben Roethlisberger (discussed in the next chapter), Patrick Kane,[25] or Mark Chamura,[26] it is clear how race shapes representative, narrative, and public consumption.

To note how white privilege played out within the media narrative surrounding accusations of sexual assault against Montague, Roethlisberger, or Peyton Manning[27] or how rape culture leads to male exoneration inside and outside the courtroom[28] speaks to the ways that ideology and history operate within media, public discourse, and the criminal justice system. Yet, to highlight these racial dimensions, or the ways that misogyny and rape culture exist within and beyond sports culture,[29] isn't simply about guilt or innocence in specific cases. Yet, so often, these discussions devolve into "crime dramas," deliberations about evidence, and who is entitled to be believed.

Importantly, these conversations so often repel necessary intersectional analyses that recognize both race and gender while invariably denying voice and justice to victims. As such, white male athletes accused of sexual violence receive minimal yet humanizing coverage, which serves as the basis for exonerating and even freeing them from public outrage, which along with the confinement of crime to black bodies, contributes to rape culture, thwarting examination of broader social issues. To talk about the intersections of race and gender, to look at the interworkings of racism and sexism, is to create a framework for justice.

Writing about the difficulty in acknowledging both the realities of racism within these discourses and the realities of sexual violence, rape culture, and the voices of those victimized, Jessica Luther, in the aftermath of accusations levied at three African American student athletes at the University of Oregon, wrote about the importance of dealing with race while speaking about the horrors of sexual violence within sports and beyond:

> The rub here is that sexual assault cases involving student athletes often end up being high-profile cases and black men on campuses are greatly overrepresented on athletic teams. According to the 2013 report, "Black Male Student Athletes and Racial Inequalities in NCAA Division I College Sports," "Between 2007 and 2010, black men were 2.8 percent of full-time, degree-seeking undergraduate students, but 57.1 percent of football teams and 64.3 percent of basketball teams." The report states that, at Oregon, black men make up 1.1 percent of the overall UO undergraduate population but account for 54.5 percent of football and basketball team members. Louis Moore, assistant professor of history at Grand Valley State University, says that unfortunately these disproportionate numbers mean that "the face of rape and criminality" in sports is often "going to be the black male" (though, of course, not exclusively). Additionally, the lack of black men on campuses, Moore argues, feeds into the idea that they are outliers in the community. "So there is this sense that they don't belong, that they never belonged," Moore said, "and when the crime happens, it becomes, 'See, I told you so.'"[30]

The hyperfocus on black athletes, whether because it fits the prevailing scripts and stereotypes or because of the hyper-visibility of black athletes within big-time college sports, not only embodies the racist history of the criminal justice system but also is a part of rape culture. Put differently, to reduce sexual violence to sports, to localize it within black athletic bodies, and thus not consider it as part and parcel to American culture writ large, contributes to the reproduction of a culture of violence. The media, in their sensationalized coverage, have spun simplistic narratives that consistently deny that race matters in the media coverage of the rape allegations against three Oregon basketball players.

Alternatively, some interpreted the coverage of the Oregon case as proof that histories of racism were coming to bear against the accused. In response, the UO Coalition to End Sexual Violence pushed back, demanding that we both see racism and hear the cries of victims of sexual violence, that we recognize the ways in which race operates within the media and criminal justice system *and* how rape culture exists in those spaces as well:

> The history of media coverage of sexual assault is steeped in racism. Members of the UO-CESV recognize the history of white supremacist uses of rape and are very concerned about how media attention to this case may be framing our protests and concerns in a way that plays into longstanding racist narratives. It is important to note that this case does not reflect the typical demographics of race and sexual assault and we need to be scrupulous in bringing all perpetrators to justice, regardless of their race, class, or sexual identity.[31]

Although these conversations are important, especially as we begin to develop frameworks that look at the intersections of race, gender, class, and sexuality, as we begin to talk about multiple forms of injustice and violence, as we demand that every conversation doesn't turn into a debate that looks more like an "opening statement," as we push for accountability irrespective of race, class, and gender that considers multiple axes of restitution and justice, I want to spend the rest of this chapter looking not so much at the ways that antiblack racism shapes the headlines of athletes in the crime blotter, but instead at how whiteness operates within everyday law breaking and criminality.

## WHITE PRIVILEGE + ATHLETE: A CONTRADICTION IN TERMS

White privilege is one of the most misunderstood terms in contemporary America. When uttered by activists and scholars, many on the right scoff at this absurd idea. Noting that they weren't born with a silver spoon in their mouths or that things aren't easy for them either, white-privilege deniers commonly think of privilege as wealth, as referring to a life that might be profiled by Robin Leach or *MTV's Cribs*. In fact, privilege is both an "unearned advantage"[32] and the ability to navigate the world without encountering institutionally created obstacles. If we think of life as a race, privilege is the ability to run without ditches, boulders, or a headwind. Racism and sexism is running the same race but in a lane where rocks, potholes, and other obstacles are every step. Privilege is therefore an "unearned advantage," what W. E. B. DuBois described as a "psychological wage,"[33] or what Peggy McIntosh identified as an "invisible knapsack."[34]

But white male privilege also determines the ability to live as things should be. One should be able to run the race without extra obstacles; one should be able to enter a store without being followed by a store clerk; one should be able to make mistakes without being reduced to or defined by those mistakes; one should be able to fall short or simply do something accidentally without it being read as a statement and referendum on entire communities.

The sports world is littered with examples of white athletes who had the privilege to make mistakes, where they were able to throw down the unearned wages of whiteness to purchase freedom, who were able to cash in a "get out of jail free" card, provided by their whiteness. The ability to be #CrimingWhileWhite,[35] a concept that will be discussed more in chapter 8, is reflective of the power and privilege afforded white athletes. Here are but a few examples:

> Arrested with cash and pills while driving erratically, Jim
> Irsay, despite his past, faces little punishment from Roger
> Goodell and ultimately gets probation from justice system.[36]
> #CrimingWhileWhite

❖    ❖    ❖

> Mitch McGary fails a drug test and is suspended for a year.
> Despite being drafted in the NBA, he still becomes a victim
> emblematic of unjust NCAA.[37] #CrimingWhileWhite

❖    ❖    ❖

> Kevin Love steps on another player's face and receives little more
> than a short suspension.[38] #CrimingWhileWhite

❖    ❖    ❖

Maria Sharapova takes PED, a drug that manufacturer says
should be taken for four to six weeks (and not ten years), and is
warned five times; she becomes a victim.[39] #CrimingWhileWhite

❖   ❖   ❖

Arrested for a DUI and photographed with drugs, Michael
Phelps's narrative becomes a sad tale of too much pressure and
ultimately redemption.[40] #CrimingWhileWhite

With each example, privilege operates in such a way as to construct these
crimes as neither serious nor defining of the character of the athlete or that
of their community. They are mistakes that say little about the person and
much less about the broader white community.

### LACROSSE AND CRIME: AN EPIDEMIC AT DUKE?

In 2006, three Duke lacrosse players were accused of rape. "On the night
of March 13, 2006, Mangum and another woman were hired by members
of the Duke lacrosse team to dance and strip at a house party. Early the
next morning, she reported to Durham police that she had been sexually assaulted by some of the lacrosse players," writes Jessica Luther. "The
allegations riveted the nation. And then the case fell apart amid a series of
inconsistencies in accounts of the evening and various unethical actions by
Durham District Attorney Mike Nifong. All charges against the players were
eventually dropped."[41]

Rather than look at the case, or the media spectacle, I want to use this
moment to reflect on the culture surrounding the team as emblematic of
#CrimingWhileWhite.[42] Represented as "angels," as all-American kids who
were playing by the rules prior to being "falsely accused" of sexual violence,
the narrative presents them as perfect victims. Their teammates, not charged
with anything, were equally presented as victims, unfairly treated by the
media, Duke University, and the public at large because of stereotypes.

Angels and victims is how we have come to remember Duke lacrosse.
In the midst of the arrest and the spectacle of Duke lacrosse, Scoop Jackson spotlighted not only the privileges afforded to them because of their
whiteness but also the privileges of playing lacrosse given its racial and class
signifiers. Playing lacrosse is #PlayingWhileWhite, and therefore the culture of lacrosse as defined by criminality and misbehavior was non-existent.
Jackson notes that between 1999 and 2006, forty-one Duke lacrosse players

had been charged with misdemeanors in either Durham or Orange counties. While the players represented 0.75 percent of Duke's undergraduate population of 6,255, they accounted for 33 percent of arrests for open-container violations, 25 percent of arrests involving disorderly conduct, and 31 percent of all cases involving alcohol-related unsafe behavior. Worse yet, the 2004–05 team set records not just in terms of wins but also in criminal behavior, with fifteen out of forty-seven players having been charged with misdemeanor crimes including disturbing the peace, public urination, and public drunkenness.[43]

According to the *News and Observer* (Raleigh), half of the 2005–06 team has been brought up on student-conduct charges, much of which was alcohol related. Collin Finnerty was convicted of assault in 2006, in the aftermath of the rape charges, after he punched and berated two men with homophobic slurs in Washington DC. Yet the media narrative imagined him and his teammates "young men" as good kids with great futures.

Given that whiteness, as noted by bell hooks, is "synonymous with goodness and all that is benign and non-threatening,"[44] it is no wonder that the many arrests and misdeeds coming from Duke lacrosse caused little concern long before. Known for "throwing kegs through windows" and "purposely breaking bones in fight club activities,"[45] the Duke lacrosse team lived by its own rules. While sports media routinely links this behavior to other student athletes, specifically in sports dominated by black males, in wake of the 2006 lacrosse scandal few questioned how lacrosse culture, whiteness, and class privilege may have fueled this behavior. While their defenders would have you believe that this is a reflection of college culture, or that of student athletes, or that it was irrelevant to the discourse surrounding the accusations of sexual violence, such arguments are rarely afforded to countless black athletes.

Like Scoop Jackson, David Steele pushed readers to use the case as a moment to reflect on the culture of lacrosse regardless of the outcome of the case. "Too many people who are close to the sport see this as a symptom of the lacrosse culture for it not to be taken seriously," he writes. "If any group of people should understand that, it should be those close to the game here—if not just because this is the epicenter of the sport, then because this also was the epicenter of what probably was the worst team-related incident before the one at Duke."[46] Steele and Jackson, two of the few black sportswriters who wrote about the case, saw the issues as not simply about lacrosse culture or the lack of institutional accountability but also about the ways in which the lacrosse culture, media silence, and lack of accountability are manifest in the whiteness of lacrosse. It is the whiteness of the sport that produces the silence and normalization of criminal behavior. Speaking about a sport that is over 97 percent white, Scoop Jackson wrote powerfully:

> Because we don't cover lacrosse with the same intensity or passion that we cover NCAA football or basketball, because recruits from Delbarton Academy don't excite us the way recruits from Oak Hill Academy do, since lacrosse hasn't been an A-list assignment since Jim Brown revolutionized the sport at Syracuse, we also ignored the deviant behavior and allowed the administrative negligence to exist. . . . But just because the media doesn't cover lacrosse doesn't mean a university—especially one of such prestige as Duke—can absolve itself of holding student athletes to the standards of excellence documented in the school's mission statement. If Elton Brand, Grant Hill, Sean Dockery, Daniel Ewing, Corey Maggette, Chris Duhon and Shelden Williams are going to be held to a certain behavioral standard while attending Duke, then Collin Finnerty, Reade Seligmann and Ryan McFadyen needed to be held to the same level of responsibility. Because they, too, represent the Duke University. Just as much as their parents' endowments.[47]

In other words, while much of the discourse initially focused on "did they do it?" and in its aftermath presented the three men accused, their teammates, and their coach as victims, I want to point out how before, during, and after the sexual-assault case many misdeeds, criminal activities, and problematic behaviors were excused and ignored. This is evident in the dismissal of the various indiscretions, arrests, and other civil violations perpetrated by members of Duke lacrosse long before the international spectacle. This is evident of their presentation as angels, as examples of what is good about college sports. Such consequences are commonplace in the examples of #Criming-WhileWhiteAndAthlete. To be white, especially a white collegiate and professional athlete, is to live with power and privilege. When breaking the law one rarely becomes a criminal, a threat, or unredeemable blight on society.

Everyday crime, whether it be drug use by Michael Phelps and Mitch McGary, or DUIs from Lenny Dykstra,[48] whose long rap sheet has not thwarted endless opportunities, Abby Wambach,[49] or any of the other various crimes committed by college athletes in sports like baseball, swimming, and lacrosse, get normalized and excused, while "real" crime is projected onto their black and brown athletic counterparts.

Whereas whites commit crimes all of the time, they are rarely defined by those decisions, and their crimes are reduced to 'mistakes'; compare that to African Americans, who irrespective of behavior are rendered as criminals, as perpetual suspects. The differential media attention and the types of narratives seen in the sports world illustrate these broader cultural practices.

To further illustrate #CrimingWhileWhite in terms not only of the decriminalization of white crime but also of the ways in which white crime is framed as a mistake, as a bad choice, as an unfortunate circumstance, and as something that neither defines whiteness or the individual, I now turn to a discussion of Johnny Manziel.

## THE SUMMER(S) OF JOHNNY'S DISCONTENT

On the heels of his Heisman Trophy win, Johnny Manziel spent the summer after his freshman year in the headlines. When he was not on Twitter, he was causing havoc at frat parties at the University of Texas. He also quickly left Peyton Manning's passing camp, where he purportedly missed a wakeup call because he was hung over. Questions about his travel on private jets to various events or his encounter with police (he pled guilty for failing to identify himself to a police officer) were of little consequence compared to reports that appeared about his receiving pay for autographs. Captivating the national media attention, these reports that Manziel may have received money for autographs, a major NCAA violation, did little to change the narrative surrounding him. In fact, in each case, these indiscretions or mistakes were dismissed as either "much ado about nothing" or evidence of the media "crusade" against him. Manziel was a kid and therefore should be allowed to have fun; he was a nineteen-year-old college student and was simply doing what other college students were doing.

In each instance, there was some "explanation" as to why Manziel's behavior was neither a problem for him nor an indication of a larger issue of crime or deviance in sports: he was clearly not a black athlete, and therefore he clearly wasn't a problem.[50] The message was clear: move along, Johnny is an all-American kid partaking in some all-American fun, so there's nothing to fret over with respect to Johnny Manziel. At least, that was the message.

His behavior, therefore, inspired a wide range of defenders who went to every length to explain his every move—Manzielsplaining. Some denied the accusations while others questioned the sources; others simply offered reasons to explain why his indiscretions were no big deal. Still others focused on how Manziel was being held to unfair standards, subjected to an unseen level of scrutiny because he is brash, because he's a Heisman winner, because he's rich and white, and because the media likes to bring guys down. In other words, the criticism was not about his behavior or the need for accountability, maturity, discipline, or punishment, but because "haters gonna hate."

A common refrain was that Johnny Manziel is just like everyone else, which itself embodies the normalization of whiteness.[51] He's just like other college students or any number of the quarterbacks who played before him. In an era of twenty-four-hour sports news and Twitter, his antics were simply more visible and thus prone to be overblown. Alex Endress, in "Manziel Heavily Criticized in Today's Age, but Peyton Manning Got in Trouble Too," makes this point:

> In today's world, a picture of the mooning incident would've been on Twitter in less than an hour and maybe even a video of it on YouTube. It's flat-out ridiculous to say Manziel's production will drop off this season because of photos or videos seen of him on the Internet. Does he drink alcohol? Sure. Given some of his chosen locales, it's almost certain—but so do 80 percent of college students, according to the National Institute on Alcohol Abuse and Alcoholism.[52]

Similarly, Chris Dufresne concludes that Johnny Football has every right to act like any other college student:

> Johnny got into a bar fight and was caught with a fake ID. (Welcome to a large club.) Johnny sent a tweet saying he couldn't wait to get out of College Station. (Have you ever been there?) He jetted around the country with Daddy's money to crash parties from Denver to Dover. (As if he's the only spoiled-brat child son from a Texas oil-money family.) Johnny also was tossed from a frat party at Texas while wearing a Tim Tebow jersey, and he might have had a hangover when he missed his wake-up call for the Manning Passing Academy. He's just a kid, under enormous pressure, trying to blow off some steam. The problem is not Manziel's right to act like a kid or a fool. The problem is the full portrait that's forming of a young man seemingly lacking even a base level of accountability or responsibility. Manziel is not a golfer or tennis player—he's the most important player on his football team. There's no "I" in t-e-a-m, but there is one in Manziel.[53]

While acknowledging that his off-the-field indiscretions might negatively affect his relationship with teammates, Dufresne positions Manziel's behavior as a team issue rather than a moment to wax sociological, offer parenting advice, or reflect on today's youth. Manziel's behavior did not warrant an intervention from the criminal justice system or even Texas A&M: "Manziel isn't required to be a role model for the public or any of us, but he will have to answer to the players and for the season he is hanging out to dry in the Texas heat."

Indeed, Manziel wasn't required to do anything to make amends or *be* anything, which is the definition of white privilege. He was representative of himself, immune from grandiose theories, panics, stereotypes, and a discourse that emphasizes necessary disciplinarity and punishment. Even in the aftermath of public exposure of his missteps, he remained an individual whose actions said little about other quarterbacks, white youth, or the sons of wealthy families. He was "Johnny Football." This discourse led not only to a pass for certain behaviors but also to an inability to see him as anything but an individual.

By 2016, Johnny Manziel had experienced two professional years that included several off-the-field incidents, encounters with police, and perpetual distractions. He had gone from celebrated recluse to pitied cautionary tale. Sure, he spent more time in Las Vegas partying with friends than studying his playbook; sure, he reportedly lied to his coaches and his employer; sure, he was a regular on Sports Center's police blotter over and over again; nonetheless, much of sports media demanded Johnny receive empathy and understanding. Never mind the incessant coverage afforded to him, which questioned whether he should be playing more or should get another chance, and another chance despite being a mediocre professional and a distraction.

#PlayingWhileWhite means forgiveness and excuses. In the aftermath of two lackluster seasons of endless off-the-field issues, the sports media establishment was still making excuses for Johnny. Brian Billick offered the explanation of all explanations, lamenting how privilege and entitlement was having negative consequences for Manziel. It was leading to bad decisions and hurting his performance on and off the field. "Off the field he reminds me of that affluenza kid. He just doesn't get it. And again, maybe the way he was raised he just doesn't have the reference frame. For whatever it's worth, I've seen nothing on the football field athletically, and the way he plays his game, to indicate he can last in the NFL."[54] Similarly, Tim Baffoe, in "Johnny Football: The NFL's Affluenza Teen" lets Manziel off the hook, portraying him as a victim of white-male privilege:

Manziel is a privileged disaster; the disaster negates not the privileges. The latter is a safety net ensuring that no matter how off the rails the Johnny Football train gets, Johnny Rich Kid—save for any physical harm's way he puts himself in—will be just fine. The great irony of the nickname is that Johnny Football doesn't *need* football. He needs it even less than the mouth-breathing inhaler of reality television needs him. . . . Football doesn't drive Manziel. Sure, he might like playing it a hell of a lot. Certainly it greases the wheels for his lifestyle off the field. Any frosh in a Psych 101 class could spit out a term paper on the game's perks feeding his obvious narcissism. But he has a constant understanding that once the game leaves him—probably sooner than later—there's no worry of a Plan B or sweating not having dressed in enough games to qualify for a pension.

The efforts to compare him to Ethan Couch, the white wealthy teen who avoided a twenty-year sentence for killing four people while driving intoxicated, are very revealing. According to a psychologist, Couch's wealthy parents spoiled him rotten, so he didn't know any better when he drove drunk. As reported by Jessica Luther, Dr. Miller described the teen's diagnosis of "affluenza" in the following way: "The teen never learned to say that you're sorry if you hurt someone. If you hurt someone, you sent him money." Arguing that his parents failed to establish proper boundaries and mechanisms of accountability, Dr. Miller concluded that Couch had the emotional age of twelve, leading to poor choices with deadly consequences. "He never learned that sometimes you don't get your way. He had the cars and he had the money. He had freedoms that no young man would be able to handle."[55] While denying the legal, cultural, social, and economic roots of these lessons, and failing to note the irony in putting on a defense that cites the lack of accountability and responsibility as the basis of limiting accountability and responsibility, his defense team was successful. The audacity of the "affluenza" defense and its ultimate success embodies the entrenched nature of white supremacy and class privilege: This equals #CrimingWhileWhite. As Luther reminds us,[56] our collective ability to see Couch (and Manziel, Phelps, Lochte, Josh Hamilton) as innocent, to see this young boy as having a future, and as someone who can be rehabilitated, helps us to understand such a "slap on the wrist," especially in comparison to the draconian criminal justice experienced by youth of color. "But there is something else going on here. It matters that Judge Boyd saw Couch as someone that not only could be rehabilitated but whom it was worth it to rehabilitate," she notes. Couch has the values, the culture, the family, and the whiteness that bestows him second chances; his redemption is possible, especially because his parents are able to foot the $450,000 bill for inpatient treatment at a California center, which "specializes in equine assisted psychotherapy where patients get to ride horses and also offers mixed martial arts lessons, opportunities for massages and cooking lessons."[57]

The parallels between Couch and Manziel are clear in the efforts to explain away their behavior, to deny responsibility and accountability. Each becomes a victim. Others offered similar excuses that elicited sympathy, all while humanizing Manizel as a victim who deserved another chance. Deion Sanders, showing that sexism and patriarchy are not simply a thing of *Mad Men*, sought to declare Manziel's innocence, blaming his girlfriend and their "relationship," which was "inflammatory," as the source of his problem.[58]

Others focused on his problems, expressing sympathy and shock at his behavior. Over and over again, the emphasis on how his behavior was out of character and some outside issue was contributing toward bad decisions.[59] After Manziel was pulled over "by the police for domestic argument" Mike Florio described the situation as follows: "Browns quarterback Johnny Manziel has shown tremendous maturity and growth this year, but he apparently is still struggling with the medical condition that arose from a series of personal choices regarding the use of alcohol."[60]

Although he is a good kid, his demons produced all of these difficulties. This is what #CrimingWhileWhite looks like: being seen as a kid; being given third and fourth chances; a lack of accounting of a person's history of misbehavior within discussions so that each incident becomes an isolated instance requiring only limited explanation; sympathetic and humanizing media representations; efforts to explain "WHY"; and an overall effort to narrate each and every indiscretion and criminal activity as unrepresentative of core character and values.

## EVERYTHING BUT THE BURDEN

"Marshall Henderson is the Charlie Sheen of college basketball—an unapologetic poster-child of white privilege," notes Charles Modriano in an email to me. "Despite a litany of on- and off-court behavior that normally send sports media pundits into 'what about the kids' columns with African-American athletes, Henderson has been most often described as passionate, colorful, and entertaining." Greg Howard similarly depicts the double standard that anchors media responses:

He messes with any racially essentialist expectations of what a white basketball player is supposed to be. He's an incessant shit-talker who tosses up 30-footers, rarely passes, and has a conspicuous lack of "hustle" stats. He tokes an invisible joint after making [sic] three-pointers . . . Marshall Henderson by all rights shouldn't exist. And if he were a black athlete, he wouldn't—not as far as big-time basketball is concerned.[61]

Henderson, despite embracing the aesthetics and practices of hip-hop (which is criminalized when attached to black bodies), is imagined as charismatic and a new sort of athlete. He is the walking embodiment of "everything but the burden"[62] who not only can talk trash and play with a reckless swagger without consequence from the media or his coach but can engage in criminal behavior with relative impunity. This is #CrimingWhileWhite, a set of privileges that are the antithesis of the experiences of African Americans. According to C. L. Cole and David Andrews, "African American professional basketball players . . . are routinely depicted in the popular media as selfish, insufferable, and morally reprehensible."[63] Henderson does not live under this burden, but is instead celebrated for his "swagger" and "passion." When arrested, he was able to cash in on the wages of whiteness; when he transferred from school to school and the media recast this behavior as part of his "journey," he tasted the power of whiteness.

Henderson, like Manziel, like Michael Phelps, Grayson Allen, Hope Solo, and so many others, are not problems; they are not seen as products of a culture of poverty or a "broken family." They are not shamed, told that their mistakes are hurting the kids who don't have fathers and uncles[64] and therefore need them to be good role models. Sure, they may do drugs, drive drunk, get into fights, get arrested, or give the finger to fans; they may talk trash, or engage in other indiscretions but they are ultimately good, innocent, and redeemable. In America, it's about #PlayingWhileWhite, not #BeingDisciplinedWhileWhite or punishing whiteness.

The privileges afforded to many white athletes discussed within this book, including the recasting of arrest records as "evidence of his maturation," is not simply about the power in narratives of whiteness that focus on intelligence, civility, and inherent innocence (and the corresponding potential redemption); it is also about entrenched antiblack racism. This is true for Johnny Manziel, whose record is expunged from the public imagination before the next incident; or for members of the Duke lacrosse team; or for countless other college teams whose "rap sheets" are lengthy yet unseen so that if and when a "BIG" case comes along, the past is rendered invisible, offering no context for judging these angels.

Henderson, as with Michael Phelps, Josh Hamilton, and Johnny Manziel, is only legible as a "good kid," a "competitive and passionate baller," and as someone "who may have made mistakes," because blackness is only legible as disruptive, uncontrollable, and as a source of "cultural degeneracy." Studies like the one in the *Journal of Alcohol and Drug Education*, in which ninety-five percent of respondents pictured a black drug user when prompted to imagine a drug user or another that found that "60 percent of viewers who saw a story with no image falsely recalled seeing one, and 70 percent of those viewers believed the perpetrator to be black" illustrate the power of antiblack racial framing.[65] In America, there remains a persistent link between perceptions of blackness and assumptions of criminality. Irrespective of whether the sports media is purposely affirming these stereotypes, or whether the ubiquitous focus on black athletes reflects the popularity and cultural importance of those sports dominated by black athletes, the end result is the perpetuation of a culture that sees crime and blackness as interchangeable; the exoneration and dismissal of criminal activities by the police, the criminal justice system, and the media for white athletes and their non-participating peers furthers antiblack racism.

The "production of social knowledge about" blackness "establishes a library or archive of information."[66] The hegemonic representation of black bodies "[describe] a state of mind and a way of life," reflecting "as much a cultural as an economic condition."[67] Henderson, Manziel, and countless other examples, no matter what their actions on or off the courts, exist apart from these racial narratives and representations.

To be black in America is to be "reduced to individual pathologies and the poverty of culture that generates the social disease of deviance";[68] it is to live with an "absence of the moral virtues disabling individuals from deferring gratification, planning ahead and making sacrifices for future benefit."[69] In the contemporary United States, a "secluded, camouflaged kind of racism" that ultimately "naturalizes black people as criminals,"[70] leads not only to the mass incarceration of black and brown youth but also to the second chances offered to Johnny Manziel, Marshall Henderson, Michael Phelps, and countless others. It leads to the redemptive narratives afforded to Henderson and Hope Solo amid the "thugification" of black bodies—including Metta World Peace and Trayvon Martin, Richard Sherman and Alton Sterling, Serena Williams and Rekia Boyd, Colin Kaepernick, and Korryn Gaines. It leads to sympathetic media coverage and the daily message that white lives matter even as black bodies, star athlete or not, are seen as problems, criminals, and threats to social order. To be white is to exist as an Angel even in the face of counter evidence. To be black is to be a "thug" and a "pariah."

## CONCLUSION: WHO IS THE REAL THUG?

Responding to the ubiquitous demonization of him and other black athletes, Richard Sherman challenged the applicability of the thug label:

> What's the definition of a thug? Really? Can a guy on a football field just talking to people [be a thug?] . . . There was a hockey game where they didn't even play hockey! They just threw the puck aside and started fighting. I saw that and said, Ah, man, I'm the thug? What's going on here? So I'm really disappointed in being called a thug. I know some thugs, and they know I'm the furthest thing from a thug. I've fought that my whole life, just coming from where I'm coming from. Just because you hear Compton (Calif.), you hear Watts, you hear cities like that, you just think thug, he's a gangster, he's this, that, and the other, and then you hear Stanford, and they're like, oh man, that doesn't even make sense, that's an oxymoron.[71]

Evident from Richard Sherman to Barack Obama, from Trayvon Martin and Serena Williams to countless other nameless and faceless black youth,[72] the "thug" label embodies antiblack racism, a worldview that consistently sees black bodies as dangerous criminal threats deserving discipline and punishment.[73] It's the language of white supremacy that renders black people as undesirable pariahs.

Calling white men or women "immature" or "troubled" in the wake of an arrest is equally a part of the language of white supremacy. While African Americans are defined—irrespective of individual guilt—by the worst behavior of highly publicized and even sensationalized offenders, whites are seen as inherently innocent and benign. The trope of black criminality, which is central to the white racial frame[74] and its imprint on society, is that the danger and deviance of blackness have been used to justify inequality, to rationalize high rates of incarceration, and to sanction various forms of institutional violence. The history of America is defined by the criminalization of black bodies, not to mention the systemic policing that results from these entrenched ideologies,[75] and the inoculation of whiteness.

Whether seen in graduates of Stanford University and Harvard Law, or in black youth forced out of school and hunted down by racist vigilantes as criminals,[76] the "thug" label furthers the normalization of antiblack violence in the name of white supremacy. To be a "nobody"[77] within the white imagination is antithetical to white life. To be invisible unless seen as an athlete, celebrity, or criminal is unimaginable by white Americans.

In a moment where police shootings and police brutality are seen yet not felt by white America, it is crucial that we question and challenge racially criminalizing language within sports culture and the "thugification" of black youth on every corner. This moment requires challenging the ways that whiteness comes to represent the anti-thug, the angel, and the innocent. To dismiss vandalism as (white) kids being (white) kids, (white) drug use as a mistake, a form of experimentation, or a health crisis, and a street fight as a sign of (white) immaturity furthers this criminalization process that profiles whiteness as innocent and blackness as criminal. It not only exonerates, letting those #CrimingWhileWhite off the hook, but establishes an index for understanding white misdeeds as isolated and insignificant. To ignore history, and to ignore patterns, is to reproduce narratives of whiteness as innocence. To isolate is to characterize white deviance as innocuous and unworthy of attention by the police, criminal justice, parents, schools, or countless other institutions. This is the story of Marshall Henderson, Johnny Manziel, Josh Hamilton, Michael Phelps, Abby Wambach, Hope Solo, Brock Turner, the NY Giants' Josh Brown[78] and countless college athletes.

If crimes committed by white athletes or even someone like me are no big deal, it is no wonder that when African Americans commit these same crimes a different story is told. Racial meanings, not the behavior itself, shape demands for intervention by the police or the commissioner. To commit crimes while white is to be seen as still playing, as doing things of little consequence or significance. It doesn't need to be named or made visible— that is, unless it becomes evidence of victimhood or personal growth. The absence of accountability, the denied justice for crimes involving all too many white athletes, and the racially stratified privileges anchor the experience of #PlayingWhileWhite.

# CHAPTER 5

# GETTING HIGH

*The New Jim Crow and White Athletes*

J ONATHAN Hargett *could* have been the next Michael Jordan. Amar'e Stoudemire, a high school teammate at Mt. Zion Christian Academy in Durham, North Carolina, once described him as "the best player I've ever played with. I've never seen a point guard as fast as him, jump as high as him and dribble better than him. . . . That boy was something else."[1]

Yet, his basketball career would never develop much beyond legends and stories of what could have been.[2] Instead, he became yet another cautionary tale about the elusiveness of the American Dream that too often ends in America's prison graveyard.[3] Following a heroic high school career, Hargett was arrested on drug-possession charges shortly after the end of his freshman year at West Virginia University. Although he joined a plentiful group—college students caught with marijuana—he faced unusual consequences: forty-five days in jail.

Upon his release, things took a turn for the worse. He had lost his collegiate eligibility, having received improper benefits as a result of his signing with an agent. Shortly thereafter, he entered the NBA draft, only to be passed over by every team. After a failed attempt to get the NCAA to reinstate him, Hargett took his talents to the World Basketball Association, joining the Southern Crescent Lightning squad in Peachtree City, Georgia.

Struggling to make ends meet, Hargett began to sell drugs as well, which ended after his arrest in 2008 for "possession of cocaine and marijuana with the intent to distribute."[4] Having been let down by collegiate sports, having been left behind by a dysfunctional educational system, having suffered because of poverty and countless other injustices, Hargett found himself on the inside looking out. His "choice" to break the law, to sell and use drugs, had consequences; the war on drugs, the nation's misplaced priorities evident in America's "New Jim Crow,"[5] the criminalization of (black) drug addiction, and poverty all have consequences; Jonathan Hargett was one such casualty.

Garrett Reid, son of then Philadelphia Eagles coach, Andy Reid, who is white, is also a causality of racism's entrenched place in the sporting landscape and beyond. Despite arrests from drug use and multiple drug infractions including smuggling drugs into jail and testing positive while incarcerated, not too mention his involvement with selling drugs, Reid spent less than two years in prison. "In the midst of his legal troubles in his early 20s, Reid said he 'got a thrill' out of being a drug dealer in a lower-income neighborhood just a few miles from his parents' suburban Villanova mansion," noted an ESPN story.[6] "I liked being the rich kid in that area and having my own high-status life," Reid confessed to a probation officer in 2007. "I could go any-where in the 'hood. They all knew who I was. I enjoyed it. I liked being a drug dealer." Whereas Reid was seen as a kid with a problem, a kid who needed help, Hargett was a "thug," a criminal without potential for redemption. Whereas Reid's drug use was dismissed with limited accountability, Hargett was sent to prison, ultimately dying of an overdose. Two stories, two tragic outcomes, both evidence of the differences between #PlayingWhileWhite/#LivingWhileWhite and #PlayingWhileBlack/#LivingWhileBlack.

According to Michelle Alexander, "racial bias in the drug war was *inevi-table*."[7] Its inevitability rests in the false narratives, stereotypes, and mis-information disseminated throughout every corner of American society, turning the problem of drugs into a problem of blackness. From *Locked Up* on MSNBC to ESPN, from the world of politics to the world of sports to the halls of Congress, America's drug habit has been defined through and around blackness, rationalizing and sanctioning a war on blackness rather than a war on drugs. This racial coding shapes discourses around sports, from the collegiate ranks to extreme sports.

It is evident in the 1986 overdose of Len Bias, then a University of Mary-land superstar on the verge of an NBA career,[8] which galvanized a nation toward militarized policing and a racialized war on drugs. His death prompted discussions about drug culture within inner cities, despite the fact that Bias grew up in a middle-class Maryland community. His overdose led to public scrutiny and bouts of panic regarding drug use in sports, result-ing in greater surveillance, despite no evidence that the issue was specific to sports. As Theresa Runstedtler notes in "Racial Bias: The Black Athlete, Reagan's War on Drugs, and Big-Time Sports Reform":

In a matter of days, the conversation shifted dramatically, as his death became the center of a national conversation about the dangers of cocaine, especially the new "demon drug" of crack cocaine, and the need for a more concerted war on drugs. Bias's tragic death and its aftermath typically garner a line or two in most histories of President Ronald Reagan's war on drugs and the so-called crack epidemic, as a catalyst for the increasingly punitive turn in drug policy and the concomitant criminalization of African Americans. The fallen Bias proved to be a flexible symbol that government and university officials from across the political spectrum used to support various types of policy reform. At the same time that Bias's death became a justification for the criminalization of black youth beyond the university, it also inspired calls for the more systematic disciplining of black athletes, along with the expansion of policing on college campuses.[9]

The racial nature of America's war on drugs is equally evident in the decriminalization of high white bodies inside and outside the sporting area. It is evident in the muted outrage directed at Michael Phelps,[10] golfer Dustin Johnson,[11] or Tim Lincecum[12] following reports of drug use, especially in comparison to both the media coverage and punishment directed at the likes of the NFL's Josh Gordon, Rickey Williams, or countless other NBA players[13] who spent their careers dodging defenders and media reports lamenting their addictions, selfishness, and lack of discipline.

It is reflected in the multiple chances afforded to former Major League Baseball outfielder Josh Hamilton, who will be discussed in greater detail in the next chapter, and pitcher Steve Howe,[14] who seemingly had more drug suspensions (seven) than hits during his career.[15] Like Reid and Hamilton, the media reports about Howe focused on his "drug problem" and his demons, never mind zero tolerance inside and outside the sports world. Sadly, Howe died in a car crash in 2006—toxicology reports found methamphetamine in his system.

Sports mirror society; this is no different with the war on drugs. This can be seen in the normalization of drug use in some sports, its ubiquity in others, its dismissal as 'no big deal,' and even its being cited as evidence of the creativity and countercultural ethos of certain sports. Examining specific examples within both professional leagues and the NCAA, media narratives surrounding Texas Christian University, the University of Oregon, Marshall Henderson, and other examples, this chapter looks at the "New Jim Crow"[16] nature of drugs within contemporary sports. It reflects on the power of the sports media and discourses surrounding the playing field to shape our collective understanding of drugs.

Whereas "selfish" black athletes who cannot "stay off the weed"[17] become representative of broader pathologies within and beyond the black community, the white athlete has a problem and needs help. Serving as a microcosm for a nation that has thrown African Americans and Latinos into jail as part of the "war on drugs" while calling for compassion and treatment with respect to white America,[18] sports has its own "New Jim Crow."

Evident in narratives surrounding both "recreational" and "performance-enhancing" drugs, #PlayingWhileWhite means not only getting high with relative impunity but also basking in a level of innocence even when caught on the drug train. Reflecting broader cultural and criminal-justice discourses, this chapter examines the pedagogical implications of crime and the panic that results from pot-smoking ballers in the NBA compared with praise and adoration ("they are free" and "creative") when white athletes partake in similar high times. Who is allowed to get high is evidence of the wages of sporting whites.

## STUDENTS (ATHLETES) GETTING HIGH OR CRIMINAL-ATHLETES?

Following a six-month investigation by the DEA, eighteen students from Texas Christian University (TCU), including four football players, were arrested for allegedly selling a myriad of drugs—marijuana, cocaine, prescription drugs, and ecstasy—on and off campus. Describing it as a "stain on the football program"[19] and "an especially embarrassing blow to the school because it included four members of the high-profile football team,"[20] the media narrative homed in on the arrest of the four student athletes (three out of four appear to be white although only a few stories included images). Ignoring the other twelve non-athletic participating students involved, the media made the football team the story, a fact that isn't surprising given the fallout from Len Bias's death less than twenty years before.[21]

In "TCU Will Survive Shameful Day," Jean-Jacques Taylor denounced the players as "[s]hameful, [e]mbarrassing, [s]tupid,"[22] giving their peers a pass. Taylor, like many in the media, used the opportunity to celebrate the coach for his handling of the situation. He was bringing discipline to these unruly "criminal-athletes": "Patterson should be applauded for having the gumption to reportedly order team-wide drug testing when a recruit told him that he was declining a scholarship offer because of the drug culture."[23] The story was thus less about drugs, police investigations, and university culture, and more about crime and football, blackness, and undisciplinarity. The facts were pushed aside for a story, which ultimately exhibited the power of racial profiles that simultaneously criminalized black bodies and declared whiteness as innocent.

When black athletes do something wrong whether on or off the court, they find themselves ensnared in what Joe Feagin has described as the "white racial frame":[24] "a comprehensive orienting structure, a 'tool kit' that whites and others have long used to understand, interpret, and act in social settings."[25] These TCU athletes, like Len Bias, were trapped in this entrenched white racial frame. The dominant white racial frame actually consists of "stereotyped racial knowledge, racial images and emotions and racial interpretations" along with "several 'big picture' narratives that connect elements into historically oriented stories with morals."[26] Ideas about cultural values, hard work (meritocracy), the American Dream (rags-to-riches), equal-justice-under the-law, and of course, colorblindness all operate within this context. These "selected bits" that encompass the dominant white racial frame are deployed in an effort to "interpret society" in ways that legitimate and sanction this master narrative and the corresponding racial order.[27]

Much of the media identified TCU as evidence of a drug culture ravaging college athletes. In the narrative that developed, the fluidity between "drug user" and "drug dealer," between someone who simply smokes weed and a drug pariah speaks to the racial discourses here. With TCU, the arrest of players for selling became a moment to lament drug culture within (some) college sports.

Eric Olson, in "TCU Bust Sign of Increased Pot Problem," pointed to the arrests as an indication of a larger problem.[28] Highlighting that 22.6 percent of student athletes reporting use of marijuana during the last twelve months—a number that is up from 21.2 percent in 2005—Olson sounds the alarm about athletes getting high. Ignoring the fact that marijuana use is up throughout society, Olson and others frame big-time sports as the problem irrespective of facts. Entitlement, immaturity, and criminality propelled the problem of the drug criminal-athlete corrupting collegiate sports and the campus as a whole.

Despite countless rules that make sure student athletes don't garner special advantages otherwise unavailable to their nonparticipating peers, the NCAA has seen little problem in punishing student athletes for activities that are normalized and accepted within university culture. The demonization and surveillance of (black) student athletes getting high is nothing new. Along with the death of Len Bias, a 1985 point-shaving scandal at Tulane would contribute to dramatic changes in NCAA's own drug policies. According to Aaron Gordon:

> In April 1985, eight Tulane basketball players were indicted in a
> point-shaving scandal and investigators found that one player,
> Gary Kranz, used cocaine as a means of luring the other members
> of the team into the scheme. The NCAA pulled a classic bait-
> and-switch, blaming cocaine for the scandal and not the obvious
> economic incentives facing unpaid college players.[29]

In its aftermath, then-NCAA President John Toner pushed for policy shifts, announcing, "I'm scared to death about the combination of gambling and drugs. We have the responsibility to regulate the safety of the student athlete and the integrity of the sports.[30] Increased policing of drug usage among student athletes was necessary because of fears about point shaving and fixing games; the additional surveillance, a fact of life unknown to their non-participating peers wasn't purportedly about treating student athletes differently but instead about protecting them from shady outside characters. This is also why the focus had to be on basketball and football rather than lacrosse or swimming—these were the student athletes who criminals would prey on because of the potential financial gains. The war on drugs within athletic dorms and within the locker room was about protecting them from gangstas and bad choices, like the one that led from Len Bias's transformation from the embodiment of the American Dream to a reminder of the horrors of an American nightmare. This was the message justifying the policy shifts on campus.

The NCAA would simultaneously justify its targeted drug policies with tried and proven racial paternalism. According to then athletic director of the University of Pittsburgh, Edward E. Bozik, "We are more in the public sector, and the youngsters are subjected to more opportunities to be in that culture than the normal student. I feel a special obligation to deal with this."[31] Similarly, then University of Southern California athletic director Mike McGee called for the NCAA to rid sports of the drug scourge: "It is my view that an institution such as USC needed to show that concern for our athletes. The university is in a position of exerting some positive influence on the whole drug abuse problem in athletics."[32] Similarly, John Jacobs identified athletics as an important staging ground for the war on drugs, one that needed to target African Americans: "If star athletes and molders of opinion use drugs for 'recreational' purposes how will we ever contain the raging epidemic in the streets? Hopefully Len Bias's tragic death may help change the climate that tolerates drugs."[33] For Jacobs, a columnist at the *Baltimore Afro-American,* the NCAA and others needed to focus on the epidemic within the black athletic community not only for their sake but also for the safety and future of the broader black community:

> Their white peers may be able to get away with dabbling in drugs, but they [black players] can't. Aside from the personal dangers, they are role models in the community, worshipped among young blacks as white athletes never are in their communities. So they have to stay clean and act clean, or they'll be implicity [*sic*] responsible for further tragedies.[34]

This sort of racial logic and praxis continues today. In 2015, Georgia Athletic Director Greg McGarity explained the NCAA's "father knows best" approach: "It's just an institutional philosophical approach to what is best for your youngsters. We've always felt that if we can correct behavior that is against the law as quickly as possible it's going to help them when they move on. I'd say it's had a positive effect on our kids, those who have made mistakes, they learn pretty quickly in the majority of cases."[35] A receiver's coach from the University of Oregon further emphasized the importance of teaching student athletes proper values and instilling discipline with respect to the drug policies of the teams and the NCAA:

> It's a demanding culture and you can never investigate and know every single detail about a guy, but we try to do the best job we can and when they get there it's not just coaching football it's coaching life skills. We do as much as anybody if not more educating guys on decision making on a daily basis. You can't make decisions for a person, but it's something we stress every day.[36]

While this stance appears to be race neutral, the context and subtext tells a different story. For example, in "ESPN's 'Higher Education': Rampant Use of Marijuana in College Football Isn't the Least Bit Shocking," Adam C. Biggers, writing about ESPN's feature story on the "college football's pot problem,"[37] exemplifies the ways that race works here:

> One part of the story that should be looked into is the players' backgrounds. Many of the athletes in the ESPN report are African-American and come from disadvantaged backgrounds.

Based on my experience, marijuana isn't considered a "drug" by many in the urban community. I've been around college athletes, even coached at the prep level in Flint, Mich., and it's clearly evident that marijuana is "nothing" when compared to other illicit substances. That may be true, but it's still illegal.[38]

Never mind the views of marijuana from white suburban youth or on college campuses; never mind collegiate athletes in sports dominated by whites; never mind drug use throughout the nation, including states where medical marijuana and recreational is permissible under the law. The hyperfocus on black culture, on those who have "so much to gain," on those whose links to "crime," and those from "disadvantaged backgrounds" shapes the narrative of not only who is a drug user but who is most potentially harmed by drug use. The narrative plays on longstanding racial stereotypes about who are most likely to be preyed upon by gamblers and criminal enterprises. Yet, at the same time, it holds (black) football and basketball student athletes to a higher standard regarding drugs since they are visible role models. These racial elements, based in history and hegemonic "racial scripts"[39] define both the NCAA's approach to and media discourses about the issue.

Following the suspensions of two student athletes from the University of Oregon prior to the 2015 National Championship, Pete Thamel took aim at Darren Carrington and Ayele Forde for seemingly behaving like regular college students. "The intention of this column isn't to offer a pass to Carrington or Forde; both made immature mistakes that could cost their team the national title."[40] They "let down their school, coaches and teammates."[41]

Oregon offensive coordinator Scott Frost offered a similar denunciation that blamed the players for poor choices: "I think any time you put something in your body that doesn't belong there it's a bad decision," Frost said.[42] Others, while empathetic given shifting societal views on marijuana, were equally judgmental, focusing on the student athletes' personal failures.[43]

Despite football and basketball having some of the lowest rates of drug usage, the media narrative turned this incident into yet another spectacle worthy of panic and intervention. While acknowledging marijuana use in lacrosse at almost fifty percent and a culture of getting high in other (white) sports, David Ubben still lamented how "drug scandals marred the football year" in 2012.[44]

For some, these panics and the outrage is justifiable. With popularity comes increased attention to student athletes in revenue sports; with that comes headlines and judgmental columns, calls for harsher punishments, and policing and surveillance through drug testing.[45] Of course, the profit-ability and popularity of their sport doesn't produce any tangible advantages; worse yet, because of the racial nature of the war on drugs, and entrenched racial stereotypes, such stories result in more narratives that locate drug use and criminality within black bodies, fulfilling Alexander's promise that a racialized war on drugs was "inevitable." Once the profile of a drug user has solidified as black—a process that is impacted by sports media—not only do stories of black athlete drug use become hyper-visible in the public eye, but that same public, through the sports media, also excuses and ignores the rampant drug culture among white athletes and their nonpar-ticipating peers.

### THE DRUG EPIDEMIC AND COLLEGIATE SPORTS

In a feature story on University of Oregon football that depicted the pro-gram as plagued by rampant drug use exacerbated by failed drug-testing programs within college sports, Mark Schlabach concludes: "College foot-ball players smoking marijuana is nothing new. Coaches and administra-tors have been battling the problem and disciplining players who do so for decades."[46] Schlabach highlights the purported epidemic plaguing college football by citing the following:

> NCAA statistics show a bump in the number of stoned athletes.
> In the NCAA's latest drug-use survey, conducted in 2009 and
> released in January, 22.6 percent of athletes admitted to using
> marijuana in the previous 12 months, a 1.4 percentage point
> increase over a similar 2005 study. Some 26.7 percent of football
> players surveyed fessed up, a higher percentage than in any other
> major sport.

Sadly, the facts got in the way of this narrative. An NCAA study found that marijuana use was least common amongst Division I student athletes at 16.9 percent, with Division II student athlete use at 21.4 percent and those from Division III having the highest level of usage at 28.3 percent. As drug usage declined at the Division I level, the other two levels of usage saw increases. Reflecting the separate and unequal approach to America's drug "problem," the NCAA has equally embraced a racially stratified approach. In Division III, which is not only the whitest college division and a space where the NCAA and its sports media partners have not peddled narratives about rags-to-riches and sports as the great racial equalizers, the NCAA quietly loosened its own rules about illegal drug use. Allie Grasgreen, in "Athletes, Drugs and Entitlements," described the cultural and policy shifts in the following way:

> The NCAA's Committee on Competitive Safeguards and Medical Aspects of Sports proposed the idea for a few reasons: marijuana is not performance enhancing and is not considered "cheating," so its use should carry a punishment different from those for other drugs; officials want to focus more on helping athletes overcome use and less on punishing them for it; and many who have been punished under the current policy have lost much more than a year of eligibility.[47]

Yet, the proposed changes would only impact Division III athletes; in the suburbs of college sports, as in the NHL, with its lack of testing for marijuana, drug use is neither policed nor seen as a problem.

As participation in DIII sports isn't tied to the allure of future earnings, the NCAA clearly sees little issue in (white) kids getting a little bit high. In exchange for their athletic labor, they get to enjoy the collegiate experience of their peers. Where they are "paying for the party,"[48] these white Division III student athletes are *playing* to party. While about money and the false dreams that are being sold to rationalize exploitation, this is also about race. #PlayingWhileWhite allows one to get high with relative impunity—no media shaming, community outrage, or institutional consequences.

Marijuana (and drug) use isn't unique to college sports, and despite entrenched and racialized "sincere fictions"[49] and media spectacles, drugs aren't endemic to basketball and football. While a 2014 study found usage rates declining across all divisions of men's basketball (10.6 percent) and football (17.4 percent), mirroring the usage rates of several other sports (in basketball, usage being less common than in other sports and significantly less than among non-athletic participating student peers), men's lacrosse (35.8 percent), men's swimming (29.3 percent), women's lacrosse (23.1 percent), women's swimming (21.1 percent) and men's golf (21 percent), might as well each receive a feature article in *High Times*.[50]

In fact, an NCAA study found that almost 7 percent of college swimmers admitted to using amphetamines.[51] The only higher rates came from wrestling, lacrosse, and baseball—clearly not sports dominated by black athletes. According to the NCAA, 85 percent of white student athletes reported use of alcohol in the last twelve months, compared with less than 65 percent of black student athletes. For a range of illicit drugs, the disparities are even greater: 5.4 percent of whites reported using amphetamines, while only 1.7 percent of black student athletes did so. With cocaine, 2.1 percent of whites used within the last twelve months, compared to 1 percent of blacks. Over 25 percent of white student athletes smoked some weed, compared with 18 percent for black student athletes.[52]

Yet, these facts do not penetrate media narratives, the NCAA's own policies, and the public discourses of both outrage and panic #PlayingWhite-White. No headlines or exposés on swimmers and lacrosse players getting high. There is little concern with the rule of law and its violation here #PlayingWhileWhite. Few commentators use the issue of drug use from student athletes playing lacrosse or swimming as a moment to moralize about how being a student athlete is a privilege that requires greater responsibility. There is no discussion of role models and the dangers to self, sport, and university that come with poor choices. Not surprisingly, one would be hard pressed to find a discussion about the cultures of these sports, the pathologies of today's (white male) youth, the influence of Keith Richards, Ozzy Ozborne, Charlie Sheen, Robert Downey Jr., or Bill Maher, or the rampant criminality within these sports.

Take this headline in an article about swimming: "NCAA: Swimmers Biggest Users of Sleep Aids . . . ; #2 in Marijuana Use." Amphetamines and illicit narcotics are refashioned as "sleep aids." This isn't simply a rhetorical sleight of hand, one that displaces narratives of crime; this headline frames drug use as a response to the demands of school and performance at an elite level within one's sport. This same article sought to explain the excessive drug use within swimming in three ways: 1) that because swimmers and lacrosse players have less to lose, they can smoke weed; 2) swimmers and lacrosse student athletes could be honest about their use because of their anonymity—nobody cares that they are getting high, so they are able to confess their sins, whereas elite basketball and football student athletes lie because they have to; and 3) because swimmers get up early they are clearly dealing with exhaustion through drug usage.[53] #PlayingWhileWhite means that in the face of wrongdoing—in other words, criminal misconduct—something must be wrong with the data. Even if true, there is a legitimate reason and context that we must look at before we pass judgment.

These reports and headlines illustrate how the phrase "what it means to be criminal in our collective consciousness" translates into "what it means to be black." As argued by Michelle Alexander, "the term black criminal is nearly redundant," so much so that "to be a black man is to be thought of as a criminal, and to be a black criminal is to be despicable—a social pariah."[54] Still, to users and dealers, blackness is essential in the dominant white imagination.

Given the high rates of drug usage on college campuses, it shouldn't be surprising that drug distribution occurs on college campuses, too. It shouldn't shock anyone that white middle-class students are slangin' dope between classes. While rarely in the news, cases at San Diego State,[55] UC Santa Cruz,[56] Columbia,[57] Reed,[58] and Union[59] highlight how students don't need to venture off campus to get their high on. So often, these busts result in outrage at the unfair targeting of college students, whose indiscretions should have been handled "internally."[60] They aren't criminals. They are "adorable",[61] "kids from next door."[62] They are college kids, with bright futures, who needed to sell drugs given the cost of attending today's universities. These cases and broader research[63] demonstrate that criminal elements are not invading college campuses; those who otherwise wouldn't be there without "affirmative action" or athletics don't bring dysfunction and pathologies onto campus; on the contrary, the criminal element is the very people seen as "real" college students.

Dismissed as harmless youthful fun, celebrated as "part of the college experience,"[64] and sanctioned by a war on drugs in someone else's backyard— except when involving non-students, student athletes from certain sports, and those who fit the drug user/dealer profile—it shouldn't be surprising that white middle-class students often stand above the law. Seeing TCU or Oregon as a story about football and drugs, as a consequence of athletic entitlement and the recruitment of "ghetto stars," is just another "get out of jail free" card. The story begins and ends with the black athlete: As W. E. B DuBois asked, "How does it feel to be a problem?" Marshall Henderson would not know.

## TROUBLE ON AND OFF THE COURT

Marshall Henderson's career was one defined by troubles on and off the court. Despite appearing to lack a conscience about a good shot or the accepted societal rules and laws, Henderson spent a career getting a pass, regardless of the transgression.

In the aftermath of a breakout season in 2013, Marshall Henderson spent his off-season battling the criminal justice system. Over several months, he had several face-to-face visits with the police, including a May stop where, after being pulled over for speeding, he was found to be in possession of both marijuana and cocaine. Ultimately, he wasn't charged with any drug crimes, but instead was cited for not having insurance. Given his history and the draconian nature of American drug policy,[65] the lack of intervention from the criminal justice system should give pause. It is a telling reminder of America's "New Jim Crow."[66]

Reports of this and other incidents only surfaced after Henderson's coach announced that he would be suspended indefinitely for violating "team rules." Yet media reports indicated that, in fact, Henderson had violated state law as well as school policies. Notwithstanding his popularity and visibility within the national media, little was made of his rap sheet and his ongoing troubles with the law.

The media response to Henderson's suspension and to the reported arrests was muted, to say the least. At worst, he was called a "knucklehead"[67] and a dude who dealt with "drama."[68] He was described as an average college student who "liked to enjoy himself,"[69] as someone who is "battling a beast"[70] and a sickness, as just a kid who for some reason keeps messing up. He's a troubled kid, with baggage; someone who needs to (and can) get his life together, if he gets the right help.

Chris Herren, a former basketball player at both the collegiate (Fresno State) and professional (Boston Celtics) levels, whose battles with addiction have been well documented and celebrated as reasons for redemption, furthered the "Poor Marshall" narrative: "You can never minimize the fact that you're jeopardizing your future. It's tragic for me to see his situation knowing what I know, what I went through, what I did." Herren, who like Henderson was afforded many second chances, further noted: "Ultimately, he needs to get down to the reason why a substance is more important than yourself, your family and your future. . . . Whether it's basketball, football, baseball or any sport at a high level, the price to pay is a lot of pressure. That's why he needs to incorporate some balance in his life and surround himself with people who have the same dream he does."[71] Similarly, ESPN's Andy Katz encouraged Ole Miss (and America) to give Henderson another chance, to help him overcome his personal demons:

> Ole Miss may be doing its best to help Henderson. And it should.
> The Rebels shouldn't completely dismiss him as an individual
> with a drug problem without offering assistance. There should
> be suspensions for games/practices, and there should be athletic
> department and academic punishments. . . . Many athletes don't
> get second chances. Henderson can still overcome his latest
> setback.

Henderson was not cast as a thug, as a menace, or as a criminal—he was not someone who should be kicked off the team, kicked out of school, or sent to jail. He was just a "kid" who "made mistakes."[72] Henderson deserved a lifeline; he had "earned" a chance at redemption.

The empathetic and supportive response to his 2013 brush with the law was nothing new. This was usual course for Henderson, whose rap sheet has neither impacted his access to the basketball court, his standing as a student, nor his place in the media. In 2009, according to a statement given to the Secret Service, Henderson, then a senior in high school, used "$800 of counterfeit money given to him by a friend to buy 59 grams of marijuana in two separate transactions."[73] A year later, while a freshman at the University of Utah, the Secret Service knocked on Marshall's door to notify him of his impending arrest. "They came to Utah and they were like, 'Blah and blah and we got this and surveillance camera,' and I threw up," recalled Henderson. "That was my first thing, because I thought I was done for." Yes, he was scared; yet his description of the encounter and his memory resting with "blah blah" speaks to the pass that was around the corner. With help from his coach and father, he was able to plea to a forgery charge, which led to a probation sentence.

After one year, which also included a one-game suspension for punching a Brigham Young University player in the face, Henderson decided to transfer to Texas Tech, since the team's rules didn't mesh with "his individualism." Then, in 2011, Henderson violated his probation by testing positive for alcohol, marijuana, and cocaine,[74] which resulted in his serving twenty-five days in jail along with seven weekends of work release. Still, he kept on playing basketball. Notwithstanding his history, he faced few consequences for his actions; he faced little accountability from Ole Miss, the NCAA, or the criminal justice system.

When one compares his experiences (and lack of accountability) with those of a countless number of black athletes[75] who have been criminalized in the media and pushed aside by their coaches and universities, the power of race and white privilege become quite evident. In 2011, both Klay Thompson and Reggie Moore were suspended from the Washington State University basketball team following their arrests for marijuana possession.[76] While guilty only of a "crime" that is commonplace on college campuses, they faced widespread media scorn—which situated their arrests in the context of collegiate basketball—and a suspension. Although the charges were dropped, the suspensions and the stained reputations remained; worse for Thompson, his father went on a national radio show to lament his son's poor decision-making.

Tyrann Mathieu faced a worse fate. In 2012, following a suspension for drugs, he was dismissed from the Louisiana State University football team for violation of "team rules": another failed test.[77] That September, he was also arrested for possession while no longer a member of the team. According to Greg Howard, Mathieu's experience, in comparison to Henderson's, reveals a lot about race in America, about the criminal justice system, and about the white racial framing and regimes of policing:[78]

> Mathieu, in case you've forgotten, was crowned the top defensive player in college football in 2011, like Henderson, an undersized athlete getting by primarily on balls and guile. But Honey Badger was kicked off the Tigers before the 2012 season for a series of failed drug tests that found traces of marijuana in his system. He withdrew from school and went to rehab, before enrolling again at LSU later in the fall, with hopes of playing in the 2013 season. On Oct. 25, he was arrested again for possession.
>
> What followed was a shitstorm whipped up mainly by the media, who turned a commonplace story about recreational pot smoking into a narrative about a troubled black athlete on the verge of entering a very dark wood. *Sports Illustrated*'s Thayer Evans and Pete Thamel, in maybe the single dumbest piece of sportswriting last year, went so far as to compare the Honey Badger to his father, Darrin Hayes—a convicted murderer who is serving out a life sentence in prison without the possibility of parole. They wrote: "If the crossroads he has arrived at—between redeeming his football career or squandering it, between old loyalties and new priorities—feels familiar to him, it should: Three decades ago his father came to the same point and washed out in a spiral of drugs and violence."
>
> Mathieu has never done time. He's never killed anyone. He smoked pot. Synthetic pot. Shitty pot.

The racial stratification of America's war on drugs and its separate and unequal policies addressing drug use in collegiate sports can be seen in the differential standards at Ole Miss as well. Coach Andy Kennedy dismissed Dundrecous Nelson and Jamal Jones, both African American student athletes, following an arrest that resulted from an officer's discovery of "eight roaches of marijuana made from cigarillos."[79] While Jones was released, both were dismissed from the team. As with Tyrann Mathieu,[80] Nelson and Jones were held accountable in ways Marshall Henderson and Bo Bowling can only imagine.

Like Henderson, Bo Bowling, a wide receiver from Oklahoma University, who is white, was given multiple chances. In 2009, police entered his residence where they discovered 108.6 grams of weed, and a myriad of prescription medications—alprazolam, ephedrine, and the anabolic steroid Stanozolo. They also found evidence of potential distribution, including several plastic bags containing marijuana residue, a digital scale, and over $1,000 in cash.[81] He eventually plead guilty, spent time in jail, and was dismissed from the team, only to be allowed back on the team a year later and afforded a path to redemption.[82]

The double standards—within the criminal justice system, from athletic programs and student conduct, and from the media and criminal justice—are nothing new. The numerous "get out of jail free" cards that Henderson owns are evidence of the broader social forces that encompass a separate and unequal war on drugs.

"Let's imagine the counterfactuals: If Henderson were black, the arrest alone likely would have ended his NCAA career," writes Greg Howard. "An attempt to pick up 50-plus grams of marijuana using fake currency isn't exactly a mere youthful transgression. Would a black 18-year-old have gotten off with just probation? Would he have gotten another chance to play Division I ball?"[83] If we look at the experience of countless black athletes and many more outside the scope of collegiate sports, then we can begin to see the power in playing, smoking, or #BreakingTheLawWhileWhite.

The power of #PlayingWhileWhite is advanced when discourses of protest bubble up against the NCAA's draconian drug policies. For example, in 2014, University of Michigan student athlete Mitch McGary tested positive for marijuana and was subsequently suspended. The media story did not focus on his poor choices, his breaking the law, or how he was unable to leave behind those negative influences; instead, it focused on the hypocrisy and callousness of the NCAA. "The NCAA is a hard-liner on a lot of issues, but there aren't many things it's stricter on than marijuana. Okay, maybe that's not true—it's pretty tough on caffeine intake, as well. But Mitch McGary's one-year suspension for a failed pot test brought the NCAA's absurd rules regarding recreational drugs to light once again," writes Kevin Trahan. "Thank goodness for the NCAA, maintaining its strong policy on marijuana when basically everyone else has created much more lenient punishments. If they didn't, we might have pilots getting high on the job. These are the stakes."[84]

Compare this to the reactions directed at Darren Carrington, Tyrann Mathieu, Klay Thompson, and any number of black student athletes, whose arrests or media reports about possible misconduct resulted in sanctimonious outrage at how student athletes represent the university and how breaking the law should have consequences. It produces articles on the epidemic of drug use among college athletes.

In isolating its attention to college athletics, and even more narrowly to football and basketball teams, while scrubbing Henderson, McGary, Bowling from the conversation (they are individuals, never representative of collegiate sports or white behavior), the national media discourse surrounding drugs consistently imagines the problem of drugs and criminality through the prism of blackness. In erasing the illicit activities of *students* while blaming/isolating criminal activity on/to student athletes—assumed to be black—this case provides a reminder of the legibility of black criminality[85] and white innocence.

Even when athletes like Henderson are violating the nation's drug laws, the narrative stays in place. Initially ignoring his criminal record, giving him multiple chances, and then focusing on redemption, the media discourse imagined his drugs as insignificant to whiteness. When read alongside the sports mediated coverage on drugs and athletes, the Henderson narrative not only perpetuates stereotypes but also normalizes the racially waged war on drugs.

While Henderson may be an extreme example, the seeming acceptance of drug use, particularly marijuana use, from white college students is both indicative of the power of playing while white and evidence of the shared power of whiteness inside and outside the arena. Just as marijuana has long been legal within "whitopias,"[86] from Colorado[87] to New York,[88] for white middle-class college students, white student athletes are able to get high, free from the consequences of stigma, media outrage, or the long-reach of the criminal justice system. Sure, swimming, lacrosse, and wrestling don't compare in popularity to basketball and football, but the power of whiteness can nonetheless be seen in the relative silence about the widespread drug cultures of these sports.

#PlayingWhileWhite is immunity from the push for zero tolerance and a culture of hyper-policing and the punishment of black bodies, particularly those seen as undisciplined and disruptive. The narratives surrounding the University of Oregon, TCU, and countless student athletes should give us pause to think about the ways in which the war on drugs, the racial language of disciplinarity and punishment,[89] the hyper-legibility of black criminality and illegibility of white criminality[90] that operate in both media narratives and NCAA policies. Only extreme-sports athletes seem to get a more lucrative "get out of jail free" card—including celebration—for drug use than do their collegiate brethren.

## EXTREME SPORTS

Despite the endemic drug culture in colleges and universities, (black) student athletes are neither afforded nor able to cash in on narratives that normalize drug use as merely a reflection of a regular facet of college life. Some sports, whether they be lacrosse or swimming, are afforded this privilege, evidenced in their normalization and acceptance of drug use, so much so that #PlayingWhileWhite means partying, breaking laws, and otherwise engaging in behavior that in circumstances colored by race would be read as signs of pathology, dysfunction, and potential harm.

Other sports, those imagined as "white sports," such as NASCAR (discussed in chapter 8), lacrosse, swimming, and extreme sports, are able to participate in illicit behavior without consequence. In fact, in those sports dominated by white bodies, drug use is often celebrated and normalized. Look no further than the culture and media discourse surrounding extreme sports.

Within several extreme sports, drug use is refashioned as evidence that these athletes are creative, free-spirited, counter-cultural, and otherwise pushing boundaries. Nowhere is this truer than within extreme sports,[91] imagined as a countercultural movement, a revolutionary underground culture, all of which is wrapped up in the scripts and profiles of whiteness, masculinity, and heteronormativity, not to mention the potential profitability and its value as a commodity. For example, Greg Burton is one who celebrates the culture of extreme sports in the following way:

> Goatees. Studs (the tongue-piercing kind). Ear-busting guitar riffs and patchouli oil.
> And talk about lighting the fire.
> Fans here also burn coals at the ends of their cigarettes, or something that smells sweeter, hempy even.
> This could be an outdoor concert for the ska-punk band Save Ferris.
> In fact, it is that and more.
> Entering its second Olympic Games, snowboarding has lost none of the edgy, underground devotion that made the sport a hit at the alternative X Games.[92]

Similarly, in writing about the reluctance of extreme sports athletes to represent the United States at the Olympics because of the "rules," including the prohibition of drugs, Allen St. John describes the lawlessness of extreme sports as harmless and almost cute:

> The party is taking off, but Danny Kass is nowhere to be found.
> At Trax, a dance club on a Bend, Ore., highway, a couple hundred snowboarders are unwinding while a band called Red i Rider

pumps out its own twisted brand of rockabilly, a twangy cover of Ice-T's "Cop Killer," the drummer pounding out the beat wearing a sequined face mask that's two parts Hannibal Lecter, one part Liberace. It's a snowboarder's nirvana—$1.50 Buds, cute local girls and a band so loud you can't hear yourself think. Most of the riders partying tonight were eliminated in the afternoon's qualifying rounds.[93]

According to St. John, Kass, then a star in snowboarding, prepared for qualifying for the main event as only an extreme sports athlete would:

> Kass summons a white-haired volunteer from the registration desk.
> "Is there drug testing today?" he asks.
> "Yes, I think so," the lady replies sweetly.
> "Are they testing for S.T.D.'s?"
> Kass's joke goes right over her head. "I don't know; I'll go find out," she says, as Curt and Danny chuckle conspiratorially on their way out the door.
> This weekend's drug testing is just a symptom of the controversy that is plaguing the selection process for the United States Olympic snowboard team.[94]

Here, drug tests—not drugs, not illicit activities, not crimes that prompt panic and widespread punishment in other "neighborhoods"—is what plagues the sport. #PlayingWhileWhite is playing in a place where the marijuana and drug culture is "a badge of honor demonstrating that snowboarding has not lost its antiestablishment roots."[95] It is sold as part of its charm and uniqueness; it is what makes it an alternative to basketball and football.

This positive drug narrative is clear in extreme-sports discourse.[96] For example, in a video on the *Snowboarder Magazine* website, Pat Bridges asks snowboarders: "Have You Ever: Smoked Weed on a Chairlift?" Can you imagine the media storm and the kind of discourse that would result from a video asking NBA or NFL players, "Have you ever smoked weed in the locker room?" Metta World Peace once noted that he drank before games, resulting in a media firestorm that recycled narratives of "out-of-control thugs."[97] With respect to extreme sports, the narrative is not just about the world-class athletes who can conquer mountains and execute gravity-defying jumps even on a diet of pot and beer; it is also one about uptight squares who are unfairly punishing extreme-sports athletes.[98] Rather than a narrative of crime and the lack of punishment, so much of the story becomes one focused on generational conflict, about how the mainstream is disconnected from youth culture. Eschewing discussions of role models and respect, the discourse reduces the issue of marijuana to that of out-of-touch suits thwarting the creativity and freedom of extreme-sports athletes.

Reflecting on "the identity crisis" and the conflicts between those who embrace pot culture within snowboarding and those who see it as an impediment to acceptance, Higgins writes:

> Doping. The word conjures images of Mark McGwire, the Tour de France and world-class sprinters. In sports such as baseball, cycling and track and field, performance-enhancing drugs have skewed any sense of fair play.
>
> But snowboarding? Not so much. Any cloud of suspicion among shreds consists in gray ribbons of pungent pot smoke. From decriminalization of marijuana in mountain towns, to positive drug tests at the Winter Olympics, to the Grenade Games festival famously held each year on April 20—the unofficial "National Pot Smoking Day"—snowboarding seems to embrace stoner sensibilities. "Marijuana is a part of snowboarding culture," said Pat Bridges, editor of *Snowboarder Magazine*.[99]

Similarly, Pete Thomas couches drug use in terms of the tension between snowboarding's mainstream aspirations and the accepted drug culture of the sport. "Snowboarding has been an Olympic sport since 1998, and from the start the disconnect between the rigidity of the Olympic movement and a sport clothed in the counter-culture attire of free-spirited youth collided," writes Thomas. "In fact, the first gold medal ever awarded in snowboarding went to a Canadian shredder who later tested positive for marijuana."[100]

Neither "side"—those who celebrate the pothead ethos of the sport versus those who see it as obstacle—reflects on the criminality of its participants or the pathology of white masculinity. The discourse is concerned neither with the role models nor their negative influence on youth. Clearly, the discussions are not about whiteness and the pathologies of suburban, middle-class identity; rather, they are a debate about the identity of extreme sports and whether getting high is part of the "extreme" in extreme sports. In either case, it is not a big deal.

Whether rationalized as simply part of the "norms" of extreme sports, or because extreme sports athletes deal with ample injuries and thus use "medical marijuana"[101] there is consistency throughout much of the public discourse surrounding extreme sports and drug use that works to downplay and minimize that use. The rhetoric of "the rule of law," "role models," "maturity," "discipline" is nowhere to be found. While the acceptance of drug use within snowboarding is extreme in nature, it points to the power and privilege of whiteness. Criminal activity is no big deal; it is accepted and even normalized. This counterculture is embraced as colorful and even an alternative to the selfish, me-first, and "show me the money" (black) athlete.

The acceptance AND celebration of drugs is not unique to snowboarding; it can be seen in surfing, BMX, skateboarding, and countless other extreme sports. Seeing athletes getting extremely high as an integral part of extreme sports is representative of what it means to be white in America, to be exempt from the profile of drug user and criminal. #PlayingWhile-White is a microcosm of #LivingWhileWhite. Despite a war on drugs, and widespread drug use, smoking while white has always been no big deal, not worthy of societal concern much less interventions from the criminal justice system. To look at extreme sports is to look at the "New Jim Crow," to look at the separate and unequal war on drugs.

### CONCLUSION: DRUG CRIMINALS
### VERSUS EXTREME ATHLETES

When you compare the normalization of drug use within extreme sports culture, the almost celebration of getting high, to the longstanding panics and policing of drug use within the NBA and the NFL, you are looking into America's racialized war on drugs. These disparate responses to drugs within these sports are a window into America's "New Jim Crow."[102] Brian Anderson and Peter Reihartz highlight the concerns about drug use in the NBA:

> The counterculture's influence, intensified by the street-hardened backgrounds of increasing numbers of pro athletes, made drug use common in sports, too. By 1982, says current NBA Commissioner David Stern, 75 percent of the league's players were using cocaine. At the same time, around 40 percent of the NFL's players were using it, too, according to former player Carl Eller, an ex-junkie himself. Because of public disgust and the obvious drug-induced deterioration of many players' skills, each of the major sports leagues began to implement drug policies of varying degrees of effectiveness in the eighties. In the fall of 1988, for example, 24 NFL players, including superstar Lawrence Taylor,

received suspensions for substance abuse after failing random drug tests. Several NBA stars—including crowd-pleaser Micheal Ray Richardson—wound up booted out of the league permanently for repeated drug violations. As a result, nobody thinks that the substance-abuse problem of sports is as bad today as it was 15 years ago—but no one thinks it is solved, either.[103]

Crime, drugs, and pathologies threatened the league; drug use was ruining careers: the problems of the NBA were a window into the broader crime epidemic plaguing the black community. This #DruggedBlackBody, especially read in comparison to the #HighExtremeSportsBody, reveals the racial work being done in sports. Whereas drug use in extreme sports (and lacrosse, swimming, and wrestling) are ignored, normalized, and even embraced as part of their counterculture ethos, drug use within the NBA and NFL elicits panic, criminalization, and demands for interdiction. This is a microcosm of America's racial landscape.

The drug-using basketball player is a threat; whereas the extreme sports star getting high is benign and harmless. Herman Gray reminds us, "The black other occupies a complex site, a place where fears, desires, and repressed dreams are lodged."[104] Whiteness, on the other hand, embodies hopes and possibilities, one where the violations of social norms and laws are recast as signs of exceptionality. Whiteness, as evident in NASCAR, extreme sports, and lacrosse, is invisible and unmarked. Yet, the normalization of #GettingHighWhileWhite demonstrates that whiteness is the ultimate wage that allows drug use or violating private property (such as skateboarding in public spaces) in the name of counterculture, fun, pushing boundaries, or living on the extreme. While blackness, for an athlete or not, maintains a dialogic existence with the stereotypes of black criminality and black drug usage, white athletes can outrun (or skate, ski, or swim) these signifiers through erasure, invisibility, or narratives of redemption.

Connecting this process to the ongoing culture wars, the Reagan revolution, deindustrialization, and the continuously expanding American prison system, S. Craig Watkins argues in *Representing* that the criminalized black body functions as a powerful marker of social decay, pathology, and danger, thus necessitating state control and intervention:

> Law and order appeals bind the nation together at the same time they divide and polarize society along lines of race and class. The merger of the criminal, lower, and dangerous classes promotes the commonsense notion that the most pernicious threats to a

harmonious society come from the bottom of the social and economic hierarchy. In this sense, then, the war on drugs deflects the anxiety and discontent of ordinary Americans and their resentment away from the corporate and political elite and against the poor.[105]

This is why reflecting on the dialectics between #PlayingWhileWhite and #BreakingLawsWhileWhite within sporting cultures is so important, as it provides a window into the broader racial practices and policies that infect every institution of society. For every Mitch McGary, Jason "White Chocolate" Williams,[106] and Steve Howe, there are countless white college students or suburban youth who are able to get high and violate any number of laws without fear of repression. For every Marshall Henderson, Tim Lincecum, Ross Rebagliati,[107] and Michael Phelps, for every lacrosse team and extreme-sports athlete who lives by different rules within the athletic world, there are countless more Bobbys and Beckys who are getting high, selling dope, and thumbing their nose at the war on drugs with impunity.

Likewise, for every black student athlete suspended for recreational drug use and every article lamenting drug use in the NBA and NFL, there are countless black men and women locked up, black and Latino youth stopped and frisked—all under the same racial logic. For every Darren Carrington, Tyrann Mathieu, Klay Thompson, and countless black athletes who have found themselves busted for drug use, there are thousands of black youth suspended and expelled from school for drug use and many more pushed into the school-to-prison pipeline or street-to-prison pipeline. For every ESPN headline about a failed drug test, there are thousands of black and Latino families and communities across the nation that have been destroyed by "the New Jim Crow."[108] The ability to get high, to make a mistake, is one overdetermined by race. That is clear in the sports world, but its impact extends beyond the playing field.

CHAPTER 6

# REDEMPTION AND CHARACTER BUILDING

*Making Mistakes While White*

WHEN the 2016 Yale Men's Basketball Team took the floor during March Madness they were missing a key member of their team. This particular Cinderella story, a narrative reserved for teams colored white and constructed as underdogs, who are assumed to lack the requisite skills, athleticism, and talent to compete with their black counterparts, didn't have a happy ending. Earlier in the season, team captain Jack Montague had been kicked off the team and expelled from the school following accusations of rape.

Amid an increased focus on sexual violence on the campus, and the Yale team's decision to wear shirts expressing their support for Montague, which prompted student protests, Montague received ample sympathetic media coverage. Reflecting the hegemony of rape culture, and promoting the lies that "false accusations" are commonplace[1] and that there is some kind of balance to a "he said/she said framework,"[2] the coverage continually painted Montague as a victim. He was a victim of false accusations, a university looking to scapegoat him, "student mobs," and an unforgiving world.

The efforts to tell his story; to provide information about his backstory; to discuss the accusations of rape in the context of basketball and expulsion from school rather than as a criminal justice issue; to call the rape a "rumor"; to emphasize all that he lost when his team played in March Madness; and to otherwise humanize him speaks to the ways that redemption is a privilege available to and unearned by white male athletes with great frequency.[3]

While there are many routes to redemption, the easiest path is never being held accountable, being seen as a victim, or being imagined as the face of injustice. As whiteness operates as a free-floating signifier of innocence and harmlessness, forgiveness and redemption can be somewhat superfluous. To be redeemed, to be lifted up, and to be embraced again presumes a level of guilt and accountability that remains antithetical to #PlayingWhileWhite. To be redeemed requires some accountability.

For others, accountability is the first step towards redemption. Past wrongs become footnotes, or provide a context for understanding the melodramatic rise from despair to glory. Mistakes are what make accomplishments meaningful and impressive as evidence of fortitude and perseverance. Ryan Braun's positive test for performance-enhancing drugs and Michael Phelps's DUI arrests were dismissed as mistakes and indiscretions, bumps in the road that each athlete was able to overcome through introspection, growth, and transformation.

When not ignoring or excusing the bad behavior of white athletes, media discourses often transform these bad choices into moments for celebration, evidence of growth and maturation. Neither defining their character nor emblematic of whiteness, these shortcomings are refashioned as evidence of character, growth, maturation, and redemption. Privilege and power allow white athletes, those who stumble because of transgressions, to move forward without interruption, stopping only to celebrate and bask in the praise about their steps taken toward redemption. Redemption remains one of the most valuable "wages of whiteness."[4]

The mistake-ridden path on the road to redemption has defined the careers of Ben Roethlisberger, Brock Turner—the Stanford swimmer whose six-month jail sentence was met with widespread outrage (the presiding judge noted: "A prison sentence would have a severe impact on him. I think he will not be a danger to others.")—Tanya Harding, Hope Solo, Josh Hamilton, Chris "Birdman" Anderson, Lance Armstrong, Josh Brown, Ryan Braun, and Mark McGwire. Accusations of rape, drug use, assault, and other transgressions have not stopped their successes on and off the field. Their careers, much less their public personas, are not defined by their actions. In fact, these obstacles, the trials and tribulations, the suspensions and the "bumps" in the road, can at times prove not to be a hindrance to success on and off the field but in fact part of an athlete's appeal. With each case, the appeal of redemption, the afforded humanity resulting from chronicling their personal demons, and the story of second chances has propelled the careers of many of these athletes to differing degrees.

This chapter explores the power of whiteness within narratives of sports as vehicles of redemption, arguing that individuals are seen apart from the normalized narrative of black athletes and therefore, in some cases, redemption and forgiveness are available. Here, I reflect on the broader consequences of living in a culture where whiteness remains a requirement for second chances, redemption, and maturation. Thinking about these narratives of redemption, in comparison the very different narratives assigned to Michael Vick, Kobe Bryant, Ray Lewis, Ron Artest, Plaxico Burress, Allen Iverson, Adrian Peterson, and Ray Rice, all of whom to differing degrees have not been able to shake the past, reveals the power of race in the construction of redemption and forgiveness narratives. This is not to say that redemption narratives and second chances do not materialize with black athletes. The ubiquitous celebration of Kobe Bryant in 2016 offered very little discussion of his 2003 rape trial in Colorado; Ray Lewis's retirement from football led to ample career opportunities despite his 2000 indictment for murder. Brandon Austin, an African American collegiate basketball player twice accused of sexual assault, was continuously afforded opportunities to continue his collegiate career amid a narrative of second chances.[5] These narratives of redemption and lived second chances are, thus, not only afforded to white athletes but anchor sporting cultures. #PlayingWhile-Masculine and the privileges of cisgender heterosexual manhood allows for redemption over and over again.

Yet many of the cases involving African American athletes, which also elicit far different and extensive media coverage,[6] redemption and the possibilities of turning over their criminal leaf to start a new chapter are clouded by the logics of race and racism. Moreover, with each, the past is never the past but an index for the person, his community, and larger discourses around blackness. For their white peers, from Lance Armstrong to Big Ben, past "indiscretions" are unremarkable, isolated, and otherwise parts of a larger narrative of triumph.

## A SURVIVOR: OUR NEED TO REDEEM LANCE

Lance Armstrong captured America's imagination for almost a decade. After battling cancer, he became America's most celebrated athlete of the late twentieth century. Dominating cycling, and winning the Tour de France seven straight years, Armstrong tapped into a myriad of tropes from those based in nationalism ("America leaves the rest of the world in the dust even in its sport") to rugged individualism ("he was able to pull himself up, beating back cancer and any number of opponents"), from those that saw him as "a breath of fresh air" (compared to other black athletes, Armstrong was humble, selfless, and more about others than himself), to those who yearned for a white male superstar, thought to be something of a dinosaur in the modern world. Despite longstanding accusations about performance enhancing drugs, Armstrong's status as America's shining cyclist on the hill defined the sporting landscape several years past 9/11.

In the face of available evidence and public knowledge, Lance Armstrong was able to ward off punishment and widespread condemnation for most of his career. At worst, he was bogged down by rumors, innuendo, and speculation of "doping." Redemption was neither necessary nor part of the discourse for many years as Armstrong's innocence was preserved within the public square.

Ultimately, as the evidence became so irrefutable, so overwhelming, and so threatening to the profitability of Armstrong Enterprises and its media and corporate subsidiaries, we had no choice but to see his guilt. Ultimately his acknowledgment of guilt offered a necessary stop on the pathway toward redemption. The media was ready and waiting to help. Framing his story as one of "doping," "transgression,"[7] and "alleged use of performance-enhancing drugs" preserved a framework about actions and choices rather than one about Lance Armstrong, his character, or whiteness.

What is striking with Armstrong is how much of the media discourse focused on Armstrong's redemption from day one. Acting as if the end of the Armstrong story had already been written, an ending in which forgiveness, redemption, and second chances were bestowed without question, much of the media framed the discussion as one about when and how Armstrong would secure his rightful redemption.[8]

This is not to say that Armstrong was without his critics or that the media response to his "apology tour" did not have plenty of naysayers. Yet, even those who questioned his motives, who poked holes in his redemptive story, who wondered if Armstrong deserved our collective forgiveness, still carved out space for Armstrong's voice. In the end, the discourse created by both critics and apologists humanized Armstrong, told his story on his terms, and provided the necessary ingredients to cook up redemption.

Inside Armstrong's "invisible knapsack"[9] of redemption lays the widespread focus on the hegemony of doping in cycling. Lance Armstrong was the product of the culture of cycling where doping was "commonplace,"[10] "pervasive,"[11] and widespread. The mantra of "it's not cheating if everyone is doing it" provided an important subtext for understanding Armstrong's use of performance-enhancing drugs.[12] His desire to compete on a level playing field, to excel in a grueling sport, and to make America proud were claimed to be the reasons behind why he used the drugs. In "Why I'm Not Angry at Lance Armstrong" Sally Jenkins encapsulates this line of thinking:

> Maybe I'm not angry at Lance because, though I hoped he was
> clean, it's simply not shocking or enraging to learn that he was

like all the other cyclists who sought a medical advantage in riding up the faces of mountains. Or because I've long believed that what athletes put in their bodies should be a matter of personal conscience, not police actions—when we demand unhealthy, even death-defying extremes of them for our entertainment, it seems the height of hypocrisy to then dictate what's good for them.

During an interview with *Le Monde*, in response to a question on whether it was "possible to perform without doping?" Armstrong focused on his lack of options: "That depends on which races you wanted to win. The Tour de France? No. Impossible to win without doping. Because the Tour is a test of endurance where oxygen is decisive."[13] During an interview with Oprah Winfrey, Armstrong acknowledged that knowing what he knows now, he would still probably cheat. "When I made the decision, when my team made that decision, when the whole peloton made that decision, it was a bad decision and an imperfect time."[14] In other words, he was doing what everyone else was doing. Similarly, during an interview with Jeremy Whittle, Armstrong focused on how his choices reflected the culture and values of cycling. They weren't an indicator of his moral compass; his actions were not a window into his values and his white male ethos. "I didn't stand over my teammates telling them to dope. That's 100 percent false. The sport fostered that culture. You had a substance, EPO, that was so efficient and if they have an equivalent tomorrow that is undetectable, everyone would be on it."[15]

With Armstrong, redemption became increasingly possible with his delivery of each explanatory factor that seemingly offered him protection from judgment, a certain level of responsibility, criminalization, and outrage. The sport made him do it; the cancer led him to do it; others on the team led him to do it. Even when acknowledging his own choices, the discourse continually reminded the public that his decisions fit within the values and culture of cycling.

The media discourse also demanded that we read his poor choices within the larger context of his life's work. In other words, his decision to use drugs and to engage in a several year cover-up was merely finite examples of bad behavior in a sea of righteousness. From his charity work to his beautiful relationship with his children, at his core Lance was a good guy. In "Livestrong Bracelet: To Wear or Not to Wear?" Emanuella Grinberg noted a tweet from Eric Liu that emphasized that the collective good from Armstrong outweighed his bad decisions. "Casting the doping allegations aside, Lance Armstrong did more good than bad, he changed a generation's view on cancer."[16] Sally Jenkins similarly wrote about her efforts to declare

Armstrong not guilty as a cheating cyclist. His "win at any cost" ethos should not revoke his humanity; the body of his good work should define Lance Armstrong:

> Maybe I'm not angry at Lance because I believe the athlete in him is a situational personality—a facet, not the whole. . . . Maybe I'm not angry at Lance because I don't understand those people who are bitterly angry to discover that he is not Santa Claus, while ignoring the very real and useful presents he delivered. Not toys, not hagiography, but the simple yet critical lesson that a third medical opinion can save your life. Or that the more educated a sick person is about their disease, the greater their statistical chance of survival. Who not only preached those lessons, but built an organization through which anyone can get the information and education about cancer for free that he was fortunate enough to be able to afford. And who put his money and incalculable amounts of time where his mouth was, raising $500 million for research and donating $7 million of his own fortune.[17]

The demand not to reduce Armstrong to the worst of his actions highlights a key tool in the redemption formula, one that is most often available for those #PlayingWhileWhite.

Others wondered if he was crazy, sick, or pathologically incapable of controlling himself. During his sit-down with Oprah,[18] Lance Armstrong admitted that "he was 'sick' and 'narcissistic.'"[19] According to Matt Majendie, "Some have suggested Armstrong might even have psychological problems—displaying behavior associated with 'narcissistic personality disorder' according to psychotherapist and author Joseph Burgo, a throwback to a difficult upbringing, a father who was not part of his life, and being raised by a single mother."[20] As is evident in these examples, much of the media continued to embrace and disseminate a narrative that explained why Lance drugged, all while emphasizing the pain he felt because of these mistakes.

Another key dimension in the redemptive discourse was the ubiquitous emphasis on how much he had lost, the suffering he endured, and the price that he paid: he was stripped of his titles; he lost millions of dollars; he fell out with friends; he faced lawsuits and criminal investigations. For example, Matt Majendie paints a devastating picture of a life torn apart:

> It's a year and a half since Lance Armstrong sat in front of Oprah Winfrey and admitted it was all a lie, every single word of it.

> In the fallout, everything that had been built on that lie came crashing down around him.
>
> From being virtually deified for his cancer survival and subsequent seven successive Tour de France wins, a record achievement which has now been erased from the history books, the American was demonized.
>
> The fallout has left him persona non grata in the cycling fraternity and vilified on social media but, somewhat surprisingly, he claims to still be well received in society.[21]

The resulting narrative was one that placed blame elsewhere, emphasizing his immense loss, and otherwise turning him into a sympathetic figure. His life was in shambles; we should not only feel sorry for his fall from the peak of the mountain but should forgive him and help him climb back to his rightful place in not only the sport world but society as a whole.

For Lance, redemption was always inevitable. Whether focusing on the drug culture of cycling or his contributions to cancer research, whether noting his own battle with cancer or his tumultuous life, the privileges of whiteness are not simply the possibility of redemption but the availability in those very narratives that offered context or reasons for one's behavior that makes redemption almost inevitable.

The desire to tell Armstrong's story, to bring his humanity to light, reflect the power in his whiteness; yet, the desire to redeem Armstrong, to highlight the understandable reasons for his choices, was about the persona that Armstrong had come to represent in our national consciousness. Framed as the scrappy fighter, as fearless, as the embodiment of the American Dream, as determined, as smart, as a leader, and the consummate worker, his redemption story was about preserving our vision of Armstrong. It was about protecting these tropes and their association with whiteness. His innocence protected the Armstrong mythology and the narrative that came with each victory. Those victories were not simply celebrated because of America's love of cycling or the athletic marvel that is the Tour de France, but because of what Armstrong signified and because of the cultural, ideological, and economic value of white athletic success. Lance Armstrong had made sports great again. His use of PEDs and his behavior threatened his utility; his redemption and the hegemonic efforts to provide him with repentance was about preserving his meaning to us.

The sometimes unfulfilled desire to redeem Lance Armstrong speaks to the power of whiteness. It highlights the financial and ideological value in the Armstrong narrative or, as Alex Gibney describes it, "the Armstrong

Lie."[22] It speaks to the pleasure and utility of not only Armstrong but also his whiteness and its bodily male signifiers. Kyle Kusz highlights the ways that Lance Armstrong capitalized on his white sporting masculinity, which not only afforded deference and denial,[23] but also forgiveness and redemption:

> Armstrong was cast as a living, breathing example that recovery was not only possible, but that one's future could be better.
>
> But each of these views was a product of the broader heroic narrative that fabricated Lance Armstrong as Lance America.
>
> Through this narrative, Americans were also urged to admire Armstrong in specifically masculine terms, whether as a modern-day American cowboy, Superman, or "miracle man." On the cover of his autobiography, Armstrong was cast not only as the "winner of the Tour de France" and a "cancer survivor," but as "husband, father, son, human being." In the slang of the era, Armstrong displayed "swagger": an unspoken, yet distinctly masculine coolness, confidence, and certitude. His athletic prowess on his bike demonstrated his indisputable masculine bona fides.[24]

Armstrong's popularity was grounded in what he signified as a white male athlete within a sports world seen as increasingly controlled by African Americans, feminists, and media elites on the coast. "Armstrong's performance of idealized white masculinity also helped to facilitate the widespread presumption of Armstrong's innocence as well as the corresponding shock and dissonance associated with his eventual confession," writes Kusz.[25] His success, his ascendance, and his ultimate redemption "was a product of his white skin coupled with his particular way of performing white masculinity as a productive, hard-working champion who gave back to, and provided for, others in need."[26] His commercials and the Oprah confession, his larger than life persona and transcendent sporting identity, were all productions of "his superhero-like actions on and off of his bike." The constructed media narrative "enabled many Americans to perceive him through a prism of white racial stereotypes as essentially innocent, virtuous, and good," not to mention scrappy, smart, and caring, "rather than through the more complicated details of his life." [27]

#RidingWhileWhite propelled Armstrong to the front of the peloton as well as to the pinnacle of sporting celebrity. It also protected him from accusations surrounding PED, and limited his accountability. The power in his narrative and its value to us necessitated his ultimate forgiveness. We needed Lance more than Lance needed us; he was America, he was the American Dream; he was a rugged individual who conquered the road and cancer; he was a man, who made mistakes. He was white. As such, he was the living embodiment of the United States and therefore he was forgiven over and over again.

### JOSH HAMILTON: A SICK MAN

Like Lance Armstrong, Josh Hamilton has been forgiven over and over again. In 1999, the Tampa Bay Devil Rays selected Hamilton as their number one draft pick. In fact, he was the overall number one selection and the first straight from high school (yes, when you are white, from suburbia, and play baseball, concerns about going to college are absent as opposed to in the NBA).[28] He was a budding star that experts saw as the future of a league in search of marketable stars.

This all changed in 2001, or at least that would become the core of the story of Hamilton's fall from grace. That year, he and his parents, who had moved from their West Virginia home to follow him around the minor leagues, were involved in a car accident. His parents would leave Florida, returning home to deal with their own injuries, leaving Hamilton, alone without his family and baseball. Without baseball and family, in physical and emotional pain, he turned to drugs. In "Josh Hamilton's Battle: From Cocaine Cravings and 26 Tattoos to Faith and Rangers," Evan Grant describes the downward spiral as epic and tragic:

> He eventually ended up on the disabled list that May because of lingering back issues, probably from the accident. Someone used to constant activity and who had been somewhat sheltered from teammates suddenly had nothing but time and money on his hands. He started hanging out at a tattoo shop, where he had earlier had Hammer inked on his right arm.
>
> One tattoo led to another. He has himself inked with flames, tribal signs and blank-eyed demons, 26 images in all. He started hanging out with the guys from the place, too. He joined them one night at a strip joint. That, Hamilton says, is when he took his first drink and snorted his first line of cocaine.

The all-American boy, the "can't miss kid,"[29] the future star of baseball, and someone who didn't even drink, was now an addict hanging out with people with tattoos in strip clubs. Was it the pressure of being a number one draft pick or that which comes with being a sports legend before he was able to drive? Was it the physical pain he lived with or some other demons that made him turn to drugs and alcohol? Or was it the bad crowd that he fell into? Under their influence, this formerly clean-cut boy turned to tattoos and then drugs and alcohol to fill the void and deal with his pain. Ultimately he would be suspended from the league. Worse, he had become estranged from his wife. Having lost his career, a healthy relationship with his family, and his health, he was on the fast track to death.[30]

If this story wasn't enough, with its tropes of white male innocence corrupted by outside influences, of the unfulfilled promise derailed by injury, loss, and addiction, the emergent story of redemption took things to yet another level. Bryan Curtis summarizes Hamilton's story and its ideological power beautifully:

> It's worth pausing right here to review why the Josh Hamilton
> Story was so powerful, so mesmerizing, to begin with. First, it was
> a really good story! It was divided into three acts: Youthful Prom-
> ise, Fall From Grace, and Big Comeback. It starred Hamilton's
> pretty wife, Katie. It had a saintly grandma, Mary, next to whom
> Hamilton knelt when he finally began to turn his life around. It's
> no wonder Casey Affleck is turning The Story into his version
> of *The Blind Side*. Second—and speaking of *The Blind Side*—The
> Story was an amazing Christian redemption narrative.[31]

The comparison to *The Blind Side* is illustrative in that Hamilton, who engaged in criminal activity, who broke the law and exhibited behavior often derided as pathological is compared to Michael Oher, who simply grew up in poverty. Hamilton had much handed to him, only to lose it because of drugs. Oher, on the other hand, was the product of deindustrialization, mass incarceration, and neoliberal post–civil rights policies that left him behind. In America, to be white means that bad behavior and mistakes can be forgiven and even compared to #LivingWhileBlack.

Curtis further notes how the redemptive story wasn't simply a result of the riches-to-rags-back-to-riches narrative and Hamilton's ultimate greatness on the field, but the ways that religion became the basis of his ascendance back to his "rightful" place as a superstar:

> Third, that Christian redemption narrative turned out to be an
> amazing *sportswriting* redemption narrative, too. Interesting how
> that works, isn't it? Both parables require a man—preferably strong

and on top of the world—who has been felled by what Bob Lipsyte called the termites of the soul. Both need a vivid description of the descent into hell. (In his book, Hamilton says he remembers seeing Satan's grinning face in a cloud formation.) Both require a man who, in his post-hell, partially rebuilt state, is very humble. There's something beguiling about an athlete who's at our level—who might even be, we think in a low moment, *beneath* us. As Hamilton once put it: "Nobody can insult me as much as I've insulted myself."

Fourth, The Story was mesmerizing because it had no gray areas. Old Josh: selfish, unholy, crack house. New Josh: devoted, godly, home run. Even though Hamilton was quick to admit he was still an addict who couldn't even carry around lunch money, there was no question about which Josh we should root for. Fifth—and this is crucial to all of the above—Josh Hamilton was willing to tell The Story again and again and again.[32]

Of course, part of each of those reasons and most certainly the final reason for why this story galvanized so many fans and media commentators is his whiteness. Whereas the white body, even if plagued by demons and misdeeds, is rendered as innocent and therefore desirable, the black body is criminal and suspect. "The primary objective of scripture as a process within current popular cultural media is to constitute the utopic American self in an effort to minimize the other, thus being consistent with what it means to be a centralized, rather than a marginalized being," writes Ronald Jackson.[33] Rendering the black body as toxic and destructive, and the white body as inherently good and therefore able to right past wrongs, media discourse shapes who is afforded the opportunity to return from mistakes. According to Jackson, "Black bodies that are defiant and decentralized, as in the case of some Black males, may be understood not necessarily as dystopic structures or delinquent nobodies, but marginalized identities seeking agency, affirmation, conjoinment, and recognition within an unfamiliar place."[34] As noted in chapter 5, we live in a nation where people of color are disproportionately incarcerated for drug use, where whites are afforded treatment while blacks and Latinos are sent directly to jail, where the stigmas of drug use are racially stratified;[35] it is clear that Josh Hamilton's redemptive story is one where his whiteness is a central ingredient.

Tellingly, Curtis sees Hamilton as a "prisoner" of his story of redemption and not a prisoner of the state. Able to reach into his athletic gym bag ("invisible knapsack"[36]) he cashed in on his whiteness; his accountability was minimal in part because of the narrative appeal of the high school baseball phenom throwing it all away because of crack and cocaine addictions only to find religion, which saved not only his life but his family and his baseball career too.

Ultimately signing with the Rangers, Hamilton would become a superstar. His story of redemption wasn't just a feel-good Hollywood movie, but one that played into our narratives of personal responsibility, forgiveness, religion, and hard work being the ultimate safety nets, and the American Dream, which are readily available for those #PlayingWhiteWhile.

Hamilton's whiteness made such a story possible. From seeing him as an innocent all-American boy to the celebration of Christianity allowing him to return to his true self, from the celebration of his difficult past as character building to diminished coverage of his relapses,[37] #PlayingWhileWhite enabled Josh Hamilton to not only stay on the field in spite of his multiple drug issues,[38] but to be celebrated as an example of hope and change. He would make millions of dollars for his performance on the field, which was also reflective of the power of his story. Both were an outgrowth of what it means to play, live, and exist while white. In a moment where white drug use has garnered national attention, from media exposés to political intervention, where white drug use is seen as a public health crisis rather than a criminal threat to law and order, the forgiveness, the lack of accountability, and the focus on helping Hamilton get better reveals the depth and scope of white privilege inside and outside of the sports world.[39] Redemption and second chances remain one of the most powerful wages of whiteness.

### BIG BEN: A CHANGED MAN

In 2010, Ocmulgee Judicial Circuit district attorney Fred Bright announced that Pittsburgh Steelers' quarterback Ben Roethlisberger would not face charges following a complaint from a twenty-year-old woman that he had sexually assaulted her in a bar bathroom. Leading up to the announcement the dominant narrative from media, fans, and the league had already focused on Big Ben's innocence. Indeed, given that less than a year before, after accusations that he sexually assaulted a woman in Lake Tahoe, ESPN issued a "do not report" memo,[40] while others within the blogosphere went on the offensive against the alleged victim, what else could one have anticipated? In this context, Ben was regularly characterized as at worst immature and simply needed to grow up following the 2010 allegations.

Over and over again, the discourse focused on how he was "innocent until proven guilty," (or innocent until the prosecutor decided not to press charges, which in this context "proved his innocence"). So often, within public discourse and media representations, such a protected right is one reserved for white athletes. In fact, the rights afforded by the Constitution have historically been out of reach for African Americans inside and outside the sporting arena. As such, redemption has also proved illusive in as much as declaring one legally innocent and therefore legally exempt from accountability embodies the most powerful tool of redemption. Outside the legal system, Ben Roethlisberger was equally protected. Initially, the league and the Steelers called for the formal investigation to be concluded prior to any decisions. They called for calm and cautioned against a rush to judgment.

Jemele Hill, one of the few commentators to bring race into the discussion, directed attention to Commissioner Roger Goodell and his decision to wait to meet with Roethlisberger until the "appropriate time." Hill rightly noted a double standard. The Commissioner had not afforded black NFL players similar patience:

> When Goodell sat [Adam "Pacman"] Jones down for a year, he wanted to send a message that irresponsible behavior could cost an NFL player his livelihood. If Goodell doesn't schedule a meeting with Roethlisberger immediately, it feeds the perception that white NFL stars under criminal investigation are treated differently and will receive more benefit of the doubt than their black counterparts.[41]

Whereas several black players, including the late Chris Henry, Michael Vick, Adam Jones, and Brandon Marshall, were suspended prior to the conclusion of their criminal cases, with others being cut or suspended by their respective teams immediately after their arrest(s) or the release of damaging information (Cedric Bensen, Tank Johnson, Greg Hardy, Ray Rice, and Plaxico Burress), Roethlisberger was initially immune from the long arm of the NFL's law (On April 13, 2010, the NFL announced it would "review all the facts and follow up at the appropriate time."). Not surprisingly, Jemele Hill's insistence at looking at race prompted ample criticism and accusations that she was "playing the race card." The outrage directed at Hill rather than at Roethlisberger (or even the Steelers or the NFL), like the NFL's response, elucidated the ways that he benefited from the culture of presumed innocence available to white athletes.

Compare his experience to that of Santonio Holmes. In the wake of an alleged assault of a woman at a bar and his suspension for violating the league substance abuse policy, the Pittsburgh Steelers traded Santonio Holmes to the New York Jets. Media accounts suggest that this was in large measure because of "his rap sheet"; team owners were tired of Holmes's bad behavior, which included illegal drug use and a previous suspension. Fans and analysts, moreover, referred to the MVP of the 2008 Super Bowl as "a problem child" with "a sense of entitlement" and as "a bad boy" "infected by low morals" and made regular connections between Holmes and new teammates best known for their transgressions—Braylon Edwards, who had previous run-ins with the law, and Antonio Cromartie, who was lampooned for having seven children with five different women and needed a large signing bonus to pay off overdue child support. The *New York Daily News* went as far as to describe the team as "[Coach Rex] Ryan's halfway house for misbehaving millionaires."[42] Similarly, Andrew Brandt questioned the logic behind the Jets' acquisitions, noting "management feels this coach can take a potentially combustible mix of players and mold them into a productive group."[43] He and others wondered whether or not the Jets father figure could redeem and reform their abject and pathologically dysfunctional black bodies.

While one may quibble about the relative value of Holmes and Roethlisberger to the franchise, the differences in their treatment is telling: the former was traded, rapidly punished for violations, and marked as deviant and a cancer on the team; the latter was retained and counseled. He was rendered a broken work in progress who could be fixed, even redeemed, with minor intervention.

Whereas Holmes fits neatly within preexisting accounts of blackness—disobedient, transgressive, criminal, unredeemable, childlike—that must always be policed without the possibility of redemption, Roethlisberger took on the role of the tragic hero, wounded by immaturity, hubris, and wrong action. Unlike Holmes, Roethlisberger had the potential to be redeemed and otherwise grow up. His eventual suspension would be part of the healing and maturation that would lead to his redemption. More recently, a similar comparison is evident in the differential treatment, media representation, and the public outcry to Josh Brown and Ray Rice (or Greg Hardy).

Where Roethlisberger enjoyed and had the potential to earn respect back from his teammates, his boss, fans, and perhaps even his critics, Holmes became doomed to exile and damned to condemnation. Failing to stay within confines of the politics of respectability in order to become a racially transcendent commodity, Holmes was sent packing. Writing about black masculinity and the politics of respectability in wake of the election of Barack Obama, Mark Anthony Neal argues that cultural inclusion and the calls for proper behavior and respectable "performances will ultimately falter under the weight of their pretensions. Like a suit that no longer fits, their performances are coming apart at the seams."[44] For Holmes, his blackness and the associated signifiers within the dominant racial scripts and frames precluded him from navigating the paths toward respectability. Yet for Roethlisberger, in the journey toward acceptance, the efforts to perform an acceptable identity were just coming together, albeit with the powerful threads of whiteness.

None of this is to say that the accusations against Roethlisberger didn't elicit criticism. Much of the outrage understandably focused on the media and the league for its failures to address sexual violence, letting Roethlisberger off the hook in some regards. He was innocent until proven guilty, whereas the media and the league were guilty as charged. Jaclyn Friedman identified those who refused to cover the Lake Tahoe incident and those who made excuses as "apologists." Accordingly, "the apologists are no laughing matter. They're an essential ingredient" within modern sports culture. These apologists, and those who make jokes and otherwise undermine the seriousness of the epidemic of sexual violence, contribute to rape culture, which "protects and lionizes male athletes at all costs."[45] Rape culture, inside and outside of sports, in turn, breathes oxygen into their misogynist rationalizations. Similarly, Anna Clark linked the media silence and the presumption of innocence to sports media culture that privileges athletes with innocence, that celebrates a certain inscription of masculinity: "Maybe, however, this inattention is dangerous; an implicit message that if you are athletically heroic enough (and Ben Roethlisberger is certainly that, if nothing else), then we as a culture will look the other way when you are accused of terrible, brutal acts."[46]

Given the widespread focus on the alleged crimes of black athletes within the media, from serious cases of sexual violence and intimate partner violence to the more commonplace traffic infraction and drug possession, given the ways that race shapes prosecutorial discretion,[47] given the ways that league suspensions are doled out to black athletes, and given the ways in which fans, pundits, and commentators have rallied to the defense of white athletes like Roethlisberger while convicting countless black athletes, claims that society doesn't take seriously criminal misconduct within contemporary sports might be an overstatement. Some accusations are taken seriously whereas others are not. As Jackson Katz has argued, "media coverage seems to increase when black males are alleged perpetrators."[48] According to Berry and Smith, "The truth about African American athletes' representation in crime may parallel the pattern of distorted representation of African American non-athletes in crime."[49] In other words, just as African American non-athletes become scapegoats, demonized menaces, and disproportionately imagined as dangerous criminals in society at large, black athletes function, as Herman Gray has argued, as "a site of spectacle, in which whites imagine blackness as a potential measure of evil and menace."[50] Blackness within dominant society and within the world of sports represents a sign of "social decay," disorder, and "danger";[51] whiteness is thus innocent and uncorrupted.[52] As whiteness signifies goodness, civility, and innocence within the broader culture, Ben Roethlisberger's ability to remain relatively immune from accountability, media condemnation, fan outrage, and criminal prosecution reflected the power of #PlayingWhileWhiteAndMale.

Ultimately, because of the extent of the accusations, given commissioner Roger Goodell's emphasis on "player conduct," which has been disproportionately directed at the league's black players,[53] and heightened external pressure from critics that honed in on the double standards, Goodell suspended Roethlisberger. According to Goodell, "There is nothing about your conduct in Milledgeville that can remotely be described as admirable, responsible, or consistent with either the values of the league or the expectations of our fans."[54]

As soon as Roger Goodell suspended Roethlisberger for six games (which was later reduced to four games), and as soon as he returned to the field, the discussion quickly turned to his redemption story. The silence and declarations of innocence that had preceded the resolution of the criminal justice system and the league's decision to suspend Roethlisberger for violating the league's conduct policy (not a criminal offense) were quickly replaced by narratives of change and redemption.

The ubiquitous redemption song would increase significantly once the Steelers made the Super Bowl during the 2010–2011 season. In "Winning Is Not Redemption," Lynn Zinser highlighted the cottage industry developing around Roethlisberger's redemption: "You know those national debt counters, the neon things on the sides of buildings that display a huge number that's rising really quickly? We would like to see a Ben Roethlisberger redemption counter, representing every time the word 'redemption' is mentioned in the same sentence as the Pittsburgh quarterback, and watch a huge number quickly rise. The bulbs may even short out."[55]

Rather than giving specific voice to past accusations, or his accusers, his past was often reframed as one of "mistakes," as "checkered,"[56] where "he fell short,"[57] where he "fell off," and one where "immaturity" caused problems. Roethlisberger was rarely defined by the multiple accusations of criminal activity. He had been accused of misconduct and "lambasted and despised by many for disrespecting women."[58] Within the media narrative, there was no possibility that he was a criminal, predator, or a thug; rather than framing the investigation around whether he may have broken the law, the focus remained on whether he may have made some bad decisions or broken some rules. It is no wonder that he was labeled a "work in progress,"[59] a person that had gotten into a "jam."[60]

The effort to distance Roethlisberger from the criminal justice system was part of the story of redemption. Likewise, the focus on his past "immaturity" and "youthfulness" (a twenty-eight-year-old man accused of sexual violence cashing in on the excuse of youthful indiscretion) and his growth from the experience speaks to the redemptive qualities of white masculinities. While his past "mistakes" did not define him, his growth and maturation were illustrative of the type of person he had become in just a few months. He learned and grew from the experience and became "a better person."[61]

"He's more open to a lot of guys," noted teammate Hines Ward. "For years, he only hung out with certain people. Maybe that was his defense mechanism or whatever. But he's opened himself up to everybody, playing basketball with all the rookies, hanging out with offensive and defensive players, special teams guys. Coming over, conversing. It's good to see him making a conscious effort to better himself."[62]

Similarly, Brett Keisel, then a defensive lineman with the Steelers, noted that Ben had become a better teammate and person in light of the accusations and suspension. "He has changed. I think he's slowed down a little bit. He's stepped back and put his slippers on at his house and made a nice, warm fire and just slowed down a little bit. He's turned a negative into a positive, and he's playing for his third Super Bowl, and that's great."[63] The hyper-focus on his redemption (and the erasure of any victims) is illustrative of the way that race operates. While the narrative presumed redemption to be an inalienable right for Ben, the pathway was overwhelmingly seen as one that starts and ends with winning.

According to Drew Jubera, early in the 2010 season Ben had "been called a rapist, a sexual predator, a serial idiot, and a bore." Worse, "the NFL suspended him. Eminem rapped about him ('Get as rowdy as Roethlisberger in a bathroom stall'). Even his own team's former Hall of Fame quarterback publicly dissed him." By the end of the season, the narrative and perception had changed. "Much could depend on Sunday's outcome—and if the Steelers win, the outcome of the game after that," noted Jubera. "How the still-young Roethlisberger handles even more accolades, or the criticism sure to be heaped on him if the Steelers lose, could set the tone for the rest of his career."[64]

Similarly, Adam Lazarus focused on the redemptive power in success. "In some ways, returning to the Super Bowl has helped repair his image. People can see that he is saying all the right things, but to some, no number of championships will be enough to undo his poor decisions and possibly criminal behavior. As for many 'embattled' athletes, time will help Roethlisberger make amends. For others, time isn't enough of a magic potion."[65] Indeed winning contributes to forgiveness and redemption; however, #WinningWhileWhite is priceless.

While narratives of second chances exist for the Armstrongs, Hamiltons, and Big Bens, they circulate amidst antiblack narratives that convict and accuse black players of wrong doing in a way that allows neither space for redemption nor any possibility of corrective accountability. Their indiscretions are rarely seen as mistakes, shortcomings, or transgressions. Their pasts are not afforded enough worth to win the game of redemption and second chances on the field or in the court of public opinion.

### FORGIVENESS: RILEY COOPER: A SAD TALE OF RACISM TO RICHES

The necessary ingredients for redemption—victimhood; the changed man; the crisis resulting in growth and maturation; the sense of already having lost too much; unfair persecution—were fully evident with Riley Cooper. While not accused of a crime, his violation of social protocol and etiquette (showing racism in public) led to a full-court redemptive press, further demonstrating the power in #PlayingWhileWhite and #MessingUpWhileWhite.

During a 2013 Kenny Chesney concert, then Philadelphia Eagles wide receiver Riley Cooper was caught on video using the N-word. Apparently angry at being slighted and not afforded the red-carpet treatment deserved by a mediocre NFL receiver, Cooper threatened to "fight every N-word" at the concert.[66]

The video prompted shock and surprise. Given the widespread belief in a post-racial America,[67] the sight of racial slurs, particularly from a football player who interacted with his black teammates daily, put into question the possibility of a post-racial America. Accordingly, as with Armstrong and Hamilton (and Roethlisberger, to a lesser degree), the redemption story of Riley Cooper was more about us than about him. It was about redeeming a nation, a post-racial fantasy, and the belief that sports remain an invaluable tool in fulfilling King's purported promise of a colorblind future.

At the same time, the power and appeal of the Cooper video rests with its affirmation of narratives of the "declining significance of race."[68] New racism is defined by racism seen through slurs uttered by the likes of Riley Cooper, Richie Icognito, Don Imus, and Paula Dean. In this context, racism becomes the vestige of "bad intentions, ideas, and actions anchored in malice and prejudice to express animus, foster exclusion,"[69] which doesn't define the structures and everyday interactions of America's "post-racial" twenty-first century.

With Cooper, no less, this narrative was even more prominent as racism became embodied in the actions of a drunk and angry country music fan. Rather than seeing the moment as a window into "backstage racism"[70]—the utterances, slurs, racial jokes, and other dehumanizing language that are rarely seen or heard—that has interpersonal, social, cultural, and institutional consequences, Cooper's use of the N-word was reduced to an aberration. It was neither reflective of America's possessive investment in antiblack racism nor Cooper's core character. This framing, and the corresponding necessity of imagining of Cooper's "racial faux pas" as an anomaly, made his redemption inevitable. Just as the history books imagine America's racial history as one of progress, growth, and maturation, the story of Cooper would also become one of personal and collective transformation, forgiveness, and redemption.

Not long after the video surfaced, the Eagles released a statement emphasizing the unacceptability of his behavior and the need for corrective intervention:

> Riley Cooper will be seeking counseling and we have excused him
> from all team activities. This is all new territory and we are going
> to evaluate this timetable every step of the way. He will meet with
> professionals provided by the Eagles during this period of time
> to better help him understand how his words have hurt so many,
> including his teammates.[71]

Cooper offered a similar assessment of the situation, making clear that while his actions weren't reflective of his values he would be "seeking help" to address the issue:

> The last few days have been incredibly difficult for me. My actions
> were inexcusable. The more I think about what I did, the more
> disgusted I get. I keep trying to figure out how I could have said
> something so repulsive, and what I can do to make things better.
>  Right now, I think it's important for me to take some time to
> reflect on this situation. The organization and my teammates have
> been extremely supportive, but I also realize that there are people
> who will have a tough time forgiving me for what I've done. The best
> thing for me, and for the team, is to step away for a period of time.

During this time I'm going to be speaking with a variety of professionals to help me better understand how I could have done something that was so offensive, and how I can start the healing process for everyone. As long as it takes, and whatever I have to do, I'm going to try to make this right.[72]

The emphasis on his personal transformation, on counseling, and on diversity training[73] was core to Cooper's redemption story. Beyond imagining the moment as incongruous to his true self and the values of the United States, he and others would define his behavior as a symptom of a disease that could be cured through training and counseling. His accountability plan would be neatly commodified so that what he needed to do to make amends could be done in short order. Like Armstrong, his redemption was inevitable.

By the end of the year, Cooper was both forgiven and redeemed, celebrated for his journey, perseverance, accountability, and ultimate transformation. According to Elizabeth Merrill:

> Months after he was caught on video uttering a racial slur at a Kenny Chesney concert—temporarily becoming the most hated man in the NFL—Cooper is having the best season of his career. . . . Cooper is now being called a good teammate and a catalyst for an 8-6 Eagles team on the verge of its first playoff berth in three seasons.[74]

The crisis resulting from his use of a racial epithet had made him a better football player, teammate, and person.

Redemption was possible because he made the changes he was allowed to make; redemption was also possible because he was forgiven by his black teammates.[75] At least that was the central theme of the plot of Cooper's season of redemption. What had been a difficult reminder of the unresolved racial issues facing America, would quickly become a reminder of the hope and possibility resulting from racial reconciliation and forgiveness.

Two mediocre professional seasons later, the story was still about Cooper's transformation. He had grown from the experience and become a better friend and teammate. According to Phil Sheridan, Cooper was a "good teammate, one who puts team first. A mentor to younger receivers, all of whom are black."[76]

The availability and utility of Cooper's redemption story is not surprising because it also provided an opportunity to celebrate the power of interracial cooperation. "But Cooper's story is about more than redemption. It's about a team with strong leadership," writes Merrill. "It's about forgiveness. It's about a young athlete who was seemingly born with everything waking up one day and realizing he was on the verge of winding up with nothing."[77] Focusing on Michael Vick's public acceptance of Cooper, much of the media discourse focused on how Vick, whose involvement with a dogfighting operation led to his incarceration and his place as one of the most hated athletes in modern history, facilitated Cooper's reintegration onto the team. "What if your son or daughter made a mistake of this factor? How would you want people to perceive it? I've been there before," noted Vick. "We talked about it man to man, one on one. We just know that we have to [find] some way [to] move on. It's a very delicate situation. But we all understand. Somehow we all have to find a way to get past it. That's maturity in itself."[78] If Vick could move on, and his black teammates were willing to accept Cooper after he used one of the vilest words in the English language, shouldn't the rest of us embrace the spirit of forgiveness? Vick made this clear: "Riley is still my teammate. And he just stood in front of us as a man and apologized for what he said. And somewhere deep down, you have to find some level of respect for that. Riley wished he never said it."[79]

Riley Cooper was evidence of the power of America's Huck Finn fixation. The interracial characteristics of his (our) redemptive story anchored the discourse in profound ways:

> The Huck Finn fixation articulates a fantasy of interracial male
> bonding that "wipes away any fears about tensions between black
> and white." As the name implies, it draws on the lessons learned
> from the relationship between Huck Finn and the slave Jim, in
> the Mark Twain novel. While the efforts of Huck to free Jim are
> consistent with the white man's burden, their friendship and
> adventures together illustrate the reassuring idea that blacks can
> be non-threatening friends and helpmates to whites. In fact, they
> can morally and physically save and redeem whites. Since blacks
> are the supporting players in these interracial relationships, they
> reassure whites that interracial friendships enhance rather than
> reduce white power.[80]

Cooper's redemption allowed for the celebration of interracial reconciliation, where racial conflict becomes a teachable moment that ultimately leads to growth and redemption for everyone involved, from Riley Cooper to Michael Vick.[81] Likewise, it became a moment for Michael Vick's partial redemption, where he could atone for his dogfighting sins to save his white teammate. It demonstrated American exceptionalism at its finest: social justice through conversation and apologies within commodity culture is the ultimate expression of neoliberalism. We see this with Cooper, we see it in the aftermath of a mass shooting in Charleston,[82] or in the discourse surrounding Paula Deen, Don Imus, or Michael Richards, whereupon justice and transformation are pushed aside for individual forgiveness and white redemption.

In "Eagles Forgive Riley Cooper after Racial Slur; So Should We," the authors speak about the lessons from Cooper:

> Just as the furor about the Trayvon Martin/George Zimmerman
> case began to subside, along came Riley Cooper. . . . Slavery is
> America's original sin and racism was its root. Much progress
> and reconciliation have been made, especially in recent decades.
> A family of color lives in the White House. But the poison still
> festers, until it bubbles to the surface once again. Much work still
> has to be done. Fortunately, this is a country that also was born to
> give people second chances. Forgiveness has always been one of
> its best qualities. It's one that is still desperately needed today.[83]

To redeem Cooper was to redeem white America. No wonder redemption was a guarantee. It is fundamental to playing, living, breathing while white.

At the same time, Cooper's pathway to redemption came through imagining him as a victim. He was a victim of the media, "Internet lynch mobs," and America's racial double standards. He was a victim of heightened racial tensions, as just two weeks earlier a Florida jury had acquitted George Zimmerman in the killing of Trayvon Martin. He was a victim of society's refusal to see racism experienced by whites, of political correctness run amuck. As noted by teammate Jason Avant, not only was Cooper subjected to a level of criticism never experienced by black athletes who had used the N-word or homophobic or other types of prejudicial slurs, but the racism he experienced as a white receiver was swept under the rug:

> I can tell you this, that Riley experiences more racism than any-
> body. Being a white receiver in the NFL, that's not a . . . I'm out
> there with him. For years, I've heard some ridiculous things, that
> he doesn't deserve to be out there. That's happened way before this
> incident. I don't want to say it to be a cop-out, but what I'm saying
> is that him being in the position that he's in, it happens in this
> league. So you have to have that mindset to have a merciful heart.[84]

Never mind facts, and history; Cooper was a victim. The tides had turned.

From the narrative depicting Cooper as an aggrieved white receiver to the widespread focus on double standards that allow black players to say the N-word[85] and "anti-white slurs"[86] with impunity, Cooper often became *the* victim. He was held to a standard that black athletes, who used other racial, homophobic, or sexist slurs, were not held to. According to Alan Black:

> If we as a sports culture had set a precedent for holding athletes 100 percent accountable and ostracizing them and jeopardizing their careers for making unacceptable remarks that hurt a subset of society, then the reaction to Cooper's inexcusable use of the N-word would be acceptable. That's not the road we have chosen to go, however, and we can't just suddenly switch that because it was a comment offensive to the black community instead of the Asian or LGBT+ communities.
>
> A clear precedent has been set, and holding Riley Cooper to a harsher standard because he was a white athlete dehumanizing the black community instead of a black athlete dehumanizing the Asian or LGBT+ communities is just plain wrong. Much like what Cooper did in the first place.
>
> So it's time to quit crucifying Riley Cooper at a level beyond that which we have established as the appropriate punishment for this sort of offense. It's hypocritical and unacceptable. If we continue to treat Riley Cooper disproportionately harsh, we are just dehumanizing fellow human beings ourselves.[87]

One NFL player similarly questioned the criticisms directed at Cooper given how many black players used the word:

> I know there are more than a few guys angry on my team [at what Cooper said], you would think that after all of these years people would be past this, but I wouldn't be surprised if someone acts like an idiot and takes a shot at his knees if he's on special teams. The league wants to keep a lid on this as much as possible, and hopes it goes away. The "n-word," as they like to say, is all over. I will tell you this, it's said all over—on the field, definitely in locker rooms. This is really nothing new.[88]

A victim unfairly subjected to a double standard, Cooper deserved forgiveness and redemption. He deserved a second chance. He may have made a mistake but that mistake reflected his drinking on that fateful night and his temper not his (or our) racism. More important, it was our racism, evident in the double standards and the demonization of Cooper, that deserved outrage.

The redemption story was complete as Cooper accepted responsibility. He made himself accountable. He fulfilled his responsibilities so redemption was necessary; for his sake, for our sake. This was a core message throughout the media, which ignored the most important privilege of whiteness: that he didn't need to be redeemed. He didn't need to win or be successful on the field; he didn't even need to apologize or pay penance, although all of those things would help.[89] He just needed to be white. The constant depiction of Cooper as a good guy being unfairly demonized, as a man who at worst made a bad choice because of too many beers and a bad temper, who was humble enough to apologize and make amends, whose good nature could be seen in the love from his black teammates made it so Cooper didn't need to walk the pathway toward redemption. His redemption was inevitable. #MakingMistakesWhileWhite makes that always the case.

CONCLUSION

The ubiquity of stories about redemption, of stories that seemingly celebrate misdeeds, criminal misconduct, indiscretions, poor choices, and bad behavior, tells us a lot about sports culture. It speaks to the ways that masculinity is framed through rags-to-riches, perseverance, and toughness. It speaks to the ways American exceptionalism focuses on the rugged individualism of white, heterosexual, cisgender middle-class men, and the importance of pulling oneself up by one's bootstraps even if one's fall was self-induced.

Whiteness is central to these redemptive stories. Blackness has long been imagined as inherently deviant, pathological, and incapable of prospering within a republican democracy that requires self-governance and discipline; whiteness has been framed in opposite terms. The power of white redemptive sports stories rests with legitimizing these sorts of frames, highlighting how even in error whiteness gets it right.

The dialectics between redemption and sports reflects the centrality of winning, at any and all costs, and "the victory culture"[90] that is central to American life. Writing about the redemptive song played by the media leading up to Roethlisberger's appearance in the 2011 Super Bowl, several commentators offered important critiques of the hyperfocus on winning as the tool in securing forgiveness and redemption.[91] Victory as redemption, as opposed to justice and accountability, can be seen as the ultimate expression of white American exceptionalism. In denying Roethlisberger the imagined path toward redemption, Zinser bemoans the lack of accountability or responsibility to atone:

> [Let] us pause for a moment to remember what "redeeming" actually is: atoning or making up for some mistake or wrong-doing. How exactly is winning football games making up for mistreating women (to use the mildest possible term for whatever Roethlisberger wrought on his accusers)? It's redemption only in the sports world, where athletic success magically papers over all manner of sin. Now, if Roethlisberger were to take his playoff winnings and use it to make the lives of abused women better, or to help teach young athletes to avoid his loutish ways, *that* would be redemption.[92]

Granderson similarly makes it plain:

> There are two words in the English language that the sports world just can't seem to get right. The first is "ironic," which often gets confused with "coincidental." The second is "redemption," which often gets confused with "The guy who got in trouble in the offseason is playing really well now." I don't know, maybe it's laziness, maybe it's the by-product of our decaying education system or maybe we misuse the word "redemption" because it makes us feel better about cheering for a troubled athlete. Far be it from me to play God, but it would seem the currency needed for moral restoration is not earned on an NFL field. . . . We may hear the word redemption used a lot this weekend, but it's doubtful we will see an example of it on the field. A kicker missing a crucial field goal can redeem himself in a later attempt. But the kind of personal upheaval Roethlisberger's trying to come back from? That is a process only a select few people are privy to see and, ultimately, only he will know even happened.[93]

Rightful in their exasperation, what both authors ignore is Roethlisberger's whiteness. His redemption emanates from his white-skinned pores, flowing through a narrative that has afforded him a level of innocence, righteousness, and goodness long denied to black bodies.

His story is not uncommon. While the power and possibility of redemption is most certainly connected to winning, the ability to #WinWhileWhite is central to this process. The desire to celebrate athletes, those imagined as moral and righteous, to reconcile sporting pleasures alongside of knowledge of misconduct and criminal behavior, is entrenched by whiteness.

To outrun the past requires victories; yet, to be fully redeemed, celebrated because of past indiscretions and immorality, reflects the unearned privileges resulting from white maleness. Sure, Kobe Bryant's on-the-court success, his MVP award(s) and titles, contributed to a level of redemption in the face of allegations of sexual violence in Colorado. Yet, for Bryant, despite his longstanding place as a "breath of fresh air," as someone seen as antithetical to the modern black hip-hop athlete,[94] the accusations always defined him in both the comment section and within media narratives. More revealing, while Kobe Bryant was, in many ways, able to overcome and "move past" the allegations, in an effort to reclaim his place as a transnational sporting icon, few have constructed rape allegations as transformative, as something that led to his growth and maturation.

Redemption comes through narratives that both deny accountability and allow athletes to move away from the past, but that in fact see the past as worthy of celebration. For Ben Roethlisberger, accusations of sexual violence were part of his story of growth, of why we should celebrate him (for Kobe, we are told to celebrate *in spite* of the accusation). Following the "ordeal," Big Ben was "humbled," "modest," and "matured."[95] He became "a different man when he acts respectful towards women, no longer feels he's above the law, no longer behaves as if he's superior with a powerful mind to influence weak-minded women into his abnormal trap."[96]

Similarly, for Lance Armstrong and Ryan Braun, whose PED use became a moment to not only forgive and forget but to celebrate how each grew from their difficult situations, their terrible choices led them to become better people. A similar story developed for Josh Hamilton and numerous other white athletes whose recreational drug use became evidence of their (our) illness, even as black and Latino athletes and non-athletes alike were sent to prisons.

#BeingRedeemedWhileWhite becomes a moment to celebrate the American spirit, one that not only forgives but lifts up those who have fallen. Whether lying on the ground, addicted to painkillers, lying before the nation asking for forgiveness for "being racist" or using PED, these redemptive stories encapsulate what it means to be white in America. The tumultuous past becomes reason for celebration of success, transformation, and the betterment of sports and society as a whole.

CHAPTER 7

# (WHITE) WOMEN AND SPORTS

*Selling White Femininity*

Sex sells sex, not women's sports.

—MARY JO KANE

**C**HALLENGING the idea that sex is able to sell women's sports, Mary Jo Kane argues that in selling sex, America's sports media is selling sex rather than sports.[1] It is selling white female bodies to the male heterosexual gaze. Sports may be the vehicle but sex, sexuality, and body are the commodities bought and sold within the sporting marketplace. The appeal to white heterosexual men, and their sexualized gaze, anchors the sporting marketplace.

Title IX, passed in 1972, states that "no person . . . on the basis of sex, be excluded from participation in, be denied the benefits of, or be subjected to discrimination under any educational program or activity receiving Federal financial assistance." This landmark decision opened up doors, providing women and girls with increased opportunities to participate in sports. Not only did Title IX challenge the privileges afforded boys and men in sports, it offered the hope of transforming society. If athletic doors were opened, maybe the barriers of sexism, misogyny, hyper-sexualization, and rape culture would ultimately disappear as well. Unfortunately, opportunities of participation have not produced necessary change in terms of sexism either inside or outside of sports.

More than forty years after Title IX, women athletes remain subjected to the logics of sexism. In their analysis of *Sports Illustrated* and its representation of women, Janet Fink and Linda Jean Kensicki found that over 55

159

percent of all images of "female athletes were non-action photographs" and in a "non sport setting."[2] In comparison, male athletes were found to appear in *Sports Illustrated* 65 percent of the time in "athletic action shots" (with only 25 percent of photographs being non-athletic). While "female athletes are becoming stronger, faster, and more talented," the representational field that depicts them for public consumption has languished in deleterious ways. Building on the work of Gaye Tuchman, who described the invisibility of female athletes as a form of "symbolic annihilation,"[3] Fink and Kensicki demonstrate that this treatment renders female athletes "removed from the athletic arena in which they participate."[4] This not only results in more sexualized images but also in ones that remind readers of the stable family structure where women remain as wives, mothers, and caregivers. Throughout the sports media, women athletes are routinely presented through traditional femininity, with make-up, sexualized clothing, and other exotic markers. Too often, they exist as a source of sexual pleasure for heterosexual male fans than as athletes deserving attention and celebration because of their athletic prowess, physical talents, and successes on the field.

In their recent study, Cooky, Messner, and Musto conclude that media coverage of women's sports has not increased in more than twenty-five years.[5] While the coverage has grown less wedded to hyper-sexualized images and narratives,[6] this has led to a sporting landscape that is less interested in the sports successes and athletic talents of women athletes.

Patricia Hill Collins offers equally powerful insights, arguing that contemporary sports media works "simultaneously to celebrate and 'feminize' their athleticism by showing women in action and showing their navels."[7] Reflecting on the WNBA's marketing campaign, she notes that WNBA "ads all shared another feature—unlike their basketball uniforms that provide more than adequate coverage for their breasts and buttocks, each woman was dressed in fitted sweat pants and in a form-fitting top that, for some, exposed a hint of their midriffs and an occasional navel."[8]

Despite the importance of this work, given its illustration of the entrenched patriarchy in sporting cultures and of the ways that sports reproduce hegemonic understandings of masculinity and femininity, the absence of an explicit intersectional framework (minus Collins) limits our ability to talk about progress with respect to the representation of women in sports. In other words, the ubiquity of "selling sex" within the scant "coverage" of female athletes continues to limit the options and representational possibilities for women athletes, although race and sexuality overdetermine its specific effects. The sexualization of female athletes remains part of the experience of white cisgender women athletes that fulfill certain beauty standards, while for others erasure, invisibility, and masculinized narratives remain the norm. #PlayingWhileWhite, at least when doing so includes a ponytail, large breasts, a skinny waist, and the other requisite signifiers that fulfill male heterosexual desire, provides visibility and media attention within sporting cultures.

To become a popular female athlete requires sex appeal; this sex appeal has been modeled on white, heterosexual, cisgender women so much that when black female athletes, transgender athletes, and lesbian athletes ascend into national consciousness, receiving endorsements, media coverage, and widespread opportunities, they don't do so as sexualized black female (or lesbian) athletes but rather as sexualized female athletes. In the white imagination, forms of discourse and media representation that sexualize female athletes erase race, fulfilling not only a sexual fantasy but also a post-racial one. To put it simply: to be a desirable female athlete, one must be heterosexual and "sexy," and since sexually appealing, heterosexual femininity has been defined through whiteness, those black female athletes who have been able to transcend, to cash in on their athletic talents as celebrities—like Skylar Diggins, Lolo Jones, or Candace Parker[9]—are imagined outside the margins of blackness. Of course, a corollary exists for those black female athletes who don't enter the marketplace as sexual icons, who are not sexually appealing athletes by these standards; these athletes are defined precisely by their blackness.

Given the entrenched misogyny, homophobia, and patriarchy within a sports world that "sells sex," that provides limited visibility to the handful of women athletes that legitimize these ideologies, it is hard to describe being able to "make it in the sports world," to "crossover," or to find sports celebrity a "privilege." Yet, as we look at the available representations, narratives, and media coverage we see a world in which white cisgender athletes and other athletes seen to fulfill "white beauty standards"[10] are commodified in ways not available to a majority of female athletes or even on-camera sports journalists like Erin Andrews or Lindsay Czarniak. The examples are endless: Danica Patrick (NASCAR), Maria Sharapova (tennis), Anna Kournikova (tennis), Ashley Harkleroad (tennis), Sophie Horn (golf), Natalie Gulbis (golf), Blair O'Neal (golf), Lauren Jackson (WNBA), Kayte Christensen (WNBA), Gina Carano (MMA), Ronda Rousey (UFC), Summer Sanders (swimming), Amanda Beard (swimming), Hope Solo (soccer), Alex Morgan (soccer), Julie Johnston (soccer), Jennie Finch (softball), Allison Stokke (track), Emma Coburn (track), and Lindsey Vonn (skiing). The hyperfocus on sexy, hot, and otherwise "beautiful" female athletes illustrates the ways in which sexism operates within contemporary sports media. The purportedly innocuous conversations on sports talk radio or during games, the inclusion of "Lovely Lady of the Day" on *SI*'s Extra Mustard, or the advertisements found on sports pages speak to the ways in which the sports media creates the hyper-sexualization of women and capitalizes on it.

The public recognition afforded to Lindsey Vonn, Hope Solo, Danica Patrick, and the many others listed above illustrates not just how sex and sexuality act as the primary vehicles for both the commodification and consumption of contemporary female athletes, but also the centrality of whiteness. While there are examples of black female athletes who are similarly objectified and propelled into this sexualized spotlight, they are celebrated as "exceptions." For example, Alison Glock, in *ESPN: The Magazine*'s issue dedicated to contributions of women in sports, celebrated the greatness of the WNBA's Candace Parker with a discussion of her body and her "feminine charm":

> Candace Parker is beautiful. Breathtaking, really, with flawless skin, endless legs and a C cup she is proud of but never flaunts. . . . She is a woman who plays like a man, one of the boys, if the boys had C cups and flawless skin. She's nice, too. Sweet, even. Kind to animals and children, she is the sort of woman who worries about others more than about herself, a saint in high-tops.[11]

Evident in their treatment not only of Parker but also Lolo Jones, Sydney Leroux (soccer), and Skylar Diggins, the media affords a few black women athletes the "privilege" to be both women and athletes, both physically gifted and sexually appealing, and both a "beauty and a beast." Such narratives are not available to all female athletes. Parker, Diggins, Leroux, and Jones are imagined as the exceptions for women of color, reinforcing the white-only avenue of entry for female athletes. Their embodiment of Western standards of beauty, their light skin, and their fulfillment of hegemonic ideas about the exotic help us understand their positioning within sporting cultures.

This chapter brings into focus the ways in which whiteness operates in the trafficking of sexualized female bodies. It looks at the value of whiteness and assumed heterosexuality within the sexualized world of sports. It highlights the limited opportunities and spaces afforded to white female athletes, the even fewer options available to women of color, and the exclusion forced on those seen as sexually undesirable to white heterosexual men. Reflecting on the privileging of heterosexual white male desire within the sports world, this chapter looks at beauty, white femininity, the roots of misogyny, racism, and homophobia within contemporary sports media. To be legible as a female athlete requires fulfilling hegemonic beauty standards, which is wrapped up in dominant discourses of race, sexuality, body, and gender. The visibility of white heterosexual female athletes, especially in comparison to women of color, queer athletes, and those who otherwise fail to embody the requirements of a sexualized misogynistic culture, points not only to the wages of whiteness but also to the importance of intersectional discussions.[12]

Following a discussion about the ways in which the sports media sells white, cisgender, heterosexual, white-sexualized femininity through lists, narratives, hyper-visibility, images, and everyday discourses, this chapter finishes with a discussion of the ways in which race, gender, and sexuality define the consumption of both the Williams sisters and Brittney Griner, arguing that each are seen through their blackness, which renders them as sexually unappealing, demonized athletes, and objects of hyper-surveillance. Whiteness asserts power and privilege even in the heteronormative, misogynistic, and hyper-sexualized sporting landscape.

### SHE'S HOT: ATHLETIC VISIBILITY
### AND THE POLITICS OF BREASTS

Embracing a feminist ethos and "marketability of feminism,"[13] the post-Title IX sports media has recast itself as "feminist"; simultaneously selling female athletes and challenging the ideas that women in sports are hypermasculine, unattractive, and no longer "women," sports and their media partners see their sexualized presentations as transformative. In this context, "selling sex"[14] becomes a feminist project, one that honors the desires of women like Ronda Rousey, who are "okay with being called pretty."[15] According to UFC president Dana White: "She's changing the way we look at women. And she's changing the way women look at themselves, definitely little girls. When we were growing up, you were told, 'You little girls play over here and boys play over here.' Ronda Rousey smashes that whole thing."[16] By embracing her sexuality, by getting "dolled up,"[17] Rousey and the UFC are challenging stereotypes of what it means to be a woman athlete. This marketing strategy play, which relies on her athletic talents, body, and sexuality, recasts MMA and sports as activists tearing down walls of inequality.

During a 2012 interview with Jim Rome, Rousey spoke about the purported taboo of having sex before a fight. "For girls it raises your testosterone, so I try to have as much sex as possible before I fight actually," Rousey noted. "Not with like everybody, I don't put out Craigslist ads or anything, but if I got a steady I'm going to be like, 'Yo, fight time's coming up.'" The power and privilege of her perceived whiteness (in 2016, it was reported that Rousey's great-grandfather was the first African American physician in America), of her perceived heterosexuality, and of her cisgenderness is on full display here. In this perception, her fulfillment of her heterosexual obligation and her embodiment of heterosexual fantasies makes her a great athlete. That is, she is a great fighter because she has sex. While fighting locates her beyond traditional expectations of women, her sexualized point of entry in this space and in the broader media landscape (her appearance in the film *Entourage* or any number of photo spreads) firmly places her within the parameters for heterosexual women. Rousey's marketability, her ability to cross over into Hollywood films, late-night television, and the world of advertising, reflects her ability to contribute to the "production, content and messages" that "perpetuate notions of sexual difference, gender difference, and gender hierarchy," based on the commodification of "sexuality and femininity."[18] Could we imagine the media's reaction, had this been Brittney Griner, Fallon Fox,[19] Caster Semenya,[20] or Serena Williams?

Sex isn't the only point of entry for discussing the athletic accomplishments of white women athletes. In an article in the *Sporting News* comparing Danica Patrick and Ronda Rousey, Jeff Owens and Troy Machir juxtapose terms like "media buzz," "marketing prowess," "attitude," "sex appeal," and "success." While discussing their shared successes, Owens and Machir argue that these women are defined not through their victories as much as through their transformation of their respective sports. They have broken down walls for women in sports, a narrative rarely afforded to Griner, the Williams sisters, Laila Ali, swimmers Simone Manuel or Lia Neal, and countless other athletes whose legacies are defined by both their victories and their destruction of glass ceilings.

#PlayingWhileWhite also means being celebrated for having some "attitude." Rousey has a "temper and a bit of an edge," while Patrick is "feisty" and "not afraid to stand her ground when she believes she's been wronged."[21] The dominant über-masculine ethos of MMA and NASCAR requires them to have such an attitude; to fight, to refuse to "back down" isn't simply assimilating into their sports, it is also necessary for breaking down the walls of patriarchy. Their attitudes and feistiness are also appealing because they are packaged along with their breasts and sexualized bodies.

Yet the celebration of Patrick and Rousey often comes back to their sexuality, their bodies, and their sexual appeal to heterosexual male fans. Owens and Machir compare the two stars as follows:

> Rousey has quite possibly the most unique sex appeal in all
> of sports. She is a prizefighter, perhaps the best on the
> planet. . . . Men are attracted to her because of her looks but

also because she beats up people. There is something primal about what she does, and men, whether they admit it or not, are drawn to it.

Google Patrick and you will find that she is much more than a racecar driver. She also is a model who has used her sex appeal to become a star on and off the track. . . . Though Patrick is known for her skills and success as a racecar driver, it is her looks that often garner the most attention.

As evident with Rousey and Patrick, #PlayingWhileWhite, like #Playing-WhileHeterosexual, elicits media celebration and million-dollar opportunities beyond sports, and it even buttresses narratives of progress alongside the persistent sexualization of women's bodies, the normalization of patriarchy, and the maintenance of racial hierarchies.

Online, on various sports and non-sports-related websites, the varied positioning of black and white women athletes becomes very clear. The hyper-sexualization of white women, which includes "Top 25 lists"; a fixation with their breasts, legs, and faces; sexualized advertisements; endless comments on YouTube; "Sexy Female Athletes" lists; and a myriad of other examples is comparatively different from that of black women. For example, *Men's Health* provides a list of female athletes, offering readers the opportunity to consume and "judge" the quality of beauty and sexiness of those who have "made it." Of the thirty-eight athletes listed, only four are African American, one of them being Lolo Jones, whose mixed background often results in debates about her identity and efforts to identify her as Creole, mixed, white, or otherwise not black.[22] The *Bleacher Report* published a list of fifteen women athletes. None of the featured women were black.[23] Both these lists, like so many that pollute the online sports community, do introduce readers to women athletes from a myriad of countries. The transnational exposé on the "sexy women" of tennis, golf, surfing, and skiing reveals the manner that women athletes are positioned. Also at the *Bleacher Report*, a slide show provides another list of its "25 Hottest Elite Female Athletes." Serena Williams does appear here, although the author worked hard to deny her the beauty, femininity, and sexiness afforded to the other athletes deemed worthy of inclusion:

*Sigh . . .*
I didn't want it to come to this, but after being alerted about a mistake I made about Laisa Andrioli, I am forced to put Serena Williams on here. . . .

> Personally, she isn't my cup of tea, but I do know that many
> find her stunningly attractive.
>
> So those of you who think Serena is hot, thank the a-holes on
> the internet who wrongfully claimed Andrioli was a striker for the
> Brazilian national team. And thank me for being a gullible loser
> who believes sites like these. Because now Serena is on here.[24]

Concluding that she was deserving of the supposed honor of being sexually objectified on this list, irrespective of the strange tastes of some men, the author elucidates her tennis résumé, celebrating her athleticism and further denying her access to the accepted definition of femininity and beauty. As an amazing athlete, she shouldn't be on that list.

Similarly, on another website, the inclusion of Serena Williams sparked a conversation where commenters lambasted the list's author with "Serena is a transgender:/ nasty;" "Serena looks like Patrick Ewing"; "serena? She looks like a bull!" and "Serena (and Venus) Williams look like MEN . . . at BEST!! I sometimes wonder if they've yet evolved to the Human Species." The mere sight of Serena on a list dedicated to celebrating beautiful women inspired racist and sexist rhetoric for the sake of protecting the accepted definitions of sexy and beautiful based in white supremacy.

Even ESPN, the supposed establishment sports media enterprise, provides readers with a "Hottest Female Athletes" list.[25] Revealing how mainstream the sexualization of women is within sports, this list is probably the most "diverse" list, with two out of the ten women celebrated as the "hottest" athletes being African American. This is not progress.

The hyperfocus on those female athletes seen as sexiest, hottest, and most beautiful speaks to the ways in which sexism anchors sports media. Yet, the single-minded emphasis on white women elucidates the ways in which race shapes opportunities. In many contexts, black women are seen as undesirable and incapable of fulfilling those sexualized expectations. Black women athletes are, thus, invisible within certain sporting spaces.[26] Even in a moment when the sports media landscape is dominated by ESPN (including its multiple affiliated channels) and Fox Sports, as well as channels dedicated to collegiate athletic conferences, specific sports, and countless more; even in a moment when there are a myriad of sports magazines, dozens upon dozens of websites, and a host of other forms of social media committed to reporting on and conversations about sports, there remains scant coverage afforded to female athletes. Research shows that less than 10 percent (3 to 8 percent) of sports coverage focuses on women's sports.[27] This is true for both local and national sports media. As such, female athletes are often seen within sports through a lens that sexualizes them, denying them their rightful place in the sporting landscape. Yet, this isn't the case across racial lines. While certainly not evidence of equity or justice, white women can enter into the sports world as sexual objects. For black women, acceptance, visibility, and financial remuneration prove more difficult given the ways that race privileges whiteness as sexually desirable.[28] To understand the varied realities of #PlayingWhileWhite and #PlayingWhileBlack in the context of women's sports necessitates an intersectional approach[29] that accounts for race, gender, class, and sexuality.

Women's participation within sports, a world defined by men and a narrow definition of masculinity, challenges dominant understandings of femininity. McKay and Johnson, building on the important work of Rowe,[30] conclude that female athletes by their very nature challenge hegemonic definitions of femininity. Given the ways that masculinity is defined through sports participation, physicality, and dominance, the presence and visibility of women athletes is disruptive to the established gender hierarchies within society as a whole. As participants and most certainly as sporting commodities, women athletes undermine the gendered ideas about what constitutes being "too fat, too mouthy, too old, too dirty, too pregnant, too sexual (or not sexual enough) for the norms of conventional gender representation."[31] They put into question the gendered norms that provide the foundation for misogyny and patriarchy.

Similarly, Laurie Schulze[32] concludes that the existence and sight of bulging muscles—a marker associated with authentic masculinity—on a woman's body complicates, if not disrupts, hegemonic understandings of not only femininity but masculinity as well: "The deliberately muscular woman disturbs dominant notions of sex, gender, and sexuality, and any discursive field that includes her risks opening up a site of contest and conflict, anxiety and ambiguity."[33] The potential is clear for the sight of girls and women on athletic fields and the increased visibility and popularity of women athletes to shake the stereotypes and gendered assumptions that run rampant in society. No longer would power, physical strength, muscularity, and athleticism be reserved for men. One could "play like a girl" with physical domination and muscular exertion.

While proven to be more complicated, given the ways that sexuality has defined athleticism and given sports culture's efforts to keep women in their properly sexualized place, the assumed links between masculinity and sports culture and the imagined incompatibility between heterosexual females and sports culture operates through a lens of whiteness. As desired womanhood has long been defined through whiteness, the visibility and presence of black women in a sports context did not necessarily challenge traditional gender hierarchies. Black women were already illegible as women; therefore their presence on the athletic field didn't challenge definitions of masculinity or femininity. Just as black women working in the fields or factories didn't pose a threat to gender roles, black women on the basketball and tennis courts do not necessarily pose a problem to the gendered definitions of sports. Given this history, there isn't a need to put black female athletes in their "proper place" within the "cult of domesticity," since black women were never invited to have a seat at America's patriarchal table in the first place. Within the white imagination, black women are neither seen as women nor considered worthy of protection from the purported harms of sports participation; neither worthy of celebration nor desirable as sexual objects. Sports participation isn't threatening to a gendered order defined through whiteness. While still excluded because of the history of racism, the presence of black female athletes is not necessarily jarring to hegemonic gender definitions. The place of black women as athletes is racially defined, precisely because black women historically have been denied femininity and womanhood within the white imagination.

Through slavery and Jim Crow, and into our current moment, black women have been consistently imagined as asexual and antithetical to standards of beauty within the white imagination.[34] This entrenched antiblackness shapes the sports world. As such, black women athletes are subjected to white supremacist ideologies. They exist outside the bounds of whiteness; whereas their female counterparts are seen as sexual, as desirable, and as little more than tight uniforms that expose their breasts and legs; black women athletes are illegible as the erotic and sought after female athlete. "Representations of Black women athletes in mass media also replicate and contest power relations of race, class, gender, and sexuality," writes Patricia Hill Collins in *Black Sexual Politics*. "Because aggressiveness is needed to win, Black female athletes have more leeway in reclaiming assertiveness without enduring the ridicule routinely targeted toward the bitch."[35] In denying the existence of a desired black femininity and sexuality, dominant discourses position black female athletes outside the stereotypical images that confine (white) women athletes to the playing field as hyper-sexual cisgender objects of the male gaze. Allowed to be athletes yet denied femininity or womanhood, black women are situated at the outskirts of the dominant frames and discursive articulations of female athletes. This is evident in the available representations and narratives afforded to Brittney Griner and Candace Parker, Jackie Joyner-Kersee, Taylor Townsend, and Lolo Jones. We can see this with the obstacles that the Williams sisters and Brittney Griner have been forced to navigate, with the obsession with Gabby Douglas's hair, with the ways that Florence Griffith Joyner with her long nails or Lisa Leslie and Tina Thompson with their lipstick were positioned within media coverage, and countless other black female athletes who faced the presumed contradiction between blackness and femininity, between heterosexual femininity and athletic prowess:

> The stereotype of women athletes as "manly" and as being lesbians and for Black women as being more "masculine" than White women converge to provide a very different interpretive context for Black female athletes. In essence, the same qualities that are uncritically celebrated Black male athletes can become stumbling blocks for their Black female counterparts.[36]

The dominant representations that commodify and celebrate those female athletes who embody a heterosexual beauty and appeal are otherwise unavailable to black female athletes. The characteristics that define blackness within white supremacist discourse (physicality, athletic superiority, aggressiveness, toughness, strength), that contribute to the hyper-commodification of black male bodies, limit the ability of black female athletes to fit into the category of woman athlete or the category of "hot athlete."

Against this history and the backdrop of Sharapova, Rousey, Patrick, and countless other female athletes who enter the sporting landscape as hypersexualized bodies, black female athletes must succeed in different ways. Whereas white female athletes can enter through multiple doors and multiple opportunities, black women must enter through a single door, as superstar athletes. Their ticket to stardom is not their breasts, butts, or bodies in the fulfillment of (white) male heterosexual pleasure. Success, stardom, and visibility come through ultimate success on the court, in the pool, or on the track; in fact, whereas white, heterosexual, cisgender women athletes are only legible as sex objects, women athletes of color are legible as athletes at the expense of their other identities. This defines the varied careers of Serena Williams and Maria Sharapova.

#PlayingWhileWhite means the possibility of #PlayingWhileSexy, which produces opportunities, visibility, and adoration. It is no wonder that despite Williams beating Maria Sharapova seventeen straight times, and despite Williams amassing twenty-three (and counting) Grand Slam titles to Sharapova's five, it is Maria Sharapova who has dominated the endorsement landscape. In 2015, Sharapova earned twenty-three million dollars in endorsements from Avon, Evian, Tag Heuer, Nike, Head, Porsche, and many others.[37] Serena Williams, on the other hand, took home thirteen million dollars, with Chase and Gatorade among her sponsors. Caroline Wozniacki, with zero Grand Slam titles, ranked a close third, with eleven million dollars in endorsement deals.[38] Eugenie Bouchard was named the most "marketable athlete by the British magazine *SportsPro*" in the spring of 2015.[39]

While there is a myriad of reasons that help us to understand and explain endorsement deals for Wozniacki and Bouchard, the place of Sharapova atop this list,[40] the dominance of "beautiful" white blonde women on the earnings ledger, speaks to the value of #PlayingWhileWhite, especially if one can play with blonde hair, a slender body, and heterosexual appeal. "It's not news that female athletes don't earn as much as male athletes in endorsements—even in tennis, which is otherwise the most equitable sport," writes Marc Bain in *The Atlantic*. "But another woman, Maria Sharapova, also earns significantly more, and it's likely because she's willowy, white, and blonde, while Williams is a black woman with prominent, athletic muscles—as is often pointed out, sometimes disparagingly."[41] Or as Chris Everett noted, "I think the corporate world still loves the good-looking blond girls."[42] Good-looking Blond WHITE Girls! That is: good-looking blond girls whose humanity is seen and who embody the lifestyle being sold by these corporations. "There is another, perhaps more important, discussion to be had about what it means to be chosen by global corporations. It has to do with who is worthy, who is desirable, who is associated with the good life," writes Claudia Rankine. "As long as the white imagination markets itself by equating whiteness and blondness with aspirational living, stereotypes will remain fixed in place. Even though Serena is the best, even though she wins more Slams than anyone else, she is only superficially allowed to embody that in our culture, at least the marketable one."[43]

#PlayingWhileWhite represents the American Dream; it represents idealism and the good life, providing ample marketing opportunities for white tennis players and their "beautiful" counterparts throughout the sporting landscape. The Williams sisters, on the other hand, whose careers, rags-to-riches stories, and potential marketability seem written straight out of central casting of the American Dream, are represented in distinct ways, highlighting the ways in which race, class, and gender operate intersectionally within the sexist sports media landscape.

## BLACK AIN'T BEAUTIFUL IN THE SPORTING WORLD:
## THE CASE OF THE WILLIAMS SISTERS

The Williams sisters have often been subjected to racist and sexist taunts about their bodies and looks. Compared to an idealized white femininity, the Williams sisters are consistently depicted as distinct from their white female peers. Whereas athletes like Sharapova, Rousey, Kournikova, and Patrick are represented as athletic but girly, powerful but sexy, able to exist in two worlds, the Williams sisters are seen as muscular, aggressive, and natural athletes—in other words, as men, sexually undesirable, and antithetical to a certain feminine ideal.[44] Throughout their careers, Serena and Venus Williams have not only had to deal with the race and class dynamics of tennis, but with a hegemonic ethos and ideology that positions them as antithetical to beauty, desirability, and the American Dream. "Imagine that you have to contend with critiques of your body that perpetuate racist notions that black women are hypermasculine and unattractive. Imagine being asked to comment at a news conference before a tournament because the president of the Russian Tennis Federation, Shamil Tarpischev, has described you and your sister as 'brothers' who are 'scary' to look at. Imagine."[45] As femininity is imagined through sexuality, sexual desirability, and beauty—all of which are located in proximity to whiteness—the Williams sisters are denied womanhood and humanity: "The embodiment of preferred femininity in U.S. culture, Kournikova has publicly derided the physiques of the Williams sisters," writes Jamie Schultz.[46] Remarking on the ways in which Kournikova juxtaposes herself against the Williams sisters, Schultz illustrates how whiteness and blackness, femininity and masculinity, heterosexuality and asexuality operate as binaries within the sports world. Kournikova defines feminity through her body and looks: "I hate my muscles. I'm not Venus Williams. I'm not Serena Williams. I'm feminine. I don't want to look like they do. I'm not masculine like they are."[47]

Throughout her career, Serena's body has faced hyper-surveillance. Jason Whitlock once referred to her as an "unsightly layer of thick, muscled blubber, a byproduct of her unwillingness to commit to a training regimen and diet that would have her at the top of her game year-round."[48] The constant references to her body, weight, and specific body parts, along with references to her being manly and muscular, speak to not only the larger history of black women athletes but the ways that black women have been subjected to a regime of racial and sexualized violence throughout history. The focus on her physicality, strength, and power,[49] as opposed to her intelligence, hard work, or talents as a tactician of the game demonstrates the bifurcated narrative between white and black women athletes. "Black bodies have long been objects of scrutiny, the recipients of inordinate attention and discussion for over a century. Black bodies were seen as the site and source of black pathology, as boundaries against which one could determine acceptable sexuality, femininity and morality (Giddings 1984; Gilman 1984)," writes Delia D. Douglas "Historically, white supremacist racial logic has long relied on 'the use of a dichotomous code that creates a chain of correspondences both between the physical and the cultural, and between intellectual and cognitive characteristics' (Hall 1997). In this context, blacks were understood as more body than mind."[50]

As many female athletes are generally defined through their perceived beauty and sexual appeal, both of which are imagined through a white (heterosexual) prism, Serena Williams and Venus Williams, as well as other women such as Simone Biles, Jackie Joyner-Kersee, Ibtihaj Muhammad, Gabby Douglas, and Simone Manuel are positioned in alternative spaces, denied a certain level of visibility and acceptance that is otherwise offered to white women who are able to fulfill a particular role in sexist sports culture:

> The dominant male, white culture drew a direct correspondence between stereotyped depictions of black womanhood and "manly" athletic and physically gifted females. Their racialized notions of the virile or mannish black female athlete stemmed from a number of persistent historical myths: the linking of African American women's work history as slaves, their supposedly "natural" brute strength and endurance inherited from their African origins, and the notion that vigorous or competitive sport masculinized women physically and sexually.[51]

Efforts to compare the Williams sisters to their black male counterparts rather than to their white female peers are visible throughout their careers. In fact, much of the demonization and mocking of the Williams sisters emanates from (a)sexualizing tropes that deny them access to acceptable feminine identities and commodification within sports. Jim Rome historically referred to them as "Predator 1 and Predator 2."[52] Likewise, Ben Rothenberg imagined Serena as distinct from her peers because of her body. "Williams, who will be vying for the Wimbledon title against Garbiñe Muguruza on Saturday, has large biceps and a mold-breaking muscular frame, which packs the power and athleticism that have dominated women's tennis for years," he wrote in "Tennis's Top Women Balance Body Image with Ambition." "Her rivals could try to emulate her physique, but most of them choose not to."[53] Similarly, Sid Rosenberg, a longtime sports commentator who in 2001 joined the Don Imus Show, which will be discussed further below, announced during one segment his disdain for the Williams sisters because of their looks. "I can't even watch them play anymore. I find it disgusting. I find both of those, what do you want to call them—they're just too muscular. They're boys."[54] He also argued that it would be more appropriate for the Williams sisters to appear in *National Geographic* than in *Playboy*.[55]

As evidenced in this history, within the white imagination the Williams sisters (and countless other athletes) are seen as black athletes first and foremost. Their blackness, which signifies strength, raw athleticism, physical bodies, fearlessness, a lack of vulnerability, and masculinity sets them apart from their athletic sisters. As such, as sports continue to be for and about male accomplishment, black women athletes remain at the periphery of sports and women's sports.

The burden is felt at the other end of the spectrum as well. After Serena Williams appeared on the cover of *Sports Illustrated* as "sportsperson of the year," she faced ample criticism for perpetuating the sexualized image faced by women athletes. Mansplainer of the year, Rick Morrissey, in "Serena Williams Doesn't Help Female Athletes with Racy *SI* Cover Shoot," wrote:

> In the photo, she's wearing a black, lacy, leotard-like outfit,
> legs draped suggestively over a golden chair. It in no way helps
> the cause of women looking to be recognized for their athletic
> abilities. . . . It objectifies women. Her intent won't line up with
> the reception, which will be a bunch of men leering at her the way
> they do at every *SI* swimsuit model. She might be selling power,
> but they're buying sex.

Beyond his focus on Serena and making it all about her choices, Morrissey not only ignores the structural constraints faced by all women athletes but also erases the ways that black women athletes have been treated differently from their peers. While making a very different intervention, Elizabeth Daniels, Mary Jo Kane, Cheryl Cooky, and Nicole M LaVoi, in "*SI* Sportsperson of the Year Cover Image of Serena Williams: Opportunity Missed," similarly fail to account for the ways in which black women athletes have never been afforded the opportunity to be sexualized like Sharapova or Patrick:

> In spite of Williams's unprecedented accomplishments as argu-
> ably the greatest female tennis player in U.S. history, she was
> featured on the cover in a sexually provocative pose. . . . The

choice to feature Williams dressed in an all-black lace bodysuit and patent leather power pumps perched on a throne as Queen of the Court has been supported by some who see this portrayal as empowering.

Given the refusal to see Serena (and Venus) Williams as a female athlete and a sexual being, and given the context of ongoing history, the image is particularly powerful. It works against the representations and narratives that are afforded to black women inside and outside the sports world.

Sports culture is one that normalizes whiteness within (and beyond) the arena. It is also an institution that normalizes masculinity and heterosexuality, both privileging and defining certain ways of being a heterosexual male. Women athletes must contend with this space. Yet, black and white women athletes enter into this space in very different ways. #PlayingWhile White&Female allows for and requires different sorts of positioning; whiteness and heterosexuality afford different types of intervention against the hyper-sexualized woman athlete. For the Williams sisters, and so many other black women athletes, including Brittney Griner, the game is different.

## GRINER: CHANGING THE GAME

Brittney Griner
Average 22.7 points/game
Sixty percent from field and over 80 percent from the line
Almost 10 rebounds each night
Record 155 blocks after 30 games in season
Team undefeated and ranked No. 1
Outscore opponents by 30+ points/game

With numbers like this—and the level of dominance seen throughout her college career—you would have thought that she would be the talk of the town, with magazine covers, lengthy biographic pieces on ESPN, and endless celebrations of her achievements. However, these numbers and her successes never translated into "Britsanity," a fact that reflects the power of race, gender, and sexuality within sports culture.

Unable to transform the available narrative, and in spite of her amazing (revolutionizing) collegiate play, Brittney Griner remained an afterthought within the basketball world. Unable to embody traditional feminine beauty and its aesthetic, yet able to fulfill the stereotypes usually afforded to black male ballers—a fact even more visible after Griner was arrested on domestic violence charges[56] after turning professional—the national imagination had little use for Griner.

Compared with Brittney Griner, Hope Solo, who is also an exceptional athlete who has faced an arrest, has cashed in on the power of cisgenderness, heterosexuality, and whiteness. Even in difficulty, she was able to take advantage of how she fulfilled hegemonic beauty standards. Amid the news coverage of Solo and Griner's arrests for domestic violence, three distinct narratives emerged. First, among the numerous articles on Griner's arrest, many featured her mug shot (and that of her partner, Gloria Johnson). In contrast, Hope Solo is presented through on-the-field images. Thus, Griner is imagined exclusively through her criminalized black body; Solo's desirability as a sexualized subject is confirmed, whereas Griner's pathology and undesirability is made visible over and over again. Second, only a few articles provided a backstory for Griner, instead focusing exclusively on her arrest. The little backstory provided often referenced a past incident in which she punched a player. In Solo's case, the backstory was central, often highlighting her childhood difficulties or her "tumultuous" relationship with Jeremy Stevens, who had been previously arrested on charges of domestic violence against Solo. In many regards, she was presented as a victim whereas Griner was a perpetrator of violence. Third, the media constructed Griner's pathway toward redemption and forgiveness as narrow at best, whereas Solo's was almost inevitable.

The sports media's positioning of Brittney Griner as a criminal, as a threat, and as the fulfillment of fears about what happens when women play sports is further enhanced by the lack of coverage that was afforded to her before and after this arrest. Whereas the discourse from Parker and Skylar Diggins, from Alex Morgan and Solo, consistently reminds fans that in spite of their athletic excellence they still are able to be beautiful women, sexual objects, mothers, and wives, Griner doesn't offer anything in this regard. This narrative, while bubbling to the surface in the aftermath of her arrest, was nothing new, demonstrating the ways that Griner's inability to fit the accepted female athlete identity precluded her rightful place as one of the nation's great athletes.

Throughout her career, Griner's greatness has been relatively invisible, because she simultaneously fits and repels our expectations about female athletes. When still in high school, Griner emerged on the national scene. Early media narratives were not limited to her game: they positioned her as a player who was challenging the expectations of both female and black athletes. Unlike the vast majority of celebrated female athletes, she was, according to this narrative, a less feminine, "androgynous female" who challenged the "rigidity of sex roles."[57] Often comparing her to males, these media narratives consistently imagined her as a "freak"[58] and an aberration, contributing to a story of shock, amazement, and wonderment that Griner was indeed a woman. According to Lyndsey D'Arcangelo, "The world of women's basketball has never seen a player like this before. Griner has the athletic skills and build of any budding male college basketball star, which has brought her 'gender' into question."[59]

In "Brittney Griner, Basketball Star, Helps Redefine Beauty," Guy Trebay highlights the ways in which she was seen, not as a baller or student athlete but instead as a gender and sexuality counternarrative:

> Feminine beauty ideals have shifted with amazing velocity over the last several decades, in no realm more starkly than sports. Muscular athleticism of a sort that once raised eyebrows is now commonplace. Partly this can be credited to the presence on the sports scene of Amazonian wonders like the Williams sisters, statuesque goddesses like Maria Sharapova, Misty May Treanor and Kerri Walsh, sinewy running machines like Paula Radcliffe or thick-thighed soccer dynamos like Mia Hamm.

While celebrating the potential in her offering an alternative feminine and aesthetic, the emergent storyline put her into the box limited to (black) female athletes—she was confined by the stereotype of women athletes. Focusing on her body image, her sartorial choices, and her swagger and how each meshed with beauty standards, all while defining her "as a tomboy," the public inscription of Griner did not challenge the conventional image of female athletes. At one level, it defined her as the exception, thereby reinforcing ideals of femininity. At another level, it refused to see her, as a tatted black woman with dreads, as representative of a paradigm shift for women athletes.

Thus, claims of a sea change were unfulfilled. The scant national attention afforded to Griner when she led her Baylor squad (not a national powerhouse) to a national championship and during her pro career reflected the profound ways in which her emergence did not usher in a new moment for women's sports. Unable to appeal to male viewers, to fulfill the expectations of femininity and sexuality, Griner remained outside the already illusive coverage of women's sports.

Griner did not fulfill the eroticized prerequisites for female athletes in the white male heterosexual imagination. Only those who are #PlayingWhileWhite can capitalize on the misogyny and heteronormativity ubiquitous to sports culture. One has to look no further than YouTube comments to see the interconnection between the perceived masculinity of Griner, the lack of desire for her as a sexual object, and her erasure from the sporting landscape. Unable to fulfill the expected role prescribed for female athletes within US sports culture, Brittney Griner is either dismissed as a "male" or a "freak," or she is used to normalize the Anna Kournikovas, Allison Stokkes, and Candace Parkers of the world—women who fulfill male expectations.

Reflecting the values of our heteronormative patriarchal society, female athletes who appear on ESPN and *Girls Gone Wild* are those who win sports titles *and* wet t-shirt contests. Griner lacks access to the whiteness and heterosexuality necessary to receive accolades and celebration from gawking fans and media interlocutors. Notwithstanding the initial efforts to elevate Griner to the status of "game changer," as someone who would redefine gendered expectations of sports, her outsider status highlights the difficulty of such a process.

Griner's inability to cross over, to secure mass appeal, wasn't purely about gender and sexuality or the predominant expectations of female athletes; it was also about the ways in which her blackness profiled her in profound ways. Described as tough, masculine, and physical, much of which comes from a 2010 incident in which she hit an opponent, Griner has faced the burden of race, gender, and sexuality. Able to dunk and brawl, rocking braids and tattoos, Griner exists in greater proximity to the black male athlete than to her white female counterparts. Her point of entry is through her physicality, athleticism, and "freakish" body as opposed to her breasts, butt, and beauty.

Her place at the periphery of male and female sports coverage fits within a larger history of sports media that speaks to the ways in which race and gender infect the experiences of athletes. The efforts to describe, contain, and represent Griner through both racial and gendered language is illustrative of a larger history of black female athletes. Those who are able to fulfill the expectations of the dominant white imagination regarding female athletes enter into the public sphere as sexual objects, while athletes like Griner, who don't embody the sexualized aesthetics of white male pleasure, find themselves on the outside looking in at the few opportunities afforded to female athletes. It is no wonder that she never galvanized the nation, even when her game merited widespread attention from men and sponsors alike. Brittney Griner has game but not the *right body*. #PlayingWhiteWhite, even in the most messed up game, is to play with the *right body*.


CONCLUSION

On April 4, 2007, following a hotly contested championship game between Rutgers and the University of Tennessee, Don Imus turned his attention to sports, using the previous day's event not only to mock the Rutgers squad and women's basketball as a whole, but to recycle longstanding images and tropes that often deny womanhood to black women:[60]

> IMUS: So, I watched the basketball game last night between—
> a little bit of Rutgers and Tennessee, the women's final.
> ROSENBERG: Yeah, Tennessee won last night—seventh championship for [Tennessee coach] Pat Summitt, I-Man. They beat Rutgers by 13 points.
> IMUS: That's some rough girls from Rutgers. Man, they got tattoos and—
> MCGUIRK: Some hard-core hos.
> IMUS: That's some nappy-headed hos there. I'm gonna tell you that now, man, that's some—woo. And the girls from Tennessee, they all look cute, you know, so, like—kinda like—I don't know.[61]

Given the treatment of the Williams sisters and other black athletes through history, Imus's reference to these student athletes as "nappy-headed hos" should spark little surprise. #PlayingWhileWhite means being immune to such venom. And while being a female athlete produces a barrage of sexism and misogyny, the experiences of black women athletes, whether looking on the court, online, or in the media, remain distinct. The antiblack demonization and disparagement of the women of Rutgers in racial terms demonstrates the unique treatment faced by black women athletes. Imus and his cast of characters did not target the women of the University of Connecticut, which because of its demographics, its geographic location, history, and its place within the national imagination reads as white. The pairing of "nappy-headed" and "ho" speaks to the unique experiences of black female athletes.

"Thus, the negotiation of the contradictions in women's sport participation differs qualitatively for African-American female athletes given the ways in which African-American women have long been portrayed in the media, and specifically sports media, as both hyper-sexualized and less feminine," write Faye Wachs, Cheryl Cooky, Michael Messner and Shari Dworkin. "As a result, African-American female athletes are subject to particular 'controlling images' in the media."[62] From the Williams sisters to Simone Manuel, from countless black women in the WNBA to Gabby Douglas, black women athletes confront the sexist demands that women athletes be sexual, that they satiate heterosexual male desires, and that they meet a particular standard of beauty. Yet, they must confront a reality whereupon the definitions of beauty and the standards of sexual desire so often exclude black women.

The "controlling images"[63] governing black female bodies shape which doors are available and open. The crossroads of antiblackness, misogyny, and heteronormativity not only defines their experiences but constrains opportunities. Melissa Harris-Perry, in *Sister Citizen: Shame, Stereotypes, and Black Women in America*, makes this clear, arguing that, "the internal, psychological, emotional and personal experiences of black women are inherently political." She goes on to write: "They are political because black women in America have always had to wrestle with the derogatory assumptions about their character and identity. These assumptions shape the social world that black women must accommodate or resist in an effort to preserve their authentic selves and to secure recognition as citizens."

Writing about Serena Williams, Claudia Rankine chronicles the burdens that Serena Williams (and countless others) carry on and off the court.[64] In addition to the racism and sexism they feel in both virtual spaces and everyday realities (resulting from both systemic racism and divestment from black communities) and the overt hyper-sexualization and denial of sexuality afforded to black women, "The daily grind of being rendered invisible, or being attacked, whether physically or verbally, for being visible" is taxing. Serena is never able to be herself. She is always signifying, representing, and otherwise embodying not only the hopes and dreams of the black community but also the fears, anxieties, and hatred of white America. Brittney Griner is always representing; Venus, Sloane Stephens, Lia Neal, Simone Manuel, Allyson Felix, Ibtihaj Muhammad, Flo Jo, Jackie Joyner-Kersee, and countless others are always embodying, signifying black femininity and what that means in a racially segregated America. "She understands that even when she's focused only on winning, she is still representing. 'I play for me,' Serena told me, 'but I also play and represent something much greater than me. I embrace that. I love that. I want that.'"[65]

This is also the story of #PlayingWhileWomen—white men are unburdened with the responsibilities of breaking down doors, of empowering all boys, and otherwise reimaging what it means to be a man. Yet, for white women athletes the power and privileges are never left too far behind either, for in the world of sports white women reinforce narratives of masculinity and femininity, heterosexuality, and patriarchy, all while reaffirming what whiteness means on and off the court: to be desirable, to be celebrated, to be innocent, to be the norm, and to otherwise be sought after is to be white.

# CHAPTER 8

# DRIVING WHILE WHITE

*NASCAR and the Politics of Race*

D ESPITE its embrace of multiculturalism and diversity, NASCAR remains overwhelmingly white and male; its aesthetics, culture and practices are not only tied to a particular set of reactionary politics but also contingent upon the embrace and privileges of whiteness. This chapter focuses on the white world of NASCAR, reflecting on its history and culture of segregation; it looks at NASCAR's resistance to diversity initiatives and a culture that prides itself on being inhospitable to drivers and fans of color.

In looking at the whiteness of NASCAR, we also see how whiteness becomes a source of benevolence and progress rather than a signifier of dysfunction, pathology, violence, and segregation. Whiteness is what is changing NASCAR, leading to cultural shifts, which in the end not only combats Southern racism but also facilitates opportunities for black drivers. Whiteness, therefore, becomes the source of the change. In this context, whiteness allows NASCAR to define its narrative, to define its history, and to deny its racism except when citing change and progress.

At the same time, the hegemony of NASCAR's whiteness not only results in a nod to racism whether in the Confederate flag, its white work force, or the spews of racism found at events[1] or in creating a sporting environment that tolerates, if not celebrates, its lack of diversity. "As much as any sport in America, NASCAR has roots tied to a certain culture: white Southerners."[2] As noted by Josh Newman and Michael Giardina, NASCAR is made important, and simultaneously problematic, by its Southern dialects and dialectics."[3] This whiteness (and its related class and geographic identities) finds its appeal in both nostalgia and white supremacist ideologies. It also becomes valuable because in whiteness NASCAR can embrace its trash-talking, drunkenness, violence, sexism, and criminality.

The dominance of those #DrivingWhileWhite allows NASCAR to embrace a countercultural identity, an outlaw ethos without ideological or material consequence. It allows it to perform diversity even while appealing to its roots in whiteness.

This chapter takes up these issues, highlighting the ways that race—both profiles and privilege—operate within the white yet colorblind world of NASCAR. It concludes with a speculative critical race-theory-inspired allegory entitled "What If NASCAR Was Black?"—in which I argue that the resistance to diversity within NASCAR and the protection and exoneration of whiteness reflect not only the power of white sporting identities, but also the yearning for transgressive, violent, and conservative political sporting identities, as long as they come through a white body within a white sport.

### DIVERSITY IN NASCAR?

In NASCAR's sixty-plus year history, only six African American drivers have started a race. Since 1986, only one African American driver—Bill Lester—has taken the green flag.[4] NASCAR's "diversity problem" is "exemplified by the significant overrepresentation of white fans in the grandstands, white drivers in the cars, white owners in the luxury boxes, and white administrators at NASCAR's corporate luxury boxes and white administrators at NASCAR's corporate headquarters."[5]

In 1999, Jesse Jackson raised the stakes on a segregated NASCAR, shining a spotlight on the whiteness of NASCAR. He questioned the lack of diversity in America's premiere motor sport as not happenstance but reflective of a discriminatory culture: "The fact of the matter is there is frustration because of exclusion. We must now turn that pain to power. We were qualified to play baseball before 1947. We are qualified to race cars now."[6] Four years later, Jackson described NASCAR as "the last bastion of white supremacy" in sports.[7] Charles S. Farrell, then director of Jackson's Manhattan-based Rainbow Sports, similarly spoke of an entrenched culture of racism that limited opportunities for African Americans. "No one has physically come up and said, 'You're black. You cannot race.' But the lack of sponsorship is tantamount to saying, 'No, you cannot race in NASCAR.'"[8] Despite increased media attention and organizing efforts, NASCAR remained a white world. It had a racism problem and recognized the lack of diversity part of it.

Despite outrage from its fans and conservative media, who saw such protests as more evidence of anti-white affirmative action and political correctness,[9] NASCAR partnered with Jackson's Rainbow/Push organization to develop diversity programs to usher in change.

In 2000, it formed the NASCAR Diversity Council, which worked along-side other motor sports organizations to change the racial demographics of racing. By 2004, NASCAR also had created the Executive Committee for Diversity. Co-chaired by Earvin "Magic" Johnson, the Committee for Diversity introduced several initiatives, including scholarship, internship, and "Drive for Diversity" programs, all of which were organized to "develop diverse and female drivers and crew members."[10] The Committee for Diversity also focused on changing the perception of NASCAR, spotlighting its commitment to greater diversity on the track and in the stands. Diversity was said to be part of its mission and vision:

> NASCAR is committed to making our sport—on and off the race-track—look more like America. No other issue is more important for NASCAR to succeed and to grow. NASCAR's role in diversi-fying the sport is to take steps to better educate new fans about NASCAR; to provide meaningful opportunities; and to facilitate greater participation within the industry.
>
> In order to better educate new fans about the sport, NASCAR has developed and is supporting several important initiatives that encourage diversity throughout the industry.[11]

These efforts prompted widespread outrage. Critics were quick to criticize Jackson for his "race hustle" and for the mere accusation of racism within NASCAR. Citing double standards, a betrayal of tradition, and disrespect toward its Southern roots, all while embracing narratives of colorblindness and post-raciality, critiques of Jackson often came in the form of an ardent defense of NASCAR as a sport where race didn't matter. "As a devoted fan of NASCAR, I am troubled by Jesse Jackson's latest exploits," noted Reginald Jones, a member of the black conservative organization Project 21. "I never once have paused to consider the racial make-up of the drivers or other fans. Like white fans of the NBA, racial proportions are irrelevant to me. NASCAR is a juicy target because of its Southern heritage and vast financial resources. Fans should be outraged by NASCAR's cowardice in the face of Jackson's latest hustle. People like me who have supported the sport do not appreciate our money going to him."[12] Similarly, Deroy Murdock used the opportunity not only to celebrate NASCAR as free from racial animus but also to deploy false equivalences and explanations that seemingly rational-ized the absence of black drivers:

What NASCAR should explain and Jackson will not admit is that some avocations skew black while others lean white. Gospel choirs rarely feature white singers. In turn, symphony orchestras do not exactly overflow with black cellists. If an overwhelmingly white fan base signifies bigotry, the (integrated) Allman Brothers owe blacks an apology. Conversely, the entire rap industry (except for Academy Award winner Eminem) should beg whites' forgiveness. More than anything else, these racial imbalances reflect diverse cultural tastes rather than prejudice. Besides, why is Jackson so worried about the racial make-up of auto racing? If tomorrow 13 percent of NASCAR's drivers woke up black (proportionate to America's black population), how would that help students at Washington, D.C.'s Anacostia High School, where 71 percent scored below basic in reading last year, and 92 percent similarly botched math? How would a corporate NASCAR sponsorship help rural blacks improve dreadful health conditions?[13]

#DrivingWhileWhite wasn't merely the ticket to corporate sponsorship, Confederate-flag-waving fan support, and opportunities to race each week; it was also the privilege to see one's opportunities and success as the result of hard work, talent, and dedication to skill. With #DrivingWhileWhite comes the belief in meritocracy and a level playing field: a racetrack without racially-determined or gendered obstacles. In 2014, Danica Patrick lamented diversity programs within NASCAR, calling them unnecessary given her success. She noted, "I have never benefited from the Diversity program. Well, clearly then I wouldn't think that there needs to be a diversity program if I'm here and I didn't get in. It wasn't like they asked me to be in it. They didn't give my team or me any money. They didn't say we'd love you . . . you know? So I would say that you have to just make it. And I'm not saying I'm here, just like, I'm not saying that being a girl hasn't helped, but I didn't need a program to make it happen."[14] This ethos that results in seeing the whiteness of NASCAR as organic and natural reflects not only white privilege but also a belief in meritocracy and inherent white excellence.

This part of the discourse embraced the myth of meritocracy and other narratives that see the intrusion of those who couldn't succeed on their own as discriminatory and unfair. White privilege is white drivers claiming the checkered flag because of their talent and doing things the right way even as drivers of color lack the same opportunities.[15] White privilege is claiming that the lack of diversity is the result of different choices and types of talent.

#DrivingWhileWhite is driving on what appears to be flat road; it is driving with a mirror that distorts and obscures the many obstacles that have insured the continued dominance of white drivers in NASCAR, whereupon diversity efforts are imagined as an assault on white drivers, fairness, and the traditions of NASCAR. It is denying a history of individual and systemic racism. It is ignoring the history of NASCAR as a "Southern, white sport" that "has integrated slower than any other major American sport after decades of racism and discrimination."[16] It is questioning the need for change, citing the beauty and greatness of previous generations even as white male drivers dominated the sport, because of their talents. Reflecting this entrenched white privilege and the power of nostalgia (Keeping NASCAR Great), the reactionary voices were loud.

NASCAR, more concerned about corporate sponsors, waning fan interest, and demographic shifts, pushed forward with its "diversity plans" with minimal success. Through the 2000s, NASCAR maintained its efforts to increase the number of black drivers. Yet, not wanting to alienate fans and corporate sponsors, it resisted any push to address racism in the stands, in the press box, and on the track. Few efforts were made to address a culture that empowered and privileged a particular type of white masculinity. NASCAR was no Martin Luther King Jr. or even Branch Rickey. Diversity efforts were about profitability and long-term viability in the sports-media marketplace (almost 10 percent—six million—NASCAR fans are African American). The focus on the goals of diversity and increasing the number of African American drivers, as opposed to transforming the culture and climate, reflect these motives and NASCAR's refusal to kowtow to some of its fans and conservative/white nationalist critics.

In 2004, NASCAR also hired Access Marketing and Communications with the sole purpose of operating a program that will "conduct a combine for minority drivers to showcase their skills for team owners in NASCAR's weekly racing series."[17] Operating from the pretense that the only obstacle to a more diverse NASCAR was "exposure," the showcase would introduce NASCAR teams to these potential drivers. To further incentivize teams to embrace their efforts, Access would provide each team with $150,000 to offset costs.

For many in NASCAR, cost represented one of the biggest obstacles to a more diverse sport. According to Joe Gibbs, NASCAR had struggled "because of the barriers" that result from the cost of participation.[18] Similarly, former NBA player, NASCAR team owner, and ESPN commentator Brad Daugherty identified "the clear-cut color barrier in NASCAR as 'not black or white' but 'green.'" For him and so many others, it is simply about access, and that has everything to do with both class and the cowardice of corporate America: "They've never been standing and guarding the gates from anyone of color coming in and participating. It's all about corporate dollars. If you don't have corporate partners, I don't care who you are, you're not going to participate in this sport. It's just not going to happen."[19]

Invoking how Bubba Wallace's family spent "$1 million plus," and was forced to move around,[20] the diversity narrative around NASCAR consistently focuses on a sport that isn't accessible to the vast majority of African Americans. While recognizing the immense financial costs of race-car driving, the focus on these purportedly colorblind barriers further elides the ways in which the whiteness of NASCAR exists as a substantial obstacle to diversity. Seemingly erasing the black middle-class and class prohibitions that exist within other communities, the emphasis on opportunity and financial barriers furthered the shift toward the normalized whiteness of sports.

The third commonplace explanation for NASCAR's behavior identifies the lack of role models as the reason for the lack of drivers. That the absence of black and Latino drivers leads youth to other sports, to dream of becoming the next Tiger Woods or LeBron James or NFL star rather than a race-car driver.[21] According to Maurice Bobb, "There are no black superheroes in NASCAR. There's no Tiger Woods or Ray Lewis or LeBron James strapped in Legends and Bandolero cars rollin' with the winners at your local Speedway."[22] For others, it is about making NASCAR cool and showing black success on the track:

> [Darrell] Wallace Jr., a confident 19-year-old from Alabama,
> knows the best way to create opportunities for other minority
> drivers is to win. NASCAR hasn't had a black driver who could be
> a role model for aspiring athletes, like Tiger Woods in golf.
>    "(Young African Americans) want to see who they can be like,"
> Wallace said. "They look at NASCAR, (and) is there anybody
> there? No."[23]

With visibility, access, and lack of role models anchoring the discourses surrounding the persistent whiteness of NASCAR, it is no wonder that the organization's diversity efforts have worked through the framework of Drive for Diversity. The focus on exposure, financial obstacles, role models, and NASCAR's limited popularity within the black community put the burden of change on the black community, seemingly blaming them for the persistence of Jim Crow within the sport. After all, NASCAR should have known it had a problem with racism in its ranks, as evidenced by several lawsuits.

David Scott, a former motor-coach driver, filed a lawsuit following an incident in 1999. During a race, two white crewmembers from another team allegedly confronted Scott, wearing white pillowcases (Klan costumes) while using the N-word. While the case was settled several years later, it highlights the racial climate plaguing NASCAR. In 2008, Mauricia Grant, a black woman who worked as a technical inspector in the Nationwide Series, filed a lawsuit alleging racial and sexual harassment, accusing "two NASCAR officials, Tim Knox and Bud Moore, of exposing themselves" and others of calling her "Nappy Headed Mo" and "Queen Sheba."[24] Despite their history and purported diversity efforts, NASCAR officials went on the offensive, blaming Grant while at the same time attacking her for being audacious enough to accuse NASCAR of racism.

With the lawsuits and increased media spotlight, not to mention sports leagues across the nation (and even globally) capitalizing on diversity as a powerful commodity in the face of waning fan interest,[25] NASCAR in 2008 changed its diversity course.

Without much success, NASCAR ended its attempts at outsourcing diversity efforts and hired Max Siegel, former president of Dale Earnhardt Inc., to take over its program to diversify the NASCAR ranks. Siegel, rather than encouraging other teams to add single drivers, took a different approach: he started his own team, Revolution Racing, which would bring together drivers of color in "an academy-like setting."[26] Siegel also maintained the original model of single-driver recruitment and breaking down boundaries between drivers and sponsors. Each year, fewer than ten drivers from underrepresented groups are invited to a combine, in which they go through a series of tests—driving, physical fitness, media readiness, and communication—to determine readiness for the NASCAR circuit. According to Paulie Harraka, a one-time NASCAR driver and participant in the Drive for Diversity Program, "The diversity program creates an opportunity to climb that ladder. It increases the likelihood. That's how I ran the Late Model (weekly) series and the West Series and got here. I wouldn't be here without that program, but it still takes a lot of work, a lot of luck."[27] In eight years, forty drivers have participated in the program.

Some critics have lamented the lack of success with their diversity programs as a consequence of the failure of drivers of color to win. Attracting black fans and prime future racers required a black driver who could cross over into the mainstream. To do that, he (or she) needed to win. The failures were, thus, not on NASCAR shoulders but instead on those black drivers who failed to deliver even with opportunity.

Other critics of the program agreed that visibility and lack of opportunity posed significant obstacles, given the ways in which old (white) boy's networks had operated within NASCAR, the program did little to address the racial politics surrounding corporate sponsorship or extend its efforts beyond neoliberal capitalism.[28] Because of the program's reliance on corporate sponsors, who have shown an unwillingness to invest in drivers of color, the problem wasn't with NASCAR. "(Companies think) why support somebody who might have 10 percent, 20 percent or 30 percent of the audience behind you when you can support somebody else that will have everybody behind you," noted Mike Vasquez, a NASCAR insider. "That's been the stigma on NASCAR in the eyes of corporate America that really is not there. The fans love everybody who races. The fans don't look at the color of your skin as much as the speed of your race car."[29] Similarly, Dylan Smith told CNN:

> There are people of different ethnicities in NASCAR, you just
> don't see them at the forefront, so now it's time to get some
> traction. . . . I think it's funny that people associate NASCAR
> so much with racism. I think there's less of it in NASCAR than
> people really know. There's a lot of fans that pull for me and pull
> for other drivers of different ethnicities and genders, and it's truly
> awesome to see that. I've got into altercations with people on the
> track but I've never thought for one minute that it was because of
> the color of my skin.[30]

It is no wonder that Susie East, in "Driving for Diversity: The NASCAR Racers Breaking Boundaries," concluded, "Things have progressed from when Smith's hero Wendell Scott was racing in the '50s and '60s." While some pined for the good ol' days, others celebrated a liberal narrative of racial progress, giving NASCAR all the credit.

This narrative was also clear about the impediments to a multicultural NASCAR: it was not racism within its structure; nor did the problem of racism come from NASCAR fans. Rather, the obstacle to diversity was the perception or misperception from corporate sponsors and NASCAR leadership, who assume that Southern white fans will not cheer for black or Latino drivers. "Still NASCAR's biggest problem is their reputation and the appearance of being a sport that doesn't embrace diversity like other forms of racing," writes Charles Johnson.[31] "NASCAR has tried to walk a fine line of still having its Southern heritage while doing just barely enough to bring in a handful of people of color to the sport, but it's 2009, the President of the United States is African American, its time more drivers, crew members and fans look like him and are welcomed to the sport."[32] Racing was a true meritocracy, so as soon as New York corporations, NASCAR bosses, and media types moved beyond their stereotypes, things would change.

#DrivingWhileWhite is the power to look around and deny the whiteness on the track, in the boardroom, and in the stands, to offer excuses and rationalizations. As such, few have focused on the fundamental limitations in NASCAR's diversity initiatives, which did little to address the racist climate and culture endemic within NASCAR. They did little to address racism among fans.[33] They did little to challenge the centrality of white masculinity in what NASCAR was selling on and off the track.

The experiences of African American drivers have been those of racial hostility from fellow drivers, track officials, and fans. An internship program can do only so much to transform cultural values, when both racism and white masculinity lie at the core of the NASCAR project.

In 1986, four years before his death, Wendell Scott recalled waiting to receive payment from an event's promoter. After every other white driver received payment, Scott stood alone in the infield, empty handed. Forced to demand payment, he was told, "Nigger, you better git yo' ass down the road!"[34] Scott was never paid. In a profile of NASCAR driver Darrell Wallace Jr., Viv Bernstein paints a picture that hasn't changed much in sixty years:

> But if Wallace's racing has set him apart, so has his race. He said he had been subjected to years of abuse from fans, even track officials, in the sport's lower levels. It eased, his father said, when he stepped up to the K&N series.
>
> "I've experienced that since Day 1 of racing," the younger Wallace said. "It doesn't hurt me. It bothers my parents more than anything. For me, it's just something I hear through one ear and it goes right through the other and just keep moving along and don't even dwell on it. Because the more you dwell on it, the more it affects you."[35]

Rather than transforming the culture of NASCAR, with its "possessive investment in whiteness,"[36] rather than address racism and sexism, rather than critically examine the ways in which whiteness operates within the organization, NASCAR has focused instead on bringing in a few drivers of color. NASCAR might as well have retitled its diversity initiatives as tokenistic. Despite claims to the contrary, the presence of drivers of color, especially if one becomes the Jackie Robinson or Tiger Woods of NASCAR, would not automatically transform a culture of racism that is part and parcel of NASCAR's history.

The responsibility for change lies with African American or Latino drivers, who must endure, win, and do so in the *right way*. NASCAR chairperson Bill France has made this clear, highlighting the importance of success as an antidote to reluctant sponsors and racist fans. Speaking about the immense potential of Darrell Wallace Jr., a mixed-race driver who participated in the Drive for Diversity internship program, France noted: "He's somebody with the most promising talent who is an African-American come through our diversity program. Look, that's a breakthrough if it materializes, and if not him, there'll be somebody who's going to walk in the door and be a star and it's going to be good for us."[37] White drivers and NASCAR officials have limited responsibilities to change the culture and demographics of *their* sport. This is what white privilege looks like.

The message is clear: racism will no longer be an issue, nor will race matter any longer, once a driver of color captivates the imagination of fans with his greatness on and off the track. The demand for exceptionality, the burden on drivers of color, and the focus outward is emblematic of diversity while white. At best, NASCAR has pushed for cosmetic diversity, the illusion of progress in spite of "possessive investment in whiteness," in spite of Confederate flags, racial discrimination lawsuits, and drivers of color complaining about a culture of bigotry and prejudice.[38]

Moreover, the push for diversity wasn't (and still isn't) about transforming NASCAR or embracing some forms of equity and social justice; instead it's a crude calculation. As NASCAR's fans are older and white, NASCAR has sought to expand its reach. Looking to African Americans and Latinos, given the increased market potential of Latinos inside and outside sports[39] as potential fans, NASCAR's embrace of diversity is about green, a neoliberal corporate approach to integration driven by demographics and profits.[40]

NASCAR's racial issues and the realities of racism are reflective not simply of the lack of diversity and the experiences of drivers and officials of color but also of the privileging and centrality of whiteness. Whiteness is necessary because of what NASCAR represents: an "outlaw" mantra with an embrace of criminality and lawlessness on and off the track. The resistance to diversity isn't simply about discrimination, about corporate sponsors placating the racism of fans, or about the assumptions made about the skills of black drivers; it's also about a need to preserve the whiteness of NASCAR. "NASCAR grew up lawless and positively redneck—the sport traces its heritage to moonshiners outrunning the law," writes Sean Gregory.[41] Its appeal, its culture, and its existence are predicated on whiteness, on a sport of #DrivingWhileWhite.

## FIGHTING WHILE WHITE

In 2006, Jeff Gordon pushed Matt Kenseth, who had plowed into him during a race in Bristol. At the time, NASCAR was taking seriously such infractions. Gordon was fined $10,000 and given five months' probation.[42] Today, he would surely be featured on SportsCenter and given a gold star, since "Boys will be boys."[43] In 2012, following a crash with Matt Kenseth, Tony Stewart Jr. jumped out of his car so that he could throw his helmet—a deadly projectile—at his opponent's windshield.[44] That same year, NASCAR fined Jeff Gordon, an ascendant superstar, $100,000 for intentionally crashing his car into Clint Bowyer's vehicle. It also docked him twenty-five points for intentionally causing a wreck at the Phoenix International Raceway, which led to a brawl between the pit crews of each team.

In NASCAR, neither fights nor one racer intentionally wrecking another's car are uncommon. For example, in 2010, despite being 157 laps behind, Carl Edwards plowed his car into Brad Keselowski, causing "his car to spin, then lift into the air at around 190 mph. It smashed into the barrier in front of the stands roof-first, then flipped back onto the track right side up."[45] His punishment was nothing more than a "tongue-lashing."[46] In 2014, just back to racing following an incident where he crashed into and killed Kevin Ward Jr. during a race, Tony Stewart Jr. decided to voice his anger toward Brad Keselowski with the ultimate weapon: his car. After Keselowski hit his bumper, Stewart chased him down. "Stewart stopped his car, put it into reverse and rammed into Keselowski, destroying the front end of his car. And on and on it goes. . . . This is NASCAR, and the drivers can't help themselves."[47] Such crashes are looped over and over again during post-race highlights, packaged as part of the sports excitement, bravado, and countercultural ethos. Similarly, massive brawls between pit crews are routinely celebrated on ESPN and throughout the sports media.[48]

The embrace of fighting fits NASCAR's brand, since the spectacle, the violence, and the wreckage is what the sport and its corporate partners are selling to fans. It is sold as evidence of the competitiveness, rebellious spirit, and everyman ethos of the sport and its fans. Sure, it may be a mainstream sport, one with ample Fortune 500 company sponsorship and investment; yet it promotes a culture that celebrates any effort to win. Part demolition derby, part drag race, and part white fraternity party, NASCAR is selling an image based on a set of masculine practices that center on violence, destruction, fearlessness, and winning-at-all-costs.

What is important here is how the normative culture of NASCAR, one that sanctions fights and purposeful car crashes, requires whiteness. The sight of professional athletes throwing their helmets at opponents doesn't elicit widespread panic about sportsmanship and role models, because they are #PlayingWhileWhite. The sight of a millionaire sport star intentionally crashing his car into an opponent does not prompt debates about fairness on the track. It doesn't compel debates in answer to the question: "Such behavior would never be allowed on the streets, so why is it acceptable on the track?" Nor does it lead to discussions about whether drivers and their crews fighting is evidence of an out-of-control sport. There are no references to riots, brawls, mayhem, or destruction. "A white athlete, like Kurt Busch, is under investigation for assault, and no one asks what kind of music he's listening to or the bagginess, or lack thereof, of his jeans," writes Dave Zirin. "When Jeff Gordon—another NASCAR hero—tries to assault another driver, 'thug' is the furthest word from anyone's mind."[49] It is striking to look at the ubiquity of intentional crashes or pit crew brawls and the muted responses in comparison with the sporting discourses surrounding the NBA and the NFL.[50] How often does an incident in the NBA or NFL lead the media and league commentators to lament the "criminals in the league" who are failing to be role models for *the kids*? How often does a fight or even a hard foul in the NBA lead to outrage that notes how such behavior would not be accepted in the streets or at any other workplace and why it should not be allowed in pro sports.

Yet, as we look at NASCAR, we don't see outrage, condemnation, discussions of these role models, or even arguments that note how intentionally crashing one's car into another car and driver, throwing a helmet at another person, or otherwise fighting would not be accepted in another space and would likely result in arrests had it been done on the streets. No hand-wringing over today's athletes or denunciation of single-parented homes, country music, or video games. The double standards reveal the privileges of whiteness; to be white, to be NASCAR, is to be empowered to behave without much of a consequence. This is what NASCAR is selling: a particular inscription of a white Southern sporting masculinity. According to Maury Brown:

NASCAR, and motor racing in general, has been a world where machismo runs deep. Verbal and physical confrontation has been a part of the landscape, likely from racing's inception. The first full telecast of a NASCAR race in 1979 highlighted this when, Donnie Allison and Cale Yarborough got tangled up in the final lap of the race, and a fight broke out in the infield after. In fact, Stewart's popularity has been one of "old-school" toughness by being at the center of such conflicts.[51]

Writing about a massive fight between Jeff Gordon and Brad Keselowski, as well as their pit crews, Christine Brennan lamented the acceptance and celebration of a culture of fighting within NASCAR:

> We can all understand why Gordon was angry, but seeing him—a cool California pitch-man—in a NASCAR fight at this stage of his illustrious career is a bit jarring. . . . What we have here, unfortunately, is a sport trying to appeal to the lowest common denominator among us. And for what? For TV ratings, that's what.[52]

NASCAR is commodifying a white masculine Southern identity, one that can and is all about *boys being boys*. Its ability to sell this sort of product is made possible only because of the sport's whiteness, maleness, and particular class politics. NASCAR is able to get away with, and in fact profit from, promoting a violent and "thuggish" sport because of its embrace of a Southern white cultural politics. Irrespective of fights and crashes (not to mention Confederate flags, the lack of diversity, its embrace of alcohol as both a key sponsor and an integral part of its festive experience, and its violence), NASCAR has successfully sold itself as wholesome, family-friendly, and a sporting alternative because of its clear linkages to white Southernness. "In contemporary discursive formations of U.S. conservatism, where policies and rhetoric are created to stimulate economic growth under the free-market regimes of (corporate) capital accumulation, the Symbolic South has been transformed into cultural tender for reproducing *the conditions of production and consumptions*," write Newman and Giardina. "The South, in its numerous discursive iterations, has been refinanced as the cultural currency of corporate capitalism by way of identity politics."[53] In other words, NASCAR exists because "as much as any sport in America, NASCAR has roots tied to a certain culture: White Southerners."[54]

Fights and car crashes, as part and parcel of NASCAR, as an outgrowth of regional cultural practices like demolition derby, come to represent the tradition of the South. They are normalized and celebrated with "best of" lists and widespread coverage.[55] They are evidence of the rugged, masculine individualism of the sport; the fights point to a sport where men have each other's back. More than that, the fights, the crashes, and everything in between, become a moment to celebrate "tradition." Preserving them, along with the Confederate flag and the overall whiteness of NASCAR, becomes a moment to protect "tradition" and the mythologized South from the intrusion of multiculturalists, feminists, and others who want to deny the South its rightful place in American social and sporting landscapes.

The celebration and promotion of off-track fighting as part and parcel of NASCAR culture, as emblematic of its rough and rebel cultural ethos, and as evidence of the team mentality guiding this individual sport isn't limited to pit crew brawls; it happens in tandem with the acceptance, normalization, and almost glorification of purposeful crashes. As noted by C. W. Nevius:

> NASCAR [is] a breakout sports sensation. It is also—let's just come right out and say it—the Whitest sport in America. The drivers are White, the pit crews are White, and it has become a cliché to note that at most races, Confederate flags outnumber African American fans. For good or bad . . . at a time when professional sports seems to be embracing hip-hop culture, NASCAR is heading in precisely the opposite direction.[56]

Because it is the "Whitest sport in America," NASCAR is also a sport where violence and unsportsmanlike behavior gets framed as tradition and evidence of everything from the rugged masculinity of the sport to its competitive spirit. Fighting becomes evidence of its difference, as an alternative place apart from those other sports. Likewise, as the "Whitest sport in America," the arrests and criminal activity garner little attention, much less outrage. As evident in NASCAR, the military, colleges, fraternities, and Wall Street, white spaces and those who inhabit them play by a different set of rules.

### NASCAR CULTURE: #CRIMINGWHILEWHITE

In the aftermath of the decision not to indict Daniel Pantaleo or any officer within the NYPD in the death of Eric Garner, protestors gathered in the virtual streets not only to demand justice for Garner and countless other victims of police violence but also to hold up a mirror in America's face. In one instance, white protestors sought to reveal the entrenched profiling of whiteness as innocence, as harmless, as nonthreatening, and as protected even when transgressing rules and laws. "The hashtag #CrimingWhileWhite is a play on 'driving while black,' the phrase used as an explanation of why black motorists are stopped and questioned by the police for no apparent reason," wrote Noam Cohen. "People posting under the hashtag explored the opposite situation: when police officers ignore obvious crimes in front of their eyes, presumably because the offenders are white. In thousands of posts on Twitter, users talked of being caught driving drunk, smoking marijuana, shoplifting, driving without a license and being given a warning by a police officer, if that."[57]

One tweet noted: "Shoplifted when I was a teenager. Was apprehended but never charged because I looked 'like a good kid' #CrimingWhile-White."[58] Such themes are commonplace; when white people break the law, their actions are often excused. They are provided second and third chances with little accountability. To fit the description of a white law-breaker is to prompt a general attitude which sees these violations as indiscretions or mistakes not worthy of overreaction or harsh punishment.

While few of the tweets have focused on sports, the protests could just as easily have focused on white athletes (this is covered in greater detail in chapters 4 through 6), particularly the wild world of NASCAR. #CrimingWhileWhite is part and parcel of NASCAR culture. The acceptance of assault on the track speaks to this, as does NASCAR's drug problem.

The issue of drugs, which given the nature of car racing and the dangers posed by an impaired driver (from drugs or alcohol) is unique compared to other sports, has garnered little attention from NASCAR, the media, and the public at large. There are but a handful of articles about drug use or the fear of drug use in NASCAR. Even in these few cases, the narratives have focused on what NASCAR was doing to "clean up the sport." Little attention has been provided during the era of non-testing and multiple chances. For example, Shane Hmiel tested positive not once—not twice—but *three times* for everything from heroin to marijuana. Each positive test resulted in a short suspension followed by reinstatement. A similar story relates to Kevin Grubb and Jeremy Mayfield.[59] Zero tolerance has in this case often actually meant second chances and numerous shots at redemption. This is #CrimingWhileWhite personified, a lived illustration that in both sports and the criminal justice system, white lives matter the most, and #AllLivesMatter is a lie that we have convinced ourselves is the truth.

By 2009, NASCAR made some changes, following a report in *ESPN The Magazine* that Aaron Fike admitted to "using heroin on the same days that he'd been behind the wheel of a NASCAR Truck Series ride." Using illicit drugs could be excused and handled with minimal disruption, but corrupting the sport and potentially endangering the lives of others took things to another level in terms of lawsuits, governmental intervention, and media scrutiny. In response, NASCAR quickly adopted a new "zero tolerance policy." According to Ryan McGee:

> In an instant, NASCAR was being attacked from all angles—media, drivers and drug-testing experts—for the gaping holes in its two-decades-old zero tolerance substance abuse policy. That criticism was absolutely justified. Terms such as "reasonable suspicion" and "we can test anyone at anytime" were groundbreaking when they were introduced in 1988, but in today's more advanced OxyContin and meth-fueled age, the effectiveness of the rarely updated policy had all but vanished. Within days NASCAR chairman Brian France formed a team to investigate the problem. Five months later he announced the new random drug-testing policy that went into effect this season.[60]

While its drivers would continue to benefit from the privileges of whiteness, from being profiled as antithetical to criminality, NASCAR as an organization also cashed in on its whiteness. Few would hold it responsible for its institutional failures and its implicit promotion of drug culture within its ranks. At one level, drugs were normalized and celebrated as part of its rebel and countercultural ethos. At another level, its ineptitude with respect to drug policy became evidence of its success. Its failures would come to light only as it became TOUGH, and thus worthy of celebration.

Compare this to the NBA, where drug usage has resulted in draconian league policies, widespread media outrage,[61] and public laments about the culture of the NBA. Compare this to the panic that followed the death of Len Bias,[62] or the media spectacle surrounding drugs and college football and basketball that regularly focus on the intrusion of urban culture, the ghetto, and the drug pathologies of the inner city. No outrage resulting from the toxic convergence of a pathological white masculinity and drugs; no lamenting the dangers of drug tolerance from NASCAR, the sports media, and society as a whole—when done so by white males. The dialectics between the whiteness of NASCAR and the acceptance of drug use as a non-problem speaks to the privilege that extends beyond NASCAR. The absence of any discussion of pre-2009 NASCAR as a reflection of the power in #PlayingWhileWhite only further underscores the privileges of whiteness.[63]

#CrimingWhileWhite is akin to driving while white: to be nonthreatening, to be an individual, and to be otherwise invisible. Despite violence, drugs, criminal activity, and so much more, NASCAR is consistently imagined as synonymous with mainstream American culture, as wholesome, and as a counter to the selfishness, criminality, dysfunction, and anti-role models that are the NBA and NFL.

NASCAR is consistently imagined as a place of angels; never mind the countless examples to the contrary, such as the arrests and the normalization of violence. Whiteness allows for mistakes that neither define whiteness nor create an obstacle to realizing one's dreams on and off the track. Whiteness equals humanity, and that humanity is the ultimate "get out of jail free" card, both metaphoric and real. Whiteness allows for the erasure of indiscretions and the celebration of deviance and criminality as evidence of the counterculture's ways.

#CrimingWhileWhite means that each arrest, each news report, and each crime is never seen as indicative of a larger cultural or communal issue. It is never about NASCAR, whiteness, or masculinity. In fact, if by chance the media does spotlight an incident, it does so in a way that isolates the indiscretion, claiming a level of exceptionality while scrutinizing for real crime and dysfunction in sports like basketball and football. For example, in the aftermath of the suspension of Kurt Busch following the issuance of a protective order in favor of his ex-girlfriend, Patricia Driscoll, Louis Brewster lamented the bad behavior of other (black) athletes. Rather than contextualizing the arrest within a larger history of domestic violence and drug arrests within NASCAR, Brewster instead linked Busch's story to those sports in which criminals are expected:

> Little did Ray Rice know that when he clobbered his fiancée in an Atlantic City elevator early in 2014, he would also knock out NASCAR Sprint Cup Series driver Kurt Busch just days before the 2015 season opener.
>
> When Adrian Peterson took the switch to his young son in Texas, it also left a mark on Busch. Welcome to the new world of domestic violence in pro sports. It will no longer be ignored or tolerated. It's taken such a long time, perhaps too long, for high-profile organizations to react to these situations, but now there is no turning back. . . . It's not a criminal case yet, but enough for NASCAR to take action. The sanctioning body doesn't want to be confused with the NFL.[64]

While his suspension was short-lived, the lack of media and public outrage speaks to the privileges of driving (and committing crime) while white. Even this moment became an instance in which one could distinguish the white world of NASCAR from those crime-ridden cesspools of the NFL and NBA.

Following the arrest of Sprint Cup driver Travis Kvapil for assault and false imprisonment after he allegedly dragged his wife by her hair when she attempted to leave the house, Jordan Bianchi reiterated the commonplace frames regarding NASCAR: it is a sport of rebels and outlaws, which sometimes goes too far but that is still better than other sports:

> Long priding itself as a family institution, NASCAR wanted to be seen as a slice of Americana where mom, dad and the kids could all be fans and not be concerned about the seediness that has consumed the stick-and-ball sports.
>
> Unlike baseball, NASCAR hasn't seen performance-enhancing drugs decimate what was once a storied record book filled with magical numbers. Or had its moral compass called into question like the NFL, where the brutality that was long celebrated is now decried because of the stark realization of the consequences from repeated blows to the head. NASCAR was supposed to be the wholesome alternative.[65]

Bianchi demands further perspective and historic context:

> This isn't a referendum on the decorum of drivers suggesting that NASCAR was once a sport filled with choirboys. After all, the origins of stock-car racing are vastly intertwined with bootlegging and men who fled from the federal officers during the week and then used those same cars to race on the local bullring on Sunday. . . .
>
> A sport that has long wanted to be considered on par with the NFL, NBA and other professional sports leagues has now done just that. Unfortunately, it's for all the wrong reasons.[66]

NASCAR and its media partners has used occasions of violence and criminal misconduct within its ranks as an opportunity in which to highlight its exceptionality by lamenting the (black) NFL and NBA. The power in profiling whiteness lies in the fact that these realities are never seen or identified as evidence of a troubling culture; instead, NASCAR retains its image as a family-friendly sports alternative, which at worst needs to deal with some bad apples.

In 2010, Tim Wise and Jasiri X called upon their readers and listeners to imagine "if the Tea Party was Black." Wise described the "game" as follows:

> Let's play a game, shall we? The name of the game is called "Imagine." The way it's played is simple: we'll envision recent happenings in the news, but then change them up a bit. Instead of envisioning White people as the main actors in the scenes we'll conjure—the ones who are driving the action—we'll envision Black folks or other people of color instead.[67]

Let's play!

Can you imagine if NASCAR was black?

Can you imagine the reaction if fans in black power shirts lined the racetrack as flags from the Black Panther Party and those representing "red, Black, and green" blanked NASCAR events? Whereas the Confederate flag, a symbol of Confederate secession and white supremacy, is commonplace at NASCAR events, even celebrated as a symbol of tradition. To be sure, such symbols of Black pride would surely bring about condemnation despite a disparate history, with the Confederate flag being a symbol of hate and violence, and the Panthers and the African colors being sources of pride, unity, and justice.*

Can you imagine if an African American driver had purposely crashed into another driver's car, sending him airborne as Carl Edwards did to Brad Keselowski in 2010?

Can you imagine if Cam Newton, Josh Norman, Odell Beckham, Yasil Puig, LeBron James, Metta World Peace, Barry Bonds, Kobe Bryant, or Terrell Owens were race-car drivers? How the public might respond if they were participating in intentional crashes, trash-talking, fist fights, and helmet throwing? Would the narrative acquit them with "Boys will be boys" or condemn them by citing such incidents as evidence of the sports outlaw ethos? Or would media discourse focus on their criminality, describing them as thugs and as gangstas? If Allen Iverson or Cam Newton, or one of NASCAR's handful of black drivers were the face of the sport, and they were

---

* Please note that given the power of white supremacy, given the history of racial terror and violence, there is no equivalent. The power and privileges of whiteness means there is no parallel. So in many ways, this exercise is a series of false equivalences deployed for analytical purposes.

found guilty of any number of transgressions commonplace in America's premiere racing sport, then hip-hop would fall in the media's crosshairs. Few seek to explain the behavior of Gordon or Kenseth through discussions of country music or rock 'n' roll.

During a Camping World Truck Series race, Kyle Busch rammed Ron Hornaday's truck into the wall, ostensibly wrecking his car. While Busch received a single-race suspension and a $50,000 fine, can you imagine the outrage, moral posturing, and punishments another driver would have met had he not been white?

Can you imagine the reaction that would have erupted had a black NAS-CAR fan booed the First Lady of the United States? Whereas white fans booed Michelle Obama and Jill Biden during an appearance at the Homestead-Miami Speedway, attracting little public and media criticism. It is almost impossible to imagine Melania Trump and Karen Pence receiving similar treatment at a black NASCAR event. If NASCAR was black, such behavior would surely elicit national outrage and condemnation. Can you imagine the reaction from the likes of Sean Hannity and Rush Limbaugh, if such disrespect was "minimized" or dismissed?[68] In reality, Limbaugh took to the airwaves to describe Michelle's boo birds as justifiable and understandable. According to Limbaugh:

> People that go to NASCAR races are the very people her husband called bitter clingers. . . . We don't like being told what to eat; we don't like being told how much to exercise; we don't like being told what we've got to drive; we don't like wasting money; we don't like our economy being bankrupted. We don't like 14 percent unemployment. The question is, what the hell is there to cheer for when Miss Obama and Ms. Biden show up? I'll tell you something else. We don't like paying millions of dollars for Mrs. Obama's vacations. The NASCAR crowd doesn't quite understand why when the husband and the wife are going to the same place, the first lady has to take her own Boeing 757 with family and kids and hangers-on four hours earlier than her husband, who will be on his 747. NASCAR people understand that's a little bit of a waste. They understand it's a little bit of *uppity-ism.*[69]

This sort of disrespect wouldn't fly if NASCAR were black; nor would a group of black drivers who refused to meet with the president. In 2012, several white NASCAR drivers passed on an invitation to the White House, citing scheduling conflicts.[70] If NASCAR drivers were black, and refused to meet with the president, would it be understandable? Or would they be another Craig Hodges? In 1992, Hodges, while visiting the Bush White House, not only wore a dashiki but also "handed the President a letter that asked him to do more to end injustice toward the African-American community."[71] The media denounced Hodges. Shortly thereafter he was out of the league. The treatment of Patriots players refusing to visit the Trump White House after their Super Bowl win tells us what the response would be.

Can you imagine if the black CEO of NASCAR, or if a group of black drivers, endorsed a presidential candidate who had referred to an entire community as "rapists,"[72] proposed the development of a policy that excluded an entire religious group from entering the United States,[73] and spent a lifetime spewing bigotry?[74]

We know that many in the media would call on them to "stay in their lane" and not "mix politics and sports," because only a white male could leverage racism, sexism, xenophobia, and a politics of fear to become leading candidate for the presidency. And as for white NASCAR drivers and their CEO, their endorsement of Donald Trump was done without controversy or handwringing.[75]

Given the entrenched whiteness of NASCAR; given how symbols of whiteness are as important to NASCAR as the cars themselves; given how important white masculinity is to the sport, and how it gives life to the very culture of NASCAR; it is hard to imagine NASCAR as black. For NASCAR without whiteness is just a bunch of cars driving fast in circles.

CONCLUSION

Over the last fifteen years, NASCAR has embraced a number of reform measures to address everything from the lack of diversity among its drivers and crews to the racism that exists in its stands. NASCAR has started an internship program and supported efforts to diversify its squad of drivers, pit crew members, and ownership. Additionally, it has worked toward the ultimate removal of the Confederate flag,[76] and it has developed potential partnerships with LeBron James.[77] All of this represents a new chapter in NASCAR's history. However, none of these changes address the powers and privileges affecting the sport that result from white supremacy. These reforms don't alter what NASCAR is selling, which is the same thing that Donald Trump sold during the 2016 presidential campaign: the wages of whiteness.

Reflecting its embrace of multicultural corporatism, NASCAR has worked to cross over into both the mainstream and communities otherwise disconnected from NASCAR. In maintaining its regional appeal and its ties to Southern traditions, NASCAR's dynamic approach to drug use, or even fights, is part of an overall strategy to connect with fans across the nation as it tries to appeal to more and more corporate sponsors.

Yet, as we look at these changes, it should be clear that these reforms do little to challenge the privileges inherent in #DrivingWhileWhite. NASCAR is ultimately selling a particular inscription of white masculinity, based on a certain set of class, regional, and ideological politics, which are not simply about the whiteness of the drivers, but also about the culture, ethos, and spectacle of a sport that embraces fighting, crashes, antihero role models, and destruction. No matter the behavior, NASCAR, and its good ol' boy drivers, is given a pass. It continues to be seen as the right kind of sporting practice, a topic that will act as the foundation for the next chapter. Irrespective of reform, NASCAR cannot usher in changes that address structural and cultural advantages afforded to white drivers, because in the end NASCAR is a sport based on and driven by whiteness.

# CHAPTER 9

# PLAYING THE WHITE WAY

*From the Cardinals to the Badgers*

*He's a throwback.*
*He has a passion for the game.*
*Old-School*
*From a different era*
*He plays the right way.*

SPORT clichés are ubiquitous in the press box, on the field, on talk radio, in sports media, and within public discourse. At the core of this book's project lies the effort to show how these sport clichés embody a racial lexicon, discourse, and index for understanding sports and the pedagogies of whiteness. From *He has the heart of a champion*, to *He has a nose for the fall*; from *He's the heart and soul of the team* to *He's their floor general*; the sporting landscape is littered with racial clichés that come together in the profiling of white athletes.[1]

This chapter continues this discussion by looking at the profiling of white athletes and teams imagined through their whiteness as *playing the right way*. According to John Baker, "The most overused, overwrought cliché in baseball? Play the game the right way." The former MLB catcher further argued, "The longer I played baseball, the more I realized that across America, that cliché—*Play the game the right way*—actually means something very specific: *Play the game MY way*."[2] While transcending baseball and ignoring the ways that race, gender, and nation operate here, Baker's emphasis on the power, on the ability, and on the privilege to define *the right way* is important.

Focusing on the Cardinals, the 2014–2015 Wisconsin Badgers basketball squad, and Jordan Spieth, I argue that the narratives surrounding *playing the right way* rely on the racial scripts that consistently imagine white athletes as "hard workers," as "cerebral," and as team players. Equally important is that a level of nostalgia that harkens back to a bygone time in sports when athletes approached the game in the *right way*: for love, for tradition, and for community. Intentional or not, the narrative emphasis on the past embodying the *right way* further reinforces the dialectics between whiteness and righteousness, between a productive white masculinity and the beauty in sports. To play the *right way* becomes synonymous with playing the white way, and with being white.

## THE CARDINAL WAY

In their 2013 remix of a late-1968 cover issue,[3] *Sports Illustrated* placed five members of the St. Louis Cardinals' pitching staff on its cover. Wearing button-up dress shirts and denim-stained jeans, Adam Wainwright, Lance Lynn, Shelby Miller, John Mozeliak, and Jaime Garcia pose for the camera while sitting in the team's locker room. Like the original, the magazine cover's image could easily lead one to mistake the five ball players for a law firm or a group of frat boys.

*Sports Illustrated* used this image to nostalgically define "the Cardinal Way." This term, which appears in bold white letters on the cover, has become a notion that represents the Cardinals as emblematic of doing things the *right way*. As a narrative, this idea represents a racialized script for how players and organizations should conduct themselves in today's sports world.

At the core of this representational and narrative device is race (as well as class, geography, and gender). The Cardinal Way is not simply a descriptor of a team but rather an index, filter, and trope of white masculinity. References to "Midwestern values,"[4] the focus on players like Matt Carpenter, Matt Adams, and several pitchers including Adam Wainwright, Lance Lynn, and Shelby Miller, and the rhetorical devices employed point to the way that whiteness functions within the Cardinal Way narrative: the Cardinal Way is the white way, the white way is the Cardinal Way, providing a subtext to the lore surrounding the St. Louis Cardinals.

The Cardinal Way is anchored by a belief that as an organization, which has won eleven World Series titles, nothing has been given to them; everything gained on and off the field has been earned through hard work, good planning, teamwork, selflessness, and a culture of winning.[5] "Ask any person in St. Louis to define 'the Cardinal Way,' and they will tell you that it's a style of play that both pays homage to and respects the fundamentals of the game dating back to when the team began playing baseball in this city in 1882," writes Tony Calandro. "The style of play is described in phrases like 'old school' and 'respect for the game.'"[6]

Others have emphasized "perseverance," "doing things right," "playing hard," "not beating themselves," and doing all this with humility as key to the Cardinals' success and evidence of their exceptional culture.[7] According to Cardinals general manager John Mozeliak, "I think when players decide they want to play here or look to play in St. Louis, there's certain expectations that a player wants to see done. And so when you think about building a business, you want that culture to represent success, and when we look at things and you hear people say, 'Cardinal Way' it's about tradition, it's about respect, and it's about doing things right. That's what we try to really impart onto our players."[8] Despite the fact that "cultivating talent" or "teaching the fundamentals" is not unique to the Cardinals' organization, these descriptors have come to define the organization.

As such, Paul White describes the Cardinal Way as being all about growth, maturation, and commitment to nurturing talent: "Identify and draft talented and versatile players. Teach them a wide variety of skills. Impart consistent franchise philosophies across all affiliates. And watch previously unheralded players flourish at the major league level."[9] Since they are not "able to out-talent teams," they rely on "fundamentals" and "playing the right way" because these values, along with hard work, allows them "to maximize their talent."[10]

In a subtle critique of today's globalized MLB economy, the success of the Cardinals is about challenging a culture of entitlement and shortcuts. According to Cardinals outfielder Matt Carpenter, "The Cardinal Way is simply being held accountable for your actions." It is about "integrity, playing hard, working hard, doing all the little things right."[11]

At the time, Carpenter emerged as the living embodiment of the Cardinal Way. "With his lack of batting gloves, he looks like an old-school ball player—and his talents stand out like one too. No matter what the situation, Carpenter is a pest to opposing pitchers. Just when a game looks like it is over, he comes through," writes Schwichtenberg. "He runs hard, plays with all-out effort, does not give up an at-bat and is the perfect example of what the Cardinal Way really is."[12] Representing itself as a selfless team, one where success is the result of hard work, determination, character, and heart, the Cardinals, through its own narrative, constructs an origin story where a team and its players pull themselves up by their bootstraps, proving the possibility of ascending from rags to riches in titles. In many ways, the Cardinal Way resembles what is constructed as the "American Way."

The Cardinal Way is a metaphor for American exceptionalism. The embrace of its neoliberal logic, which focuses on individualism, self-reliance, and free markets, highlights why the Cardinal Way resonates with so many; it builds upon core themes in American ideologies, whether it be meritocracy, the Protestant work ethic, or rugged individualism. The Cardinal Way exists as a metaphor for the United States. Success is imagined as the result of unique attributes and doing things the right way.

While the Cardinals' mythologizing is longstanding, its place in national folklore reached new heights during the 2013 MLB playoffs. The Cardinals and Dodgers squared off in an epic series to decide the National League Pennant. Not satisfied with a narrative focused on two storied franchises battling for the right to go to the World Series, nor interested in celebrating the greatness of both teams, the media and the Cardinals both seized upon the trope of St. Louis (White American) exceptionalism to turn the series into a referendum on the values of sports, suggesting a culture war of sorts. It posited a struggle between the tradition of St. Louis and the new generation global baseball players in Los Angeles.

Clarifying what was meant by the Cardinal Way also came through its definition in opposition to the Dodgers and what it signified: flashy, overpaid, transnational, ignorant of traditions, brash, and all talk. According to Bernie Miklasz, "Supposedly the Dodgers of Adrian Gonzalez and Yasiel Puig were going to make baseball more appealing by hotdogging, taunting opponents with mouse impersonations, striking a home-run pose in the batter's box (while hitting a triple), showing up umpires, throwing the ball to the wrong base or sailing it to the backstop."[13] While the Dodgers were all about "flash," the Cardinals were all about winning. The Cardinal Way— "fundamentals," "fresh leadership," and "competitive character"—once again proved victorious. The Cardinals provided a "breath of fresh air," different from the "trash-talking, spit-hurling, head-butting sports millionaires."[14] Bill McClellan described this narrative as a farce and a media fabrication: "The series against the Los Angeles Dodgers was framed as a morality play. The Dodgers were the bad guys, the show-offs. The Cardinals were the good guys who believed in the Cardinal Way. They were a bunch of Luke Skywalkers playing baseball. May the Way be with you."[15] A fabrication, yes; its ingredients were race and nation. The racial codes within this comparison are clear, as is the effort to juxtapose the humble, "happy"[16] and hardworking Cardinals with the trash-talking, "chest pounding," egotistical show-off Dodgers[17] named Puig, Carl Crawford, Adrian Gonzalez, and Hanley Ramirez.

The signification within the Cardinal Way trope emanates from the racial tropes that govern the sports landscape and the place of black and Latino players within it—players whose "deficient" understanding of tradition, corrupted values, and propensity for "flash" are bad baseball, especially if you want to win. Dominant stereotypes about black and Latino athletes shape Cardinal Way discourse; the *right way* is defined through their underlying binaries and the backdrop of the steroid era. The right way, the winning way, and the Cardinal Way are refreshing and needed because of Barry Bonds, Alex Rodriguez, and the steroid era. The beauty and power of the Cardinal Way comes through its departure and differentiation from these impure influences on the game. Yet again, whiteness is imagined as savior and protector of the American way.

Tropes for whiteness—"respect for the game," "fundamentals," and "old school"—are not limited to how the Cardinals approach the game or the types of players they put on the field; they also include their ability to manage the financial constraints they purportedly live under. Whereas other teams cash in on global marketing, television deals, and a league that privileges big-market teams, the Cardinals have won with heart and intelligence. Despite 230 million dollars in annual revenue, the Cardinals are consistently represented as a team that succeeds without money.

Not surprisingly, Forbes estimates their worth at 1.2 billion dollars. William DeWitt Jr., the team's principal owner, is also a partner at Reynolds, DeWitt & Co., a company that owns, among other things, sixty-three Arby's franchises. In 2001, as debates raged over whether the City of St. Louis should fund a new stadium, media estimates put the collective worth of all of the Cardinals' owners at four billion dollars.[18] In fact, the deep pockets of the Cardinals are nothing new, having been owned by Anheuser-Busch until 1995.

Yet, the mythology of the Cardinals is premised on a narrative that sees them as David in a league full of Goliaths. Their player payroll in 2015 was over 122 million dollars, the thirteenth highest in MLB. Nonetheless, the discourse continually positioned the franchise as disadvantaged and forced to operate without the benefits and privileges others enjoy. Whereas other teams are able to sign free agents—those blue-chip "natural" athletes—and pay for international talent because of their financial advantages, the Cardinals draft their players. Unable to buy championships, they are forced to win in the old-fashioned way, through making intelligent recruiting choices and then working hard to develop their talent.

According to Tony Calandro, the Cardinals offer a model not simply for baseball and sports but for America as a whole. They are the embodiment of American exceptionalism:

Like any successful business, the team has a proven track record of managing talent, mitigating threats and capitalizing on opportunities. If one translates the sports language that is used to describe the success of the organization into the language of what it means to be a well-run business, both financially and socially, the St. Louis Cardinals should be considered to be in the same category as other popular consumer brands like Starbucks or even Unilever.[19]

To celebrate the Cardinals as a model franchise ignores their abysmal racial and gender diversity.[20] While not alone in this trait, the 2015 Cardinals employed a total of only two people from underrepresented groups in executive and administrative capacities: Michael Hall, vice president of Cardinals Care and Community Relations and Victoria Bryant, vice president of Event Services and Merchandising. Additionally, they had one woman working on the field, serving as a Minor League Strength and Conditioning Coordinator. Hardly a model of exceptionality and progressive hiring practices; at best, like the rest. At worst, the Cardinals, with its commodification of "tradition," remain intransigent to demands to bring down the racial and gender barriers within modern sports.[21]

While the Cardinals are certainly not MLB's whitest team—in 2015, they had three players born in the Dominican Republic and six American-born players of color—the marketing and perception of the team centers on its whiteness. Its praise ignores how the Cardinal Way reflects the waning African American presence within MLB. It even becomes an indirect way to celebrate the resegregation of baseball. As of 2016, the percentage of black MLB players was 8 percent,[22] a significant drop from 17 percent in 1990.[23] The increased popularity and potential financial windfall of the NFL and NBA, as well as the necessity of specialization within youth sports, has shaped the racial landscape of MLB. Globalization[24] and MLB's reliance on exploitable and cheap labor from places like the Dominican Republic and elsewhere throughout Latin America[25] has further impacted the African American presence within MLB. The lacking sense of urgency coming from MLB, with its celebration of diversity in the absence of certain kinds of diversity, with its entrenched commercialization of Jackie Robinson, and with its celebration of "the Cardinal Way" further contributes to this ongoing resegregation. More than anything else, closed parks, divestment from parks and recreation and public schools, and mass incarceration have all contributed to the waning black presence in "America's Pastime."

Beginning in the 1970s, and continuing today, American society has seen the systematic defunding of public institutions. These policies have shifted, along with a decreasing tax base in inner city communities, due to middle-class flight, shrinking home values, high unemployment rates and devastating levels of poverty, leaving training grounds in shambles. For example, during the 1970s, the Department of Recreation in Cleveland, Ohio was forced to close down 250 million dollars worth of recreation facilities. New York City experienced similar spatial contraction, with a 60 percent decline (a forty-million-dollar drop in its annual budget for recreation). From 1976 to 1980, the number of park employees in the city dropped as well, from 6,100 to 2,600.[26] Throughout the 1990s, Los Angeles and a number of other cities including St. Louis saw a virtual end to park baseball leagues, and opportunities shift to private leagues and traveling teams. In cities with poverty rates exceeding 20 percent, and as much as 40 percent of city budgets coming from fines for traffic violations and other minor infractions, investment in green space and parks and recreation is in short supply.[27]

This trend continues today with the overall privatization of space, play, and recreation, leaving America's poor youth of color literally out in the cold. As evident in a number of studies published in the *American Journal of Preventive Medicine* (AJPM), African Americans don't have equal access to spaces of play, exercise, and recreational sport: "that unsafe neighborhoods, poor design and a lack of open spaces and well constructed parks make it difficult for children and families in low-income and minority communities to be physically active."[28]

On the ground and in *right way* narratives, baseball represents a racialized sporting culture. Baseball, played the *right way*, embodies and signifies through whiteness. Just as space is racialized, leading to very different types of investment and development,[29] sporting bodies and practices are normalized in racial ways. This impacts not only what we see on the field but also types of institutional development or underdevelopment. Writing in "Soccer, Race, and Suburban Space," David Andrews, Robert Pitter, Detlev Zwick, and Darren Ambrose highlight this issue:

> Particular sports and particular physical activities became synonymous with the emergence of this "consumerists body culture" (Ingham, 1985, p. 50), whose various physical manifestations represent compelling markers of normalized suburban existence. The most celebrated derivatives of the rigidly class-based fitness including jogging, aerobics. . . . The rise of soccer within suburban America

cannot be divorced from the metamorphosis of the body into a corporeal commodity through which self-worth is expressed.[30]

Baseball's confinement to suburban and upper middle-class communities, as well as its prohibitive cost, furthers this process of segregation and black athletic underdevelopment. For example, while only 33 percent of school-aged kids play organized sports in Boston, over 90 percent of those residing in suburban Boston do. "Parks and ball fields are well developed in the suburbs," notes a black baseball coach, comparing them with America's urban centers. As such, black youth are "growing up without the facilities or equipment," leaving them with a limited number of athletic choices.[31] To celebrate the Cardinals or baseball in general as sports role models, as illustrative of sporting aspirations, simultaneously ignores persistent inequality and normalizes white middle-class sports participation as ideal.

All of this furthers the marking of spaces and sports as white, and therefore normalized as unavailable to black and US Latino youth. As white youth and middle-class youth of color develop their talents in private batting cages, with technology, and with professional pitching coaches, youth of color confined to America's working-poor communities are left with few spaces to even play, much less the resources needed to develop their athletic talent. The reality of access to both these informal and formal spaces is startling and dramatic. White kids have more opportunities in both youth and high school sports, which subsequently offer greater career choices and the increased likelihood of an athletic scholarship. In other words, the chance to play baseball offers not only an opportunity to play in the World Series but also a window into the differential investment afforded to the Little League generation.

While certainly part of a larger history, it is also important to reflect on the racial history of MLB and its participating organizations within these discussions about the lack of diversity. Antiblack racism and the celebration of franchises with fraught racial histories reflect a culture disinvested in equitable diversity. For example, the Cardinals organization has a specific racial history defined by exclusion of black players and antiblack hostilities that continue into the twenty-first century.[32] Despite being celebrated as "the best fans in baseball," a Chicago Cubs and former Cardinals all-star was greeted with racial slurs in his first game back at Busch Stadium:

> According to the *New York Daily News*, their microphones happened to pick up some unfortunate language from some unhappy, ignorant and racist Cardinals fans. While there doesn't seem to

be any footage available, numerous people took to Twitter last night saying that they'd heard the N-word thrown in Heyward's direction.[33]

The decision of the team's mascot to attend a "Police Lives Matter"[34] event directly in response to the protests of Black Lives Matter speaks to the racial politics that define the Cardinal Way.

Paired with the nostalgia for "tradition" and the "old school," which inadvertently transports us into the era of segregation and racial discrimination, the Cardinal Way also embodies the unexamined history of racism within sports. Was it the *right way* when the St. Louis Browns refused to play against the New York Cubans, a team of black players, in 1887?[35] Does the Cardinal Way include the history of racism directed at Jackie Robinson and the Dodgers' other black players? Don Newcombe told George Vecsey about their experiences in 1949 or 1950 at St. Louis Sportsman Park, which remained segregated after Robinson's arrival in 1947:

> Thousands of Negroes, as they were called, were milling around the street, unable to pay their way into the game because the outfield pavilion, where blacks had been confined, was sold out. By some accounts, the stands had been legally integrated a few years earlier, but apparently, many of Robinson's fans were not exactly welcome there.
>
> "Jackie looked out and saw a bunch of people in the street with radios on," Newk said, recalling how Robinson summoned Burt Shotton, the manager, who said, "I never saw anything like this." Newk said a Dodgers official informed the Cardinals that the Dodgers would not take the field until the fans were inside.
>
> "You made money for the Cardinals," I said.
>
> "We just wanted them to watch us play, not stand out in the streets with radios," Newk said somberly.[36]

Although a reflection of the Cardinal Way, this history is often scrubbed from historic memory in celebrating the Cardinals as a model progressive franchise. Likewise, the integration of the Cardinals in 1954, which is often mythologized as evidence of the transformative and forward thinking of the organization, is rarely seen in the context of capitalistic motivations exerted from beyond the diamond. The decision to sign an African American player was not about racial progress or benevolence but profits and markets.[37] In 1953, Gussie Busch, the Cardinals' new owner, arrived at spring training.

"Where are our black players?" he asked. "How can it be the great American game if blacks can't play? Hell, we sell beer to everyone." Is selling beer to generate profit across racial color lines not also part of the Cardinal Way? What about the experiences of Curt Flood, who was sold to the Philadelphia Phillies without so much as a phone call—is that part of the Cardinal tradition? This racial history is bypassed for the sake of spotlighting Branch Rickey, who played an instrumental role in the integration of baseball, started within the Cardinals' organization, and was mentored by Bill DeWitt, Sr. Rather than acknowledging the racial animus that has been part and parcel of the organization's history, the narrative works to center Bob Gibson, Curt Flood, or Ozzie Smith so as to highlight the team's racial acceptance and promotion of diversity.

By ignoring this history, the *right way* is constructed through erasure, repackaging the Cardinals as a moralistic fable where the values and tenets of American exceptionalism propel greatness. In reality, the Cardinals' history, like that of America itself, is a story of success through racism: domination through racial exclusion.

The superiority of the Cardinal Way is achieved through imagining the Busch family as racial reformers rather than as opportunists; the values of the Cardinal Way are conjured through erasing their opposition to free agency and their role in the steroid era. This focus on "Midwestern values," and the connection between the "community" and team/players rather than the history of fan racism, from Jackie Robinson to Ferguson,[38] embodies the revisionist narrative construction that is taking place within the idea of the Cardinal Way. It speaks to the ways in which nostalgia operates within these spaces, ones that locate the ideal in moments, teams, and spaces dominated by white bodies. It speaks to the ways in which white sporting practices are profiled as the embodiment of the best that sports can be both on and off the field.

The Cardinal Way represents not just Cardinals wins, but how they win with less talent, how they cultivate their talent, and how they overcome limited resources (resulting from the unfortunate poverty in the area) through hard work and ingenuity. The white way is the right way; the Cardinal Way is the right way. The Cardinals are both a throwback team and the team of the future, celebrating what whiteness has been and will be for sporting cultures. Conversely, the Cardinal Way is pure fantasy that relies on the erasure of its own racial history and larger structural realities from globalization to structural adjustment programs. The Cardinals are the Hoosiers of baseball; just as the Wisconsin Badgers are the Rudy of college basketball. And what anchors the narratives and mythologies around each as playing the right way, as approaching the game in a way worthy of celebration, is whiteness.

The St. Louis Cardinals are not the only team doing it the right way. The Wisconsin Badgers, after two straight appearances in the Final Four (2014 and 2015), dethroned Gonzaga as the poster child for the right way to play basketball, for the right way to run a collegiate basketball program. The Badger way not only has led to success on the court, but it also embodies what is good about college basketball.

While clearly about victories (few teams are celebrated for doing it the right way when they are 6-40) much of the discourse has focused on the Badgers' approach to the game as reason itself for celebration. In the media and on social media, Wisconsin's success has been seen as the result of hard work, teamwork, intelligence, and ruggedness; in other words, although they lacked a superstar and "athletes," their greatness came from their defense prowess, from effort, and from playing together. Reflecting the dialectics of nostalgia, whiteness, and style of play, the narrative that surrounds Wisconsin continually invokes the belief that when the game was white, it was a game of fundamentals; that when college sports were white, it was a sport of ethics and amateurism; and that when the game consisted of a bunch of "average Joes" it was played the right way.

The greatness of the Badgers is not simply about their success or about how they play the game, but about their demeanor. They are great because they are a group of "average Joes." According to ESPN's Eamonn Brennan "They are also the comedy kings of the Final Four—witty, self-deprecating, down to Earth and irresistibly goofy. Except for the whole being awesome at basketball thing, the 2013–14 Badgers seem, all in all, like pretty normal dudes. You could chill with them."[39] They are different: "Egos aren't managed; they simply aren't tolerated. Smarts are prized. Everyone needs to get along."

Led by power forward/center Stanley "Frank" Kaminsky, who would go on to graduate in four years, Wisconsin was depicted as a collection of college students who happen to play basketball. In a story about Kaminsky, who was celebrated for taking his mother to the 2015 White House Correspondents' Dinner, Mike Lucas describes a year in which all of the basketball awards and accolades could not compare with the ultimate accomplishment of graduating in four years from an elite school like the University of Wisconsin.[40] For Frank, graduation is everything:

> It's going to be a pretty fulfilling feeling. I always wanted to
> get a college degree; it's something that my parents pushed on
> me. They said it was a priority and something I should take

very seriously. It will be a nice way to end my college career . . .
Basketball is only going to last for X-number of years . . . a degree
from a great institution, one of the top schools in the country, is
something that you can't take away from someone.[41]

For Lucas and others, his choices reflect the influence of his parents and the
Badger program.

Imagined as (un)remarkable, Kaminsky represents the type of student
who plays for Wisconsin. In another profile on Kaminsky, Daniel Tran makes
clear how he and his teammates (if the star is without ego, then these other
role players must surely be even less assuming) are unique and exceptional:

> As much as college athletes are encouraged, even badgered at
> times, to be normal students, the exposure to national media
> surrounding high-profile players like Kaminsky can induce a lot
> of hype, causing athletes to be looked at and perceived as above
> the rest of the student body. This kind of worship can inflate
> athlete's egos and convince them that they are in fact more
> important than other students.
>
> In that sense, Kaminsky is a rarity. The big 7'0" point-center
> who can seemingly do it all has the appearance of a normal college
> student that just happens to [be] the best basketball player in the
> country, not the other way around.
>
> He's not afraid to let his weirdness show and there is no fear
> of backlash of public perception because that's just who he is. I
> mean, what other college basketball player would start his own
> blog after his fame exploded last season to talk about his love of
> the HBO hit "Entourage" or how the basketball team would be
> look [sic] as a baseball team?
>
> He never hesitates to declare himself a video game master,
> though the rest of his teammates are quick to squash that notion.
> By all accounts and appearances, he's just a regular college kid
> placed in an extraordinary position and loving every minute of it.[42]

An artist on the court, successful in the classroom, and cool enough to
drink a beer with or to date, Kaminsky and his Badgers teammates represent
everything that is good about basketball and college students.

While imagined as a victim of stereotypes[43] and racial double standards,[44]
as consistently underestimated, and as a team that is seen as "boring to
watch, really slow," not to mention "white, slow, and unathletic,"[45] in reality

the Badgers' basketball team provided yet another moment to celebrate real student athletes. To play the *right way* is evidence that a team is overwhelmingly white.

During a press conference at the 2015 regional final, one reporter asked members of the Wisconsin team, "How would you want Arizona Starters to describe you?"

> "Resilient" and "Disciplined," noted two of the Badger student athletes.
> Two additional Badgers went with, "Unselfish" and "Tough."
> Kaminsky, however, offered another descriptor, which was visible to most: "White guys."[46]

Interestingly, the four adjectives each signify whiteness within the culture of basketball.[47] In fact, while only Kaminsky explicitly invoked his whiteness as part of their collective identity, the other four descriptors also signified the team's whiteness.

The team's embrace of their whiteness,[48] alongside the simplistic narrative that imagines basketball as organically black,[49] contributed to an explicit racial discourse that surrounded the team.

Not surprisingly, one of the prominent questions surrounding the Badgers was: Why was the team so white? With only a few African American players on the 2014 and 2015 Final Four teams and a longer tradition of racial homogeneity; in a sport that African Americans have dominated over several decades; much was made not only of their success but also their whiteness.

According to Josh Peter, "A number of factors contribute to Wisconsin's predominantly white teams, including: state and university demographics; coaching at the lower levels; and Ryan's system, which features a methodical, half-court offense that is key to his success but according to players and coaches can make it a challenge to recruit top African-American players."[50] Similarly, Roger Groves identified the Badgers as "methodical. They are mature. They do not lose their mind in difficult circumstances. To the contrary, they are mentally stronger than many of their opponents. Saliently, they are so fundamentally sound they do not beat themselves."[51] Playing on hegemonic stereotypes of both white and black players, Peters, Forbes, and others reduced the racial make-up of the Badgers to their "style" and their approach to the game.

The emphasis on fundamentals by then head coach Bo Ryan, and even by his predecessor Dick Bennett, contributed to a predominantly "white team."

According to DeShawn Curtis, a basketball coach in Milwaukee, black players were not learning fundamental skills, and instead relied on their athleticism, making it difficult for them to fit in under the system and coaching of Bo Ryan. Whereas AAU teams and coaches "don't teach their kids how to play basketball,"[52] Ryan offered something different:

> The majority of the programs, it's about, "We've got better athletes than you." Top recruits—regardless of race—also tend to favor an up-tempo style because they think it will help them get to the NBA, according to Curtis, other high school coaches and former Wisconsin players.[53]

In other words, it is not just about style, tempo, or different approaches to the game; it is also about the fact that Wisconsin embraces the *traditional way* of playing basketball. This emphasis on fundamentals speaks to the racial binary that juxtaposes "street ball" against "organized" basketball. The former signifies extemporaneous and individualized—blackness—while the latter signifies team, rules, fundamentals, and order: whiteness. Todd Boyd argues that, within the dominant basketball lexicon, race anchors the signifiers and meaning embedded within these varied styles of play. As such, he describes "white basketball" as one "in which adherence to a specific set of rules determines one's ability to play successfully and 'correctly.'"[54] Aaron Baker builds on this idea, arguing: "since basketball functions as a metaphor for racial identities, the style suggests a white ideology that accepts the rules of the game."[55] The aesthetic bifurcation is premised not only on the reification of whiteness and its linkage to teamwork and intelligence but also on the valorization of white, working-class identity. "Baseball and football were already predetermined to be extensions of the American blue-collar ethos, and at some point, the Cold War ethic," argues Todd Boyd. "Individuality was subsumed, contained, in the name of group productivity. This was the White American way of life writ large, and Blacks need only be concerned to the extent that they were useful."[56] Whereas media and sporting discourse consistently bestow direct praise for the intelligence and fundamentals of white players from Tom Brady to Steve Nash, the celebration of African Americans playing for athleticism and creativity re-inscribes a critique of a lack of emphasis on fundamentals, team-orientation, strategy, and basketball intelligence.[57]

A significant part of the narrative about the Badgers doing it the *right way* focuses on how, because of racial stereotypes, Wisconsin players are forced to go out and prove themselves. Never given the benefit of the doubt, the Badgers use the court to defy and counter the prevailing stereotypes about whites and basketball. Embodying a post–civil rights narrative that sees anti-white discrimination as a dominant reality,[58] the focus on anti-white stereotypes is significant, because it suggests that their whiteness is part of the reason why Wisconsin is victimized and why they are successful. Of equal importance is the idea that even faced with the obstacles resulting from stereotypes and discrimination, the Badgers still succeed, demonstrating that if they can do it, anyone can. No excuses!

During another exchange with a reporter, Kaminsky spotlighted that the talk, the disrespect, and the underestimation coming from the press, fans and even fellow competitors, all of which was the result of being seen as "a bunch of white guys" pushed the team to focus on silencing its critics and haters:

> REPORTER: Frank . . . last week you mentioned the whole white guy thing. Do you think it's a form of disrespect because guys will see you guys on the court and it's like, "Oh well, these white boys can't play?" But at the same time you guys go out and you show that you're just as athletic and as talented as everyone else.
> KAMINSKY: Obviously, I said it last week, sometimes we kind of fail that eye test. I know that me personally, I've heard comments about how I look like I'm asleep all the time. I don't know where that came from. . . . But, you know, it doesn't matter once the game starts. It doesn't matter what we look like. It matters how we play.[59]

Success comes as they are forced to disprove the stereotypes; rather than wallow in self-pity in reaction to anti-white prejudice, they instead pull themselves up by their bootstraps to prove wrong the doubters and those blinded by their own racial prejudices.

Conclusively, when it comes to the Wisconsin Badgers, a value judgment lies at the center of the narrative; Wisconsin plays the way the game is "supposed to be played"; their players act the way student athletes are supposed to behave; their program mirrors what college sports is *supposed* to be. Imagined as an ideal on so many levels, the power and privilege in the players' whiteness should be crystal clear. Despite the claims of color-blindness and the belief that success comes because of merit, and because of hard work, Wisconsin, like St. Louis, finds celebration in whiteness. Wisconsin's narrative about the Badgers celebrates their whiteness AND makes clear that its whiteness—and the culture of whiteness— is part of its recipe for success.

Even more than imagining Wisconsin as a bunch of tough yet affable students who happen to play basketball, even more than describing them as a hardworking team, the placement of Wisconsin as the embodiment of *collegiate* athletics speaks directly to the dialectics between #PlayingWhile White and *playing the right way*, between the stereotypes about black and white athletes, and between the widespread narratives that depict black student athletes as semi-professional and white students who play sports as "regular students."

In the absence of "stars" and "athleticism," players stay at Wisconsin. At least that is the narrative peddled by both Bo Ryan and much of the media. Following a 2015 championship loss to Duke, a school that has embraced the "rent-a-player" approach,[60] Bo Ryan noted that while their approach, doing things the right way, put them at a competitive disadvantage, the culture of his program was important and necessary:

> Every player that's played through the program, okay, we don't do a rent-a-player. You know what I mean? Try to take a fifth-year guy. That's okay. If other people do that, that's okay. I like trying to build from within. It's just the way I am. And to see these guys grow over the years and to be here last year and lose a tough game, boom, they came back.[61]

Whereas the Kentuckys and Dukes of the world, both opponents of Wisconsin during the 2015 Final Four, "rent players" and are ostensibly semi-professional, Wisconsin is the embodiment of collegiate sports. Similarly, in "Celebrate? Sorry We Are Studying," the 2014 Badgers were described as a team where the "term student athlete is not an oxymoron."[62] Chronicling their days spent practicing, dealing with the media, and studying for their accounting, history, and Italian classes, this story makes clear that Bo Ryan's Badgers not only play the right way but do collegiate athletics the right way. Conducting themselves in the classroom appropriately, they remind us what collegiate athletics is truly about.

Jay Miller concludes that, despite the apparent success of Kentucky's "one-and-done" approach to collegiate basketball, it is possible to reach the heights of basketball success *and* be a top-notch program of student athletes:

> So am I saying that participating in big-time collegiate athletics is incompatible with being a student? Actually, no. . . . The University of Wisconsin team somehow continues to keep up with its studies. These students are really that, and they typically stay in

school. Over the past two years, Wisconsin has graduated all of the seniors on its team and looks to do it again this year.[63]

Similarly, Roger Groves gushed over the exceptionality of Wisconsin:

> But they did not get that way through the instant recruiting of the top McDonalds' All-Americans. They had a core group who prioritized academics and continued to grow physical and academic maturity each season. . . . So for the Badgers to win the crown would be validation that playing the "right way" is indeed the way to winning it all. Other teams may even mimic them instead of the one-and-doners.[64]

Over and over again, the media discourse elevated Wisconsin as both the embodiment of an authentic basketball program of student athletes and also as the anti-Kentucky. Whereas Kentucky and Duke brought in (black) kids for a year, barely on campus long enough to pick a major much less to gain maturity, the University of Wisconsin recruited student athletes who invested time in their game, scholarly pursuits, and community. Rife with racial subtext, this sort of narrative positioned the predominantly white Wisconsin squad as a group of students who happened to play basketball in opposition to Kentucky's primarily black semi-professional team.

Irrespective of the narrative, Wisconsin is hardly doing it the *right way* educationally; that is, if graduating student athletes is a goal. "If the 68 teams were seeded by graduation rates, the Badgers would be a bottom seed," wrote Derrick Jackson. "They have the lowest Graduation Success Rate for black men of zero and the third-lowest overall at 40 percent. They were one of 16 teams that should be disqualified for historically graduating less than 50 percent of either black or white players or having an overall rate under 50 percent."[65] Facts be damned.

The Badger way/white way is clearly the *right way*; entrenched stereotypes about investment in education overdetermine the narrative afforded Wisconsin (and Kentucky). As with the Cardinals, the *right way* was imagined through a racial binary, one that pitted Kentucky/Duke versus Wisconsin. Their role as the embodiment of the *right way* reflects the power of whiteness and the ways that the meaning, ideas, and signifiers of whiteness permeate discourses of antiblackness. Beyond the major leagues and college basketball, the 2015 ascendance of golf's Jordan Spieth further reveals how #PlayingWhileWhite invariably means playing the "right" [American] way,[66] in part because playing while white means *not* playing while black.

Described as "root-table,"[67] as "humble,"[68] as "polite,"[69] as living by a "code of sportsmanship,"[70] and as an "all-American hero,"[71] Jordan Spieth emerged as the great white golfing hope following his 2015 victory at the US Masters. "He's gracious. He's kind. He's humble and polite," wrote Vince Johnson.[72]

Tiger Woods's fall from grace, alongside the longstanding search for the great white golfing hope, propelled Spieth into the national spotlight. His success in the aftermath of the era produced a narrative of him *playing the right way*. He would become America's next great (white) athletic story. In "What Makes Jordan Spieth Golf's New Leader? More Than His Skill," Jena McGregor makes clear that the hoopla is not just about his record-setting Masters performance in 2015, or even about his emergence as a top-ranked golfer, but rather about the person that he is:

> Yet just as impressive as what Spieth did last week on the course was how he did it. He handled himself with humility, for one. He gave credit to his lucky breaks, such as a ball that landed in the middle of the fairway after bouncing off a tree branch. He shrugged off a string of birdies. He asked a former sixth-grade teacher to serve as his caddie, rather than someone seasoned. He refers to older golfers as "Mr."
>
> Spieth has said he attributes his grounded nature to his 14-year-old sister, Ellie, who has a neurological disorder that places her on the autism spectrum. It's humbling to see the struggles she goes through every day, he has said—things he and others take for granted. His father also reminded him before this year's Masters that it's just a game.[73]

More than anything else, Spieth's story is one of family. According to Jeff Schultz, family is not only why Spieth is great but also indicates his core character and values:

> There's the hug from his caddie, who used to be a high school math teacher and a girls' soccer coach. There's the hug from the parents, who played college sports and went on to raise a beautiful family of five. There's the hug from his high school sweetheart, and his brother, and his college friends, and seemingly half the state of Texas.[74]

During the course of the 2015 Masters Tournament, announcers consistently celebrated that he was staying with his family during the event, watching movies and playing games. Yet, there was no golf talk. Compared to Tiger, a robot almost obsessed with the game, Spieth was a *normal* kid. Even his relationship with a caddie, who previously worked as a math teacher and a soccer coach, was an indication of his laudable morality. Citing his game and his values, his fellow golfers and the media went to great lengths to anoint him as the future of golf, as someone who could carry the game left in shambles because of the moral failing, mental weakness, and overall failures of Tiger Woods.

Representing "traditions" and "values golf," Spieth was positioned as both the game's future and the past. Celebrated with reverence and nostalgia, his transformative possibilities came from his different approach to the game, one mirroring golfers of the past. Never mind the fact that the celebration of him as an "old-school" player representing a bygone era indirectly waxes nostalgic for a time of segregation and white dominance in golf. In "Spieth Played, and Won, the Right Way," Vince Johnson praised Spieth as the right kind of champion:

> Immersed in our self-absorbed culture, and especially in the athletic world, Spieth stands out as the role model for others, a role, as Masters champion, he'll now fully realize.
>
> His wardrobe is subtle. His commercials promote social responsibility, like his AT&T commercial speaking out against texting and driving. His on-course demeanor is competitive, but without flash. When his tee shot went into the pine needles on the 12th hole Sunday, he subtly thanked each patron for moving for his ensuing shot.
>
> Upon entering Augusta National, the map of the course comes with this message:
>
> "In golf, customs of etiquette and decorum are just as important as rules governing play," Bobby Jones wrote in 1967. "Everyone is requested to display the proper customs of etiquette, decorum and behavior." Spieth fits the proper mold.
>
> "It's how the game was founded," Spieth said. "It's a game of integrity. There are no referees out there. We all respect each other . . . I learn from my examples, and I have great examples.". . . Jordan Spieth is a Masters champion, and it feels right.[75]

❖    ❖    ❖

Without Flash?

Proper?

Integrity?

Feels right?

Not Tiger Woods?

In many ways, Jordan Spieth's greatness, his potential, and his place in the future of golf is *not* Tiger Woods. Unlike Tiger Woods, he doesn't swear on the course; he is soft-spoken and humble. He doesn't make a spectacle after sinking a putt but simply moves on to the next task. Unlike Tiger, he's still with his high school sweetheart. Tiger has gone through many caddies and coaches, throwing them out like an old pair of shoes; Spieth loves his teacher-turned-caddie.

Tiger Woods changed golf; his mere existence on the course ruptured the whiteness of this country-club sport. From Orange County, California, and raised on public courses, Tiger Woods signified a rupture, one that transported golf from its segregationist 1 percent roots to a game representing "multicultural America,"[76] a game that embodied the narratives of the American Dream, that could cross over onto the commercial sports landscape. Yet, he came with baggage: his blackness.

While the ascendance of both Tiger and Spieth share many similarities: both won multiple junior titles; both played collegiate golf; both grew up in tight-knit families; both their fathers played collegiate baseball; both grew up in suburban communities—Orange County and outside of Dallas—they were often positioned as polar opposites. Spieth is situated as the anti-Tiger, as a rupture to Tiger Mania.

Unlike Tiger, he is more concerned about life outside of golf.

Unlike Tiger, who started playing golf at the age of two, Spieth didn't come to the game until a teenager. He was too busy playing baseball and doing other *normal* teenage things.

Unlike Tiger, his relationships with his parents are positioned as *normal*.

He is not in every commercial and dominating the media landscape, but instead is excelling as both a golfer and a person. While Tiger was a pitchman for Nike and countless other corporations, Spieth—endorsements not withstanding—was not selling anything to anybody; he's too busy with his family.

Jordan Spieth offered a return to the roots of golf, bringing a level of humility unseen in Tiger. He had the potential to bridge the past with a future that maintained golf's crossover possibilities.

In all, narratives surrounding Spieth were very much about Tiger. Christine Brennan chronicles America's love affair with Jordan Spieth as the result of his values and character *and* because he's not Tiger Woods:

> Spieth doesn't succumb to the uber-fist-pumping and extracur-
> ricular swearing of Tiger, so he is far less flashy and outwardly
> intimidating than Woods. But he's even more impressive as a
> person because he knows he doesn't need the window-dressing
> and the nonsense to play the game. I think they call it respect. . . .
> Spieth's vocabulary is as G-rated as Tiger's is not. There was a big
> and bold "dang it" on his tee shot at 16 Sunday. He tried to coax
> a few shots out of the trees this week by asking them to "get an
> ounce right." He failed to add the "pretty please."[77]

Anti-Tiger:

> Ask Spieth about this, about these conversations he has with his
> golf ball during every round, and he gets a bit sheepish.
>     "I don't really try to," he said. "I mean, I guess it's just the
> competitor in me, just wanting it sometimes. I'd like to think I
> don't do it the most of anybody, but if that's the case, then maybe
> I should dial it down a little bit."
>     Tiger would never, ever, ever say that.[78]

Anti-Tiger:

> Then there's the way Spieth treats his opponents, which is decid-
> edly old school. He gave a big thumbs up to playing partner Justin
> Rose for a shot Rose hit on the seventh hole Sunday that allowed
> him to shave a stroke off Spieth's lead.[79]

Anti-Tiger:

> There also was Spieth's new TV commercial. Tiger's commercials
> were always about Tiger, which is really not all that unusual. That's
> the way it is with most superstar athletes. Spieth's? The one that
> was airing between his shots Sunday was the AT&T commercial
> about not texting while driving, the kind of commercial any
> mother loves.[80]

According to Bill Burt, Jordan Spieth may "be the anti-Tiger Woods."[81]
Whereas "like Tiger, he is an athlete" who "looks like he could pitch for the

Red Sox or shoot jumpers like Danny Ainge" he doesn't come with the "baggage." "His road to Masters history had very little collateral damage. He had two parents at home and has an autistic sister, Ellie. In fact, his grandparents made an appearance, too. Spieth also still dates his high school sweetheart."[82] All-American, he's the "boy next door," whose ascendance didn't come at the cost of his family, his relationships, and his morality.

Just as Tiger's ascendance as "America's multicultural son"[83] played upon hegemonic definitions of the selfish, crude, cocky, and unredeemable black athlete from other sports, Spieth's place in the cultural landscape emanates from his juxtaposition to Woods as well. Whiteness is at the core of this comparison; playing the white way is the *right way*.

Following the 2016 Masters Tournament, which saw Jordan Spieth's "nightmare collapse,"[84] we once again witnessed how Spieth had become the anti-Tiger. On the verge of back-to-back, wire-to-wire victories, Spieth would bogey holes ten and eleven. He would follow this up with a seven, quadruple bogey on the twelfth hole, which included two balls in the water —an epic collapse. Poised to make history, Spieth's "monumental implosion"[85] ironically propelled the mythology surrounding his career and persona forward. Celebrated for not only regaining his composure but also making a comeback that almost allowed him to snatch victory from defeat, the emergent narrative emphasized his humility, grace, and professionalism following the loss. According to Kyle Porter, while the "point is not that Spieth is classy or a media darling . . . because he shook somebody's hand after a golf tournament" (then why highlight it here? This point was made over and over again), the main takeaway is "that Spieth is thoughtful." Moreover:

> He is self-aware and reflective. He knows you want to know what
> he knows, and for some reason, he gives it to you. He is thought-
> ful about his game and about what he wants you to know about
> his game. He is (along with dozens of other stars in golf) just
> generally thoughtful. It's a rarity among humans (much less ath-
> letes). And it's one of the many things to love about his future.[86]

Similarly, Andrew Joseph praised Spieth for his performance at the conclusion of the event: "This was undeniably the biggest disappointment of Spieth's career, and he didn't run away from the moment. He knew it was coming and presented the green jacket to Danny Willett."[87] Others like Mark Schlereth used the moment to celebrate Spieth for his professionalism, unlike Cam Newton, who according to some didn't handle the 2016 Super

Bowl loss with the requisite grace and professionalism. "I hope Cam Newton is watching Jordan Spieth's interview right now. To be a true professional you have to be able to face the music," he tweeted.[88] As he reclaimed his rightful place as America's top golfer, Spieth was teaching his peers the "right way to play," reminding us all what makes sports great. The anti-Tiger . . . the anti-Cam . . . the anti-Beckham . . . the anti-Kaepernick . . . the white way is the right way/the right way is the way.

### CONCLUSION

What we see with each of the three examples presented here—the Cardinals, the Badgers, and Jordan Spieth—is that, even in loss, they *play the game the right way*. Even failure becomes further evidence of their success and their greatness.

The focus on character, on role models, and on approaching their sport in a way that mirrors athletes of yesteryear, highlights the ways that hegemonic constructions of whiteness operate within these narratives. Equally important is how understandings of blackness, rooted in antiblack racism, prop up their profiles, providing meaning and legitimacy to mythologies worthy of celebrating.

While about winning—few have celebrated the Cardinals or Badgers over the last year with waning success on the court—the identities of the teams and athletes, and the mythologies surrounding them, the *right way* trope reflects the racial politics that Spieth, the Cardinals, and the Badgers signify within the dominant white imagination. Leading up to the 2016–2017 season, Nigel Hayes, who is African American, and Bronson Koenig, who is a member of the Ho-Chunk Nation, have both been in the news. Neither has been celebrated for doing things the *right way*. Hayes, who has protested against the exploitation of student athletes[89] and been active in his support of Black Lives Matter protests,[90] has faced a barrage of criticism. Koenig joined protestors in North Dakota in an effort to stop the construction of a pipeline through Standing Rock Sioux lands. This is nothing new for Koenig. Since arriving at Wisconsin, he has been active and vocal in advocating for his community. "I hope to bring awareness to the cause and give everyone there a little bit of joy and a little bit of hope," Koenig remarked in an interview with *Yahoo! Sports*. "I want to take time out of my schedule to pray with them and protest with them and show them that I'm right alongside them. They've always had my back whether I have an awful game or a great game, and this is my way of repaying the favor."[91] While their activism prompted both erasure and backlash, few cited it as examples of student athletes doing it the *right way*. However, Jon Beidelschies, in "Nigel Hayes, Bronson Koenig and the Badgers' Men's Basketball Team Are Living the Wisconsin Idea," turned their activism and courageous work into a celebration of Wisconsin athletics and the school as a whole:

> For the university, the Wisconsin Idea is pretty simple: education should influence people's lives beyond the boundaries of the classroom. It speaks to the critical need for public service and the notion that a university that divorces learning from the world with which it is supposed to engage does both its students and its community a disservice. The influence of the Wisconsin Idea, whether we see it directly or not, can be felt throughout the halls from Bascom to Babcock. It grounds the school and ties its work to the people of the state in ways that other "public ivies" don't. It is part of what makes the school so special. (And yes, UW is special in many ways). . . .
>
> These young men embody the Wisconsin Idea. They are taking their education—in the classroom, on the court—into the world and doing what they can to make it better than they found it. They are striking out bravely, confidently, because their communities need it. We all need it.[92]

Here the athletes' exceptionality, their benevolence, and their doing things the right way was ultimately about Wisconsin #PlayingTheWhiteWay. Whether protesting or playing the game with the fundamentals, whether diving for loose balls or marching for social justice, the racial signifiers associated with Wisconsin, like those attached to the Cardinals, Gonzaga, and the New York Giants (who despite claiming the mantle of doing things the *right way* initially did very little to punish Josh Brown), to Jordan Spieth, Tom Brady, Lance Armstrong, and countless others, anchor the *right way* narratives. This is power and privilege personified, cashed in over and over again.

The profiling of white athletes and those teams imagined as embodying whiteness conveys a message about the possibilities and potential of sports. Yet, it also reinforces hegemonic scripts about race, about the meanings in and difference between whiteness and blackness—which requires surveillance and policing, whether in post-game celebrations, in one's conduct during press conference or after homeruns, or in simply walking through a neighborhood. #PlayingTheRightWay is an entrenched sporting cliché; it is also a window into racial mythologies and scripts that transcends the game.

CHAPTER 10

# SPORTING CULTURES AND WHITE VICTIMS

F OLLOWING a decade of identity politics (nationalist movements), feminist struggles, the ascendance of affirmative action and war on poverty programs, and societal and cultural transformation, the 1980s and 1990s saw "the ascendancy of a new and powerful figure in U.S. culture: the white male as victim."[1] Popular culture proved particularly powerful in "the production of images and narratives of victimized and disadvantaged young white males that both reflect and reproduce the discursive logics of contemporary white male backlash."[2] Specifically, a whiteness-as-victim genre emerged, as film, music, and sporting landscapes collectively "imagined . . . the white male protagonist as underprivileged, lacking social, cultural economic or genetic privileges and under constant siege."[3] A post-civil rights, post-integration, and post-Black Power sporting landscape can thus be defined by "the production of images and narratives of victimized and disadvantaged . . . white males that both reflect and reproduce the discursive logics of contemporary white male backlash."[4]

White athletes—from Tom Brady to Duke's Grayson Allen, from Tim Tebow to Wes Welker, from Johnny Manziel to Richie Incognito,[5] from Donald Sterling[6] to members of Duke lacrosse[7]—are imagined as victims. Rather than exemplifying so-called white privilege, they embody the hegemony of whiteness under attack.

As narratives surrounding white athletes offer a racial time machine to an imagined period in sports when (white) male heroes played the *right way*, representing a clear alternative to me-first, anti-role model "thugs,"[8] claims of victimhood persist.

Despite playing the *right way*, despite embodying fundamentals, intelligence, and humility, white athletes get no love from media, fans, advertisers, competitors, and the sports world as a whole. White masculinity is

226

framed as battered, besieged, and belittled by the media, black athletes, and the masses.

By way of a conclusion, this chapter highlights the ubiquity and power of the white athlete as victim, arguing that #PlayingWhileWhite means playing in an imagined world of disrespect and marginalization, and playing uphill. Embodying new racism, the iteration of the victimized white body has become commonplace in the post–civil rights sporting landscape. Within the white sporting imagination, white males are disadvantaged not only by genetic limitations but by fans who want to root for athletes of color and women, by stereotypes, by the desire for certain types of play, and by a media world that has embraced a multiculturalist turn.[9] Under constant siege, white athletes are "victims of political correctness, multiculturalism, and a sports world that has left them behind."[10]

From the disrespected white player to the white athlete who is subject to different standards; from the white fan denied role models and the greatness of sports from years past to the white owner who gets no love; narratives of white victimhood have found significant resonance in the world of sports.

The white athlete as victim, in fact, encapsulates many of the tropes and narratives that are central to #PlayingWhileWhite: intelligence; scrappiness; the character associated with being an underdog; a persistent work ethic; and determination. The purported disdain toward the white athlete comes from contempt for the feistiness and never-die attitude that is necessary to succeed given the genetic deficiencies and the racial landscape of today's sports world.

The widespread investment in celebrating white athletes, in seeking to commodify bodies, aesthetics, eras, and sports assumed to be white also produces narratives of victimhood. Nowhere is this more evident than in the narrative surrounding Duke basketball.

POOR GRAYSON ALLEN

"'No other black player from any other school is hated as much as a white player from Duke,' former Duke point guard Jay Williams said. 'None.'"[11]

None? Of course! The white athlete is the ultimate victim—#Dont WhiteAthleteLivesMatter?

This is the central thesis of Dana O'Neil's 2016 piece, "Is Grayson Allen the Next Hated White Duke Player?" Chronicling the challenges faced by Allen, Duke's latest white star, O'Neil links the trope of white victimhood with narratives of redemption, intelligence, toughness, and nostalgia, all central ingredients to the stories we tell about white athletes.

O'Neil situates Allen's difficulty in a larger history of white ballers at Duke. His story is that of Chris Collins, who was called "Chrissy"; of J. J. Redick, who endured fans yelling about his sister. That same Redick once played against University of Maryland, where fans greeted him with "homemade T-shirts that read, 'When I grow up, I want to name my kid J. J. Redick and beat him up every day.'"[12] Allen follows in the footsteps of Jon Scheyer, who endured the creation of a website "dedicated to his many grimaces and expressions," and of Steve Wojciechowski, who once was sitting in an airport when someone walked up to him and noted "I used to watch you at Duke. God, I hated you."[13]

To be white and play basketball at Duke, is to live a tortured life. This is not just O'Neil's story about Allen, or even the broader narrative about Duke basketball that is championed by the mainstream media[14] and white nationalists[15] but about white athletes as a whole. According to O'Neil:

> Allen always checked most of the boxes, as if he'd been produced on a factory line, the latest Blue Devil cut from the Laettner prototype.
>
> Allen looks soft, but plays hard, his game filled with swagger even if he isn't necessarily the swagger type. He has had his big-stage moment: his 16-point performance outburst in last season's national championship game essentially halted Wisconsin and handed Duke coach Mike Krzyzewski his fifth title.
>
> And, of course, Allen is a white guy in a Duke uniform, the latest vessel, the reincarnation of Christian Laettner, Chris Collins, Steve Wojciechowski, J.J. Redick, Greg Paulus, and Jon Scheyer. The personas are interchangeable, and equally hard to like.

More than its centering of a white-victim-status narrative, what is striking about O'Neil's piece is how it works through a series of tropes, each of which normalizes the white athlete as hardworking, good natured, intelligent, bound by the fundamentals, and embodying all the great things about sports. White athletes are the American Dream and the signification of the American Dream; having pulled themselves up by their shoelaces and landed at one of America's great institutions of higher education, white athletes should be celebrated on Mount Rushmore, not ridiculed on memes.

Grayson Allen is the new Christian Laettner, something nobody wants. But, why? "Laettner's blue-collar parents scraped together the money to send him to prep school; Redick's bohemian parents lived on a communal farm, his dad working as a stoneware potter; Wojciechowski's dad was a longshoreman," writes O'Neil. "That doesn't matter, though. These guys looked the part, and it fit, giving rise to a legacy of loathing." In other words, they are hated and unfairly critiqued because of the stereotype that all white kids come from rich suburbs.

They purportedly are hated because of their lack of athleticism; because they made up for it in toughness, grittiness, intelligence, and work ethic.

Allen, like his white basketball forefathers, is hated because he *plays the right way*. At times, his passion for winning may lead him to trip a player or two. Sure, his determination to win might lead to bad choices, like when he refused to shake Dillon Brooks's hand following a loss to the University of Oregon in the 2016 NCAA tournament. While for others these otherwise reprehensible, "thuggish," punk acts would garner outrage and debates about "today's players," for Allen each trip, tantrum, and instance of trash-talking becomes an opportunity to reinforce the narrative of white athletes playing hard, loving team, and doing whatever it takes to win.

Similarly, the beauty (and the hatred) of the white athlete is about success. The reason Laettner, Collins, Redick, and countless other white Dukies are hated is because they win, and we don't want *them* to win. This is why we hate Tom Brady, Larry Bird, the Cardinals, the Wisconsin Badgers, and countless others. Success, toughness, and following the right path produce contempt based on jealousy and presumptions about white privilege.

It is not surprising that Allen and others embrace the white antihero persona, which is inauthentic to their true selves. J. J. Redick was hated because anti-white prejudices made him embrace the villain personality:

> Or at least he became one. Redick didn't come to Duke with the same reputation Laettner had. He was actually pretty naïve—and wildly unprepared for opposing fans. Redick admits to consciously and purposefully changing his personality, going from an unassuming middle child of a modest family to the headbobbing, trash-talking lightning rod of college basketball. Fans tormented him. So he strutted around, asking for more.[16]

Even those qualities and actions that warrant criticism, that otherwise elicit outrage, are rendered meaningless, since they don't tell us anything about Allen or Redick as a person, unless they become evidence of maturation and form a story of redemption. Authentically innocent and benevolent, whiteness remains a blank canvas that cannot be polluted.

While multicultural and feminist America purportedly hates Duke basketball because of its whiteness, because of how it plays the game, and for what its team biographies signify, no athlete encapsulates the imagined cultural shift that has rendered white athletes as the ultimate victim better than Tom Brady, the man too slow to succeed, the sixth-round pick, and the often-underestimated quarterback who rose from obscurity (Serra High School and the University of Michigan) to become a Super Bowl champion.

### AMERICA'S FAVORITE SON: TOM BRADY

Tom Brady demonstrates the unflinching power of whiteness in contemporary America. Black people are punished and demonized for cheating. White men like Tom Brady get to do all sorts of sh** for a competitive edge, and they are gaming the system. This is yet another demonstration of white privilege.

In 2015, the NFL released the Wells Report,[17] which concluded that Tom Brady—America's quarterback, its golden boy, Giselle's husband, and the man who "shut up" Richard Sherman with a 2015 Super Bowl victory—was a cheater. Commissioned by the NFL, the Wells Report looked into accusations that several members of the Patriots organization, including Brady, conspired to circumvent the league rules governing game balls. Specifically, it found the following:

> It is more probable than not that New England Patriots personnel participated in violations of the Playing Rules and were involved in a deliberate effort to circumvent the rules. Based on the evidence, it also is our view that it is more probable than not that Tom Brady . . . was at least generally aware of the inappropriate activities involving the release of air from Patriots game balls.[18]

Yet, the narrative that emerged focused on how, at worst, he made a mistake; that if the accusations were indeed true, it suggests a lapse in judgment, since Tom has "integrity," and is a "good boy."

More common has been a focus on an unfair and arbitrary process, on the morally bankrupt NFL, and on the fascism of commissioner Roger Goodell. Indeed, Tom Brady is not the first player to deal with an unjust system, to endure the hypocrisy of Goodell's NFL. Yet, the selective outrage on full display over multiple seasons reveals that Tom Brady's presumed innocence, his purported victimization, and his life matter more than those of his black counterparts.

If Tom Brady were black, people would have called him a criminal, concluding that his behavior reflected some innate values. They probably would have blamed hip-hop, single mothers, and the culture of poverty; if he had been a black player, the conversation would not have been about Goodell or the system, but instead about how a lack of morals and a work ethic led him to cut corners to win "by any means necessary." If he were black, the conversation would have turned to affirmative action and how he was forced to cheat, because he lacked the skills needed to excel at this elite level.

But Tom Brady is white. No wonder the report and the announcement of a four-game suspension, the successful appeals, the subsequent reversal of a court decision reinstating his suspension, and his eventual acceptance of the supposedly unjust ruling, led many to protest in the virtual streets:

"Tom Brady's Life Matters"
An Outrage
An Injustice
An Unjust Ruling
A Capricious Rule
Unfair and Arbitrary

Sean Gregory, channeling narratives about white victimhood, wrote: "It's actually pretty easy to pick on the cool kid. You don't come across as a bully."[19] No, it's pretty easy to brutalize the poor and to abuse the powerless; it's easy to take a black life and then blame them for their own death.[20]

During the months-long ordeal, many asked, "What's the big deal? Deflating a football cannot be much of an advantage. Besides, he has won plenty without such an advantage."

Others have acknowledged that he may have violated NFL rules, but is it a rule that really matters? Besides, everyone is doing it. As the old adage goes: "If you are not cheating, you are not trying." However, if you are white, cheating is not really cheating but merely an effort to get an edge, to garner a competitive advantage, and no big deal.

No harm, no foul.

For white athletes like Brady or his counterparts in baseball accused of using PEDs or drivers in NASCAR bending the rules, what happens in the locker room is supposed to stay in the locker room. For white athletes and coaches who don't have to compete against all forms of competition because of segregation: oh well, that's life.

For black athletes, cheating, whether by taking performance-enhancing drugs or "easy-A classes"[21] is a sign of moral and communal failure.

Not long after #DeflateGate, Little League Baseball stripped Chicago's Jackie Robinson West Little League of its title because of allegations of cheating. Many celebrated the punishment as necessary. Their crime? They had violated a ridiculous and arbitrary rule that disallowed a few kids from outside the district to play on the team.[22] Sports media commentators and the public fomented outrage. "Rules are rules," we were told. There is no excuse for cheating and not following the established rules. It doesn't matter that everyone is doing it.

It didn't matter that the kids from Jackie Robinson West didn't get an advantage. Rules are rules, and there are consequences if you break them. Their punishment was necessary, because it sent a message to kids that cheating has consequences. I guess these same concerns don't apply to Tom Brady and the Patriots. Their cheating isn't a sign of eroding values; their wanton disregard for the rules isn't a threat to our moral fabric.

But what about the kids? You would think by these very different responses that Tom Brady is not a role model.

"The truth is that many Americans have a dishearteningly high tolerance for cheating in professional sports," writes an editorial in the *Chicago Tribune*. "We dismiss the evidence. We make excuses. Sammy didn't know that bat was corked! Who can prove all those players used steroids? Everyone puts a bit of Vaseline on the ball now and then. What's the big deal about letting a little air out of a football?"[23]

This separate and racially unequal acceptance of "cheating" extends beyond the sporting landscape. White kids getting high, popping Adderall, and selling dime bags is nothing to worry about. White athletes smoking marijuana or using PEDS at most elicits shaming on the road to redemption; it's all good. White student athletes violating NCAA rules is nothing to worry about. Their cheating—or law-breaking—is seen as neither a threat nor an act in need of punishment.

While black drug dealers are dangerous "thugs," white Wall Street executives are smart businessmen working under the rules of capitalism.

Whereas black kids taking diapers are looters, those who have stolen land, resources, and so much more are patriots.

For Brady, and white America as a whole, we have been told over and over again that there needs to be proof, indisputable evidence, that "America's golden boy," its anti-criminal, is a cheater (ignore destruction of cell phone).

Brady demonstrates yet again that whites are innocent . . . until proven innocent. Any evidence to the contrary proves that the system is flawed, that we have a miscarriage of justice. Even when "convicted," Brady, like Josh Hamilton, Big Ben, Lance Armstrong, Brock Turner, Ryan Braun, Hope Solo, Riley Cooper, Michael Phelps, Ryan Lochte, and countless others are forgiven with little accountability and even less justice. Embodying what we want to think about our white selves, and about the nation, forgiveness and redemption is a gift to our white selves.

And don't even think about convictions as a result of circumstantial evidence. In a nation where video after video of white police officers killing unarmed black men and women has prompted neither arrest, much less conviction, circumstantial evidence has little chance of penetrating the Teflon power of whiteness.

If only the same rules applied to Barry Bonds or Alex Rodriguez, both of whom never tested positive for performance-enhancing drugs.

If only the same rules applied to Freddie Gray, whose looking "funny" at an officer prompted the officer to arrest him, resulting in his death.[24]

Stop-and-frisk and racial profiling is built upon the "circumstantial" evidence that justifies the harassment of black and brown youth throughout America.

The racial double standards are endless. It is no wonder that Brady and so many of his defenders have expressed shock and outrage at being held accountable for cheating. It is no wonder that he became a victim over and over again, even after his 2017 Super Bowl victory. This is part of his career.

In 2012, Tom Brady got into a heated argument with an assistant coach. The incident dismissed as no big deal and a sign of his "passion for the game," he remained the league's "golden boy." Compare this to endless examples of black athletes who have been routinely demonized at any instance when they have challenged their coach.

When Brady talked trash to his opponents, it was a sign of his competitiveness; when Richard Sherman and Cam Newton engaged in similar types of banter, by contrast, they were "thugs" who didn't respect the game.

It is no wonder that Brady and his supporters were outraged. He was being penalized despite playing by the rules of America's ultimate game, where white is always right. That is the lesson when looking at the lack of consequences for Lance Armstrong, Josh Hamilton, countless collegiate athletes, and numerous NASCAR racers. This is evident in the multiple chances afforded to Johnny Football, Hope Solo, and Ben Roethlisberger. This is the message in the celebration of Tim Tebow as an underdog or Grayson Allen as a victim.

To #PlayWhileWhite is to be seen as smart, scrappy, determined, and a leader. #PlayingWhileWhite is to win, to be celebrated in victory, redeemed in defeat, lifted up when down, and sympathized with by others as a real or imagined victim. It is to be innocent and a repository of excuses for failure.

As I am finishing this book, news has just broken that Ryan Lochte and three of his teammates, in an effort to conceal breaking down a bathroom door at a gas station and the resulting fight with a security guard—all during a night of drunkenness—concocted a story about being robbed. Playing on widespread fear—racialized fear—of criminals of color during the Rio Olympics, the Lochte narrative tapped into entrenched stereotypes of #ThugsOfColor preying on #InnocentWhites. "Here you have a group of white swimmers in a predominantly Afro-Latino country that is unfortunately known for its violence stating that they were robbed at gunpoint. Everyone rallied behind poor Lochte and the other swimmers," writes Yesha Callahan. "Why? Because white privilege."[25]

Reflecting the power and privileges of whiteness, Lochte's allegations prompted international media coverage and concern. Ultimately, Lochte's story fell apart. And while some continued to justify his claims of a robbery, others merely offered context to help understand Lochte and his mistake.

As the truth became clear, the excuses were plentiful: the stress of the Olympics made him do it; his immaturity and youthfulness (at the age of thirty-two) caused the mistake; or simply, that it was simply no big deal. This is what #PlayingWhileWhite looks like. "No apologies from him or other athletes is [sic] needed. We have to understand that these *kids* came here to have fun. Let's give these *kids* a break. Sometimes you make decisions that you regret," noted IOC spokesman Mario Andrada. "They had fun, they made a *mistake*, life goes on."[26]

Fun? At whose expense?

Was the fun in kicking down the bathroom door?

Was the fun in urinating on the bathroom wall, in damaging property*— or did the fun start with the fight with the security guard?[27] Was the fun in sparking an international spectacle that further solidified the image of Brazil as violent and uncivilized, dangerous even to Olympians, much less tourists?

I can imagine that for Afro-Brazilian youth from the favelas, for the security guard, and for those who worked at the gas station that night, this was not fun. But soon this episode will have come and gone with little consequence. Yes, Lochte would lose some endorsements; sure he would find himself suspended from US swimming, both of which were likely in any event because of his lackluster performance at the Olympics. He would also land a spot on *Dancing with the Stars*.

Just as the Olympics will have come and gone, leaving sacred burial grounds trampled upon, communities destroyed, and families torn apart by countless police shootings, Lochte and his crew will have come and gone, with memories of medals and fun all at the expense of others, which is the definition of #PlayingWhileWhite.

---

* Please note that some of the specifics and details are conflicting in this regard.

#PlayingWhileWhite means life goes on. Whiteness is the ultimate "get out of jail free" card, a lifetime pass to go on with your life without apologies or consequences. It is to call any indiscretion, failure, or even crime a mistake or a case of bad judgment, which not only affords forgiveness but represents a rhetorical effort to make clear that these actions don't define these four white *men* or their broader community, #BoysBeingBoys. "Lochte is being given the benefit of the doubt by folks who are 'waiting for all the details' before they make a determination about the swimmer's story, or arguing that what he did wasn't actually [a] lie but rather [an] 'embellish[ment of]' the truth," writes Britni Danielle,[28] who wondered how the story would have played out had the "kids" been four members of the men's basketball team. "Listen, it's clear White privilege is real. White folks don't really have to worry about getting racially profiled; they can fight, pull a gun, or shoot at police and still live; they qualify for better home loans; get called for job interviews; and apparently, they are given the benefit of the doubt when they're caught up in a blatant lie that sparks an international scandal. Must be nice."[29]

In the same week where Gabby Douglas was demonized for her failure to stand at attention during the national anthem and her insufficient smile in appreciation of her teammates;[30] in a nation where black youth are regularly seen as adults—suspected, guilty, and blamed for their own deaths[31]—the excuse-making and culture of exoneration offers yet another reminder of the power of white supremacist privilege.

Just like his access to swimming pools[32] and his celebration in the media, Lochte's ability to blame his misdeeds on the racial Other[33] and his ability to walk the pathway to forgiveness is all about the ways in which whites are profiled: as heroes, as deserving of protection, as innocent, and as always right. To understand Lochte is to understand America; to see Lochte beyond medals and swimming times is to see the lived realities of white privilege and antiblack racism. To see his experiences, along with the many others discussed in this book, is to witness white supremacy at work inside and outside the sporting arena.

The logic of American racism doesn't simply work within these sporting arenas; it governs their—our—everyday realities, from our experiences with the police to our experiences with prospective employers. We are profiled everyday: as innocent, as hard working, as fundamental, as proper, as civilized, as redeemable, as intelligent, as leaders, as free spirited, as victims, as the future, and as the embodiment of the beautiful past and a glorious future. Even when the game is over, power and privilege remain when #PlayingWhileWhite.

# NOTES

INTRODUCTION

1   Leonard 2012a; McNulty 2005.
2   Messner, Dunbar, and Hunt 2000.
3   Buffington 2005, 21.
4   Lapchick 2002; Niven 2005.
5   Leonard 2008; Kusz 2007, 2001; Price 1997.
6   R. Jackson 2006.
7   Frankenberg 2001, 76.
8   Ibid.
9   hooks 1992, 169.
10  Lipsitz 1998, 72.
11  Dyer, quoted in Kusz 2001, 393.
12  Wray and Newitz 1997, 3.
13  Feagin and Vera 1995, 296.
14  Shome 1996, 503.
15  Dyer 1997.
16  Giroux 1997.
17  Dyer 1997, 4.
18  Ibid., 1.
19  Frankenberg 1997, 1.
20  Rasmussen et al. 2001, 9; Giroux 1997.
21  Dyer 1997, xiii.
22  McCune 2014.
23  King and Springwood, 2001, 4; quoted in D. D. Douglas 2005, 259.
24  Edwards 1998.
25  Kusz 2001.
26  T. Lewis 2010.

27   I. Perry 2011; Bonilla-Silva 2006; Collins 2004; Bonilla-Silva 2001;
     P. J. Williams 1997; hooks 1992.
28   Crenshaw 2000, 554.
29   Giroux 2008, 61.
30   Ansell 1997, 20–21.
31   R. Jackson 2006.
32   McDonald 2005.
33   Leonard 2012a; King and Leonard 2010; Ferber 2007; Giardina and
     Donnelly 2007; Douglas 2005; Leonard 2004; D. L. Andrews 2001b;
     Cole 2001; Cole and D. L. Andrews 2001; King and Springwood 2001;
     Boyd 2000; Davis and Harris 1998; L. Johnson and Roediger 1997;
     Cole and D. L. Andrews 1996.
34   Giardina and Donnelly 2007, 3.
35   Boyd 2000, 60.
36   Roediger 1999.
37   DuBois 1935; 1997.
38   McIntosh 1989.
39   Kusz 2003, 2007.

## 1. THE SCRAPPY WHITE LEADER

Chapter 1 includes and builds on material published in D. J. Leonard, "Johnny
Manziel Is No Rosa Parks," *New Black Man (in Exile)*, blog, August 14, 2013,
and "Revealing the Stigma against Tattooed Athletes," *Huffington Post*,
December 5, 2013.

1    Said 1978, 36.
2    Oates 2017; Leonard 2014; Oriard 2010; Oriard 2008; Coakley 2006;
     Shropshire 1996; Edwards 1972.
3    Webber 2012.
4    Melnick 2001.
5    Ibid., 184.
6    Buffington 2005; Dufur and Feinberg 2009; Hartmann 2007.
7    Buffington 2005, 20.
8    Mercurio and Filak 2010; Hartmann 2007; Rhoden 2007; Buffington 2005;
     Murrell and Curtis 1994.
9    Billings 2004, 202.
10   Burnison 2013.
11   Webber 2012.
12   Ibid.
13   Burnison 2013; PA Sports 2009.
14   Webber 2012; Young 2010; Zimmerman 2010.
15   Doyle 2011; Pasquarelli 2006.
16   Zachariason 2014; Wesseling 2013; Wood 2013.

17  Rosenthal 2013; Dunne 2012.
18  Woodard 2014; Blount 2013.
19  Tynes 2016; Bell 2013; Lovelace 2013; M. D. Smith 2013a; Rhoden 2006; M. D. Smith 2012; Vance 2006.
20  Sando 2016.
21  S. Jenkins 2011; Wood 2012, 2011.
22  Wood 2011.
23  North 2012; Wood 2011.
24  S. Jenkins 2011.
25  Tobak 2011.
26  Rendell 2015.
27  Panchina 2009.
28  Butterworth 2010.
29  Renck 2014.
30  Howe 2012; Walker 2011; Guregian 2010a; Guregian 2010b; Guregian 2007; Harper 2007.
31  Renck 2014; Walker 2011; O'Sullivan 2008; Guregian 2010a; Guregian 2010b; Guregian 2007; Harper 2007.
32  Walker 2011.
33  Guregian 2010a.
34  Howe 2012.
35  Walker 2011.
36  Gasper 2009.
37  Howe 2012.
38  Giudice 2012.
39  Shaikin 2009.
40  Faraudo 2015.
41  Yoder 2014.
42  Strauss 2014.
43  M. Moore 2014.
44  Leitch 2014.
45  Ringo 2014.
46  Leitch 2014.
47  Quoted in Leitch 2014.
48  Hohler 2008.
49  Quoted in Hohler 2008.
50  Craggs 2009.
51  Abraham 2012.
52  Junior 2009.
53  Yoder 2014.
54  Craggs 2010.
55  Brooks 2013.
56  Baffoe 2016; R. Wilson 2016; Florio 2015; Breech 2014; Endress 2013.

57  Brooks 2013; Broomberg 2013.
58  Baffoe 2016; Endress 2013.
59  Dufresne 2013.
60  Brooks 2014.
61  Ellis 2014.
62  Ibid.
63  Lee 2014.
64  Scarborough 2014.
65  Lee 2014.
66  Brooks 2014.
67  Leonard 2012a; Boyd 2003; King and Springwood 2001.
68  "Bradshaw On WFAN" 2013.
69  M. D. Smith 2013b.
70  Elliott 2013.
71  Whitlock 2013a.
72  Petkac 2013.
73  Quoted in ESPN, 2013.
74  Whitlock 2012.
75  Gasper 2013.
76  Gregory 2013.
77  J. F. Engel 2013.
78  Barra 2013.
79  Wetzel 2013a.
80  Ibid.
81  J. F. Engel 2013.
82  Theoharis 2014.
83  McGuire 2011.
84  Feagin 2010; Giroux 2008; Bonilla-Silva 2006, 2004; Collins 2004;
     T. N. Brown 2003; Wise 2001a; hooks 1992.
85  D. Boyd 2015.
86  Freeling 2015; Halberstam 1999.
87  Wheel 2013.
88  J. F. Engel 2013.
89  Zirin 2013a.
90  Petchesky 2013a.
91  Gantt 2016.
92  Solomon 2013.
93  Whitlock 2013b.
94  Hartmann 2007, 50.
95  Silverstein 2013.
96  D. Brown 2000.
97  Khan 2012.
98  Wheel 2013.

99   Neal 2013.

100   Nocera and Strauss 2016; Arnett 2015; Branch 2011.

101   Woodbine 2016.

102   Guevara and Fidler 2002, 49.

103   Guevara and Fidler 2002, 49; quoted in Leonard 2013a.

104   Deion Sanders, quoted in Travis 2013a.

105   Travis 2013b.

106   Ibid.

107   Picca and Feagin 2007; Bonilla-Silva 2006; Bonilla-Silva 2001.

108   Barra 2013.

109   Nocera and Strauss 2016.

110   Hruby 2016.

111   Kaplan 2000.

112   Hruby 2016.

113   Whitley 2012.

114   "Kyle McNary Is the Worst NBA Fan Ever" 2009; quoted in Leonard 2013b.

115   Collins 2004, 153.

116   Ferber 2007, 20.


## 2. HE GOT BRAINS

Chapter 2 includes and builds on material published in D. J. Leonard, "'Basketball IQ' and the Racial Coding of the Word," *The Undefeated*, June 8, 2016, and "Bill Simmons and the Bell Curve: The 'Limited Intellectual Capital' of the NBA's Players," *New Black Man (in Exile)*, blog, October 20, 2011. This material was also included in D. J. Leonard and B. L. Hazelwood (2014), "The Race Denial Card: The NBA Lockout, LeBron James and the Politics of New Racism," in *Colorblind Screen: Television in Post-Racial America*, edited by Sarah Turner and Sarah Nielsen, 108–39 (New York: New York University Press).

1    B. Simmons 2011a.

2    B. Simmons 2011b.

3    Bonilla-Silva 2001; Gresson, Kincheloe, and Steinberg 1997.

4    Runstedtler 2012; Leonard 2012a; Carrington 2010; T. Lewis 2010;
     T. Boyd 2003.

5    Leonard and King 2011; Ferber 2007; P. H. Collins 2004; D. D. Douglas
     2005; Ferber 1999; Hoberman 1997.

6    Feagin et al. 2001, 188.

7    Ferber 2007, 20.

8    Coakley 2006, 288.

9    D. D. Douglas 2005, 3.

10   Mercurio and Filak 2010, 57.

11   Ibid.

12   Ibid.

13  Quoted in Hutcherson 2011.
14  Carrington 2002, 19.
15  Neal 2013.
16  Strauss 2012; Israeli n.d; Perchick 2011.
17  Ferber 2007; Bonilla-Silva 2006; P. H. Collins 2004; Ferber 1999.
18  Slover 2014.
19  Perchick 2011.
20  Slover 2014.
21  Ibid.
22  D. Coleman 2014; Santelices and Wilson 2010.
23  Golden 2007.
24  Leonard 2012a; King and Leonard 2011; Carrington 2010; Ferber 2007;
    P. H. Collins 2004; T. Boyd 2003.
25  In 2003, Marianne Bertrand and Sendhil Mullainathan published a study
    entitled "Are Emily and Greg More Employable than Lakisha and Jamal?
    A Field Experiment on Labor Market Discrimination." They concluded
    that applicants with "white sounding names" were 50 percent more likely
    to receive a callback when submitting a résumé compared to those "black
    sounding names." According to these MIT professors, whiteness was
    worth as much as eight years of work experience. #ApplyingWhileWhite
    was a distinct advantage. They argue, "While one may have expected that
    improved credentials may alleviate employers' fear that African-American
    applicants are deficient in some unobservable skills, this is not the case in
    our data. Discrimination therefore appears to bite twice, making it harder
    not only for African-Americans to find a job but also to improve their
    employability" (Bertrand and Mullainathan 2003). See C. Miller 2004 for
    further discussion.
26  Gane-McCalla 2009.
27  B. Ryan 1992.
28  Quoted in Koutroupis 2012.
29  Quoted in Zwerling 2015.
30  Fischer-Baum, Gordon, and Haisley 2014.
31  Rhoden 2006; T. Boyd 2003; Dyson 2001; King and Springwood 2001;
    T. Boyd 1997; Hoberman 1997.
32  Boyd 1997, 114.
33  Oriard 2010, 245.
34  Little 2007.
35  Tynes 2016; Mercurio and Filak 2010; Billings 2004.
36  Oriard 2010; Hartmann 2007; Rhoden 2007; Buffington 2005; Murrell and
    Curtis 1994.
37  Oates 2017; Hartmann 2007; Rhoden 2007; Buffington 2005.
38  Lipsitz 1995; Lipsitz 1998.
39  Roithmayr 2014.

40   Runstedtler 2012.

41   Cortez 2014.

42   Reilly 2013.

43   Ibid.

44   Nickel 2008.

45   Klis 2012.

46   Kiszla 2014.

47   Bernreuter 2014.

48   Sherman 2014.

49   Bernreuter 2014.

50   Dungy quoted in M. D. Smith 2012.

51   Rishe 2012.

52   V. Strauss 2012.

53   C. S. Brown 2013.

54   M. Smith 2004.

55   Thangaraj 2015; C. R. King 2014; Uperesa 2014; Zirin 2012; Kusz 2011;
     Pelley 2010.

56   Ferber 2007, 212.

57   Quigley 2010.

58   McCune 2014.

59   D. D. Douglas 2005; Spencer 2004.

60   Leonard, Davie, and C. R. King 2010; Cole and D. L. Andrews 2001.

61   D. L. Andrews 2001a, 2001b; D. L. Andrews and S. J. Jackson 2001;
     Cole 2001; Cole and D. L. Andrews 2001; Denzin 2001; C. R. King and
     Springwood 2001; McDonald 1996, 2001; McDonald and D. L. Andrews
     2001; Davis and Harris 1998.

62   Mwaniki 2017; Longman 2015b; C. R. King 2014; J. F. Engel 2014; Kang 2012;
     Yang 2012; Wierenga 2012; Zirin 2012; Kusz 2011; Kang 2010; Brock 2009.

63   See Mwaniki 2017; Thangaraj, Arnaldo, and Chin 2016; Thangaraj 2015;
     C. R. King 2014; Wang 2012a; Wang 2012b; Zirin 2012; Kusz 2011;
     Kang 2010; Brock 2009.

64   Gordon 2014a; J. B. Hill 2014.

65   Gordon 2014a.

66   Ibid.

67   J. B. Hill 2014.

68   M. Lewis 2009.

69   Kendi 2016, 456; R. D. G. Kelley 1997.

70   Kendi 2016, 456.

71   Quoted in Kendi 2016, 459.

72   Entine 1999.

73   Quoted in Reese 2000.

74   Grant and Taylor 2012, 213. See also Kendi 2016.

75   M. Grant 1916. See also Kendi 2016.

76  Herbes-Sommers 2003.

77  Kendi 2016, 311.

78  Hoberman 1997.


## 3. TALKING TRASH (WHILE WHITE)

Chapter 3 includes and builds on material published in D. J. Leonard, "Hating Marshall Henderson," *New Black Man (in Exile)*, blog, March 29, 2013, and D. J. Leonard and C. Richard King, "N-Words, R-Words and the Defense of White Power in the NFL," *New Black Man (in Exile)*, blog, February 26, 2014.

1  N. Collins 2013.

2  Quoted in N. Collins 2013.

3  Runstedtler 2012.

4  Atkins 2001.

5  Dessources 2015; Habib 2002.

6  Leli 2014; Hale 2013; Pfitzinger 2007; B. C. Anderson and Reinharz 2000; Longman 1999; Silverman 1999.

7  Leli 2014.

8  Quoted in Silverman 1999.

9  Pfitzinger 2007.

10  Quoted in Pfitzinger 2007.

11  Feinstein 2002.

12  Canzano 2009; Feinstein 2002.

13  Kerasotis 2003.

14  Silverman 1999.

15  N. Collins 2013.

16  Quoted in Feinstein 2002.

17  S. Berry 2011; Feinstein 2002.

18  Quoted in S. Berry 2011.

19  See S. Berry 2011; R. Kelley 2010; Canzano 2009; Pfitzinger 2007; Stellino 2004; Habib 2002; B. C. Anderson and Reinharz 2000; *Seattle Times* 1994.

20  See Smizik 2006; B. C. Anderson and Reinharz 2000; *Seattle Times* 1994.

21  Feinstein 2002.

22  Pfitzinger 2007; Smizik 2006; Habib 2002; B. C. Anderson and Reinharz 2000.

23  See R. Kelley 2010; B. C. Anderson and Reinharz 2000; *Seattle Times* 1994.

24  R. Kelley 2010; B. C. Anderson and Reinharz 2000; *Seattle Times* 1994.

25  B. C. Anderson and Reinharz 2000.

26  Leonard 2012a; Boyd 2003.

27  *Seattle Times* 1994.

28  See Leonard 2012a.

29  Quoted in Gray 2005, 21.

30  Hall quoted in Watkins 1998, 36.

31  Gray 1995, 35.
32  Crenshaw 1997, 104.
33  Dyson 2007; Zirin and Chang 2007; Sewell 2006; Perry 2004; Pough 2004; A. Lewis 2003; Hall 1996.
34  Chaidha 2014.
35  Buckley 1993.
36  Leonard 2012a; Canfora 2011; Cunningham 2009.
37  Feinstein 2002; Longman 1999.
38  Cunningham 2009; V. L. Andrews 1996.
39  Ferber 2007; D. D. Douglas 2005; C. R. King and Springwood 2005; T. Boyd 2003; D. L. Andrews 2001b; Cole 2001; Cole and D. L. Andrews 2001; Denzin 2001; Banet-Wiser 1999; T. Boyd 1997; Cole and D. L. Andrews 1996.
40  Longman 1999.
41  Hutchins 2013.
42  R. D. G. Kelley 1997, 4.
43  Ibid., 8–9.
44  Lipsitz 1995, 379; quoted in Watkins 1998, 24.
45  Ferber 2007; Cunningham 2009; Hughes 2004; V. L. Andrews 1996.
46  Gray 2005.
47  Travis 2013c.
48  Broomberg 2013.
49  Brooks 2013.
50  Wolken 2013.
51  Travis 2013c.
52  C. Greenberg 2013.
53  Watson 2013b.
54  Brooks 2014.
55  Travis 2014; Auerbach 2013; L. Brown 2013; Wolfman-Arent 2013.
56  While embracing his Native American identity, he is able to cash in on his whiteness in powerful ways.
57  Gleeson 2013a, 2013b.
58  Newman 2010.
59  Schwab 2013.
60  Lcy 2013.
61  Rybaltowski 2013.
62  Howard 2013.
63  Huffington Post 2013.
64  Gleeson 2013a, 2013b.
65  Sturgeon 2014.
66  Ibid.
67  ESPN.com News Services 2016.
68  Browne 2014.

69  Waldron 2014.
70  Devine 2014.
71  M. Cohen 2014.
72  Shapiro 2014.
73  Van Bibber 2014.
74  Quoted in Coppinger 2014.
75  T. Moore 2014.
76  Culp-Ressler 2014.
77  T. Moore 2014.
78  Rhoden 2014.
79  Garcia 2014.
80  Ferber 2007, 20.
81  I. Perry 2004.
82  Busfield 2011; Crunktastic 2011; Vecsey 2011; D. D. Douglas 2005;
    Spencer 2004.
83  Bradshaw on WFAN 2013; Elliot 2013; M.D. Smith 2013.
84  Augustine 2014; P. Perry 2014.
85  Sessler 2014; Florio 2010.
86  I. Perry 2011; Phillips 2011; Alexander 2010; Feagin 2010; Sullivan 2007;
    Applied Research Center 2006; Johnson, Boyden, and Pittz 2001;
    Skiba and Knesting 2001; Transnational Racial Justice Initiative 2001.
87  Hutchinson 2014; Reid 2014; ESPN.com News Services 2014a.
88  C. R. King 2015.
89  Ibid.
90  Leonard 2012a.
91  P. King 2014.
92  Banzhaf 2014.
93  Banzhaf 2014; Zirin 2014a, 2014b.
94  Whitlock 2014b.
95  R. Williams 1998, 140.

### 4. WHITE THUGS?

1   Muhammad 2011.
2   Alexander 2010, 194.
3   Leal, Gertz, and Piquerob 2015; Keane 2013; Berry and Smith 2000.
4   Gibbs 2016.
5   Crenshaw 1997; Johnson and Roediger 1997.
6   Markovitz 2006; Leonard 2004.
7   K. Armstrong 2015; Baylis 2015; McCann 2015; Solotaroff and Borges 2013.
8   Moorti 2002; Sloop 1997.
9   Bogdanich 2014; Rosenberg 2014.
10  Botelho and Sanchez 2014; Ramsey 2014; K. C. White 2014.

11 Leonard and C. R. King 2011.

12 NPR 2013; Schrotenboer 2013.

13 K. Armstrong 2015; Baylis 2015; J. King 2013.

14 Cropley 2014; C. Kelly 2014; Ludbrook 2014; Seal 2013.

15 Ridley 2014; Serino 2014.

16 Ndopu 2013.

17 K. C. White 2014.

18 Roberts 2014.

19 Luther 2016a; Bazelon 2013.

20 Moskovitz 2015; Coates 2014; McDonough 2014.

21 Goff 2015; B. Lewis 2015; Rogers 2015.

22 Doyle 2014.

23 Svrluga 2016.

24 W. Cohen 2016, 2014.

25 Zirin 2015b.

26 C. R. King and Springwood 2001.

27 Quinn 2016.

28 Luther 2016a.

29 Ibid.

30 Luther 2014.

31 UO Coalition to End Sexual Violence 2014.

32 Cherry 2013.

33 Rothman 2014.

34 McIntosh 1989.

35 Chan 2014; N. Cohen 2014; L. Williams 2014.

36 Alper 2014; Evans 2014.

37 Bonesteel 2014.

38 Leonard 2012b; Modiano 2012.

39 J. M. Jackson 2016; Sule 2016.

40 Sanchez and Watts 2014; Ruane 2016.

41 Luther 2016b.

42 Garper 2006; See W. Cohen 2016; N. Cohen 2014; Steele 2006; and S. Jackson 2006 for discussion of media narrative surround Duke lacrosse.

43 S. Jackson 2006. See also W. Cohen 2016.

44 hooks 1997, 169.

45 S. Jackson 2006.

46 Steele 2006.

47 S. Jackson 2006.

48 Associated Press 2012b; Himmelberg 1991.

49 Jones 2016.

50 P. H. Collins 2006; Leonard 2006a; Leonard 2006b; P. H. Collins 2004; Leonard 2004; M. K. Brown et al. 2003; D. L. Andrews and S. J. Jackson 2001; Cole and D. L. Andrews 2001; Cole and S. King 1998.

51  Hartmann 2007.
52  Endress 2013.
53  Dufresne 2013.
54  Heck 2016.
55  Luther 2013.
56  Ibid.
57  McCormack 2013.
58  Quoted in Gantt 2016.
59  R. Wilson 2016; Breech 2014.
60  Florio 2015.
61  Howard 2013.
62  Tate 2003.
63  Cole and D. L. Andrews 1996, 72.
64  C. R. King and Springwood 2001; Cole and D. L. Andrews 1996.
65  Alexander 2010, 103.
66  Goldberg 2000, 155.
67  Ibid., 166.
68  Ibid.
69  Ibid.
70  A. Davis 1998, 270.
71  Sherman 2014.
72  Bouie 2014.
73  Foucault 1995.
74  Feagin 2010.
75  Garcia 2015; Muhammad 2011; Alexander 2010; D. L. Andrews 2001a;
    Gray 1995.
76  M. D. Smith 2016.
77  M. L. Hill 2016.
78  Raanan 2016; Samuel 2016.

## 5. GETTING HIGH

Chapter 5 includes and builds on D. J. Leonard, "ESPN Must be High: Drugs and Jim Crow in Sports Reporting," *New Black Man (in Exile)*, blog, May 22, 2012; "Drug Culture on College Campuses and the Criminalization of Student Athletes," *Urban Cusp*, March 22, 2012; and "Real Consequences: The War on Drugs, the New Jim Crow and the Story of Jonathan Hargett," *New Black Man (in Exile)*, blog, August 23, 2012.

1   Quoted in C. V. Coleman 2012.
2   C. V. Coleman 2012.
3   Thamel 2012.
4   Ibid.
5   Alexander 2010.

6    ESPN 2012.
7    Alexander 2010, 104.
8    Weinreb n.d.; Wilbon 2009; Goldstein and Kinzie 2006.
9    Runstedtler 2016.
10   Layden 2015; CNN 2009.
11   Terranova 2015; ESPN 2014b.
12   Associated Press 2009.
13   Leonard 2012a; Povak 2006; T. Boyd 2003; Seligman 2003.
14   Associated Press 1985.
15   Crowe 2006.
16   Alexander 2010.
17   Block 2015.
18   Denvir 2016; Mauer 2016; Alexander 2010; Davis 1998.
19   Boren 2012.
20   Associated Press 2012a.
21   Runstedtler 2016.
22   Taylor 2012.
23   Ibid.
24   Feagin 2010.
25   Ibid., 13.
26   Ibid., 13.
27   Ibid., 15.
28   Olson 2012.
29   Gordon 2014b.
30   Ibid.
31   Quoted in Gordon 2014b.
32   Ibid.
33   Quoted in Runstedtler 2016.
34   Ibid.
35   Wolken 2015.
36   Ibid.
37   Biggers 2012.
38   Ibid.
39   R. Jackson 2006.
40   Thamel 2015.
41   Ibid.
42   Scott Frost quoted in Thamel 2015.
43   Waldron 2015.
44   Ubben 2012.
45   Jessop 2013; Ubben 2012.
46   Schlabach 2012.
47   Grasgreen 2014.
48   E. A. Armstrong and Hamilton 2013.

49  Vera, Feagin, and Gordon 1995.
50  Rexroat 2014.
51  Keith 2014.
52  Rexroat 2014.
53  Keith 2014.
54  Alexander 2010, 193.
55  Carless and O'Connor 2008; T. Perry 2008.
56  Short 2016; Veklerov 2016.
57  Robinson and Grove 2010; Secret and Zraickdec 2010.
58  Pein 2012.
59  WSPA Staff 2016.
60  Tilkin 2012.
61  Encalada 2015.
62  Hudson 2015.
63  Mohamed and Fritsvold 2011.
64  Daily Beast 2010.
65  Mauer 2016; Alexander 2010; A. Y. Davis 1998.
66  Alexander 2010.
67  C. S. Brown 2013; Chase 2013.
68  AOL.com Editors 2016.
69  T. Ryan 2013.
70  Gleeson 2013b.
71  Chris Herren quoted in Gleeson 2013c.
72  Quoted in McIntyre 2013.
73  McIntyre 2013.
74  Auerbach 2013.
75  Leonard and C. R. King 2011; C. R. King and Springwood 2001; D. L.
    Andrews and S. J. Jackson 2001.
76  WSPA Staff 2011.
77  Watson 2013a.
78  Muhammad 2011; Alexander 2010; Feagin 2009; Prashad 2003; Davis 1998;
    R. D. G. Kelley 1998.
79  Kellenberger 2012.
80  Kirk 2012.
81  Dohrmann and Evans 2013.
82  Mizell 2013.
83  Howard 2013.
84  Trahan 2014.
85  Neal 2013.
86  R. Benjamin 2009.
87  Patton and Leonard 2014.
88  Hamm and Vitale 2015.
89  Rivas 2011; Quigley 2001; Skiba and Knesting 2001.

90 Ingraham 2014; Tolson 2013; Drug Addiction Treatment 2011; Mohamed and Fritsvold 2011; Wise 2001b.
91 Leonard 2008; Kusz 2007; Wheaton 2004; Kusz 2003; Borden 2001; Rinehart and Sydnor 2001; Rinehart 1998.
92 Burton 2002.
93 St. John 2002.
94 Ibid.
95 Higgins 2013.
96 Baca 2015; Blevins 2013; Woodsmall 2015.
97 Knoblauch 2009.
98 Bethea 2016; Siegel 2013; Vecsey 1998.
99 Higgins 2013.
100 Thomas 2009.
101 Holland 2012.
102 Alexander 2010.
103 Anderson and Reinharz 2000.
104 Gray 1995, 165.
105 Watkins 1998, 37.
106 CBC Sports 2000.
107 Passan 2014.
108 Alexander 2010.

## 6. REDEMPTION AND CHARACTER BUILDING

Chapter 6 includes and builds on D. J. Leonard and C. R. King, "White is Right: Ben Roethlisberger and the Power of Privilege," *New Black Man (in Exile)*, blog, April 16, 2010; and C. R. King and D. J. Leonard, "Race, Redemption, and Respectability: White Racism in Athletics," *Racism Review*, April 14, 2010.

1 As noted by Zerlina Maxwell 2014. "the FBI reports that only 2–8 percent of rape allegations turn out to be false, a number that is smaller than the number 10 percent, who lie about car theft."
2 Luther 2016a; Marcotte 2014.
3 Clearly 2016; Craig 2016; Korman 2016; Martin 2016; Schow 2016.
4 Roediger 1999.
5 Kingkade 2014.
6 Coogan 2009; Berry and Smith 2000.
7 Sinnott and McGowan 2013.
8 Macur 2015, 2014; P. Johnson 2013; Newell 2013.
9 McIntosh 1989.
10 Sinnott and McGowan 2013.
11 Roan and Slater 2015.
12 Macur 2014.
13 Quoted in Associated Press 2013.

14  Quoted in BBC 2015.
15  Quoted in Clarke 2015.
16  Grinberg 2012.
17  Jenkins 2012.
18  BBC 2015.
19  Carroll 2013.
20  Majendie 2014.
21  Ibid.
22  Quoted in Kusz 2015.
23  Kusz 2015.
24  Ibid.
25  Ibid.
26  Ibid.
27  Ibid.
28  See Leonard 2012a.
29  Real Sports 2008.
30  Grant 2008.
31  Curtis 2012.
32  Ibid.
33  R. Jackson 2006.
34  Ibid., 55.
35  Mohamed and Fritsvold 2011; Alexander 2010; Quigley 2010.
36  McIntosh 1989.
37  DiGiovanna and Shaikin 2015.
38  DiGiovanna 2015.
39  Yankah 2016; DeVega 2015; Harmony 2015.
40  Rosenthal 2009.
41  J. Hill 2010.
42  *New York Daily News* 2010.
43  Brandt 2010.
44  Neal 2010.
45  Friedman 2009.
46  A. Clark 2009.
47  Alexander 2010.
48  J. Katz 2006, 137.
49  B. Berry and E. Smith 2000.
50  Gray 1995, 165.
51  D. L. Andrews 2001b, 117.
52  Coogan 2009.
53  Cunningham 2009; Simons 2003.
54  CBS News 2010.
55  Zinser 2011.
56  S. Douglas 2011.

57   Granderson 2011.
58   Bleacher Report 2011.
59   Granderson 2011.
60   Bissinger 2011. Both Granderson 2011 and Bissinger 2011 question to
     differing degrees the redemption story afforded to Roethlisberger.
61   Rosenthal 2015.
62   Quoted in A. Benjamin 2010.
63   Quoted in Covitz 2011.
64   Jubera 2011.
65   Lazarus 2011.
66   Schwartz 2013.
67   Bonilla-Silva 2006, 2001.
68   W. J. Wilson 2012.
69   C. R. King 2015, 63.
70   Picca and Feagin 2007.
71   Quoted in Sessler 2013.
72   Quoted in Keeney 2013.
73   Palmer 2013.
74   Merrill 2013.
75   Person 2014.
76   Sheridan 2015.
77   Merrill 2013.
78   Quoted in Katzowitz 2013.
79   Ibid.
80   Larson 2005, 34.
81   Adelson 2013.
82   Patton 2015.
83   Delaware County Daily Times Editorial Board 2013.
84   Quoted in Merrill 2013.
85   Romaine 2013.
86   V. Thomas 2013.
87   Black 2013.
88   Quoted in Santoliquito 2013.
89   Petchesky 2013b.
90   Engelhardt 2007.
91   Bissinger 2011; Granderson 2011; Zinser 2011.
92   Zinser 2011.
93   Granderson 2011.
94   Leonard 2004.
95   Bleacher Report 2011.
96   Ibid.

Chapter 7 includes and builds on D. J. Leonard, "Not Entertained?" *Slam Online*, February 29, 2012; and (2014) "Dilemmas and Contradictions: Black Female Athletes," *Out of Bounds: Racism and the Black Athlete (Racism in American Institutions)*, edited by Lori Martin, 209–30 (New York: Praeger), 2014.

1   Kane 2011.
2   Fink and Kensicki 2002, 328.
3   Tuchman 2000.
4   Fink and Kensicki 2002, 330.
5   Cooky, Messner, and Musto 2015.
6   Fagan 2014.
7   P. H. Collins 2004, 136.
8   Ibid.
9   Brekke 2015; Shapiro 2014; Yahoo Beauty 2015; Cardellino 2013;
    Longman 2012; S. Jackson 2011; Glock 2009; Salazar-Moreno 2009.
10  P. H. Collins 2004.
11  Glock 2009.
12  Cooper 2015; Crenshaw 1989.
13  Fink and Kensicki 2002.
14  Cooky et al. 2015.
15  Maese 2015.
16  Ibid.
17  Ibid.
18  Kane and Greendorfer, 1994, 40.
19  McNeil and Isaacson 2013.
20  Yaniv 2009.
21  Owens and Machir 2015.
22  *Men's Health* 2014.
23  Mike McD 2009.
24  Boberg 2011.
25  ESPN, page 2, n.d.
26  Wachs et al. 2012; McKay and Johnson 2008; D. D. Douglas 2005;
    Jamie Schultz 2005; McPherson 2001.
27  Cooky et al. 2015.
28  Wachs et al. 2012; P. H. Collins 2004.
29  Cooper 2011.
30  Rowe 1990.
31  McKay and H. Johnson 2008, 492.
32  Schulze 1990.
33  Quoted in McKay and H. Johnson 2008, 492.
34  P. H. Collins 2004.
35  Ibid., 134.
36  Ibid, 136.

37  Earnings are from Fox Business 2015. In 2016, she would lose some endorsements after she tested positive for a banned substance, meldonium. The media and many of her corporate partners would, however, take a sympathetic response. Whereas some companies merely suspended their relationship, pending an investigation and her return to the tennis court, others remained silent. Within the broader media landscape, which simultaneously rationalized and dismissed the positive test as unfortunate and merely a mistake, the limited damage to her brand speaks to the material benefits of Maria Sharapova #PlayingWhileWhite (Mullen 2016).

38  Badenhausen 2015.

39  Rankine 2015.

40  Chase 2015.

41  Bain 2015.

42  Quoted in Rankine 2015.

43  Rankine 2015.

44  Rankine 2015; B. Cooper 2011.

45  Rankine 2015.

46  Jamie Schultz 2005.

47  Kournikova quoted in Jamie Schultz 2005, 346.

48  Whitlock quoted in Milz 2009.

49  Milz 2009.

50  Douglas n.d.

51  Vertinsky and Captain quoted in Jamie Shultz 2005, 347.

52  Majavu n.d.

53  Rothenberg 2015.

54  Quoted in Fay 2015.

55  Desmond-Harris 2016.

56  Longman 2015a.

57  Trebay 2010.

58  Caitlin 2012.

59  D'Arcangelo 2009.

60  Harris-Perry 2011.

61  Quoted in Wachs et al. 2012, 141.

62  Wachs et al. 2012, 151.

63  P. H. Collins 2004.

64  Rankine 2015.

65  Ibid.

## 8. DRIVING WHILE WHITE

Chapter 8 includes and builds on D. J. Leonard, "What if NASCAR Was Black," *Ebony* online, May 29, 2012.

1      Newman and Giardina 2011, 103–107.
2      Livingstone 2007; also quoted in Newman and Giardina 2011, 95.
3      Newman and Giardina 2011, 95.
4      Bernstein 2012.
5      Newman and Giardina 2011, 110.
6      Quoted in Murdock 2003.
7      Quoted in C. Jenkins 2003.
8      Quoted in Murdock 2003.
9      Kersey 2012; Dieckmann 2010; Sailer 2005; Murdock 2003.
10     NASCAR 2016.
11     NASCAR n.d.
12     Project 21 2003.
13     Murdock 2003.
14     Quoted in Bianchi 2014.
15     Newman and Giardina 2011, 112-113.
16     J. Jones 2015.
17     Quoted in Pockrass 2012.
18     Quoted in Bernstein 2012.
19     Quoted in Hinton 2009.
20     J. Jones 2015.
21     Pockrass 2013; Hinton 2004.
22     Bobb 2013.
23     Gluck 2013.
24     Zirin 2008.
25     Peltz 2011; N. Ryan 2010.
26     Pockrass 2013.
27     Quoted in Pockrass 2013.
28     Newman and Giardina 2011.
29     Quoted in Pockrass 2013.
30     Quoted in East 2015.
31     C. Johnson 2009.
32     Ibid.
33     Newman and Giardina 2011.
34     Quoted in Hinton 2009.
35     Bernstein 2012.
36     Lipsitz 1995; Lipsitz 1998.
37     Quoted in Bernstein 2012.
38     Jensen 2014; Hinton 2009; J. Johnson 2009.
39     Iber and Regalado 2006.
40     Chang 2014.
41     Quoted in Newman and Giardina 2011, 194.
42     C. Brennan 2014.
43     Ibid.

44  M. Brown 2014.

45  Associated Press 2010.

46  Ibid.

47  C. Brennan 2014.

48  Ibid.

49  Zirin 2014c.

50  Leonard, George, and Davis 2016; Zirin 2014c; Leonard 2012;
    Carrington 2010; Hughes 2004; T. Boyd 2003; D. L. Andrews 2001a;
    V. L. Andrews 1996.

51  M. Brown 2014.

52  C. Brennan 2014.

53  Newman and Giardina 2011, 95; italics in the original.

54  Newman and Giardina 2011, 95.

55  Schwartz 2014.

56  Quoted in Newman and Giardina 2011, 94.

57  N. Cohen 2014.

58  Dickerson 2014.

59  Easterling 2012.

60  McGee 2012.

61  Leonard 2012a.

62  Runstedtler 2016.

63  Estes 2012.

64  Brewster 2015.

65  Bianchi 2013.

66  Ibid.

67  Wise 2010.

68  Tapper 2011.

69  Quoted in Tapper 2011; italics added.

70  Gluck 2011.

71  Berkow 1996.

72  Capehart 2015.

73  Wright 2016.

74  S. King 2015; Parham 2015.

75  Diamond 2016.

76  Pierce 2015.

77  NASCAR 2015.

## 9. PLAYING THE WHITE WAY

1  Reinardy and Wanta 2008.

2  J. Baker 2015.

3  Levin 2013; Liss 2013.

4  Megdal 2013.

5   Ibid.
6   Calandro 2013.
7   Schwichtenberg 2014.
8   Quoted in O'Neill 2011.
9   P. White 2013.
10  Goold 2012.
11  Quoted in White 2013.
12  Schwichtenberg 2014.
13  Miklasz 2013.
14  Cole and D. L. Andrews 2001, 72.
15  McClellan 2014.
16  Ibid.
17  Ibid.
18  T. Anderson and Vise 2001.
19  Calandro 2013.
20  Bogan 2012.
21  Lapchick 2015.
22  Nightengale 2016.
23  M. Engel 2011.
24  Bretón 2000.
25  Farrell 2012.
26  R. D. G. Kelley 1998, 201.
27  Balko 2014.
28  Active Living Research 2007.
29  Lipsitz 2011.
30  Andrews, Pitter, Zwick, and Ambrose 2003, 207.
31  Quoted in Ogden 2000.
32  Ley 2015.
33  Norris 2016.
34  Ley 2015.
35  DeRousse 2013.
36  Quoted in Levitt 2009.
37  Bogan 2012.
38  Sieczkowski 2014.
39  E. Brennan 2014.
40  Lucas 2015.
41  Quoted in Lucas 2015.
42  Tran 2015.
43  Whitley 2014.
44  Coppens 2015.
45  Bronson Koenig quoted in Schroeder 2014.
46  Quoted in Potrykus 2014.
47  Leonard 2012a; Boyd 1997; Boyd 2003; Platt 2000.

48  Peter 2015.
49  Woodbine 2016; Leonard 2012a; Boyd 1997; Boyd 2003.
50  Peter 2015.
51  Groves 2015.
52  Curtis quoted in Peter 2015.
53  Ibid.
54  T. Boyd 1997, 115.
55  A. Baker 2000, 225.
56  T. Boyd 2003, 26.
57  T. Boyd 2003; C. R. King and Springwood 2001; Platt 2000; Cole and Andrews 1996.
58  P. H. Collins 2004; Bonilla-Silva 2006.
59  Quoted in Potrykus 2014.
60  Bennett 2015.
61  Quoted in Mandall 2015.
62  Crouse 2014.
63  J. Miller 2014.
64  Groves 2015.
65  D. Z. Jackson 2015.
66  Baragona 2015; Dickinson 2015; Horn 2015; Jeff Schultz 2015.
67  Jeff Schultz 2015.
68  Dickinson 2015; Horn 2105.
69  Horn 2015.
70  Tunney 2015.
71  Dickinson 2015.
72  V. Johnson 2015.
73  McGregor 2015.
74  Jeff Schultz 2015.
75  V. Johnson 2015.
76  Leonard, Davie, and C. R. King 2010; Cole and D. L. Andrews 2001.
77  C. Brennan 2015.
78  Ibid.
79  Ibid.
80  Ibid.
81  Burt 2015.
82  Ibid.
83  Cole and D. L. Andrews 2001; further discussed in Leonard, Davie et al. 2010.
84  Joseph 2016.
85  Kerr-Dineen 2016.
86  Porter 2016.
87  Joseph 2016.
88  Quoted in Joseph 2016.
89  ESPN 2016.

90  Beidelschies 2016.
91  Quoted in Eisenberg 2016.
92  Beidelschies 2016.

## 10. SPORTING CULTURES AND WHITE VICTIMS

Chapter 10 includes and builds on D. J. Leonard, "#IfBradyWereBlack: Tom Brady and the Privileges of Whiteness," *New Black Man (in Exile)*, blog, May 14, 2015.

1   Savran 1998, 4.
2   Kusz 2001, 392.
3   Ibid., 396.
4   Ibid., 392.
5   Gasparino 2014; Peart 2013.
6   Chavez 2014; Travis 2014; Whitlock 2014a.
7   Zirin and Pronson 2006.
8   Cole and D. L. Andrews 2001, 72.
9   Chang 2014.
10  Kusz 2001, 396.
11  Quoted in O'Neil 2016.
12  O'Neil 2016.
13  Ibid.
14  Riccobono 2015; Abramson 2014; Austin 2010.
15  Sailer 2015.
16  O'Neil 2016.
17  Vrentas 2015.
18  Wells et al. 2015.
19  Gregory 2015.
20  P. King 2014.
21  Pickeral 2012.
22  Zirin 2015a.
23  Chavez 2015.
24  M. L. Hill 2016.
25  Callahan 2016.
26  Ngaruiya 2016.
27  Arnold 2016; Danielle 2016.
28  Danielle 2016.
29  Ibid.
30  Abad-Santos 2016.
31  M. L. Hill 2016.
32  Hackman 2015.
33  See Russell 1998 for larger history of racial hoaxes.

# REFERENCES

Abad-Santos, A. 2016. "Rio 2016: Gabby Douglas's Olympics Experience Fits the Pattern of How We Treat Black Female Athletes." *Vox*, August 15.

Abraham, P. 2012. "On Pedroia, Gonzalez and Perceptions." *Boston.com*, May 8.

Abramson, M. 2014. "Grant Hill Says People Hate Duke Basketball Because 'We've Had a Lot of Really Good White Players.'" *New York Daily News* online, March 21.

Active Living Research, 2007. "Active Education: Physical Education, Physical Activity and Academic Performance." Fall.

Adelson, E. 2013. "Michael Vick Helps Clean Up Riley Cooper's Mess." *Yahoo! Sports*, August 1.

Alexander, M. 2010. *The New Jim Crow: Mass Incarceration in the Age of Colorblindness*. New York: New Press.

Alper, J. 2014. "Jim Irsay Sentenced to Probation, Drug Testing in Plea Deal." *NBC Sports*, "Pro Football Talk," September 2.

Anderson, B. C., and P. Reinharz. 2000. "Bring Back Sportsmanship." *City Journal*, Spring.

Anderson, T., and M. Vise. 2001. "Cards Owners Worth $4 Billion." *Biz Journals* online, May 6.

Andrews, D. L., ed. 2001a. *Michael Jordan, Inc.: Corporate Sport, Media Culture, and Late Modern America.* Albany: State University of New York.

———. 2001b. "Michael Jordan Matters." In *Michael Jordan, Inc.*, edited by D. L. Andrews, xiii–xx.

Andrews, D. L., and S. J. Jackson, eds. 2001. *Sports Stars: The Cultural Politics of Sporting Celebrity*. New York: Routledge.

Andrews, D. L., R. Pitter, D. Zwick, and D. Ambrose. 2003. "Soccer, Race, and Suburban Space." In *Sporting Dystopias: The Making and Meanings of Urban Sport Cultures*, edited by R. C. Wilcox, D. L. Andrews, R. Pitter, and R. L. Irwin. 197–220. Albany: SUNY University Press.

Andrews, V. L. 1996. "African American Player Codes on Celebration, Taunting, and Sportsmanlike Conduct." *Journal of African American Studies* 2 (2–3): 57–92.

Ansell, A. E. 1997. *New Right, New Racism: Race and Reaction in the United States*. New York: New York University Press.

AOL.com Editors. 2016. "Where Has Marshall Henderson Been since Leaving Ole Miss?" *AOL.com*, March 14.

Applied Research Center. 2006. "Racial Disparities Related to School Zero Tolerance Policies." *Race Forward*, April 13.

Armstrong, E. A., and L. T. Hamilton. 2013. *Paying for the Party: How College Maintains Inequality*. Cambridge, MA: Harvard University Press.

Armstrong, K. 2015. "The Chilling Story of Convicted Murderer Aaron Hernandez and the Trail That Put Him Away for the Rest of His Life." *New York Daily News* online, April 18.

Arnett, A. 2015. "Media Fuels Negative Perception of Black Athletes." *Diverse Education*, June 4.

Arnold, G. 2016. "Video Shows U.S. Swimmer Ryan Lochte 'Fighting' with Gas Station Security Guard: Report." *Oregon Live*, August 18.

Associated Press. 1985. "Cocaine, Fame Led to Tragedy of Steve Howe." *LA Times* online, October 12.

———. 1997. "Body Work Tattoos Proliferate among NBA Players." *Cincinnati Post*, October 29, 1B.

———. 2009. "Pitcher Faces Misdemeanor Charges." *ESPN* online, November 5.

———. 2010. "NASCAR Race Marred by Accusations of Intentional Crash." *NJ.com*, March 7.

———. 2012a. "TCU Drug Bust Includes 4 Football Players." *Fox News Sports* online, February 16.

———. 2012b. "Lenny Dykstra Sentenced for Fraud." *ESPN* online, December 3.

———. 2013. "Lance Armstrong: 'Impossible' to Win Tour de France without Doping." *USA Today* online, January 26.

Atkins, L. 2001. "In This Corner: The Man Who Invented Trash Talking." *Chicago Tribune*, December 27.

Auerbach, N. 2013. "Marshall Henderson Brings Points, Passion to Ole Miss." *USA Today*, July 10.

Augustine, B. 2014. "Tom Brady Slams Richard Sherman for Taunting Michael Crabtree." *New York Daily News* online, January 20.

Austin. 2010. "Black Like Me: What Duke vs. Butler Means for the Face of Basketball." *UPPROX*, April 5.

Baca, R. 2015. "Now, X Marks the Pot." *Denver Post*, January 22, A1.

Badenhausen, K. 2015. "The World's Highest-Paid Female Athletes 2015." *Forbes*, August 12.

Baffoe, T. 2016. "Johnny Football: The NFL's Affluenza Teen." *The Cauldron*, January 7.

Bain, M. 2015. "Why Doesn't Serena Williams Have More Sponsorship Deals?" *Atlantic Monthly* online, August 31.

Baker, A. 2000. "Hoop Dreams in Black and White: Race and Basketball Movies." In *Basketball Jones*, edited by T. Boyd and K. Shropshire, 215–39.

Baker, J. 2015. "Playing the Right Way?" *Fox Sports*, June 15.

Balko, R. 2014. "How Municipalities in St. Louis County, Mo., Profit from Poverty." *Washington Post* online, September 3.

Banet-Wiser, S. 1999. "Hoop Dreams: Professional Basketball and the Politics of Race and Gender." *Journal of Sport and Social Issues* 23 (4): 403–20.

Banzhaf, J. F. 2014. "NFL Hypocrisy: Banning the N-Word, But Supporting the R-Word." *Indian Country Today*, February 24.

Baragona, J. 2015. "Rush Limbaugh Uses Spieth's Masters Win to Justify Augusta's History of Racism And Sexism." *PoliticusUSA*, April 13.

Barra, A. 2013. "Johnny Manziel, Trailblazer: The NCAA Is a Total Joke, Again." *Salon*, August 29.

Baylis, S. C. 2015. "Aaron Hernandez Flaunts New 'Lifetime' Tattoo Amid Reports of Prison Fight." *People*, May 1.

Bazelon, E. 2013. "How Did Jameis Winston Evade a Rape Charge?" *Slate*, December 6.

BBC. 2015. "Lance Armstrong Interview: An Abridged Transcript." *BBC* online, January 26.

Beidelschies, J. 2016. "Nigel Hayes, Bronson Koenig and the Badgers' Men's Basketball Team Are Living the Wisconsin Idea." *SB Nation*, September 28.

Bell, J. 2013. "Geno Smith the Latest to Pay the Black Tax." *USA Today* online, April 22.

Benjamin, A. 2010. "Big Ben's Toll: Penalty Served, the Idea Now Is to Redeem, Rebuild." *Boston.com*, November 14.

Benjamin, R. 2009. *Searching for Whitopia: An Improbable Journey to the Heart of White America.* New York: Hachette Book Group.

Bennett, C. 2015. "Bo Ryan Says Wisconsin Doesn't Do 'Rent-A-Player.'" *Heavy.com*, April 7.

Berkow, I. 1996. "The Case of Hodges vs. the N.B.A." *New York Times* online, December 25.

Bernreuter, H. 2014. "Peyton Manning 'Smartest Man in the NFL' According to Former Teammate Blair White." *MLive.com*, January 31, 2014.

Bernstein, V. 2012. "Driver's Seat Elusive for Black Racers." *New York Times*, May 19.

Berry, B., and E. Smith. 2000. "Race, Sport, and Crime: The Misrepresentation of African Americans in Team Sports and Crime." *Sociology of Sport Journal* 17 (2): 171–91.

Berry, S. 2011. "Athletes' Roles: An Investigation on Why Not All Athletes Make Good Role Models." *Bleacher Report*, December 5.

Bertrand, M., and S. Mullainathan. 2003. "Are Emily and Greg More

Employable Than Lakisha and Jamal? A Field Experiment on Labor Market Discrimination." NBER Working Paper No. 9873. *NBER.org*, July 2003.

Bethea, C. 2016. "Tanner Hall and the Athlete's Case for Cannabis." *New Yorker* online, March 18.

Bianchi, J. 2013. "NASCAR's Reputation Takes Another Hit with Kvapil Arrest." *SB Nation*, October 11.

———. 2014. "Danica Patrick Clueless in Opposition to NASCAR Diversity Program." *SB Nation*, October 29.

Biggers, A. C. 2012. "ESPN's 'Higher Education': Rampant Use of Marijuana in College Football Isn't the Least Bit Shocking." *Yahoo! Sports*, April 18.

Billings, A. C. 2004. "Depicting the Quarterback in Black and White: A Content Analysis of College and Professional Football Broadcast Commentary." *Howard Journal of Communications* 15 (4): 201–10.

Birrell, S. 1989. "Racial Relations, Theories and Sport: Suggestions for a More Critical Analysis." *Sociology of Sport* 6 (3): 212–27.

Bissinger, B. 2011. "The NFL's Silly Redemption Debate." *Daily Beast*, January 26.

Black, A. 2013. "Philadelphia Eagles' Riley Cooper Being Held to Hypocritically Harsh Standard." *Bleacher Report*, August 2.

Bleacher Report. 2011. "Changed Man? Ben Roethlisberger Defies Every Law of Redemption." *Bleacher Report*, January 26.

Blevins, J. 2013. "Acceptance of Pot Grows Like Weeds in Sports World." *Denver Post* online, December 29.

Block, J. 2015. "Stephen A. Smith Goes Off on Black Athletes for Smoking Weed." *Complex*, March 26.

Blount, T. 2013. "Russell Wilson Is Seahawks' Clear Leader." *ESPN* online, September 6.

Bobb, M. 2013. "NASCAR's Hopeless Pursuit of Diversity." *The Shadow League*, February 22.

Boberg, K. 2011. "25 Hottest Elite Female Athletes." *Bleacher Report*, June 6.

Bogan, J. 2012. "No African-Americans on Cardinals Roster, Few in the Stands." *St Louis Post-Dispatch* online, August 5.

Bogdanich, Walt. 2014. "A Star Player Accused, and a Flawed Rape Investigation." *New York Times* online, April 16.

Bonesteel, M. 2014. "Michigan's Mitch McGary Fails Drug Test, Will Enter NBA Draft." *Washington Post* online, April 25.

Bonilla-Silva, E. 2001. *White Supremacy and Racism in the Post-Civil Rights Era*. Boulder, CO: Lynne Rienner Publishers.

———. 2006. *Racism without Racists: Colorblind Racism and the Persistence of Racial Inequality in America*. New York: Rowan and Littlefield.

Borden, I. 2001. *Skateboarding, Space and the City; Architecture and the Body*. New York: Berg Publishers.

Boren, C. 2012. "TCU Drug Arrests 'a Stain' on Football Program." *Washington Post* online, February 16.

Botelho, G., and R. Sanchez. 2014. "Vikings Star Adrian Peterson Turns Himself in, Freed on Bail." *CNN* online, September 16.

Bouie, J. 2014. "Richard Sherman Is Right: Thug Is the New N-Word." *Daily Beast*, January 27.

Boyd, D. 2015. *White Allies in the Struggle for Racial Justice.* New York: Orbis Books.

Boyd, T. 1997. *Am I Black Enough for You: Popular Culture from the 'Hood and Beyond.* Bloomington: University of Indiana Press.

———. 2000. "Mo' Money, Mo' Problems: Keepin It Real in the Post Jordan Era." In *Basketball Jones*, edited by T. Boyd and K. Shropshire, 59–67.

———. 2003. *Young, Black, Rich and Famous: The Rise of the NBA, the Hip Hop Invasion and the Transformation of American Culture.* New York: Doubleday.

Boyd, T., and K. Shropshire, eds. 2000. *Basketball Jones: America above the Rim.* New York: New York University Press.

"Bradshaw on WFAN: 'Selfish' Dez Bryant Needs to Shut His Mouth." 2013. CBS New York, October 29.

Branch, T. 2011. "The Shame of College Sports." *Atlantic* online.

Brandt, A. 2010. "Holmes' Behavior Doomed His Future." *National Football Post*, April 13.

Breech, J. 2014. "Report: Browns 'Stunned' by Johnny Manziel's Nonstop Partying." *CBS Sports* online, July 14.

Brekke, K. 2015. "WNBA Star Skylar Diggins: You Can Be Both a Beauty and a Beast." *Huffington Post*, May 11.

Brennan, C. 2014. "NASCAR Fights to Stay Relevant and Loses." *USA Today* online, November 6.

———. 2015. "Jordan Spieth Is Masters Champion for the Ages." *USA Today* online, April 12.

Brennan, E. 2014. "On Biggest Stage, Wisconsin Still Laughing." *ESPN* online, April 4.

Bretón, M. 2000. "Fields of Broken Dreams: Latinos and Baseball." *Colorlines*, April 20.

Brewster, L. 2015. "Athletes' Bad Behavior No Longer Being Tolerated, Kurt Busch Latest Example." *Inland Valley Daily Bulletin* online, February 22.

Brock, G. M. M. 2009. "African Athletes Shine in the U.S. National Football League: African Players Provide Role Models on and off the Football Field." IIP Digital, United States Embassy, December 17.

Brooks, B. 2013. "Don't Throw Johnny Manziel Out with the Trash Talk." *NFL.com*, September 3.

———. 2014. "Johnny Manziel Cements His Status as Franchise Quarterback." *NFL.com*, January 1.

Broomberg, N. 2013. "Johnny Manziel Trash Talks a Rice Defender, Says He Won't Give Him an Autograph." *Yahoo! Sports*, August 31.

Brown, C. S. 2013. "One-Trick Pony." *Grantland*, January 25.

Brown, K. 2014. "The Problem with #CrimingWhileWhite." *Jezebel*, December 4.

Brown, L. 2013. "Marshall Henderson Loves JaVale McGee and JR Smith." *Larry Brown Sports*, March 13.

Brown, M. 2013. "Enjoy the Show." *Sports on Earth*, March 24.

———. 2014. "NASCAR's Tony Stewart, Machismo and a Tragic Death in Motor Racing." *Forbes* online, August 11.

Brown, M. K., M. Carnoy, et al. 2003. *Whitewashing Race: The Myth of a Color-blind Society*. Berkeley: University of California Press.

Brown, T. N., et al. 2003. "There's No Race on the Playing Field: Perceptions of Racial Discrimination among White and Black Athletes." *Journal of Sport and Social Issues* 27 (2): 162–83.

Browne, R. 2014. "Stanford Man: Richard Sherman and the Thug Athlete Narrative." *Grantland*, January 22.

Bruce, T. 2004. "Making the Boundaries of the 'Normal' in Televised Sports: The Play-by-Play of Race." *Media, Culture & Society* 26 (6): 861–79.

Buckley, T. 1993. "Turning Trash (Talk) into Treasure." *USA Today*, 7c.

Buffington, D. 2005. "Contesting Race on Sundays: Making Meaning Out of the Rise in the Number of Black Quarterbacks." *Sociology of Sport Journal* 22: 19–37.

Burnison, G. 2013. "Peyton Manning Would Make an Even Better CEO." *Capital Content*, October 31.

Burt, B. 2015. "Spieth Could be the Anti-Tiger." *Eagle Tribune* online, April 14.

Burton, G. 2002. "Boarders: Dudes With 'Tude." *Salt Lake Tribune*, February 12, O17.

Busfield, Steve. 2011. "Serena Williams Fined $2,000 for US Open Final Outburst." *The Guardian*, September 12.

Butterworth, M. L. 2010. *Baseball and Rhetorics of Purity: The National Pastime and American Identity During the War on Terror*. Mobile, AL: University of Alabama Press.

Caitlin. 2012. "The Misgendering of Brittney Griner." *Fit and Feminist*, April 3.

Calandro, T. 2013. "The Cardinal Way: Built to Last." *Huffington Post*, October 25.

Callahan, Y. 2016. "White Thugs Destroy Gas Station, Fight Attendant, but Will Get Away with It Because White Privilege." *The Root*, August 18.

Canfora, J. L. 2011. "NFL Puts Teams on Notice about On-Field Actions after Trash Talk." *NFL.com*, January 15.

Canzano, J. 2009. "When Sportsmanship Is Forgotten, We All Pay the Price." *Oregon Live*, September 14.

Capehart, J. 2015. "Donald Trump's 'Mexican Rapists' Rhetoric Will Keep the Republican Party Out of the White House." *Washington Post* online, June 17.

Cardellino, C. 2013. "US Athletes Lolo Jones and Alex Morgan's Beauty Must-Haves." *Cosmopolitan* online, March 20.

Carless, W., and A. O'Connor. 2008. "Dozens of Arrests in University Drug Sting." *New York Times* online, May 6.

Carrington, B. 2002. " 'Race', Representation and the Sporting Body." Occasional Paper Series, CUCR, Goldsmiths College, University of London.

———. 2010. *Race, Sport and Politics: The Sporting Black Diaspora*. Thousand Oaks, CA: Sage Publishers.

Carroll, R. 2013. "Lance Armstrong 'Sick' and Tearful in Second Oprah Winfrey Interview." *Guardian*, January 19.

CBC Sports. 2000. "NBA Suspends Jason Williams of the Kings." *CBC Sports* online, July 20.

CBS News. 2010. "Roethlisberger Suspended 6 Games by NFL." *CBS News* online, April 21.

Chadiha, J. 2014. "Trash Talk: All about Finding an Edge." *ESPN* online, January 29.

Chait, J. 2014. "What White People Don't See When They Watch Basketball." *New York Magazine* online, March 20.

Chan, W. 2014. "#CrimingWhileWhite, #ICantBreathe Dominate Twitter Talk in Eric Garner Case." *CNN* online, December 4.

Chang, J. 2014. *Who We Be: A Cultural History of Race in Post-Civil Rights America*. New York: St Martin's.

Chase, C. 2013. "Ten Things We Learned from Marshall Henderson's Incredible Comments." *USA Today*, March 21.

———. 2015. "Why Does Maria Sharapova Earn $10 Million More in Endorsements Than Serena Williams?" *USA Today*, September 1.

Chavez, L. 2014. "Our Selective Outrage on Racism." *New York Post*, May 5.

———. 2015. "Cheating in the NFL? Yes, It's a Big Deal." *Chicago Tribune*, May 7.

Cherry, M. 2013. "The Unearned Advantages of Racial and Gender Privilege." *The Root*, August 3.

Clark, A. 2009. "You Haven't Forgotten about Big Ben . . . Have You?" *Bitch Media*, October 22.

Clark, K. 2014. "Super Bowl 2014: Peyton Manning is Mr. Annoying." *Wall Street Journal* online, January 31.

Clarke, S. 2015. "Lance Armstrong Hits Out at Hypocrisy in Cycling's Doping Culture." *Cycling Weekly*, December 7.

Clearly, T. 2016. "Jack Montague: 5 Fast Facts You Need to Know." *Heavy.com*, March 17.

CNN. 2009. "Phelps Admits 'Bad Judgment' after Marijuana-Pipe Photo." *CNN* online, February 2.

Coakley, J. 2006. *Sports in Society: Issues and Controversies*. Boston: McGraw Hill Publishing.

Coates, T. 2014. "No, Hope Solo Is Not 'Like' Ray Rice." *Atlantic Monthly* online, September 23.

Cohen, M. 2014. "Richard Sherman's Immature Gloating Shows He's Not Ready for Sport Stardom." *Guardian*, January 21.

Cohen, N. 2014. "Grand Jury Decision Leads to Twitter Confessions of 'Criming While White.'" *New York Times* online, December 4.

Cohen, W. 2014. "The Duke Lacrosse Player Still Outrunning His Past." *Vanity Fair*, March 24.

———. 2016. "Remembering (and Misremembering) the Duke Lacrosse Case." *Vanity Fair*, March 10.

Cole, C. L. 2001. "Nike's America/America's Michael Jordan." In *Michael Jordan, Inc.*, edited by D. L. Andrews, 65–71.

Cole, C. L., and D. L. Andrews. 1996. "Look—It's NBA Show Time!: Visions of Race in Popular Imaginary." In *Cultural Studies: A Research Volume*, edited by N. Denzin, 1: 141–81. New York: Routledge.

———. 2001. "America's New Son: Tiger Woods and America's Multiculturalism." In *Sports Stars*, edited by D. L. Andrews and S. J. Jackson, 70–86.

Cole, C. L., and S. King. 1998. "Representing Black Masculinity and Urban Possibilities: Racism, Realism and Hoop Dreams." In *Sport and Postmodern Times*, edited by G. Rail, 49–86. Albany: State University of New York Press.

Coleman, C. V. 2012. "Lost 1." *SLAM*, May 7.

Coleman, D. 2014. "New SAT: Still Racist, Still Classist." *Schools Matter*, March 7.

Collins, N. 2013. "A Little (or a Lot) on the Trashy Side." *ESPN* online, April 17.

Collins, P. H. 2004. *Black Sexual Politics: African Americans, Gender and the New Racism*. New York: Routledge.

———. 2006. "New Commodities, New Consumers: Selling Blackness in a Global Marketplace." *Ethnicities* 6 (30): 297–317.

Coogan, D. 2009. "Race and Crime in Sports Media: Content Analysis on the Michael Vick and Ben Roethlisberger Cases." *Journal of Sports Media* 7 (2): 129–51.

Cooky, C., M. A. Messner, and M. Musto. 2015. "'It's Dude Time!' A Quarter Century of Excluding Women's Sports in Televised News and Highlight Shows." *Communication and Sport* 3 (3): 261–87.

Cooper, B. 2011. "Refereeing Serena: Racism, Anger, and U.S. (Women's) Tennis." *Crunk Feminist Collective*, September 12.

———. 2015. "Intersectionality." In *The Oxford Handbook of Feminist Theory*, edited by L. Disch and M. Hawkesworth.

Coppens, A. 2015. "USA Today Goes All 'White Boy' on Wisconsin Badgers on Eve of Final Four." *Madtown Badgers*, April 3.

Coppinger, M. 2014. "Roger Goodell 'Not Cheering for' Richard Sherman." *NFL.com*, January 23.

Cortez, D. 2014. "The Great White Quarterback; All Contrived and Concocted Dynasties Come to an End." *Black Athlete*, May 1.

Covitz, R. 2011. "Steelers Quarterback Ben Roethlisberger Playing for Redemption." *Seattle Times* online, February 5.

Craggs, T. 2009. "Dustin Pedroia Comes Out Swinging." *Boston Magazine* online, April.

———. 2010. "Danny Woodhead: Not Particularly Small, Just White." *Deadspin*, October 5.

Craig, K. 2016. "Sexual Assault Rumors Overshadow Yale Basketball Team." *CBS News* online, March 5.

Crenshaw, K. W. 1989. "Mapping the Margins: Intersectionality, Identity Politics, and Violence against Women of Color." *Stanford Law Review* 43 (6): 1241–99.

———. 1997. "Color-Blind Dreams and Racial Nightmares: Reconfiguring Racism in the Post-Civil Rights Era." In *Birth of a Nation 'Hood*, edited by T. Morrison, 97–168.

———. 2000. "Race, Reform and Retrenchment" In *Theories of Race and Racism: A Reader*, edited by L. Back and J. Solomos, 549–60. New York: Routledge.

Cropley, E. 2014. "Pistorius Shoves Race, Crime and Punishment in South Africa's Face." *Reuters*, October 23.

Crouse, K. 2014. "Celebrate? Sorry, We're Studying." *New York Times* online, March 29.

Crowe, J. 2006. "Steve Howe, 48; Former Dodger Pitcher Whose Drug Use Hurt Career." *LA Times* online, April 29.

Crunktastic. 2011. "Refereeing Serena: Racism, Anger, and U.S. (Women's) Tennis." *Crunk Feminist Collective*, September 12.

Culp-Ressler, T. 2014. "The Myth of the Absent Black Father." *Think Progress*, January 16.

Cunningham, P. L. 2009. "'Please Don't Fine Me Again!!!!!': Black Athletic Defiance in the NBA and NFL." *Journal of Sport and Social Issues* 33 (1): 39–58.

Curtis, B. 2012. "The Prisoner of Redemption: What Happened to Josh Hamilton?" *Grantland*, October 8.

Daily Beast. 2010. "50 Druggiest Colleges." *Daily Beast*, December 12.

Danielle, B. 2016. "The Ryan Lochte Robbery Story Is the Epitome of White Privilege." *Ebony*, August 18.

Daniels, E., M. J. Kane, C. Cooky, and N. M. LaVoi. 2015. "*SI* Sportsperson of the Year Cover Image of Serena Williams: Opportunity Missed." Nicole M. Lavoi, December 23.

D'Arcangelo, L. 2009. "Brittney Griner May Push Gender Boundaries, but Not on Purpose." *Curve*.

Davis, A. Y. 1998. "Race and Criminalization: Black Americans and the Punishment Industry." In *The House That Race Built*, edited by W. Lubiano, 264–79.

Davis, L. R., and O. Harris. 1998. "Race and Ethnicity in US Sports Media." In *Media Sport*, edited by L. A. Wenner, 154–69. New York: Routledge.

Davis, N. 2014a. "Deion Sanders Talks DeSean Jackson Release, Diva WR's, Johnny Football's Ghetto Tendencies." *Roland Martin Reports*, April 2.

———. 2014b. "Peyton Manning: More Athletic and Less Intelligent Than You Might Think." *PS Mag* online, January 29.

Delaware County Daily Times Editorial Board. 2013. "NFL: Eagles Forgive Riley Cooper after Racial Slur; So Should We (Other Views)." *Daily Local News* online, August 2.

Denvir, D. 2016. "Their 'Compassion' Is Seriously Flawed: Politicians Care about White Addicts—but Still Love the Racist Drug War." *Salon*, February 8.

Denzin, N. 2001. "Representing Michael." In *Michael Jordan, Inc.*, edited by D. L. Andrews, 3–14.

DeRousse, R. 2013. "Cardinals in History: The Rise of Racism in Baseball." St. Louis Cardinals' website, January 1.

Desmond-Harris, J. 2016. "Serena Williams Is Constantly the Target of Disgusting Racist and Sexist Attacks. *Vox*, September 7.

Dessources, V. 2015. "The Lost Art of Trash Talk." *Hoops Junction*, March.

DeVega, C. 2015. "Sympathy Is for White People: The '60 Minutes' Segment That Highlights America's Startling Double Standard on Addiction." *Salon*, November 4.

Devine, J. 2014. "Trash Talking Isn't an Art. It's Garbage. Nothing Good Comes Out of It." *Monterey County Herald*, January 22.

Diamond, J. 2016. "NASCAR CEO, Drivers Endorse Donald Trump." *CNN* online, February 29.

Dickerson, J. 2014. "#CrimingWhileWhite Explodes on Twitter Following Eric Garner Decision." *Huffington Post*, December 3.

Dickinson, M. 2015. "Jordan Spieth Masters Art of Humility after Memorable Win." *The Times (UK)* online, April 14.

Dieckmann, J. R. 2010. "NASCAR Turning Hard Left, and Not Just on the Track." *Renew America*, October 25.

DiGiovanna, M. 2015. "Josh Hamilton Will Not Be Suspended for Substance-Abuse Relapse." *LA Times* online, April 3.

DiGiovanna, M., and B. Shaikin. 2015. "Josh Hamilton Suffers Substance-Abuse Relapse; MLB Suspension Likely." *LA Times* online, February 27.

Dohrmann, G., and T. Evans. 2013. "Special Report on Oklahoma State Football: Part 3—The Drugs." *Sports Illustrated* online, September 12.

Douglas, D. D. n.d. "To Be Young, Gifted, Black and Female: A Meditation on the Cultural Politics at Play in Representations of Venus and Serena Williams." *Sociology of Sport* online.

———. 2005. "Venus, Serena, and the Women's Tennis Association: Where and When 'Race' Enters." *Sociology of Sports Journal* 22 (3): 256–83.

Douglas, S. 2011. "Buzz Bissinger Isn't Interested in Tales of Ben Roethlisberger's Redemption." *The Big Lead*, January 27.

Doyel, G. 2013. "Still a Johnny Football Fan; Not Crazy About Johnny Manziel, the Person." *CBS Sports* online, August 11.

Doyle, J. 2011. "Drew Brees, Leadership by Example." *Pro Player Insiders*, June 3.

———. 2014. "Sexism, Hope Solo and 'the Domestic Violence Case No One Is Talking About.'" *The Sports Spectacle*, September 21.

Drug Addiction Treatment. 2011. "White Teens Have Double the Rates of Drug Addiction as African-Americans." *Drug Addiction Treatment*, November 14.

DuBois, W. E. B. (1935) 1997. *Black Reconstruction in America*, 1860–1880. New York: The Free Press.

Dufresne, C. 2013. "Time for Johnny Manziel to Sign in as a Team Leader." *LA Times* online, August 5.

Dufur, M. J., and S. L. Feinberg. 2009. "Race and the NFL Draft: Views from the Auction Block." *Qualitative Sociology* 32 (1): 53–73.

Dunne, T. 2012. "Rodgers' Leadership Qualities Affirmed." *Milwaukee-Wisconsin Journal Sentinel*, September 19.

Dyer, R. 1997. *White*. New York: Routledge.

Dyson, M. E. 2001. "Be Like Mike? Michael Jordan and the Pedagogy of Desire." In *Michael Jordan Inc.*, edited by D. L. Andrews, 259–68.

———. 2007. *Know What I Mean? Reflections on Hip Hop*. New York: Basic Civitas Books.

East, S. 2015. "Driving for Diversity: The NASCAR Racers Breaking Boundaries." *CNN* online, April 24.

Easterling, J. 2012. "NASCAR Drivers That Have Failed Random Drug Tests." Website for KYGL, July 10.

Eastman, S., and A. Billings. 2001. "Biased Voices of Sports: Racial and Gender Stereotyping in College Basketball Announcing." *The Howard Journal of Communications* 12 (4): 183–201.

Edwards, H. 1972. *Sociology of Sport*. Belmont, CA: Dorsey Press.

———. 1998. "An End to the Golden Age of Black Participation in Sports?" *Civil Rights Journal* 3 (1): 18.

Eisenberg, J. 2016. "Why Wisconsin's Bronson Koenig Is Joining the Dakota Pipeline Protest." *Yahoo! Sports*, September 12.

Elliott, J. 2013. "Diva Dez Bryant's Lack of Class and Maturity Starting to Get Old." *PennLive.com*, October 27.

Ellis, Z. 2014. "Johnny Manziel Leads A&M to Stunning Comeback Victory over Duke in Chick-fil-A Bowl." *Sports Illustrated* online, January 1.

Encalada, D. 2015. "World's Cutest Drug Kingpin Is All Smiles for Drug Bust Mugshot." *Complex*, November 10.

Endress, A. 2013. "Manziel Heavily Criticized in Today's Age, but Peyton Manning Got in Trouble Too." *Bleacher Report*, July 13.

Engel, J. F. 2013. "Manziel Case Was Tipping Point." *Fox Sports* online, August 9.

———. 2014. "Jeremy Lin's Success with New York Knicks Based on Foundation of Hard Work." *Fox Sports* online, July 24.

Engel, M. 2011. "Baseball Continues to See Fewer Black Players." *Star Telegram*, July 17.

Engelhardt, T. 2007. *The End of Victory Culture: Cold War America and the Disillusioning of a Generation*. Amherst, MA: University of Massachusetts Press.

Entine, J. 1999. *Taboo: Why Black Athletes Dominate Sports and Why We're Afraid to Talk About It*. New York: Public Affairs.

ESPN. 2012. "Garrett Reid, Son of Andy, Found Dead." *ESPN* online, August 6.

———. 2013. "Kobe Bryant Urges Dwight Howard." *ESPN* online, Ferbuary 7.

———. 2014a. "Sherman Disagrees with Idea of Ban." *ESPN* online, March 3.

———. 2014b. "Tour Says Johnson Leave 'Voluntary.'" *ESPN* online, August 2.

———. 2016. "Nigel Hayes Carries Sign Asking for Money at College GameDay." *ESPN* online, October 17.

ESPN, Page 2. n.d. "Hottest Female Athletes: 2011." "Page 2" webpage, *ESPN* online.

Estes, C. 2012. "Allmendinger Got His Energy Kick, but May Never Race NASCAR Again." *Sports Illustrated* online, September 20.

Evans, T. 2014. "Jim Irsay Arrest Reports Tell of Cash, Pills, Erratic Driving." *USA Today* online, March 27.

Fagan, K. 2014. "Sex Sells? Trend May Be Changing." *ESPN* online, October.

Faraudo, J. 2015. "Cleveland Cavaliers' Matthew Dellavedova's Scrappy Play Pleases Teammates, Bothers Foes." *Mercury News (San Jose)* online, June 1.

Farrell, C. 2012. "The 'Enigma' of Dominican Baseball." *New York Daily News* online, December 4.

Fay, K. 2015. "Let's Talk About Serena." *The Odyessy* online, July 22.

Feagin, J. R. 2010. *The White Racial Frame: Centuries of Racial Framing and Counter-Framing*. New York: Routledge.

Feagin, J. R., and H. Vera. 1995. *White Racism: The Basics*. New York: Routledge.

Feagin, J. R., H. Vera, and P. Batur. 2001. *White Racism*. New York: Routledge.

Feinstein, J. 2002. "Trash-Talking Is Littering the Game," *Washington Post*, February 7, D01.

Ferber, A. 1999. *White Man Falling: Race, Gender and White Supremacy.* Lanham, MD: Rowman and Littlefield.

———. 2007. "The Construction of Black Masculinity: White Supremacy Now and Then." *Journal of Sport and Social Issues* 31 (11): 11–24.

Fink, J., and L. J. Kensicki. 2002. "An Imperceptible Difference: Visual and Textual Constructions of Femininity in *Sports Illustrated* and *Sports Illustrated for Women.*" *Mass Communication and Society* 5 (3): 317–39.

Fischer-Baum, R., A. Gordon, and B. Haisley. 2014. "Which Words Are Used to Describe White and Black NFL Prospects?" *Deadspin*, May 5.

Florio, M. 2010. "Aaron Rodgers Talks Trash to Teammate on Twitter." *Pro Football Talk*, June 11.

———. 2015. "Pulled Over by Police for Domestic Argument, Johnny Manziel Admits to Drinking." *NBC Sports*, October 15.

Foucault, M. 1995. *Discipline and Punish: The Birth of the Prison.* New York: Vintage Books.

Fox Business. 2015. "Top Seven Highest-Paid Female Tennis Stars." *Fox Business* online, September 1.

Fox News. 2014. "Danica Patrick Questions Need for NASCAR Diversity Program." *Fox News* online, October 27.

Frankenberg, R. 1997. "Local Whiteness, Localizing Whiteness." In *Displacing Whiteness: Essays in Social and Cultural Criticism*, edited by R. Frankenberg, 1–34. Durham, NC: Duke University Press.

———. 2001. "The Mirage of an Unmarked Whiteness." In *The Making and Unmaking of Whiteness*, edited by B.B. Rasmussen, E. Klinenberg, I. Nexica, and M. Wray, 72–96. Durham, NC: Duke University Press.

Freeling, I. 2015. "Black History Month 2015: Whites in the Civil Rights Movement Who Fought, and Sometimes, Died for the Cause." *New York Daily News* online, February 26.

Friedman, J. 2009. "Sports Misogyny and the Court of Public Opinion." *American Prospect* online, July 27.

Gane-McCalla, C. 2009. "Athletic Blacks vs. Smart Whites: Why Sports Stereotypes Are Wrong." *Huffington Post*, May 25.

Gantt, D. 2016. "Deion Sanders Says Johnny Manziel's Girlfriend Is a Problem." *Pro Football Talk*, February 5.

Garber, G. 2006. "Lacrosse Culture Crisis: Play Hard, Party Hard." *ESPN* online, May 25.

Garcia, A. 2014. "Richard Sherman and Respectability Politics in Sports." *Racialisious*, January 20.

———. 2015. "The Illegalities of Brownness." *Social Text*, 33 (2): 99–120.

Gasparino, Charles. 2014. "Why Didn't Ray Rice Get the Richie Incognito Treatment Right Away?" *National Review*, September 10.

Gasper, C. 2009. "No. 83 Is the Team MVP." *Boston Globe* online, December 15.

Gasper, C. L. 2013. "Johnny Manziel Case Latest Example of NCAA Hypocrisy." *Boston Globe* online, August 11.

Giardina, M. D., and M. K. Donnelly. 2007. "Introduction," In *Youth Cultures and Sport: Identity, Power, and Politics*, edited by M. D. Giardina and M. K. Donnelly, 1-12. New York: Routledge.

Gibbs, L. 2016. "The Legacy of The Kobe Bryant Rape Case." *Think Progress*, April 3.

Giddings, P. 1984. *When and Where I Enter: The Impact of Black Women on Race and Sex in America*. New York: William Morrow.

Gilman, S. 1984. "Black Bodies, White Bodies: Toward an Iconography of Female Sexuality in Late Nineteenth-Century Art, Medicine, and Literature." *Critical Inquiry* 12, no. 1, 205–43.

Giroux, H. 1997. "Racial Politics and the Pedagogy of Whiteness." In *Whiteness: A Critical Reader*, edited by Mike Hill, 294–315. New York: New York University.

———. 2008. *Against the Terror of Neoliberalism: Politics Beyond the Age of Greed*. New York: Routledge.

Giudice, K. 2012. "Welker Thrives in Leadership Role." Denver Broncos' website, June 7.

Gleeson, S. 2013a. "Marshall Henderson Has Confrontation with Coach, Throws Ice at Ole Miss Fans." *USA Today* online, January 29.

———. 2013b. "Marshall Henderson Rejoins Ole Miss, Still Will Miss Games." *USA Today* online, September 26.

———. 2013c. "Chris Herren Gives Marshall Henderson advice." *USA Today* online, July 12.

Glock, A. 2009. "The Selling of Candace Parker." *ESPN* online, March 12.

Gluck, J. 2011. "Five NASCAR Drivers Decline President Obama's White House Invitation." *SB Nation*, September 1.

———. 2013. "Black NASCAR Driver Knows He Could Change Face of Sport." *USA Today* online, February 9.

Goff, S. 2015. "U.S. Goalkeeper Hope Solo Has Kept a Low Profile in Women's World Cup." *Washington Post* online, June 28.

Goldberg, D. T. 2000. "Racial Knowledge." In *Theories of Race and Racism: A Reader*, edited by L. Back and J. Solomos, 154–80. New York: Routledge.

Golden, D. 2007. *The Price of Admission: How America's Ruling Class Buys Its Way into Elite Colleges—and Who Gets Left Outside the Gates*. New York: Broadway Books.

Goldstein, A., and S. Kinzie. 2006. "Bias Death Still Ripples Through Athletes' Academic Lives." *Washington Post* online, June 19.

Goold, D. 2012. "Now in Book Form: The Cardinal Way." *St Louis Post-Dispatch* online, May 18.

Gordon, A. 2014a. "The Rejection of Myron Rolle: The NFL Wanted Him . . . Until He Was Named a Rhodes Scholar." *SB Nation*, February 12.

———. 2014b. "The NCAA's Weed Policy: A History of Ignorance." *Vice.com*, October 15.

Granderson, L. Z. 2011. "Ben Roethlisberger's Redemption." *ESPN* online, January 23.

Grant, E. 2008. "Josh Hamilton's Battle: From Cocaine Cravings and 26 Tattoos to Faith and Rangers." *Dallas News* online.

Grant, M. 1916. "The Passing of the Great Race." New York: Scribner's.

Grant, M., and J. Taylor. 2012. *The Passing of the Great Race*. London, England: Wermod and Wermod Publishing Group.

Grasgreen, A. 2014. "Athletes, Drugs and Entitlements." *Inside Higher Ed* online, January 17.

Gray, H. 1995. *Watching Race: Television and the Struggle for Blackness*. Minneapolis, MN: University of Minnesota Press.

———. 2005. *Cultural Moves: African Americans and the Politics of Representation*. Berkeley: University of California Press.

Greenberg, C. 2013. "Johnny Manziel Taunts Rice Players with Autograph, Money Counting Gestures." *Huffington Post*, August 31.

Greenberg, M. 2001. "Selfish Kobe Should Just Go Away." "Page 2" webpage, *ESPN* online.

Gregory, S. 2010. "NASCAR: A Once Hot Sport Tries to Restart Its Engine." *TIME* online, April 26.

———. 2013. "It's Time to Pay College Athletes." *TIME* online, September 16.

———. 2015. "Why the Tom Brady Suspension Is Ridiculous." *TIME* online, May 11.

Gresson, A., J. L. Kincheloe, and S. R. Steinberg. 1997. *Measured Lies: The Bell Curve Examined*. New York: St. Martin's Press.

Grinberg, E. 2012. "Livestrong Bracelet: To Wear or Not to Wear?" *CNN* online, October 22.

Groves, R. 2015. "Why A Wisconsin National Championship Would Be Good for College Basketball." *Forbes* online, March 15.

Guevara, A. J. M., and D. P. Fidler. 2002. *Stealing Lives: The Globalization of Baseball and the Tragic Story of Alexis Quiroz*. Bloomington: University of Indiana Press.

Guregian, K. 2007. "Labrador Receiver; Criticism Doesn't Dog Welker," *Boston Herald*, June 7, 76.

———. 2010a. "Wes Welker Being Wes Welker: Again, Welker Defies Odds with OTA Return," *McClatchy-Tribune Business News* [Washington], June 3.

———. 2010b. "Deion Branch: Wes Welker Will Catch Up." *McClatchy-Tribune Business News* [Washington], February 21.

Habib. H. 2002. "The Writing on the Ball: From Petulance to Penmanship, Critics Say There's Ample Evidence of Athletes Missing Manners." *Palm Beach Post*, December 22, 1B.

Hackman, R. 2015. "Swimming While Black: The Legacy of Segregated Public Pools Lives On." *Guardian* online, August 4.

Halberstam, D. 1999. *The Children*. New York: Fawcett Books.

Hale, M. 2013. "Sports Has Long History of Players' Trash Talk." *New York Post* online, January 13.

Hall, S. 1996. "What Is This 'Black' in Black Popular Culture?" In *Stuart Hall: Critical Dialogues in Cultural Studies*, edited by H.S. Chen and D. Morley, 465–75. London: Routledge.

———. 1997. *Minimal Selves*. London: ICA.

Hamm, T., and A. S. Vitale. 2015. "Weed Is Basically Legal in New York City Now, but Only If You're White." *Vice*, October 23.

Harmony, P. 2015. "Why New Calls for A 'Gentler' Drug War Are Racist and Classist." *Black Girl Dangerous*, November 10.

Haro, A. 2016. "Olympic Athletes Have Actually Been Allowed to Smoke Weed Since 2013." *The Inertia*, August 8.

Harper, J. 2007. "Work Ethic Isn't the Only Thing That Makes Welker a Success." *NewsOK.com* (The Oklahoman), June 24.

Harris-Perry, M. 2011. *Sister Citizen: Shame, Stereotypes, and Black Women in America*. New York: Harper & Row.

Hartmann, D. 2007. "Rush Limbaugh, Donovan McNabb, and 'A Little Social Concern': Reflections on the Problems of Whiteness in Contemporary American Sport." *Journal of Sport and Social Issues* 31 (1): 45–60.

Heck, J. 2016. "Brian Billick Compares Johnny Manziel to Teen Who Killed People." *Sporting News*, February 16.

Herbes-Sommers, C. 2003. *Race: The Power of an Illusion*. Berkeley, CA: California Newsreel.

Hernstein, R. J., and C. Murray. 1994. *The Bell Curve: Intelligence and Class Structure in American Life*. New York: The Free Press.

Higgins, M. 2013. "Swifter, Higher . . . Higher." *ESPN* online, July 24.

Hill, J. 2010. "Goodell's Slippery Roethlisberger Slope." *ESPN* online, May 26.

Hill, J. B. 2014. "Former FSU Star Myron Rolle Paid Cost for Being Different." *BET* online, February 20.

Hill, M. L. 2016. *Nobody: Casualties of America's War on the Vulnerable, from Ferguson to Flint and Beyond*. New York: Atria Books.

Himmelberg, M. 1991. "A Dream Gone Awry Dykstra Discovers Baseball Success, Off-Field Problems." *Orange County Register*, May 12, D01.

Hinton, E. 2004. "The Tiger Woods of NASCAR?" *Daily Press* online, November 18.

———. 2009. "Drive for Diversity Shifts Out of Neutral." *ESPN* online, January 21.

Hoberman, J. 1997. *Darwin's Athletes: How Sport Has Damaged Black America and Preserved the Myth of Race*. Boston: Houghton Mifflin.

Hohler, B. 2008. "Most Valuable Half-Pint." *Boston.com*, September 28.

Holland, G. 2012. "Some Thoughts from Pot-Smoking Skaters." *LA Times* online, November 13.

hooks, b. 1992. *Black Looks*. Boston: South End Press.

———. 1997. "Representing Whiteness in the Black Imagination." In *Displacing Whiteness: Essays in Social and Cultural Criticism*, edited by R. Frankenberg, 65–179. Durham, NC: Duke University Press.

Hoose, P. M. 1989. *Necessities: Racial Barriers in American Sport*. New York: Random House.

Horn, B. 2015. "Jordan Spieth 'Could Carry Our Game for Decades'; Others Laud His 'Epic' Masters Performance." *Dallas News* online, April 12.

Howard, G. 2013. "How Marshall Henderson Gets Away with Being Marshall Henderson." *Deadspin*, March 27.

Howe, J. 2012. "Wes Welker Has Spent Football Life Proving Doubters Wrong, from College Coaches to NFL Executives." *NESN*, January 3.

Hruby, P. 2016. "The NCAA Lets College Olympians Collect Cash for Gold, Because Amateurism Is a Self-Serving Lie." *Vice*, August 18.

Hudson, W. 2015. "Texan Girl Next Door Caught Running College Drug Ring." *PJ Media*, November 12.

Huffington Post. 2013. "Justin Timberlake, 'The 20/20 Experience': Is There a Visual Preference for Whiteness?" *Huffington Post*, March 27.

Hughes, G. 2004. "Managing Black Guys: Representation, Corporate Culture, and the NBA." *Sociology of Sport Journal* 21 (2): 163–84.

Hutcherson, K. 2011. "Donald Trump Rejects Allegations of Racism." *CNN* online, May 2.

Hutchins, A. 2013. "Johnny Manziel Still Clowning Everyone on Twitter." *Deadspin*, July 28.

Hutchinson, E. O. 2014. "Black Players Get the Flag with NFL's 'N-Word' Ban." *Huffington Post*, February 26.

Iber, J., and S. O. Regalado. 2006. *Mexican Americans and Sports: A Reader on Athletics and Barrio Life*. College Station: Texas A&M University Press.

Ingham, A. G. 1985. "From Public Issue to Personal Trouble: Well-Being and the Fiscal Crisis of the State." *Sociology of Sport Journal* 2 (1): 43–55.

Ingraham, C. 2014. "White People Are More Likely to Deal Drugs, but Black People Are More Likely to Get Arrested for It." *Washington Post* online, September 30.

Israeli, D. n.d. "Top 10 Smartest Athletes in Professional Sports." *Men's Fitness* online.

Jackson, D. Z. 1989. "Calling the Plays in Black and White: Will Today's Super Bowl Be Black Brawn vs. White Brains?" *Boston Globe*, January 22, A25.

———. 2015. "Top on the Courts, but Wisconsin at Bottom of Graduation Rates." *Boston Globe* online, March 24.

Jackson, J. M. 2016. "It's Important That Maria Sharapova's Doping Isn't Bigger News." *Black Youth Project*, March 18.

Jackson, R. 2006. *Scripting the Black Masculine Body: Identity, Discourse, and Racial Politics in Popular Media*. New York: State University of New York Press.

Jackson, S. 2006. "Duke Administration to Blame." *ESPN* online, 18 April.

———. 2011. "The Skylar Diggins Balancing Act." *ESPN* online, December 23.

Jenkins, C. 2003. "NASCAR Ends Donations to Jackson's Rainbow PUSH." *USA Today*, July 28.

Jenkins, S. 2011. "Tim Tebow Shows That in Sports, There's No Faking Leadership (and Bruce Boudreau and Randy Edsall Could Take Note)." *Washington Post* online, December 1.

———. 2012. "Why I'm Not Angry at Lance Armstrong." *Washington Post* online, December 15.

Jensen, T. 2014. "Danica Upset after Boyfriend Misses Race, Questions Diversity Program." *Fox Sports* online, October 24.

Jessop, A. 2013. "How the SEC Can Stop the Problem of Recreational Drug Use in College Football. *Forbes* online, July 31.

Johnson, C. 2009. "Nascar's Lack of Diversity and the Impression of Racism." *Bleacher Report*, June 12.

Johnson, L., and D. Roediger. 1997. " 'Hertz, Don't It'? Becoming Colorless and Staying Black in the Crossover." In *Birth of a Nation 'Hood: Gaze, Script and Spectacle in the O. J. Simpson Case*, edited by T. Morrison, 197–240. New York: Random House.

Johnson, P. 2013. "Is Lance Armstrong on the Road to Redemption?" *Yahoo! Sports*, January 15.

Johnson, T., J. E. Boyden, and W. Pittz. 2001. "Racial Profiling and Punishment in U.S. Public Schools: How Zero Tolerance Policies and High Stakes Testing Subvert Academic Excellence and Racial Equity." Oakland, CA: Applied Research Center, ERASE Initiative.

Johnson, V. 2015. "Spieth Played, and Won, the Right Way." *Gainsville Times* online, April 12.

Jones, J. 2015. "Bubba Wallace Is Best Hope for Full-Time Black Driver in NASCAR Cup Series." *Charlotte Observer* online, May 22.

Jones, S. 2016. "Soccer Star Abby Wambach Charged with DUI." *CNN* online, April 3.

Jones, V. 2005. "Black People 'Loot' Food . . . White People 'Find' Food." *Huffington Post*, September 1.

Joseph, A. 2016. "Mark Schlereth Uses Jordan Spieth's Collapse to Take a Shot at Cam Newton." *USA Today*, April 10.

Jubera, D. 2011. "Roethlisberger's Road to Redemption." *CNN*, January 21.

Junior. 2009. "The Utterance of This Word Should Be Punishable by Death." *Deadspin*, September 16.

Kane, M. J. 2011. "Sex Sells Sex, Not Women's Sports." *The Nation* online, July 27.

Kane, M. J., and S. L. Greendorfer. 1994. "The Media's Role in Accommodating and Resisting Stereotyped Images of Women in Sport." In *Women, Media and Sport: Challenging Gender Values*, edited by P.J. Creedon, pp. 28–44. London: Sage.

Kang, J. K. 2010. "The Lives of Others." *Freedarko*, January 14.

———. 2012. "The Question of Identity." *Grantland*, March 20.

Kaplan, S. C. 2000. "The Color Gap in Girls' Sports." *Alternet*, November 29.

Katz, A. 2013. "Ole Miss Star Needs to Face His Problems." *ESPN* online, July 11.

Katz, J. 2006. *The Macho Paradox: Why Some Men Hurt Women and How All Men Can Help*. New York: Source Books.

Katzowitz, J. 2013. "Michael Vick Begins the Process of Forgiving Riley Cooper." *CBS Sports* online, August 1.

Keane, T. 2013. "The Myth about Crime and the NFL." *Boston Globe* online, July 2.

Keeney, T. 2013. "Riley Cooper Caught on Tape Saying Racial Slur at Kenny Chesney Concert." *Bleacher Report*, July 31.

Keith, B. 2014. "NCAA: Swimmers Biggest Users of Sleep Aids among College Athletes; #2 in Marijuana Use." *SwimSwam*, August 5.

Kellenberger, H. 2012. "Dundrecous Nelson, Jamal Jones Dismissed from Team." *Clarion-Ledger* online, blog, January 5.

Kelley, R. 2010. "Why Athletes Aren't Role Models." *Newsweek* online, March 10.

Kelley, R. D. G. 1997. *Yo' Mama's Disfunktional!: Fighting the Culture Wars in Urban America*. Boston: Beacon Press.

———. 1998. "Playing for Keeps: Pleasure and Profit on the Postindustrial Playground." In *The House That Race Built*, edited by W. Lubiano, 195–231.

Kelly, C. 2014. "Oscar Pistorius and the Redemptive Crime Story." *Globe and Mail* online, October 21.

Kendi, I. K. 2016. *Stamped from the Beginning: The Definitive History of Racist Ideas in America*. New York: Nation Books.

Kerasotis, P. 2003. "Decline in Sportsmanship Reflects Societal Shifts." *Enquirer* online, March 4.

Kerr-Dineen, L. 2016. "Jordan Spieth Just Had a Monumental Implosion at the Masters." *USA Today* online, April 10.

Kersey, P. 2012. "Thought for the Daytona 500: Will Diversity Kill NASCAR?" *V Dare*, February 26.

Khan, A. I. 2012. *Curt Flood in the Media: Baseball, Race, and the Demise of the Activist-Athlete*. Jackson, MS: University of Mississippi Press.

King, C. R. 2001. *Beyond the Cheers: Race as Spectacle in College Sport*. Albany: State University of New York.

———, ed. 2014. *Asian American Athletes in Sport and Society*. New York: Routledge.

———. 2015. *Redskins: Insult and Brand*. Lincoln, NE: University of Nebraska Press.

King, C. R., and D. J. Leonard. 2010. "Race, Redemption, and Respectability: White Racism in Athletics." *Racism Review*, April 14.

King, C. R, and C. F. Springwood. 2001. *Beyond the Cheers: Race as Spectacle in College Sport*. Albany: State University of New York.

———. 2005. "Body and Soul: Physicality, Disciplinarity, and the Overdetermination of Blackness." In *Channeling Blackness: Studies in Television and Race in America*, edited by D. Hunt, 185–206. New York: Oxford University Press.

King, J. 2013. "Let the Aaron Hernandez Prison Rape and Racist Jokes Begin." *Colorlines*, June 24.

King, P. 2014. "Legislating Language: Will the NFL Ban the N-Word?" *MMQB*, March 3.

King, S. 2015. "Donald Trump's Blatant, Unapologetic Racism Breeds a Dangerous Hysteria." *New York Daily News* online, November 23.

Kingkade, T. 2014. "Brandon Austin, Twice Accused of Sexual Assault, Is Recruited by a New College." *Huffington Post*, July 28.

Kirk, J. 2012. "Tyrann Mathieu Arrested: The Rise and Fall of the Hone Badger." *SB Nation*, October 26.

Kiszla, M. 2014. "Manning Plenty Tough Enough Despite Critics." *Denver Post*, September 7, W9.

Klis, M. 2012. "Hard Work Behind Manning's Genuis; 'Pretty Driven.'" *National Post*, September 6, B9.

Knoblauch, A. 2009. "Ron Artest Admits to Drinking during Games, Likes to Have Fun." *LA Times* online, blogs, December 2.

Korman, C. 2016. "Jack Montague Attends Yale's NCAA Tournament Game." *USA Today* online, March 17.

Koutroupis, Y. 2012. "Mike Brown: Steve Nash 'a Very Intelligent Leader.'" *USA Today* online, July 22.

Kusz, K. W. 2001. "'I Want to Be the Minority': The Politics of Youthful White Masculinities in Sport and Popular Culture in 1990s America." *Journal of Sport and Social Issues* 25 (4): 390–416.

———. 2003. "BMX, Extreme Sports, and the White Male Backlash." In *To the Extreme: Alternative Sports, Inside and Out*, edited by R. E. Rinehart and S. Sydnor, 153–78.

———. 2007. *Revolt of the White Athlete*. New York: Peter Lang Publishing.

———. 2011. "Much Adu about Nothing? Freddy Adu and the Politics of Neoliberal Racism in New Millennium America." In *Commodified and Criminalized: New Racism and African Americans in Contemporary Sports*, edited by D. Leonard & C. R. King 147–64. New York: Rowman and Littlefield.

———. 2015. "Lance Armstrong's Beautiful Lie." *The All Rounder*, April 6.

"Kyle McNary Is the Worst NBA Fan Ever." 2009. *Permanent Insanity*, May 26.

LaFauci, T. 2014. "Statement Game: How Johnny Manziel Silenced His Critics with Last Night's Performance." *Politicus USA*, January 1.

Lapchick, R. 2002. *Smashing Barriers*. New York: Madison Books.

———. 2015. "The 2015 Racial and Gender Report Card: Major League Baseball." Institute for Diversity and Ethics in Sport, University of Central Florida, April 15.

Larson, S. G. 2005. *Media and Minorities: The Politics of Race in News and Entertainment*. Lanham, MD: Rowman and Littlefield.

Layden, T. 2015. "After Rehabilitation, the Best of Michael Phelps May Lie Ahead." *Sports Illustrated* online, November 10.

Lazarus, A. 2011. "Ben Roethlisberger and the 25 Sports Stars with the Longest Roads to Redemption." *Bleacher Report*, January 25.

Leal, W., M. Gertz, and A. R. Piquerob. 2015. "The National Felon League?: A Comparison of NFL Arrests to General Population Arrests." *Journal of Criminal Justice* 43 (5): 397–403.

Lee, T. 2014. "Johnny Manziel: Allen Iverson on Grass." *Breitbart*, January 2.

Leitch, W. 2014. "The Unlikely Villain." *Sports on Earth*, March 21.

Leli, T. 2014. "Ranking The 15 Best Trash-Talking Athletes Ever." *Rant Sports*, March 3.

Leonard, D. J. 2004. "The Next MJ or the Next OJ? Kobe Bryant, Race and the Absurdity of Colorblind Rhetoric." *Journal of Sport and Social Issues* 28 (3): 284–313.

———. 2006a. "The Real Color of Money: Controlling Black Bodies in the NBA." *Journal of Sport and Social Issues* 30 (2): 158–79.

———. 2006b. "A World of Criminals or a Media Construction?: Race, Gender, Celebrity and the Athlete/Criminal Discourse." In *Handbook of Sports Media*, edited by A. Raney and J. Bryant, 523–42. Mahwah, NJ: Lawrence Erlbaum Associates.

———. 2008. "To the White Extreme in the Mainstream: Manhood and White Youth Culture in a Virtual Sports World." In *Youth Cultures and Sport: Identity, Power, and Politics*, edited by M. Giardina and M. Donnelly, 91–112. New York: Routledge.

———. 2012a. *After Artest: The NBA and the Assault on Blackness*. New York: SUNY Press.

———. 2012b. "Silence, Innocence, and Whiteness: The Undemonization of Kevin Love." *POPSspot*, February 9.

———. 2013a. "Johnny Manziel is No Rosa Parks." *New Black Man*, August 14.

———. 2013b. "Revealing the Stigma against Tattooed Athletes." *Huffington Post*, December 5.

———. 2014. "Beyond Black and White: Norm Chow and the Question of Model Minority with Football Coaching Ranks." In *Asian American Athletes in Sport and Society*, edited by C. R. King, 138–51.

Leonard, D. J., W. R. Davie, and C. R. King. 2010. "A Media Look at Tiger Woods—Two Views," *Journal of Sports Media* 5 (2): 107–16.

Leonard, D. J., K. George, and W. Davis, eds. 2016. *Football, Culture, and Power*. New York: Routledge.

Leonard, D. J., and C. R. King. 2011. *Commodified and Criminalized: New Racism and African Americans in Contemporary Sports*. New York: Rowman and Littlefield Publishers.

Levin, S. 2013. "Cardinals: *Sports Illustrated* Cover Draws on 1968 Lou Brock, Roger Maris, Bob Gibson Photo." *Riverfront Times* online, May 23.

Levitt, A. 2009. "When St. Louis Was the Most Racist City in Major League Baseball." *Riverfront Times* online, January 19.

Lewis, A. 2003. "Media Representations of Rap Music: The Vilification of Hip-Hop Culture." Master's thesis, Communication, Culture, and Technology, Georgetown University.

Lewis, B. 2015. "The U.S. Women's Most Controversial Player—and World's Best Goalie." *New York Post* online, June 6.

Lewis, M. 2009. "The No-Stats All-Star." *New York Times* online, February 13.

Lewis, T. 2010. *Ballers of the New School: Race and Sports in America*. Chicago: Third World Press.

Ley, T. 2013. "Who Is This Marshall Henderson Guy? Your Guide to College Basketball's Most Entertaining Gunner." *Deadspin*, January 28.

———. 2015. "Your Racist Uncle Will Love This Picture of the Cardinals' Mascot." *Deadspin*, May 20.

Lipsitz, G. 1995. "The Possessive Investment in Whiteness: Racialized Social Democracy and the 'White Problem' in American Studies," *American Quarterly*, 47 (3): 369–87.

———. 1998. *The Possessive Investment in Whiteness: How White People Profit from Identity Politics*. Philadelphia, PA: Temple University Press.

———. 2011. *How Racism Takes Place*. Philadelphia, PA: Temple University Press.

Liss, S. 2013. "'Cardinal Way' Makes Cover of *Sports Illustrated*." *Biz Journals*, May 28.

Littal, R. 2014. "Marcus Smart Says Fan He Shoved Called Him a Nigger." *Black Sports Online*, February 9.

Little, A. 2007. "The NFL Ain't Easy for Black Quarterbacks." *Yahoo! Sports*, September 20.

Livingstone, S. 2007. "NASCAR Seeks Diversity but Finds the Going Slow." *USA Today* online, April 27.

Longman, J. 1999. "Looking for Sportsmanship in Pro Sports." *Telegram & Gazette*, November 28, C1.

———. 2012. "For Lolo Jones, Everything Is Image." *New York Times* online, August 4.

———. 2015a. "Brittney Griner Arrested with Fiancée Glory Johnson." *New York Times* online, April 23.

———. 2015b. "More Nigerian-Americans Are Reaching Highest Levels of Sports." *New York Times* online, March 18.

Lovelace, S. 2013. "Black Quarterbacks Changing Perceptions in NFL Playoffs." *The Grio*, January 6.

Lubiano, W., ed. 1998. *The House That Race Built*. New York: Vintage Books.

Lucas, M. 2015. "Thought Process: Kaminsky Follows Own Path to Greatness, Graduation." *UWBadgers.com*, May 12.

Ludbrook, K. 2014. "Pistorius Cleared of Murder, Still Faces Lesser Charge." *Fox Sports* online, September 11.

Luther, J. 2013. "Affluenza: The Latest Excuse for the Wealthy to Do Whatever They Want." *The Guardian* online, December 15.

———. 2014. "Faces of Assault." *Sports on Earth*, March 23.

———. 2016a. *Unsportsmanlike Conduct: College Football and the Politics of Rape*. Baltimore, MD: Edge of Sports Books.

———. 2016b. "'I'm Broken': The Duke Lacrosse Rape Accuser, 10 Years Later." *Vocativ*, March 10.

Macur, J. 2014. "End of the Ride for Lance Armstrong." *New York Times* online, March 1.

———. 2015. "Lance Armstrong's Ugly Detour from Road to Redemption." *New York Times* online, February 16.

Maese, R. 2015. "UFC's Ronda Rousey Is Okay with Being Called Pretty. She Can Still Kick Any Guy's Butt." *Washington Post* online, February 26.

Majavu, M. n.d. "Serena Williams: Playing Tennis While Black." *The Argus Report*.

Majendie, M. 2014. "Lance Armstrong: 'Day-to-Day Life Is Positive.'" *CNN* online, August 20.

Mandall, N. 2015. "Coach K Responds to Bo Ryan's 'Rent-a-Player' Barb: 'There Is a Better Choice of Words.'" *USAToday* online, April 8.

Marcotte, A. 2014. "4 Things You Should Know About Fake Rape Accusations." *Alternet*, December 10.

Markovitz, J. 2006. "Anatomy of a Spectacle: Race, Gender, and Memory in the Kobe Bryant Rape Case." *Sociology of Sport Journal* 23 (4): 396–418.

Martin J., et al. 2016. "Expelled Basketball Captain Jack Montague to Sue Yale." *CNN* online, March 14.

Mauer, M. 2016. "Our Compassion for Drug Users Should Not Be Determined by Race." *The Guardian* online, January 7.

Maxwell, Z. 2014. "No Matter What Jackie Said, We Should Generally Believe Rape Claims: Incredulity Hurts Victims More Than It Hurts Wrongly-Accused Perps." *Washington Post* online, December 6.

McCann, M. 2015. "Aaron Hernandez Murder Trial Could Hinge on Cigarette Butt, Bubblegum." *Sports Illustrated* online, March 6.

McCarthy, D., R. L. Jones. 1997. "Speed, Aggression, Strength, and Tactical Naivete." *Journal of Sport & Social Issues* 21 (4): 348–62.

McClellan, B. 2014. "McClellan: No More 'Cardinal Way,' Please." *St. Louis Post-Dispatch* online, March 5.

McCormack, D. 2013. "Horseback Riding, Massages and Cooking Lessons: Inside the Luxury $450k Per Year Rehab Center That 'Affluenza' Teen Will Attend as Punishment for Killing Four in DUI." *Daily Mail* online, December 17.

McCune, J. 2014. "Another Missed Shot: After Collins, the NBA and the Politics of Identities." Symposia, Jason Collins in the American Sportscape: Race, Gender, and the Politics of Sexuality, Washington University, April 11, 2014, St. Louis, MO.

McD, Mike. 2009. "The 15 Sexiest Female Athletes to Watch: 2010 Edition," *Bleacher Report*, December 23.

McDonald, M. 1996. "Horatio Alger with a Jump Shot: Michael Jordan and the American Dream." *Iowa Journal of Cultural Studies* 15: 33–47.

———. 2001. "Safe Sex Symbol? Michael Jordan and the Politics of Representation." In *Michael Jordan Inc.*, edited by D. L. Andrews, 153–76.

———. 2005. "Mapping Whiteness and Sport: An Introduction." *Sociology of Sport Journal* 22 (3): 245–55.

McDonald, M., and D. L. Andrews. 2001, "Michael Jordan: Corporate Sport and Postmodern Celebrityhood." In *Sports Stars*, edited by D. L. Andrews and S. J. Jackson, 24–35.

McDonough, K. 2014. "The Domestic Violence Gender Trap: Hope Solo, Ray Rice and the Tired Myopia of 'Women Do It Too.'" *Salon*, September 25.

McGee, R. 2012. "NASCAR's Drug Policy at a Glance." *ESPN* online, July 10.

McGregor, J. 2015. "What Makes Jordan Spieth Golf's New Leader? More Than His Skill." *Washington Post* online, April 13.

McGuire, D. L. 2011. *At the Dark End of the Street: Black Women, Rape, and Resistance—A New History of the Civil Rights Movement from Rosa Parks to the Rise of Black Power*. New York: Vintage Books.

McIntosh, P. 1989. "White Privilege: Unpacking the Invisible Knapsack." *Peace and Freedom Magazine*, July/August, 10–12.

———. (1989) 2010. "Some Notes for Facilitators on Presenting My White Privilege Papers." The National SEED Project website.

McIntyre, J. 2013. "Marshall Henderson Is the Bad Boy of the SEC: Meet the Jersey-Poppin, Coors Light-Drinkin' Scoring Machine." *The Big Lead*, January 29.

McKay, J., and H. Johnson. 2008. "Pornographic Eroticism and Sexual Grotesquerie in Representations of African-American Sportswomen." *Social Identities: Journal for the Study of Race, Nation and Culture* 14 (4): 491–504.

McNeil, F., and M. Isaacson. 2013. "FSBC Reviewing Fox's MMA license." *ESPN* online, March 6.

McNulty, R. 2005. "New Code Not Racist, Just Good Business." *Seattle Post-Intelligencer*, October 25, D2.

McPherson, T. 2001. "Who's Got Next?: Gender, Race and the Mediation of the WNBA." In *Basketball Jones*, edited by T. Boyd and K. Shropshire, 184–97.

Megdal, H. 2013. "The Cardinal Way." *Sports on Earth*, August 14.

Melnick, M. J. 2001. "Race, Ethnicity, and Sport." In *Contemporary Issues in Sociocology of Sport*, edited by A. Yiannakis and M. J. Melnick, 183–86. Champaign, IL: Human Kinetics.

Men's Health. 2014. "The Hottest Female Athletes: 2011." *Men's Health* online, April 5.

Mercurio, E., and V. Filak. 2010. "Roughing the Passer: The Framing of Black and White Quarterbacks Prior to the NFL Draft." *Howard Journal of Communications* 21 (1): 56–71.

Merrill, E. 2013. "How Riley Cooper Put Slur in Past." *ESPN* online, December 18.

Messner, M.A., M. Dunbar, and D. Hunt. 2000. "The Televised Sports Manhood Formula." *Journal of Sport and Social Issues* 24 (4): 380–94.

Miklasz, B. 2013. "Cardinal Way Wins Out Over Mickey Way." *St. Louis Post-Dispatch* online, October 19.

Miller, C. 2004. "Study Finds Strong Link between Race, Employer Response: Calif. Researcher Finds Arab Americans Most Likely to Face Job Discrimination." *Michigan Daily* online, December 1.

Miller, J. 2014. "The Right Balance." *Milwaukee Journal-Sentinel* online, April 1.

Milz, D. 2009. "Serena Williams Is a Slacker, Jason Whitlock Says: It's Easy to Agree." *Bleacher Report*, July 7.

Mizell, G. 2013. "Former Oklahoma State WR Bo Bowling Talks His 'Success Story,' Place in *Sports Illustrated* Report." *NewsOK*, blog, September 12.

Modiano, C. 2012. "ESPN's Lost Week: Why White Fans Don't Hate White Athletes." *POPSspot*, February 9.

Mohamed, A. R., and E. D. Fritsvold. 2011. *Dorm Room Dealers: Drugs and the Privileges of Race and Class*. Boulder, CO: Lynne Rienner Publisher.

Moore, M. 2014. "Aaron Craft, Andrew Dawkins, McAdoo Make NBA Training Camps." *CBS Sports* online, September 2.

Moore, T. 2014. "Richard Sherman Has Only Himself to Blame." *CNN* online, January 22.

Moorti, S. 2002. *Color of Rape: Gender and Race in Television's Public Sphere*. Albany: State University of New York Press.

Morrison, T., ed. *Birth of a Nation 'Hood: Gaze, Script, and Spectacle in the O. J. Simpson Case*. New York: Pantheon Books.

Morrissey, R. 2015. "Serena Williams Doesn't Help Female Athletes with Racy *SI* Cover Shoot." *Chicago Sun-Times* online, December 12.

Moskovitz, D. 2015. "Hope Solo Is Not a Problem." *Deadspin*, June 16.

Muhammad, K. G. 2011. *The Condemnation of Blackness: Race, Crime, and the Making of Modern Urban America*. Cambridge, MA: Harvard University Press.

Mullen, J. 2016. "Maria Sharapova Loses Endorsement Deals after Failing Drug Test." *CNN* online, March 8.

Murdock, D. 2003. "Doing the Hustle (Again)." *National Review* online, May 2.

Murrell, A. J., and E. M. Curtis. 1994. "Causal Attributions of Performance for Black and White Quarterbacks in the NFL: A Look at the Sports Pages." *Journal of Sport and Social Issues* 18 (3): 224–33.

Mwaniki, M. 2017. *The Black Migrant Athlete: Media, Race, and the Diaspora in Sports*. Lincoln, NE: University of Nebraska Press.

NASCAR. n.d. "NASCAR Committed to Diversity Program Going Forward." *The Auto Channel.*

———. 2015. "Roush Taps LeBron Ties for Bubba Sponsorship." Website for NASCAR, January 28.

———. 2016. "NASCAR Drive for Diversity Unveils 2016 Driver Roster." Website for NASCAR, January 15.

Ndopu, E. 2013. "Oscar Pistorius: Salvaging the Super Crip Narrative." *The Feminist Wire*, February.

Neal, M. A. 2010. "Coming Apart at the Seams: Black Masculinity and the Performance of Obama-Era Respectability." *New Black Man in Exile*, blog, April 7.

———. 2013. *Looking for Leroy: Illegible Black Masculinities*. New York: New York University Press.

Newell, S. 2013. "The Lance Armstrong Redemption Tour Is Hitting Some Hurdles." *Deadspin*, January 15.

Newman, J. I. 2010. *Embodying Dixie: Studies in the Body Pedagogics of Southern Whiteness*. Champaign, IL: Common Ground Publishing.

Newman, J. I., and M. Giardina. 2011. *Sport, Spectacle, and NASCAR Nation: Consumption and the Cultural Politics of Neoliberalism*. New York: Palgrave Macmillan.

New York Daily News. 2010. "With Santonio Holmes and Antonio Cromartie, New York Jets Coach Rex Ryan May Have His Hands Full." *New York Daily News* online, April 12.

Ngaruiya, A. 2016. "The IOC Says 32-Year-Old Ryan Lochte and the U.S. Swimmers Were Just 'Kids' Having Fun." *UPROXX*, August 18.

Nickel, L. 2008. "Rodgers Preparing to Assume Control." *Milwaukee Journal Sentinel* online, March 9.

Nightengale, B. 2016. "As MLB Celebrates Jackie Robinson, Dearth of Black Pitchers Concern Many." *USA Today* online, April 14.

Niven, D. 2005. "Race, Quarterbacks and the Media: Testing the Rush Limbaugh Hypothesis." *Journal of Black Studies* 35 (5): 684–94.

Nocera, J., and B. Strauss. 2016. *Indentured: The Inside Story of the Rebellion Against the NCAA Hardcover*. New York: Portfolio Books.

Norris, L. 2016. "The 'Best Fans in Baseball' Reportedly Yelled Racial Slurs at Jason Heyward Last Night." *Sports Mockery*, April 19.

North, T. C. 2012. "Tim Tebow Leadership—a Fearless Leader." *Tcnorth.com*.

NPR. 2013. "Double Murder Charges Still Haunt Ex-Raven Linebacker Ray Lewis." *NPR Morning Edition*, November 5.

Oates. T. P. 2017. *Football and Manliness: An Unauthorized Feminist Account of the NFL*. Champaign, IL: University of Illinois Press.

———. 2016. "Is Grayson Allen the Next Hated White Duke Player?" *ESPN* online, February 9.

Ogden, D. C. 2000. "African-Americans and Pick-up Ball: The Loss of Diversity and Recreational Diversion in Midwestern Youth Baseball." *NINE: A Journal of Baseball History and Culture* 9 (1–2): 200–207.

Olson, E. 2012. "TCU Bust Sign of Increased Pot Problem." *Huffington Post*, February 16.

O'Neil, D. 2011. "The 'Cardinal Way' Is Team's Foundation." *St Louis Post-Dispatch* online, October 30.

Oriard, M. 2008. *Sporting with the Gods: The Rhetoric of Play and Game in American Literature*. Cambridge: Cambridge University Press.

———. 2010. *Brand NFL: Making and Selling America's Favorite Sport*. Chapel Hill, NC: University of North Carolina Press.

O'Sullivan, T. 2008. "Targeted Man: Welker a Target for Cassel as Well as Opponents." *Concord Monitor*, December 2008.

Owens, J., and T. Machir. 2015. "Danica Patrick and Ronda Rousey: Who's the Bigger Star?" *Sporting News*, November 5.

Palmer, Brian. 2013. "What Happens in Racial Sensitivity Training? How Counselors Will Try to Talk the Racism Out of Riley Cooper." *Slate*, August.

Panchina, J. 2009. "10 Scrappiest Players." *Bleacher Report*, September 9.

Parham, J. 2015. "The Collected Quotes of Donald Trump on 'the Blacks.'" *Gawker*, July 24.

PA Sports. 2009. "Colts Teammates Respect Manning's Leadership Style." *Bleacher Report*, December 9.

Pasquarelli, L. 2006. "Brees Brings Leadership to Saints." *ESPN* online, August 7.

Passan, J. 2014. "After Nearly Losing His Olympic Gold Medal to a Positive Marijuana Test, Ross Rebagliati Now Wants to Sell Weed to Canada." *Yahoo! Sports*, January 31.

Patton, S., and D. J. Leonard. 2014. "Viewpoint: Why Eric Garner Was Blamed for Dying." *BBC* online, December 8.

PBS. 2016. "There Was No Wave of Compassion When Addicts Were Hooked on Crack." *PBS* online, March 29.

Peart, C. 2013. "A Double Standard on the N-Word?" *App.com* (*Asbury Park Press*), December 1.

Pein, C. 2012. "Two Students Arrested in Drug Bust at Reed." *Willamette Week* online, February 16.

Pelley, S. 2010. "American Samoa: Football Island." *CBS News* online.

Peltz, J. 2011. "NASCAR Grapples with a Downshift in Popularity." *LA Times* online, March 21.

Perchick, M. 2011. "Steve Nash, Ryan Fitzpatrick, and the 35 Smartest Athletes of All Time." *Bleacher Report*, February 1.

Perry, I. 2004. *Prophets of the Hood: Politics and Poetics in Hip-Hop.* Durham, NC: Duke University Press.

———. 2011. *More Beautiful and More Terrible: The Embrace and Transcendence of Racial Inequality in the United States.* New York: New York University Press.

Perry, P. 2014. "Revis: Brady is a Relentless Trash-Talker." *CSNNE*, November 13.

Perry, T. 2008. "How the Police Busted a College Drug Scene." *LA Times* online, May 7.

Person, J. 2014. "Carolina Panthers' Jason Avant Led Charge to Forgive Eagles' Riley Cooper." *Charlotte Observer* online, November 6.

Petchesky, B. 2013a. "Worst Columnist in America Compares Johnny Manziel to Rosa Parks." *Deadspin*, August 9.

———. 2013b. "The Problem with Riley Cooper's Redemption." *Deadspin*, December 28.

Peter, J. 2015. "Wisconsin Doesn't Hide from 'White Guys' Reputation." *USA Today* online, April 3.

Petkac, L. 2013. "How to Be the Worst Teammate." *Bleacher Report*, March 14.

Pfitzinger, J. 2007. "Disrespect a Continuing Problem; Trash-Talking in Athletics Is a Byproduct of an Increasingly Crass Culture, Those Involved in Youth Sports Say." *Star Tribune*, February 13, 1E.

Phillips, A. 2011. "City Schools Are Suspending More Students, and for Longer." *Chalk Beat*, January 27.

Picca, L. H., and J. Feagin. 2007. *Two-Face Racism: Whites in the Backstage and Frontstage.* New York: Routledge.

Pickeral, R. 2012. "UNC Probe Reveals Academic Fraud." *ESPN* online, December 12.

Pierce, C. P. 2015. "NASCAR's Confederate Flag Ban and the Explosion of Athlete Activism." *Grantland*, June 29.

Platt, L. 2000. "The White Shadow." In *Basketball Jones: America Above the Rim*, edited by T. Boyd and K. Shropshire, 68–74.

Pockrass, B. 2012. "NASCAR Diversity: Darrell Wallace Jr. Hoping to Become Role Model for African-American Drivers after Landing Full-Time Ride." *Sporting News*, February 9.

Porter, K. 2016. "Jordan Spieth's Introspection after Historic Masters Loss Rare for Athletes." *CBS Sports*, April 12.

Potrykus, J. 2014. "Frank Kaminsky: You Can't Judge the Player by His Color." *Milwaukee-Journal Sentinel* online, April 4.

Pough, G. 2004. *Check It While I Wreck It: Black Womanhood, Hip-Hop Culture, and the Public Sphere*. Boston: Northeastern University Press.

Povak, T. 2006. "Haunted Draft." *Orlando Sentinel*, June 27, B1.

Prashad, V. 2003. *Keeping Up with the Dow Joneses*. Cambridge, MA: South End Press.

Price, S. L. 1997. "What Ever Happened to the White Athlete?" *Sports Illustrated*, December 8, 31–46.

Project 21. 2003. "Black Group Calls on Jesse Jackson to Put Money Where His Mouth Is and Sponsor a Black NASCAR Driver." Website for Project 21: The National Leadership Network for Black Conservatives, July 3.

Quigley, B. 2010. "'Felony is the New 'N-Word': Michelle Alexander on Mass Incarceration as 'The New Jim Crow' in the Age of Obama." *Black Gender Report*, June 9.

Quinn, T. J. 2016. "Documents Reveal Peyton Manning Accuser Called Sexual Assault Crisis Center to Report 1996 Incident." *ESPN* online, February 23.

Raanan, J. 2016. "Giants Kicker Josh Brown Detailed Domestic Violence in Documents." *ESPN* online, October 19.

Rainville, R., and E. McCormick. 1977. "Extent of Covert Racial Prejudice in Pro Football Announcers' Speech." *Journalism Quarterly* 54 (1): 20–26.

Ramsey, N. 2014. "Costas on NFL's Adrian Peterson: 'It's a Horrible Crime.'" *MSNBC* online, September 25.

Rankine, C. 2015. "The Meaning of Serena Williams: On Tennis and Black Excellence." *New York Times* online, August 25.

Rasmussen, B. B., E. Klinenberg, I. Nexica, and M. Wray. 2001. "Introduction." In *The Making and Unmaking of Whiteness*, edited by B.B. Rasmussen, Klinenberg, I. Nexica, and M. Wray. 1–24. Durham, NC: Duke University Press.

Real Sports. 2008. "Real Sports with Bryant Gumbel: Josh Hamilton." *YouTube.com*.

Reese, J. 2000. "Black Men Can Jump . . . and Sprint and Run Long Distances Faster Than Anyone Else. Why? Despite the Racist Overtones, One White Author Argues It's Genetic Superiority." *Daily Herald*, April 25.

Reid, J. 2014. "NFL Is Right to Ban N-Word, Other Slurs, from the Playing Field." *Washington Post* online, February 25.

Reilly, R. 2013. "A Dichotomy of Brains and Brawn." *ESPN* online, October 4.

Reinardy, S., and W. Wanta. 2008. *The Essentials of Sports Reporting and Writing*. New York: Routledge.

Renck, T. E. 2014. "Broncos WR Wes Welker Remains Motivated to Win His First Super Bowl." *Denver Post* online, June 8.

Rendell, E. 2015. "Forget His Stats, Tim Tebow Is a Great Leader." *Philly.com* (*Philadelphia Inquirer*), April 27.

Rexroat, M. 2014. "NCAA National Study of Substance Use Habits of College Student-Athletes." Website of the NCAA, July 2014.

Rhoden, W. C. 2006. *Forty Million Dollar Slaves: The Rise, Fall, and Redemption of the Black Athlete*. New York: Crown Publishers.

———. 2007. *Third and a Mile: From Fritz Pollard to Michael Vick—An Oral History of the Trials, Tears and Triumphs of the Black Quarterback*. New York: ESPN Books.

———. 2014. "Seahawks' Richard Sherman, Like Cornerbacks Before Him, Plays Man-to-Man and Goes Toe to Toe." *New York Times* online, January 22.

———. 2016. "Early Entry? One and Done? Thank Spencer Haywood for the Privilege." *New York Times*, June 29.

Riccobono, A. 2015. "Duke Basketball: Why Are the Blue Devils So Hated?" *IB Times*, April 1.

Ridley, L. 2014. "Oscar Pistorius Sentence: Tragedy Highlights Staggering Level of South African Gun Crime." *Huffington Post*, October 21.

Rinehart, R. E. 1998. *Players All: Performances in Contemporary Sport*. Bloomington: University of Indiana Press.

Rinehart, R. E., and S. Sydnor, eds. 2001. *To the Extreme: Alternative Sports, Inside and Out*. Albany: State University of New York.

Ringo, K. 2014. "Aaron Craft Wins Home Finale with Scrappy Play That Defined Ohio State Career." *Yahoo! Sports*, March 9.

Rishe, P. 2012. "Peyton Manning, Papa John's and Marijuana: A Rocky Mountain High." *Forbes* online, November 14.

Rivas, J. 2011. "Nearly All Student Arrests in NYC Public Schools Target Black and Latino Males." *Color Lines*, November 30.

Rivera, C. 2014. "The Brown Threat: Post-9/11 Conflations of Latina/os and Middle Eastern Muslims in the US American Imagination." *Latino Studies* 12 (1): 44–64.

Roan, D., and M. Slater. 2015. "Lance Armstrong: I'd Change the Man, Not Decision to Cheat." *BBC* online, January 26.

Roberts, D. 2014. "Jameis Winston Is Not a Victim." *Deadspin*, December 4.

Robinson, J., and L. Grove. 2010. "Columbia University Drug Bust." *Daily Beast*, December 8.

Roediger, D. 1999. *The Wages of Whiteness: Race and the Making of the American Working Class*. New York: Verso.

Rogers, M. 2015. "Ugly Details of Hope Solo's Arrest Come Out in Report Before U.S. Opener." *USA Today* online, June 8.

Roithmayr, D. 2014. *Reproducing Racism: How Everyday Choices Lock in White Advantage*. New York: New York University Press.

Romaine, D. 2013. "Riley Cooper and America's Double Standard on Racism." *Big Time Sports*, August 3.

Rosenberg, M. 2014. "New Jameis Winston Allegations Obscure a More Important Discussion." *Sports Illustrated* online, October 15.

Rosenthal, G. 2009. "Last Word on ESPN's Civil Lawsuit Policy." *NBC Sports*, July 21.

———. 2013."Why Is Aaron Rodgers' Leadership Being Questioned?" *NFL.com*, January 23.

———. 2015. "Ben Roethlisberger: I Wasn't a Good Teammate." *NFL.com*, August 6.

Rothenberg, B. 2015. "Tennis's Top Women Balance Body Image with Ambition." *New York Times* online, July 10.

Rothman, J. 2014. "The Origins of 'Privilege.'" *New Yorker* online, May 12.

Rowe, K. 1990. "Roseanne: Unruly Woman as Domestic Goddess." *Screen* 31 (4): 408–19.

Ruane, M. E. 2016. "Testing the Limits." *Washington Post* online, June 9.

Runstedtler, T. 2012. *Jack Johnson, Rebel Sojourner: Boxing in the Shadow of the Global Color Line.* Berkeley: University of California Press.

———. 2016. "Racial Bias: Black Athletes, Reagan's War on Drugs, and Big-Time Sports Reform." *American Studies Journal*, special issue, "Sport in the University," forthcoming.

Russell, K. K. 1998. *The Color of Crime: Racial Hoaxes, White Fear, Black Protectionism, Police Harassment, and Other Macroaggressions.* New York: New York University Press.

Ryan, B. 1992. "As Bird Goes, a Part of Every Fan Goes, Too." *Baltimore Sun* online, August 19.

Ryan, N. 2010. "Action on Track Isn't Helping NASCAR Attendance, Ratings." *USA Today* online, July 21.

Ryan, T. 2013. "Marshall Henderson Appears to Be Enjoying Himself as SEC Champion." *The Big Lead*, March 17.

Rybaltowski, M. 2013. "Marshall Henderson Taking His Act to the NCAA Tournament." *CBS Sports* online, March 13.

Said, E. 1978. *Orientalism.* New York: Vintage Books.

Sailer, S. 2005. "The White Guy Gap." *V Dare*, March 13.

———. 2015. "Top 20 Most Hated Duke Basketball Players by Race—Whites Most Hated by Far." *V Dare*, March 26.

Salazar-Moreno, Q. 2009. "Pregnant Candace Parker Graces Cover of ESPN Magazine." *bvonsports.com*, March 13.

Samuel, E. 2016. "Josh Brown Saga Is Latest Evidence That Racial Bias Is Alive and Well in the NFL." *New York Daily News* online, October 21.

Sanchez, R., and A. Watts. 2014. "Olympic Swimmer Michael Phelps Arrested on DUI Charge." *CNN* online, September 30.

Sando, M. 2016. "2016 NFL QB Tier Rankings." *ESPN* online, August 8.

Santelices, M. V., and M. Wilson. 2010. "Unfair Treatment? The Case of Freedle, the SAT, and the Standardization Approach to Differential Item Functioning." *Harvard Educational Review* 80 (1): 106–33.

Santoliquito, J. 2013. "Riley Cooper May Have Bigger Problems Ahead." Website of CBS Philly, August 1.

Savran, D. 1998. *Taking It Like a Man: White Masculinity, Masochism, and Contemporary American Culture*. Princeton, NJ: Princton University Press.

Scarborough, A. 2014. "Manziel Leaves as a Winner." *ESPN* online, January 1.

Schlabach, M. 2012. "Higher Education." *ESPN* online, April 19.

Schow, A. 2016. "Jack Montague, Free Speech and the Rush to Judgment." *Washington Examiner* online, March 17.

Schroeder, G. 2014. "Wisconsin Is Athletic Enough to Be an NCAA Title Contender." *USA Today* online, April 4.

Schrotenboer, B. 2013. "Slayings Not Forgotten, Ray Lewis Not Forgiven." *USA Today Sports* online, June 18.

Schultz, Jamie. 2005. "Reading the Catsuit: Serena Williams and the Production of Blackness at the 2002 U.S. Open." *Journal of Sport and Social Issues* 29 (3): 338–57.

Schultz, Jeff. 2015. "Jordan Spieth Is Golf's Newest 'Root-able' Champ, for Fans and Foes Alike." Website of the PGA, April 13.

Schulze, L. 1990. "On the Muscle." In *Fabrications: Costume and the Female Body*, edited by J. Gaines and C. Herzog, 59–78. London: Routledge.

Schwab, F. 2013. "Ticket Punched: Marshall Henderson Gator Chomps, Lifts Ole Miss to SEC Title." *Yahoo! Sports*, March 17.

Schwartz, N. 2013. "Eagles Receiver Riley Cooper Uses Racial Slur at a Kenny Chesney Concert." *USA Today* online, July 31.

———. 2014. "The Five Greatest Fights in NASCAR History." *USA Today* online, November 5.

Schwichtenberg, P. 2014. "St. Louis Cardinals: Matt Carpenter Exemplifies the Cardinal Way." *Rant Sports*, October 5.

Seal, M. 2013. "The Shooting Star and the Model." *Vanity Fair* online, June.

*Seattle Times*. 1994. "Basketball Trash Talking Belongs in the Trash Can." *Seattle Times* online, November 12.

Secret, M., and K. Zraickdec. 2010. "5 at Columbia Are Charged in Drug Sales." *New York Times* online, December 7.

Seligman, A. 2003. "Enforcing Drug Policy; Some Say the NBA Doesn't Do Enough with Its Testing." *The Columbian*, April 7, B8.

Serino, K. 2014. "Oscar Pistorius and the White Factor." *AL Jazeera* online, May 13.

Sessler, M. 2013. "Riley Cooper Excused from Eagles Activities, Seeks Help." *NFL.com*, August 2.

———. 2014. "Eagles' Graham: Aaron Rodgers Was 'Laughing at Us.'" *NFL.com*, November 18.

Sewell, J. I., Jr. 2006. "'Don't Believe the Hype': The Construction and Export of African American Images in Hip-Hop Culture." Master's Thesis, Department of Communication, East Tennessee University.

Shaikin, B. 2009. "David Eckstein Is More Than a 'Scrappy' Little Player." *LA Times* online, April 26.

Shapiro, B. 2014. "An Athlete Who Needs More Than a Ponytail: The W.N.B.A.'s Skylar Diggins Discusses Her Beauty Regimen." *New York Times* online, July 7.

Sheridan, P. 2015. "Riley Cooper Still Starting for Eagles." *ESPN* online, August 13.

Sherman, R. 2014. "The NFL's Smartest QBs." *MMQB*, January 3.

Shome, R. 1996. "Race and Popular Cinema: The Rhetorical Strategies of Whiteness in *City of Joy*." *Communication Quarterly* 44 (4): 502–18.

Short, A. 2016. "6 UC Santa Cruz Students Face MDMA Felonies, but Throwing Them in Prison Won't Help Anyone." *Alternet*, March 26.

Shropshire, K. L. 1996. "Merit, Ol' Boy Networks, and the Black-Bottomed Pyramid." *Hastings Law Journal* 45: 455–72.

Sieczkowski, C. 2014. "St. Louis Cardinals Fans Have a Seriously Racist Response to Ferguson Protesters." *Huffington Post*, October 7.

Siegel, A. 2013. "How a Stoned Canadian Changes Sports History." *Deadspin*, August 1.

Silverman, J. 1999. "The Art of Trash Talk." *Psychology Today* online, September 1.

Silverstein, J. 2013. "Don't Feel Your Pain: A Failure of Empathy Perpetuates Racial Disparities." *Slate*, June 27.

Simmons, B. 2011a. "Avoiding the Lockout and the Red Sox." *Grantland*, October 14.

———. 2011b. "Behind the Pipes: Into the Arms of the NHL." *Grantland*, October 25.

Simons, H. D. 2003. "Race and Penalized Sports Behaviors." *International Review for the Sociology of Sport* 38 (1): 5–22.

Sinnott, J., and T. McGowan. 2013. "Lance Armstrong's Demise: How an All-American Hero Fell to Earth." *CNN* online, February 22.

Skiba, R. J., and K. Knesting. 2001. "Zero Tolerance, Zero Evidence: An Analysis of School Disciplinary Practice." Indiana Education Policy Center, August.

Sloop, J. M. 1997. "Mike Tyson and the Perils of Discursive Constraints: Boxing, Race, and the Assumption of Guilt." In *Out of Bounds: Sports, Media and the Politics of Identity*, edited by A. Baker and T. Boyd, 102–22. Bloomington: University of Indiana Press.

Slover, R. 2014. "*SN* Names the 20 Smartest Athletes in Sports." *Sporting News*, November 5.

Smith, M. 2004. "Students of the Game Foes are Often Left Smarting," *Boston Globe*, January 18, D3.

Smith. M. D. 2012. "Tony Dungy Explains Why Peyton Manning Could Never Be a Coach." *NBC Sports* online, "Pro Football Talk," December 10.

———. 2013a. "Warren Moon Sees Biases Hurting Black Quarterbacks." *NBC Sports* online, "Pro Football Talk," April 24.

———. 2013b. "Dez Bryant Flips Out on the Cowboys' Sideline." *NBC Sports* online, "Pro Football Talk," October 27.

———. 2016. *Invisible Man, Got the Whole World Watching: A Young Black Man's Education.* New York: Nation Books.

Smizik, B. 2006. "Taunting and Excessive Celebration Show a Lack of Class from Steelers." *Pittsburgh Post-Gazette*, September 27, F1.

Solomon, J. 2013. "Texans Need Manziel's Fiery Personality." *Houston Chronicle* online, December 26.

Solotaroff, P., and R. Borges. 2013. "Aaron Hernandez: Patriots Tight End Violent Evolution." *Rolling Stone* online, August 28.

Spencer, N. 2004. "Sister Act VI: Venus and Serena Williams at Indian Wells: 'Sincere Fictions' and White Racism." *Journal of Sport and Social Issues* 28 (2): 115–35.

Staples, R., and T. Jones. 1985. "Culture, Ideology and Black Television Images." *The Black Scholar* 16 (3): 10–20.

Steele, D. 2006. "Duke Lacrosse Players Afflicted by Sense of Entitlement." *Baltimore Sun* online, March 31.

Stellino, V. 2004. "Excessive Celebration Could Lead to Ejection." *Florida Times Union*, April 1, C7.

St. John, A. 2002. "I'm on the Olympic Team? Bummer!" *New York Times* online, January 27.

Strauss, E. S. 2014. "Aaron Craft Scrapping in Summer League." *ESPN* online, July 18.

Strauss, V. 2012. "Tom Brady vs. Eli Manning: Who's Smarter?" *Washington Post* online, February 5.

Sturgeon, M. 2014. "College Basketball Is More Fun with Ole Miss Sharpshooter Marshall Henderson." *Rant Sports*, February 2.

Sule, A. O. 2016. "The Benefit of the Doubt: A Case Study on White Privilege." *Media Diversified*, March 8.

Sullivan, E. 2007. "Deprived Dignity: Degrading Treatment and abusive Discipline in New York City and Los Angeles Public Schools." National Economic and Social Rights Initiative, March.

Svrluga, S. 2016. "Expelled Yale Basketball Captain: Alleged Sexual Misconduct Was Consensual." *Washington Post* online, March 14.

Tapper, J. 2011. "Rush Limbaugh Says First Lady Was Booed Partly Because NASCAR Fans Hate Her 'Uppityism.'" *ABC News* online, November 21.

Tate, G. 2003. *Everything but the Burden: What White People Are Taking from Black Culture.* New York: Broadway Books.

Taylor, J. J. 2012. "TCU Will Survive Shameful Day." *ESPN* online, February 16.

Terranova, J. 2015. "Dustin Johnson: Binge Drinking, Not Cocaine, Was My Problem." *New York Post* online, January 20.

Thamel, P. 2008. "For Florida State Player and Scholar, Game Day Is Different." *New York Times* online, November 19.

———. 2012. "'What Happened to Him?' Basketball Star Jonathan Hargett's Promising Career Derailed." *New York Times* online, August 18.

———. 2015. "Suspensions to Oregon Players bring NCAA Marijuana Policy into Question." *Sports Illustrated* online, January 11.

Thangaraj, S. I. 2015. *Desi Hoop Dreams: Pickup Basketball and the Making of Asian American Masculinity*. New York: New York University Press.

Thangaraj, S. I., C. Arnaldo, and C. B. Chin, eds. 2016. *Asian American Sporting Cultures*. New York: New York University Press.

Theoharis, J. 2014. *The Rebellious Life of Mrs. Parks*. Boston: Beacon Press.

Thomas, P. 2009. "For Snowboarders, Drug Testing Can Be a Real Bummer." *LA Times* online, February 20.

Thomas, V. 2013. "The Hypocrisy of the Real Double-Standard with Riley Cooper and the N-Word." *The Shadow League*, August 7.

Tilkin, D. 2012. "Some Students Say Reed Should've Handled Drug Case Internally." Website for KATU, February 18.

Tobak, S. 2011. "Leadership Lessons from Tim Tebow." *CBS News* online, December 14.

Tolson, I. 2013. "Dealing with Black Boys Who Deal Drugs." *The Root*, August 28.

Trahan, K. 2014. "The NCAA's Absurd Drug Rules in Context." *SB Nation*, April 25.

Tran, D. 2015. "Wisconsin Badgers: The 'Average Joe' Player of the Year." *Busting Brackets*, April 10.

Transnational Racial Justice Initiative. 2001. "The Persistence of White Privilege and Institutional Racism in US Policy." *www.raceforward.org*.

Travis, C. 2013a. "Johnny Manziel Helps Defeat Our Ridiculous, Racial QB Stereotypes." *Fox Sports* online, April 3.

———. 2013b. "Manziel Opinions Say a Lot about Us." *Fox Sports* online, September 3.

———. 2013c. "Money, Autograph Taunts by Manziel." *Fox Sports* online, September 1.

———. 2014. "Actions Matter More Than Words . . . Unless You're on the Internet." *Outkickthecoverage.com*, May 12.

Trebay, G. 2010. "Brittney Griner, Basketball Star, Helps Redefine Beauty." *New York Times* online, April 5.

Tuchman, G. 2000. "The Symbolic Annihilation of Women by the Mass Media." In *Culture and Politics*, edited by L. Crothers and C. Lockhart. 150–74. New York: Palgrave Macmillan.

Tunney, J. 2015. "Spieth's Code of Sportsmanship." *Monerey Herald* online, April 19.

Tynes, T. 2016. Buffalo's 3 Black Quarterbacks Are Battling Each Other and History." *SB Nation*, August 31.

Ubben, D. 2012. "Drug Scandals Mar Football Year." *ESPN* online, May 29.

UO Coalition to End Sexual Violence. 2014. "Racism, Media, Protest." May 11.

Uperesa, F. L. 2014. "Fabled Futures: Migration and Mobility for Samoans in American Football." *The Contemporary Pacific* 26 (2): 281–301.

Van Bibber, R. 2014. "The Worst of the Richie Incognito/Jonathan Martin Report." *SB Nation*, February 14.

Vance, L. 2006. "The Complete History of African American Quarterbacks in the National Football League (NFL)." *Black Athlete*, February 23.

Vecsey, G. 1998. "Sport of the Times; Snowboard Dude Says: No Big Deal." *New York Times* online, February 13.

———. 2011. "From a Voice to a Roar, Again." *New York Times* online, September 11.

Veklerov, K. 2016. "UC Santa Cruz Frat, Sorority Members Suspected in Drug Ring." *SFgate*, March 11.

Vera, H., J. R. Feagin, and A. Gordon. 1995. "Superior Intellect?: Sincere Fictions of the White Self." *The Journal of Negro Education* 64 (3): 295–306.

Vrentas, J. 2015. "Ted Wells Strikes Back." *Sports Illustrated* online, May 12.

Wachs, F. L., C. Cooky, M. A. Messner, and S. L. Dworkin. 2012. "Media Frames and Displacement of Blame in the Don Imus Incident: Sincere Fictions and Frenetic Inactivity." *Critical Studies in Media Communication* 29 (5): 421–48.

Waldron, T. 2014. "Richard Sherman: 'Thug' Is 'Accepted Way of Calling Somebody the N-Word.'" *Think Progress*, January 22.

———. 2015. "Harsh: Two Oregon Players Won't Play in National Title Game Because They Were Caught Smoking Pot." *Think Progress*, January 12.

Walker, M. 2011. "Small Scale Model." *Boston.com*, October 2.

Wang, O. 2012a. "Jeremy Lin Puts the Ball in Asian Americans' Court." *LA Times* online, February 12.

———. 2012b. "Living with Linsanity." *LA Review of Books* online, March 6.

Watkins, S. C. 1998. *Representing: Hip-Hop Culture and the Production of Black Cinema*. Chicago: University of Chicago Press.

Watson, G. 2013a. "Tyrann Mathieu Said He Failed at Least 10 Drug Tests While at LSU, but Lost Count after That." *Yahoo! Sports*, April 12.

———. 2013b. "Johnny Manziel's Strong Game Overshadowed by Childish Play." *Yahoo! Sports*, August 31.

Webber, A. 2012. "Why the Patriots' Tom Brady Is a Better Leader Than Eli Manning." *Washington Post* online, February 2.

Weinreb, M. n.d. "The Day Innocence Died." *ESPN* online, n.d. Accessed May 18, 2016.

Wells, T., B. S. Karp, and L. L. Reisner. 2015. "Investigative Report Concerning Footballs Used during the AFC Championship Game." Report, May 6.

Wesseling, C. 2013. "Matt Hasselbeck: Andrew Luck Is a 'Natural' Leader." Website for the NFL, May 29.

Wetzel, D. 2013a. "Johnny Manziel's Suspension Exposes Ridiculousness of NCAA's Double Standards" *Yahoo! Sports*, August 28.

———. 2013b. "Lance Armstrong, Arrogant and Unaware, Did Little to Repair His Image in Mea Culpa with Oprah." *Yahoo! Sports*, January 18.

Whannel, G. 1992. *Fields in Vision: Television Sport and Cultural Transformation*. London: Routledge.

Wheaton, B. 2004. *Understanding Lifestyle Sports: Consumption, Identity and Difference*. New York: Routledge.

Wheel, R. 2013. "Ed O'Bannon vs. the NCAA: The Antitrust Lawsuit Explained." *SB Nation*, January 31.

White, K. C. 2014. "Adrian Peterson Is Not a Racial Symbol." *Atlantic Monthly* online, September 15.

White, P. 2013. "Cardinal Way: Unlikely Stars Emerge from Stable System." *USA Today* online, September 11.

Whitley, D. 2012. "Colin Kaepernick Ushers in an Inked-Up NFL Quarterbacking Era." *Sporting News* online, November 28.

———. 2014. "Wisconsin Badgers Defy Stereotypes En Route to Final Four." *Orlando Sentinel* online, April 2.

Whitlock, J. 2012. "Kobe's Ego Is Lakers' Big Problem." *Fox Sports* online, December 18.

———. 2013a. "Bryant's Problems Mirror Society's." *ESPN* online, November 7.

———. 2013b. "Manziel Should Be Game-Changer." *Fox Sports* online, August 7.

———. 2014a. "Culture Clash." *ESPN* online, April 29.

———. 2014b. "Throw a Flag on the N-Word." *ESPN* online, February 26.

Wierenga, J. 2012. "Jeremy Lin: Why Every American Should Be Rooting for Linsanity to Last." *Bleacher Report*, February 15.

Wilbon, M. 2009. "Revisiting Len Bias." *Washington Post* online, November 4.

Williams, L. 2014. "#CrimingWhileWhite Is the Only Thing You Need to Read to Understand White Privilege." *Think Progress*, December 4.

Williams, P. J. 1997. *Seeing a Colorblind Future: The Paradox of Race*. New York: The Noonday Press.

Williams, R. 1998. "Living at the Crossroads: Exploration in Race, Nationality, Sexuality, and Gender." In *The House That Race Built*, edited by W. Lubiano, 136–56.

Wilson, R. 2016. "Browns' Coach: 'There Are Problems to Address with Johnny Manziel.'" *CBS Sports* online, January 1.

Wilson, W. J. 2012. *The Declining Significance of Race: Blacks and Changing American Institutions*. Chicago: University of Chicago Press.

Wise, T. 2001a. "School Shootings and White Denial." *Alternet*, March 5.

———. 2001b. "A New Round of White Denial: Drugs and Race in the 'Burbs." *Alternet*, August 13.

———. 2010. "Imagine: Protest, Insurgency and the Workings of White Privilege." *Time Wise*, April 25.

Wolfman-Arent, A. 2013. "Meet Marshall Henderson, the Cockiest Cold-Blooded Sniper in College Basketball." *Bleacher Report*, January 30.

Wolken, D. 2015. "College Athletics' Approach to Marijuana Murky, Inconsistent." *USA Today* online, January 10.

Wonsek, P. L. 1992. "College Basketball on Television: A Study of Racism in the Media." *Media, Culture and Society* 14 (3): 449–61.

Wood, D. 2011. "Tim Tebow's Leadership Qualities Should Be Mode for All NFL QB's." *Bleacher Report*, December 12.

———. 2012. "Tim Tebow's Attitude and Leadership Qualities Prove He Should Start in NFL." *Bleacher Report*, December 13.

———. 2013. "Andrew Luck's Leadership Will Lead Indianapolis Colts to Deep Postseason Run." *Bleacher Report*, August 11.

Woodard, D. 2014. "Russell Wilson: Master and Commander." *Huffington Post*, February 12.

Woodbine, O. X. 2016. *Black Goods of the Asphalt: Religion, Hip-Hop and Street Basketball*. New York: Columbia University Press.

Woodsmall, M. 2015. "'98 Olympic Gold Medalist Ross Rebagliati Swears by Weed." *The Inertia*, March 24.

Wray, M., and A. Newitz. 1997. *White Trash: Race and Class in America*. New York: Routledge.

Wright, D. 2016. "Trump: Muslim Ban 'Just a Suggestion.'" *CNN* online, May 12.

WSPA Staff. 2011. "WSU Star Klay Thompson Suspended Following Arrest." *Spokesman-Review (Spokane, WA)* online, March 4.

———. 2016. "Deputies Watch Party on Live Stream, Bust 20 for Drugs in Union." Website of WSPA, February 1.

Yahoo Beauty. 2015. "Skylar Diggins on Beauty, Confidence and Life on the Court." *Yahoo! Sports*, April 7.

Yang, J. 2012. "Will Lin-Sanity Tame Tiger Moms?" *New York Daily News* online, February 15.

Yaniv, O. 2009. "Caster Semenya, Forced to Take Gender Test, Is a Woman . . . and a Man." *New York Daily News* online, September 10.

Yankah, E. 2016. "When Addiction Has a White Face: Commentary." *New York Times*, February 9, A23.

Yoder, M. 2014. "Your White Guy Code Word Power Rankings." *Awful Announcing*, January 8.

Young, S. M. 2010. "Brady Harps on Leadership." *Boston.com*, May 23.

Zachariason, J. J. 2014. "Andrew Luck: The Smartest Rushing Quarterback in the NFL." *Number Fire*, May 20.

Zimmerman, M. 2010. "Major Tom." *Men's Health*, June 1.

Zinser, L. 2011. "Winning Is Not Redemption." *New York Times* online, January 26.

Zirin, D. 2007. "Black Coaches? The NFL Drops the Ball." *Los Angeles Times* online, January 28.

———. 2008. "Who Is Mauricia Grant? NASCAR Knows." *Huffington Post*, July 11.

———. 2012. "Feel the Lin-Sanity: Why Jeremy Lin Is More Than a Cultural Curio." *The Nation* online, February 7.

———. 2013a. "No, for the Love of God, Johnny Manziel Isn't Rosa Parks." *The Nation* online, August 11.

———. 2013b. "Lance Armstrong's Discordant Redemption Song." *Edge of Sports*, January 14.

———. 2014a. "A Penalty for the N-Word, but Not for the R-Word?" *The Nation* online, February 26.

———. 2014b. "Richard Sherman Defends His Dirt." *The Nation* online, April 3.

———. 2014c. "Kurt Busch, Ray Rice and How Sport Disseminates the Burdens of Racism." *The Nation* online, November 11.

———. 2015a. "Gentrification Is the Real Scandal Surrounding Jackie Robinson West." *The Nation* online, February 12.

———. 2015b. "The Patrick Kane Case Marks a New Low in the Long History of Rape Accusations Against Athletes." *The Nation* online, September 23.

Zirin, D., and J. Chang. 2007. "Hip-Hop's E-Z Scapegoats." *The Nation* online, May 8.

Zirin, D., and K. Pronson. 2006. "Privilege Meets Protest at Duke University." *Edge of Sports*, April 14.

Zwerling, J. 2015. "The Rise of Matthew Dellavedova, the Playoffs' Unlikely Star and Biggest Pest." *Bleacher Report*, June 4.

# INDEX·

multiculturalism, 88–89, 180, 200, 221, 223, 227

Murray, Charles, 61

Musto, Michael, 160

**N**

NASCAR, 3, 6–7, 9, 77, 73, 127, 131, 164–65, 180, 181–201, 231, 233; crime and, 193–97, 198–99; diversity and, 181–90, 200–201; fighting and, 190–93; whiteness and, 189–90, 191–93, 195–96, 200–201

Nash, Steve, 42, 51, 215

National College Players Association, 36

NBA dress code, 3, 88–89

NBA lockout, 44–45

Neal, Lia, 161, 179

Neal, Mark Antony, 146

neoliberalism, 8, 142, 154, 187, 189, 205

New England Patriots, 230, 232

"New Jim Crow," the, 57, 110–12, 121, 130, 132

Newman, Josh, 180, 184, 192

new racism, 8, 12–17, 20, 35, 40, 56–60, 74, 87, 114; NASCAR, multiculturalism, and, 181–82, 185; redemption and, 150, 161; white victimization and, 216, 226

Newton, Cameron (Cam), 5, 16, 20–21, 46, 57, 84, 90, 198, 223–24, 233

NFL draft, 51–52

Nifong, Mike, 98

Nowinski, Chris, 49–50

N-word, 67–68, 83, 86–89, 150–51, 154–55, 186, 210

**O**

Obama, Barack, 15, 46, 71, 108

Obama, Michelle, 199

O'Bannon, Ed, 36, 38

Ole Miss. *See* University of Mississippi

Olympics, 41, 127, 129; Rio (2016), 65, 233–35

O'Neal, Shaquille, 46, 64

Ortiz, Steven, 69

Owens, Jesse, 46, 54

Owens, Terrell, 16, 46, 82, 198

**P**

Palace Brawl, 70, 88

Palmer, Janay. *See* Rice, Janay Palmer

Parker, Candace, 161–62, 168

Parks, Rosa, 35–36

Paterno, Joe, 9, 17, 42

Patrick, Danica, 9, 164–65, 168, 173, 183

Patriots. *See* New England Patriots

"paying for the party," 119

Pedroia, Dustin, 24–26, 29, 42

performance-enhancing drugs (PEDs), 139–40, 158, 231–32

Perry, Imani, 79, 85

Peterson, Adrian, 91, 93, 135, 196

Phelps, Michael, 7, 9, 17, 65, 73, 98, 100, 104 106–9, 112, 132, 232

Pistorius, Oscar, 6, 9, 92–93

Pither, Robert, 208–9

playing the right way, 9, 27, 50, 57, 67, 183, 189, 202–3, 204–25, 226–27, 229, 233

positional segregation, 18–19, 51, 53

"possessive investment in whiteness," 10, 53, 76, 151, 188–89

post-raciality, post-racism. *See* new racism

Pryor, Terrelle, 34–35, 37–38, 40–41

Puig, Yasiel, 7, 16, 74, 198, 205

**Q**

Quigley, Bill, 57

**R**

race: athleticism and, 8, 12–13, 23–30, 48, 50–53, 61–63, 206, 213–15, 217, 229; intelligence and, 7–8, 23–24,